# A COMPANION TO TRANSPORT, SPACE AND EQUITY

# NECTAR SERIES ON TRANSPORTATION AND COMMUNICATIONS NETWORKS RESEARCH

**Series Editor:** Aura Reggiani, *Professor of Economic Policy, University of Bologna, Italy*

NECTAR (Network on European Communications and Transport Activities Research) is an international scientific, interdisciplinary association with a network culture. Its primary objective is to foster research collaboration and the exchange of information between experts in the fields of transport, communication and mobility.

NECTAR members study the behaviour of individuals, groups and governments within a spatial framework. They bring a wide variety of perspectives to analyse the challenges facing transport and communication, and the impact these challenges have on society at all levels of spatial aggregation.

This series acts as a companion to, and an expansion of, activities of NECTAR. The volumes in the series are broad in their scope with the intention of disseminating some of the work of the association. The contributions come from all parts of the world and the range of topics covered is extensive, reflecting the breadth and continuously changing nature of issues that confront researchers and practitioners involved in spatial and transport analysis.

Titles in the series include:

# A Companion to Transport, Space and Equity

*Edited by*

Robin Hickman

*Bartlett School of Planning, University College London, UK*

Beatriz Mella Lira

*Bartlett School of Planning, University College London, UK*

Moshe Givoni

*Transport Research Unit, Department of Geography and the Human Environment, Tel-Aviv University, Israel*

Karst Geurs

*Centre for Transport Studies, University of Twente, the Netherlands*

NECTAR SERIES ON TRANSPORTATION AND COMMUNICATIONS NETWORKS RESEARCH

 Edward Elgar
PUBLISHING

Cheltenham, UK • Northampton, MA, USA

Published by
Edward Elgar Publishing Limited
The Lypiatts
15 Lansdown Road
Cheltenham
Glos GL50 2JA
UK

Edward Elgar Publishing, Inc.
William Pratt House
9 Dewey Court
Northampton
Massachusetts 01060
USA

A catalogue record for this book
is available from the British Library

Library of Congress Control Number: 2019951034

This book is available electronically in the **Elgar**online
Social and Political Science subject collection
DOI 10.4337/9781788119825

Printed on elemental chlorine free (ECF)
recycled paper containing 30% Post-Consumer Waste

ISBN 978 1 78811 981 8 (cased)
ISBN 978 1 78811 982 5 (eBook)

Typeset by Servis Filmsetting Ltd, Stockport, Cheshire
Printed and bound in the USA

# Contents

# Editors and contributors

All of the contributors are recognised or emerging researchers in research and practice in transport, city planning and social equity. Many of us have worked together previously on research projects and/or through the NECTAR research network (www.nectar-eu.eu/). Short biographies are given below.

## EDITORS

**Robin Hickman** is a Reader (Associate Professor) at the Bartlett School of Planning (BSP), University College London and Director of the MSc in Transport and City Planning. He has been a Visiting Research Associate and Research Fellow at the Transport Studies Unit, University of Oxford. He worked in consultancy as an Associate Director at Halcrow, leading on transport research; and previously at Llewelyn Davies and Surrey County Council. He completed his PhD at the BSP in 2007. He co-chairs Cluster 1 of the NECTAR network and writes a regular column in the Town and Country Planning journal.

He has research interests in transport and climate change, transport and social equity, urban structure and travel, integrated transport and urban planning strategies, the affective dimensions of travel, discourses in travel, multi-criteria appraisal and sustainable transport strategies in the UK, Europe and Asia. His most recent books are Handbook on Transport and Development (Edward Elgar, 2015) and Transport, Climate Change and the City (Routledge, 2014).

**Beatriz Mella Lira** is a PhD candidate and Research Assistant at the Bartlett School of Planning, UCL. She is an Architect with a Master's degree in Urban Development from P. Universidad Catolica de Chile. Her research interests are in urban planning, transport planning, well-being, social equity, the Capability Approach and multi criteria appraisal. Her PhD research is sponsored by Becas Chile and examines transport and social equity in Santiago, Chile.

Beatriz has worked as a Visiting Lecturer at University of Westminster and Teaching Assistant at UCL. She was Research Assistant for the British Council Newton Fund research project 'Sustainable Cities and Resilient Transport' (2014–2017). She has worked in private consultancy as External Consultant at the OECD (2017) and Project Manager at Urbanica Consultores (2011–2014) in projects related to accessibility, master planning and land use, sustainable transport, communication infrastructure and urban design. She leads the Socially Just Transport Doctoral Research Network.

**Moshe Givoni** is Head of the Transport Research Unit (TRU) and Associate Professor at the Department of Geography and Human Environment, Tel Aviv University. He is also a Visiting Research Associate at the TSU, University of Oxford and an Associate Editor for the journal Transport Reviews. He gained his PhD at the Bartlett School of Planning, University College London, in 2005, and received a Marie Curie postdoctoral fellowship which was undertaken at the VU University, Amsterdam. He co-chairs Cluster 1 of the NECTAR network.

His research interests are in the field of transport and mobility with focus on transport policy and planning; the links between transport and economic development; and transport and the environment. Most of his research is on public transport systems, and rail and high-speed rail in particular. His most recent books include The Handbook on Transport and Development (Edward Elgar, 2015), Moving Towards Low Carbon Mobility (Edward Elgar, 2013) and Integrated Transport: from Policy to Practice (Routledge, 2010).

**Karst Geurs** is Full Professor of Transport Planning at the Centre for Transport Studies (CTS), University of Twente. His research focuses on interactions between land use and transport, accessibility modelling and evaluation and the dynamics in travel behaviour. From 2009–2013 he was Associate Professor at the CTS. He worked at the National Institute for Public Health and Environment from 1997 and moved to the Netherlands Environmental Assessment Agency in 2005. In 2006, he received his PhD at the Faculty of Geosciences, Utrecht University, the Netherlands, on accessibility appraisal of land use and transport policy strategies. He teaches Master's courses on Transport Policy and Planning, Land Use and Transport Interactions and Sustainable Transport within the Master Track Transport Engineering and Management.

He is chair of the Network on European Communications and Transport Activities Research (NECTAR), Editor-in-Chief of the European Transport Research Review (ETRR) and a member of the Editorial Advisory Board of the Journal of Transport and Land Use (JTLU). His most recent books include Accessibility, Equity and Efficiency. Challenges for Transport and Public Services (Edward Elgar, 2016) and Accessibility Analysis and Transport Planning. Challenges for Europe and North America (Edward Elgar, 2012).

## CONTRIBUTORS

**Nihan Akyelken** is an Associate Professor in Sustainable Urban Development at the University of Oxford. Nihan joined Oxford as a Research Fellow at the Transport Studies Unit, School of Geography and the Environment, in 2008. Previously, she worked at the London School of Economics and Political Science (LSE) Public Policy Group. She obtained her PhD in Economic Geography from the University of Oxford, and her undergraduate and Master's degrees from the LSE in the areas of Economics and Philosophy and European Political Economy. She has worked on research projects funded by the European Commission, the UK Research Councils, the Swedish International Development Agency, the British Council and the British Academy, and held academic awards from Wolfson College, Alan Nesta Ferguson Foundation and the LSE Award Schemes. She is the winner of the 2015 OECD-ITF Young Researcher of the Year Award and was named as a World Social Science Fellow in Sustainable Urbanisation by the

International Social Science Council in 2014. Situated at the intersection of economic and social geography, development planning and political economy, Nihan's research focuses on mobility-related inequalities and the wider impacts of transport infrastructure investments.

**David Banister** is Professor Emeritus of Transport Studies at the University of Oxford. From 2006–2015, he was the Director of the Transport Studies Unit, University of Oxford, and Director of the Environmental Change Institute, University of Oxford (2009–2010). Prior to 2006, he was Professor of Transport Planning at University College London. He has spent time as a Research Fellow at the Warren Centre in the University of Sydney (2001–2002), a Visiting VSB Professor at the Tinbergen Institute in Amsterdam (1994–1997), and Visiting Professor at the University of Bodenkultur in Vienna in 2007. He was the first Benelux BIVEC-GIBET Transport Chair (2012–2013) and was the Chair of the ERC Advanced Research Grants SH3 Panel (2015–2016). He has edited the journal Transport Reviews for 20 years and has published 25 books and over 300 papers in refereed journals. His two latest books are Inequality in Transport (Alexandrine Press, 2018) and The Imperatives of Sustainable Development: Needs, Justice, Limits (Routledge, 2017).

**Christine Benna Skytt-Larsen** is Assistant Professor in social geography at the University of Copenhagen. Her research focuses on the dynamics of the uneven geography of cities and regions. Specifically, she studies how the creation of social relations and actors' involvement in specific local communities affect social relations, knowledge creation, human identity and life chances in time and space.

**Eda Beyazit** is an Associate Professor at the Urban and Regional Planning Department at Istanbul Technical University (ITU), where she teaches courses on urban transport, urban geography and inequalities, planning philosophy and urban design. She specialises in urban mobilities, especially in the ways in which transport infrastructures generate socio-spatial inequalities at different scales. She examines a range of issues from social justice and transport, to mobility cultures, issues of power, planning and decision-making. Her recent research projects include investigation of the daily travel experiences of female domestic workers in Istanbul and the spatial hierarchical organisation of disaster preparedness in Thrace, Turkey. She was a Visiting Research Associate at Transport Studies Unit, Oxford University (2013–2017). She is one of the collaborators of the UNESCO Chair in Gender, the General Assembly of Partners Habitat III, and a member of COST Network on the Wider Impacts and Scenario Evaluation of Autonomous and Connected Transport.

**Jose Bienvenido Manuel Biona** is a Full Professor at the Mechanical Engineering Department of De La Salle University (DLSU) in Manila, Philippines. He completed his PhD at DLSU, with visiting PhD research fellowships at University of Portsmouth in the UK, Technical University of Graz in Austria and Universiti Teknologi, Malaysia. His research interests include sustainable transportation policy and planning, alternative vehicles assessment, transportation technology diffusion modelling and energy economics. He has more than 10 years of consulting work experience with the Philippine national and local government agencies as well as with various local and international organisations. He is currently leading a project assessing the desirability of transportation in cities of the Philippines, and the development of the Philippine electric vehicle policy and adoption roadmap.

**Geneviève Boisjoly** is an Assistant Professor at the Department of Civil, Geological and Mining Engineering at Polytechnique Montréal, Canada. Her research focuses on land use and transport interactions and on their impacts on travel behaviour and health. She is specifically interested in urban accessibility and how land use and transport planning can contribute to more equitable and sustainable cities.

**Kristian Bothe** is a PhD candidate in economic geography at the University of Copenhagen. His research focuses on urban and regional development and specifically on the wider spatial and socio-economic impacts of urban public transport investments.

**Geert te Boveldt** is a Research Associate in the research group MOBI at Vrije Universiteit Brussel (VUB), Belgium. His research interests include the social, economic as well as the political dimensions of transport planning. Previously he held positions in several (non) governmental organisations in the fields of sustainable mobility, housing policy and strategic spatial planning, in both Belgium and the Netherlands.

**Mengqiu Cao** is a Senior Lecturer at the University of Westminster, with a PhD from the Bartlett School of Planning, UCL. He has been a Guest Lecturer and Research Assistant at UCL and at Birkbeck, University of London, and a Visiting Lecturer at University of Westminster. He has worked in academia and industry in transport and urban planning. He was a part-time Research Fellow at the Town and Country Planning Association in 2015; and previously a Logistics Executive working at Inprime Logistics Ltd. His research interests include transport planning, social equity, travel vulnerability, transport and climate change, travel behaviour and well-being, integrated urban planning and sustainable transport development, statistics and transport modelling. He has also worked with public authorities and international funding organisations, such as the British Council, NDRC, MOHURD, Changsha-URPB, Asian Development Bank, and Town and Country Planning Association.

**Yannick Cornet** is a Senior Researcher in intelligent transport systems at the ERA Chair team at the University of Žilina, University Science Park. He is also a Lecturer in sustainable mobility at the University of Aalborg, Planning Department, Centre for Design, Innovation and Sustainable Transition. He currently researches on smartphone-based, multi-modal diaries for collecting European data on the experience of travel time. His previous research includes sustainable mobility indicators, multi-actor multi-criteria decision-support tools, and case studies on high-speed rail appraisal and cycling transitions. He has also worked as a software project manager on the design of real-time carpooling apps at Nokia. His broader research interests lie in the application of novel information technologies and decision-support tools to the challenge of achieving a transition towards environmental and social sustainability of mobility systems.

**Carey Curtis** is Professor of city planning and transport at Curtin University, Perth, Australia, Director of the research network Urbanet, and Guest Professor at University of Lund/K2. Her research experience spans four decades and has included over 50 projects in both academia and the planning industry. She has published extensively in the areas of travel behaviour, transport and land use planning, accessibility planning and institutional barriers to sustainable urban development.

**Robbin Deboosere** graduated with a Master's degree in Urban Planning from the School of Urban Planning, McGill University. He was previously a Research Assistant for the

Transportation Research at McGill (TRAM) group and received his Master's degree in Engineering: Traffic, Logistics and ITS, from KU Leuven. His research interests include transport equity, determinants of mode choice, transportation from the user's perspective, and travel behaviour.

**Taotao Deng** is an Associate Professor at the Shanghai University of Finance and Economics, China. He received his PhD in Transport Studies from University of Aberdeen, UK. His main research interests are regional economics, transport geography and tourism economics. During the past seven years, he has authored 14 academic journal papers, in Transportation, Transport Reviews, Journal of Urban Planning and Development and Tourism Economics.

**Ahmed El-Geneidy** is a full Professor at the School of Urban Planning, McGill University, Montreal, Canada. He is currently serving on the board of directors of the Autorité régionale de transport métropolitain (ARTM), the regional public transport planning and financing authority for the Montreal metropolitan region and he is the elected chair of the World Society on Transport and Land Use Research (WSTLUR). He is also an editor of the Journal of Transport and Land Use. His research interests include land use and transport interaction, equity in transport systems, public transport planning and operations, non-motorised (walking and cycling) behaviour and planning and measuring the needs for disadvantaged populations.

**Eran Feitelson** is a Professor at the Department of Geography and head of the Advanced School for Environmental Studies at the Hebrew University of Jerusalem. He is a previous head of the Federmann School of Public Policy and Government. He has published extensively in the fields of transport policy, land use planning, environmental policies and water policy. In addition to his academic work, Eran has participated in several national planning teams and has been a member of many national committees. He also serves as chair of the Israeli Nature Reserves and National Parks Commission.

**Brendan Gleeson** is Professor of Urban Policy Studies and Director, Melbourne Sustainable Society Institute, University of Melbourne, Australia. His research interests include urban social policy, city planning and management and environmental theory and policy. He is the author of numerous scientific papers and chapters and his most recent book is The Urban Condition (Routledge, 2014).

**Matt Higgins** is a transport planning practitioner, with experience working at Steer, Transport for London, the London Borough of Hackney and the Department for Transport. In 2017 he graduated from the MSc Transport and City Planning (Distinction) from UCL, winning the R.B. Hounsfield Prize for his dissertation, which studied opposition to road space reallocation for cycling and the potential for behavioural economics to inform more effective planning and delivery. He has research interests in active travel and behavioural economics.

**Haoyu Hu** graduated from the School of Geography Science at Nanjing Normal University. He is now a PhD candidate at Peking University, China. His research area is focused on Geographic Information Systems, regional geography and regional transport systems.

**Imre Keseru** is a transport planner and geographer in the MOBI research group at Vrije Universiteit Brussel, Belgium. He has a PhD in Earth Sciences from the University of Szeged in Hungary. He previously worked at the KTI Institute for Transport Sciences in Budapest as a deputy head of unit managing several international projects on urban mobility and cross-border public transport. Currently, he is a postdoctoral researcher and team leader for urban mobility at MOBI.

**Shengxiao Li** is a PhD candidate at the School of Design, University of Pennsylvania, USA. He obtained his bachelor degrees in urban management and economics, and Master's in urban planning from Peking University in China. His research interests lie within transport equity issues, the interaction between land use and travel behaviour and international transport planning. He has published 10 papers in peer-reviewed journals on transportation and planning, including Transportation Research Part A and D, Transportation and Journal of Transport Geography.

**Lixun Liu** is a PhD graduate at the Bartlett School of Planning, UCL. Her research focuses on urban rail development and social equity issues. She holds an MSc and BSc in Architecture from Tsinghua University, China.

**Neil Stephen Lopez** is an Assistant Professor at the Mechanical Engineering Department of De La Salle University (DLSU) in Manila, Philippines. He completed his PhD from DLSU, including Visiting Research at the Transport Studies Unit, University of Oxford, UK; Bartlett School of Planning, UCL, UK; and the Sustainable Transportation Energy Pathways Institute, University of California, Davis. He is also a member of the Transportation Science Society of the Philippines, and of the Network on European Communications and Transport Activities Research. His research interests include transportation policy and planning, alternative vehicles assessment and energy economics. He is currently working on a project assessing the desirability of transportation in cities of the Philippines, and evaluating policies for future electric vehicles deployment in the Philippines.

**Karen Lucas** is Professor of transport and social analysis at the Institute of Transport Studies, University of Leeds, where she is also the Deputy Director of the Leeds Social Science Institute. She has more than fifteen years of international experience as a social researcher in transport. Her research focuses on developing better understandings of the relationship between transport and social outcomes with a particular emphasis on low-income and socially disadvantaged groups and communities.

**Glenn Lyons** is the Mott MacDonald Professor of Future Mobility at UWE Bristol. He is seconded for half of his time to Mott MacDonald, creating a bridge between academia and practice. Throughout his career he has focused upon the role of new technologies in supporting and influencing travel behaviour both directly and through shaping lifestyles and social practices. A former secondee to the UK Department for Transport and more recently to the New Zealand Ministry of Transport, Glenn has led major studies into traveller information systems, teleworking, virtual mobility, travel time use, user innovation, road pricing, public and business attitudes to transport and future mobility. He is now actively engaged in examining the future prospects for technological innovations including Connected Autonomous Vehicles and Mobility as a Service. He has been involved in a number of strategic futures initiatives and recent engagements have included helping transport authorities address future uncertainty in their planning, policymaking and investment; and examining the need for transport planning practice to evolve.

**Cathy Macharis** is Professor at the Vrije Universiteit Brussel, Belgium. Her research group, MOBI, is an interdisciplinary group focusing on sustainable logistics, electric and hybrid vehicles and urban mobility. Her research focuses on how to include stakeholders within decision and evaluation processes in the field of transport and mobility. She has been involved in several regional, national and European research projects dealing with topics such as the implementation of innovative concepts for city distribution, assessment of policy measures in the field of logistics and sustainable mobility, and development of a multi-actor, multi-criteria analysis framework.

**Anthony Perl** is Professor of urban studies and political science at Simon Fraser University in Vancouver, British Columbia, Canada. Before joining SFU, Anthony worked at the University of Calgary, the City University of New York and Université Lumière in Lyon, France. He received his undergraduate honours degree in Government from Harvard University, followed by an MA and a PhD in Political Science from the University of Toronto. His research crosses disciplinary and national boundaries to explore policy decisions made about transportation, cities and the environment. He has published in dozens of scholarly journals and authored five books. His work has been awarded prizes for outstanding papers presented at the World Conference on Transport Research and the Canadian Transportation Research Forum. He has advised governments on transport and urban policy, and is currently a member of the Vancouver City Planning Commission.

**Jan Scheurer** is a Senior Research Fellow at the School of Built Environment, Curtin University and a member of the Future Cities Lab, an Honorary Associate at the Centre for Urban Research (CUR), RMIT University and a frequent visitor at the University of Amsterdam (UvA) and RMIT Europe (Barcelona). Jan's areas of expertise are urban design, transport and accessibility planning, sustainability policy and mobility culture.

**Rebecca Shliselberg** is a researcher at the Transportation Research Unit, Department of Geography and Human Environment and PhD candidate at the Porter School of Environmental Studies, Tel Aviv University, Israel. She holds an MSc in Urban and Regional Planning from the Technion. After over 25 years of consulting in Israel and abroad, she has recently assumed a position leading a strategic planning unit for transport in Israel under the auspices of the Ministry of Transport. Rebecca's research interests focus on furthering well-being as a policy objective, particularly focusing on operationalising motility as a means of promoting more socially sustainable transport systems. Rebecca has specialised in public transport planning having developed national planning standards, and has led several strategic sustainable transport planning initiatives in the Tel Aviv region.

**Emilia Smeds** is a PhD candidate at the Department for Science, Technology, Engineering and Public Policy (STEaPP), University College London and a Researcher at the UCL City Leadership Laboratory. Emilia's research area is urban and transport governance, with a focus on experimentation and innovation for sustainable and socially just mobility. Emilia has been a Research Assistant at Imperial College London for the EUFP7-funded PASTA (Physical Activity Through Sustainable Transport Approaches), and has also worked as a practising transport planner in Helsinki, Finland. She holds an MSc in Transport and City Planning from the Bartlett School of Planning, UCL and a BSc in Environmental Policy from the London School of Economics and Political Science.

**Janet Stanley** is Associate Professor and Principal Research Fellow in urban social resilience at the Melbourne Sustainable Society Institute, University of Melbourne, Australia. She specialises in social inclusion, transport, climate change and equity and bushfire arson. She has many refereed journal and book publications; her latest co-authored book is How Great Cities Happen: Integrating People, Land Use and Transport (Edward Elgar, 2017).

**John Stanley** is Adjunct Professor and Senior Research Fellow in sustainable land transport, Institute of Transport and Logistic Studies, The University of Sydney, Sydney, Australia. John was a former Deputy Chair of Australia's National Road Transport Commission. He co-authored Introduction to Transport Policy: A Public Policy View, and How Great Cities Happen. His research interests focus mainly on integrated land use transport policy and planning, social inclusion and public transport policy.

**Jingwei Sun** received his Master's degree in Geography from University College London and now works as an urban planner at the Jiangsu Institute of Urban Planning and Design, China. His research interests include transport geography, urban planning and economic geography.

**Ceyda Sungur** is a Visiting Researcher at the Geography Department of the Université Paris 1 – Panthéon-Sorbonne and at the UMR Géographie-Cites. She received her Bachelor's degree in City and Regional Planning from Middle East Technical University, and her Master's degree in Urban Design from Istanbul Technical University. Her research focuses on the everyday experiences of women service workers in Istanbul. She specialises in labour geography, mapping and ethnographic inquiry by exploring the everyday experiences of the 'invisible' women workers who keep the city 'sanitary and functional'. Recently she has been involved in a research expedition on the daily travel experiences of women domestic workers.

**Imogen Thompson** is a City Planner at Transport for London, specialising in the relationship between transport investment and urban growth. Her work examines the impacts of transport on housing delivery, regeneration and growth opportunities. Previously, Imogen has worked as a development planner in Vancouver, Canada, leading on regeneration and transport-oriented development projects. She holds an MSc Transport and City Planning (Distinction) from the Bartlett School of Planning, UCL and a BA (First Class) in Urban Studies from the University of British Columbia, Canada. During her studies, Imogen worked as a researcher at UCL and UBC on a range of international projects including the Sintropher European transnational project and the Vancouver Downtown East Side regeneration study.

**Florencia Rodriguez Touron** is an urban mobility specialist from Buenos Aires, Argentina. After graduating in Sociology at University of Buenos Aires, she pursued a Master's degree in Urban Economics from Torcuato Di Tella University and an MSc Transport and City Planning from the Bartlett School of Planning, UCL. She has worked for the public sector in Argentina at the national level, in public transport performance assessment and then moved to the consultancy field working for national and local governments and development banks throughout Latin America. She contributes with NGOs developing mobility planning strategies and policy recommendations in Argentina. Her research topics focus on transport equity and social, economic and urban effects of disruptive technologies in transport.

**Qiyan Wu** is Professor of the School of Public Policy and Administration, Xi'an Jiaotong University. He was a Professor at the East China Normal University from 2016 to 2017, the Nanjing Normal University from 2010 to 2016 and Academic Dean and Professor at Yunnan University from 2002 to 2010. He was also a Visiting Professor at the University of British Columbia in 2007–2008. His teaching and research over the past five years has focused on the areas of education-led gentrification (e.g. he coined the term *jiaoyufica-tion*), urban residential segregation, urban housing policy and urban political economy, and has recently included the impact of the high-speed rail system on urban and regional restructuring.

**Yongping Zhang** is a PhD candidate at the Bartlett Centre for Advanced Spatial Analysis (CASA), University College London. He has an academic background in geography, urban planning and environmental policies. He has research interests in sustainable cities, urban modelling, spatial analysis using urban big data and various issues related to Chinese urbanisation.

**Yuerong Zhang** is a PhD candidate and Teaching Assistant at the Bartlett School of Planning (BSP) and the Bartlett Centre for Advanced Spatial Analysis (CASA), UCL. Her research interests are public transport network resilience and vulnerability, street networks and urban morphology.

# Acknowledgements

Many thanks to all those who have helped us with this edited collection. First, thanks to our contributors, who have sent through excellent chapters covering very different interpretations of the transport, space and equity topic; and responded efficiently and patiently to our reviews and requests. Most have even kept to the time schedule! Second, to the Commissioning Editors at Edward Elgar, Katy Crossan and Alex Pettifer. Thanks for the very effective production of the book. Finally, to our families and friends – in particular to Helen, Martha and Oscar; Damián and Rafael; Helena, Daniel, Ella and Alex; Annemarie, Jonah and David. You allow us to disappear into the various offices to write and edit the books, when we really should be doing other things. Thanks and love to all.

# PART I

# INTRODUCTION

# 1. Transport and space and social equity impacts

*Robin Hickman, Beatriz Mella Lira, Moshe Givoni and Karst Geurs*

## UNDERSTANDING THE LINKAGES BETWEEN TRANSPORT AND SPACE AND SOCIAL EQUITY IMPACTS

> Bleak, dark, and piercing cold, it was a night for the well-housed and fed to draw round the bright fire, and thank God they were at home; and for the homeless starving wretch to lay him down and die. Many hunger-worn outcasts close their eyes in our bare streets at such times, who, let their crimes have been what they may, can hardly open them in a more bitter world.
> Charles Dickens (1837) *Oliver Twist*, p.174.

In the 1800s, in Victorian England, Charles Dickens famously highlighted the problems of poverty, of the large inequity in living standards across the population, of the weaknesses of human behaviour – and of the role of government institutions in protecting the status quo and ignoring the disadvantaged. These may be distant times, when there was little protection against the harshness of life circumstance. But, look around in our cities and we see increasing inequity, in income, activities and life opportunities. A focus on supporting economic growth, the financialisation of development, and overlooking of distributional issues, has led to very unequal lifestyles. We seem not to have progressed far in society – with significantly unequal participation in activities across many cities globally.

Social equity has been the focus of research in geography, development studies and economics for decades, and in recent years has been given greater consideration in transport and city planning. Research considers how transport systems facilitate access to activities, in a differential manner by population group. Hence, the availability of transport systems is closely linked to social inequity.

Transport systems and infrastructure investment can lead to inequitable travel behaviours, with certain socio-demographic groups using particular parts of the transport system and accessing particular activities and opportunities. Transport planning has conventionally focused on providing for increased levels of mobility, initially in terms of highway capacity for the private car, but increasingly with infrastructure for public transport, walking and cycling. A problem has been that the appraisal and evaluation of projects has focused on metrics of mobility, such as vehicle kilometres travelled and time savings. This has led to investment in projects that enhance levels of mobility – and there has been relatively limited consideration given to other important policy objectives, such as transport's contribution to spatial and social goals.

In terms of definitions, there is much confusion and conflation of key concepts in the literature, but we understand the following terms, in this edited book, as below:

- Transport: 'to transfer or convey from one place to another' (transitive verb); or 'an act or process of transporting' (noun).

- Space: 'a continuous area or expanse which is free, available, or unoccupied' or 'an area of land' (noun).
- Social equity: the quality of 'being fair and impartial' (noun), including fair access to activities, opportunities, livelihood, education, income and resources, as facilitated, in this case, through transport.
- Social justice: the fair relation between the individual and society, including 'a fair distribution of activities and opportunities within a society' (noun).
- Disadvantaged groups: a group 'in unfavourable circumstances' (adjective), including by income, age, gender, ethnicity; and by area and temporally.

(Merriam Webster Online Dictionary, 2018)

There are interpretations of horizontal equity, where individuals and groups should be treated the same in the distribution of resources, benefits and costs; and vertical equity, where disadvantaged groups are favoured in order to compensate for inequity, i.e. through progressive policy interventions.

Transport is not the only contributor to social equity, indeed unlikely to be the most important factor, but it can play a significant role in facilitating access to activities. Different transport systems, including modes, extent of networks, running times and cost of access, all contribute to differential travel experiences and impacts by socio-demographic groups, spatially and temporally. The objective, in policy terms, is that transport governance and investments can be better understood and shaped to contribute more positively to social equity.

There is, of course, a problem in empirical terms in understanding what level of social (in)equity is appropriate in different contexts and how this might be measured. The concept of social equity can be interpreted and understood in different ways, is relational, spatially and temporally, hence there can be no agreed overall threshold across contexts.

The aim of this book is to explore these issues and the differential impacts, relating transport to social equity. We use international case studies to explore the spatial and social equity impacts associated with transport systems, city planning and infrastructure investments.

Contributions are made in 21 chapters, from 42 leading and newly emerging researchers, each addressing the issues from a particular angle or viewpoint. This publication brings together, in one volume, wide-ranging evidence from the field, and in doing so fills a major gap in the literature. The book draws on competing viewpoints to highlight the range and dimensions of the debate, the complexity and tensions, and the progression in argument over time. The volume will serve as a guide for undergraduates and graduate students, researchers and academics wishing to find a comprehensive reference to research on transport, space and equity impacts. We hope too that the debate will reach a wider audience, including consultants, policy makers and wider practitioners. In this way the book can gain a wider reach, including achieving some influence on practice.

There is an increasing understanding that transport can be more than a derived demand – that transport has distributional impacts, indeed the journey itself can be useful, and increasingly so, as travel can be used in useful ways, including to access work, leisure and other activities, and to participate in life. Equity impacts associated with transport investment are very different relative to context and there are no general rules to be found in terms of the expected impacts of infrastructure investment – there are many factors involved. The 'static' intervention of infrastructure is inserted into a complex and dynamic context, hence empirically this is a difficult research area to conceptualise and test empirically. Appropriate urban planning, infrastructure, pricing, education and training, and wider factors, need to be considered to ensure that socially and spatially-equitable impacts are realised.

Beyond this introduction, this book is structured into five further parts:

## PART II TRANSPORT AND SPATIAL IMPACTS

Part II contains six chapters, and examines spatial impacts concerned with transport, including how public transport investments are associated with changes in socio-economics; city and neighbourhood development and regeneration; and development value.

Robbin Deboosere, Geneviève Boisjoly and Ahmed El-Geneidy consider the impact of improved accessibility on employment opportunities in the Greater Toronto and Hamilton region, using the concept of competitive job accessibility, defined as the number of accessible jobs by number of workers who can access them. Increases in transit accessibility for low and medium income neighbourhoods are associated with higher increases in income, yet lower increases in income for the higher income areas. This is perhaps explained by the migration of higher income groups out to the car-dependent suburbs, and reflective of the continuing flight to the suburbs in this context.

Jan Scheurer and Carey Curtis examine socio-spatial equity and transit investment in Melbourne. Following inner-urban gentrification trends over several decades, Australia's larger cities show a strong pattern for socio-economically disadvantaged groups to reside at the urban fringe, where they are also transport-disadvantaged. Spatial data compares socio-economic disadvantage against indicators of public transport accessibility to illustrate how current public transport investment programmes in Melbourne could be modified and expanded to address spatial inequalities. It is argued that a greater geographical reach of high-quality public transport and of opportunities for low-car living must coincide with dedicated housing affordability programmes if a reversal of social-spatial disparities is to occur.

Lixun Liu explores the case of Chongqing, asking what factors influence people choosing rail transit and how these vary over space. Geographically weighted regression is used to show differences in travel between old and new neighbourhoods. Longer commuting distance is associated with reduced use of transit, particularly in the old city neighbourhood. Here, the wealthy established residents tend to use the car and migrants tend to use the bus. However, it is important to understand the role of the planning strategy and the development planned around the transit investment – this is critical to the developmental benefits that follow the transit investment.

Qiyan Wu, Anthony Perl, Jingwei Sun, Taotao Deng and Haoyu Hu explore the development of the high-speed rail (HSR) network in China and the associated impact on accessibility, mode choice and spatial structure. Cities that gain intercity connections through HSR have higher accessibility enhancements, such as Huzhou. Daily commuting catchments have increased, thus more cities are absorbed within the commuting catchments of the major cities such as Shanghai and Beijing. The city region expands to the scale of the supercity, representing a new scale of urban development and interaction.

Emilia Smeds considers journeys to school in relation to social practices and the dimensions of material, meaning and competency. This is viewed as a more complete framework for assessing social change than psychological theories which concentrate on attitudes at the individual level. Two schools are analysed, using interviews, in Ealing, West London. The prevalence for driving to school is based on a range of issues, including lack of suitable walking and cycling facilities, space-time constraints on parents' mobility, poor public transport provision, availability of school choice, and negative meanings such as fear of traffic. Hence the difficulties in moving people away from the use of the private car for journeys to school – they are much more fundamental than changing individual behaviours and very often involve deeper, structural issues.

Imogen Thompson examines the link between transport investment and housing development and value, using hedonic modelling of connectivity to the Jubilee Line Extension and the East London Line in London, and associated house sale values. House prices increase with improved public transport connectivity, particularly where they were previously low. There also seems to be a distance component, with housing located 320–640 metres from the station gaining greatest price uplift.

# PART III TRANSPORT AND SOCIAL EQUITY IMPACTS

Part III contains six chapters, and examines social equity impacts associated with transport, including spatial restructuring and social dynamics, access to healthcare, the travel of working women, children and young people, and the potential for innovations in reducing inequality.

Eran Feitelson puts forward an approach to examining the equity implications of public transport, discussing the attributes of different transport systems, the types of trips made and attributes of travellers – and hence summarises the likely equity implications. There are important impacts on accessibility and life prospects. The hyper-mobile benefit most from travel, and these use air and high speed rail in particular. The most obviously progressive mode is the use of the bus (alongside walking), which is subsidised by taxpayers and, in the main, serves lower income groups.

Kristian Bothe and Christine Benna Skytt-Larsen examine Metro investment and socio-spatial impacts in Copenhagen, suggesting that residents within the catchment of the Metro have higher levels of education, lower unemployment rates and higher mean incomes than the reference group beyond. However, the largest differences are between neighbourhoods within transit catchment, reflecting the different socio-economic characteristics of each area. Amagerbro and Ørestad, for example, experience large increases in mean incomes. Much of the change in social composition of the station catchments is driven by differences between the stayers, in-movers and out-movers relative to the conditions before the Metro investment. Impacts of the Metro hence reflect a combination of the Metro investment, the local context, provision of urban amenities, type of housing provision and supporting urban policies.

Neil Stephen Lopez and Jose Bienvenido Manuel Biona assess cumulative accessibility to healthcare services in Metro Manila, using Google Maps. Access to health car provision differs by mode and travel budget, particularly under 100 Philippines Pesos (PhP). Almost half of zones do not have access to a healthcare facility by private car for a travel budget of 100 PhP. Public transport has advantages over private modes at lower travel budgets; and the private car becomes more advantageous at higher budgets. The peripheral areas have high costs of accessing healthcare, and this is where public transport access is often very limited.

Eda Beyazit and Ceyda Sungur explore gendered mobilities in the periphery of Istanbul, within a capitalist-based and patriarchal society. Higher paid work in central areas is often not possible for females due to the lengthy journeys from suburban areas, cost of travel and household responsibilities; whereas males are able to choose higher paid jobs from a wider geographical area across the city. Poorly educated females are particularly disadvantaged in the poor periphery, experiencing higher levels of walking to work and use of company shuttle services, often to lower paid employment.

Janet Stanley, John Stanley and Brendan Gleeson examine transport and social equity impacts from the perspective of children and young people. They examine the theoretical contributions from authors such as Rawls and Sen, the use of needs identification in transport planning, and the importance of transport for children and young people in helping them to participate in activities and social interaction. They suggest that the needs of children and other groups in society should be better catered for, instead of solely focusing on improving the journey to work for commuters.

Karen Lucas, Nihan Akyelken and Janet Stanley put forward the livelihoods approach as a method for assessing the social impacts of transport projects in relation to the Sustainable Development Goals. A number of criteria are developed, including issues of social progress, distribution and justice, to help consider the requirements of different populations and areas into which projects might be introduced. Case study material is used from South Africa and Brazil.

Perhaps the next stage here is to think what benchmarks might be achieved? Beyond encouraging progress against key criteria, we should also think what we should be aiming for in terms of our 'future' state?

## PART IV EMERGING APPROACHES TO SOCIO-SPATIAL EQUITY ANALYSIS

Part IV contains seven chapters, and examines emerging approaches to socio-spatial equity analysis, including capabilities-based approaches, behavioural interventions, motility and multi-actor appraisal.

David Banister, Yannick Cornet, Moshe Givoni and Glenn Lyons critique the commodification of travel time savings in transport planning and project appraisal. They ask for less focus on travel time and, instead, that consideration should be given to the door-to-door journey, the experience of travel and type of activities at the destination. A case study of High Speed Rail is used to discuss the issues. The concept of reasonable travel time is developed, reflecting a difference between useful and non-useful travel.

Mengqiu Cao, Yongping Zhang, Yuerong Zhang, Shengxiao Li and Robin Hickman apply different social equity measures, including the Capability Approach, Gini coefficient, Atkinson index, Palma ratio, Pietra ratio, Schutz coefficient and Theil index, in relation to transport and social equity in the neighbourhood of Tuqiao, Beijing. This is a migrant-rich, low income neighbourhood, adjacent to the East Sixth Ring Road and

Batong Subway Line One extension. Gender, age, hukou, incumbent population, personal income and car ownership are related to travel and travel experience.

Beatriz Mella Lira discusses the use of the Capability Approach in relation to transport and social equity. The concepts of capabilities and functionings are used to help consider the things a persons may value doing and being, including the activities that they are able to perform. A list of social indicators is developed, including life, bodily health, bodily integrity, sense and emotion. The lower the levels and higher the gap between the current and expected achievement of opportunities are seen as reflective of social inequity, with transport viewed as a facilitator in the development of fairer societies.

Geert te Boveldt, Imre Keseru and Cathy Macharis discuss the use of greater participatory approaches in transport appraisal, specifically through the application of Competence-based Multi Criteria Analysis (COMCA). This allows the use of multi-actor viewpoints where different actors have varied roles, tasks or levels of responsibility. The Brussels North–South railway corridor is used as a case study, with project options rated against a do-nothing alternative.

Matt Higgins discusses the potential of behavioural economics, and particularly the Mindspace framework, for use in consultation processes around transport projects. The Walthamstow Village Mini-Holland cycle scheme in London is used to explore the potential for framing projects in a way that might reduce public opposition. The role of the messenger, incentives and salience are seen as particularly important in project development and in limiting any public controversy that might follow.

Rebecca Shliselberg and Moshe Givoni discuss the concept of motility as an emerging objective for transport policy. Motility is defined as the capacity to engage in travel, including the elements of spatial and social mobility. Semi-structured interviews are used to discuss personal narratives and a survey to understand cognitive processes in travel, experience and activity participation.

Finally, Florencia Rodriguez Touron examines the concept of motility and the linkage to eudaimonic well-being, using a case study of Buenos Aires. Telephone surveys and interviews are used to assess motility (using factors such as transport availability, access to activities, personal safety and travel cost) and well-being is hence (in terms of human flourishment), across different communes in the city. The findings reveal that increases in the motility scale are significantly associated with increases in well-being.

## PART V CONCLUSIONS

Part V contains the final chapter, bringing the edited collection to a close, synthesising the wide field, and providing reflections on the implications for research and practice. It discusses the rich literature, puts forward the current 'state-of-the-art' in our understanding, and asks 'What next?' in terms of the emerging issues for future research and practice.

There are some very interesting contributions here – we hope you enjoy the read!

## REFERENCE

Dickens, C. (1837) *Oliver Twist*, London, Vintage Books [Republished 2013].

# PART II

# TRANSPORT AND SPATIAL IMPACTS

## 2. Understanding the relationship between changes in accessibility to jobs, income and unemployment in Toronto

*Robbin Deboosere, Geneviève Boisjoly and Ahmed El-Geneidy*

## 1. INTRODUCTION

In many urban areas, transport agencies are trying to provide all citizens with greater access to opportunities as a means to improve residents' well-being (Boisjoly and El-Geneidy, 2017; Handy, 2008; Proffitt, Bartholomew, Ewing, and Miller, 2015). Several cities particularly intend to increase access to opportunities in socially deprived areas, in order to support social inclusion and enhance the quality of life of residents in these neighbourhoods (Mayor of London, 2018; NSW Government, 2012; San Diego Association of Governments, 2011). In this context, research suggests that improvements in access to opportunities by public transport can bring considerable benefits to vulnerable populations, as they are more likely to rely on this mode for accessing their destinations (Stanley and Lucas, 2008).

To quantify access to opportunities, accessibility, or the ease of reaching destinations, is increasingly being used in research and practice as a key land use and transportation performance measure. From a social equity perspective, accessibility has been used as a tool to assess the socio-spatial distribution of public transport services (Bocarejo and Oviedo, 2012; Delmelle and Casas, 2012; Golub and Martens, 2014; Kawabata and Shen, 2007), and to evaluate how changes in accessibility differ across socio-economic groups as a result of projected or new infrastructure projects (Foth, Manaugh, and El-Geneidy, 2013; Manaugh and El-Geneidy, 2012; North Central Texas Council of Governments, 2016; Paez, Mercado, Farber, Morency, and Roorda, 2010; Southern California Association of Governments, 2016). While a large body of literature has assessed accessibility levels for different socio-economic groups, or changes in these accessibility levels over time, little research has been conducted to assess the outcomes of such improvements in accessibility.

The goal of this study is, therefore, to assess the relationship between improvements in the levels of accessibility to jobs by public transport and the resulting socio-economic benefits, measured by changes in median household income and unemployment rate over time in the Greater Toronto and Hamilton Area, Canada. For this purpose, competitive accessibility levels to employment opportunities by transit and by car are calculated for all census tracts in 2001 and 2011. Competitive accessibility discounts the number of accessible jobs by the number of workers that can access them, thereby accounting for the demand potential for each job. The vertical equity of accessibility by transit is then assessed for both years by comparing competitive accessibility levels across median household income deciles. Vertical equity is used to measure the provision of service to vulnerable groups compared to the general population. Two linear regressions are subsequently performed to examine the relationship between accessibility changes and income and unemployment at the census tract level, while controlling for the movement of residents. This study contributes to the literature on accessibility and the equity of outcome resulting from these accessibility levels, and is of relevance to planning professionals and researchers wishing to investigate the effects of accessibility improvements across neighbourhoods, especially low income ones.

The rest of the chapter is organized as follows. Section 2 explains the concept of accessibility, examines how equity is incorporated in academic literature on this concept, and presents previous literature on accessibility, employment and income. Section 3 considers the data and methodology used to investigate the relationship between improvements in transit accessibility and changes in income and unemployment, and Section 4 presents and discusses the findings. Section 5 then concludes the chapter and provides recommendations for further research.

## 2.   EQUITY OF ACCESSIBILITY AND EQUITY OF OUTCOME

### 2.1   Accessibility

Accessibility was first defined by Hansen (1959) (p.73) as "the potential of opportunities for interaction". In contrast with mobility, accessibility also considers land use factors such as the variety and number of destinations that can be reached, instead of only examining an individual's ability to move through the transportation network (Handy and Niemeier, 1997). Geurs and van Wee (2004) posit that accessibility measures should comprise four interacting components: land use, transportation, time, and the individual. Accessibility thus tries to incorporate the spatial distribution of activities, the transport system connecting these activities, the time constraints of individuals and services, and personal needs and abilities to provide a more accurate picture of the performance of transport systems.

There are several commonly used measures of accessibility, most of which take into account only the land use and transportation component, as they can be more easily computed, interpreted, and communicated, increasing their chances to impact policy (Geurs and van Wee, 2004; Handy and Niemeier, 1997). Cumulative measures of accessibility count the number of opportunities that can be reached within a set time-frame, for example the number of jobs an individual can reach within 45 minutes of travel (Wickstrom, 1971). Gravity-based accessibility measures, on the other hand, take into account that people will not stop travelling at an arbitrary time-limit, and weigh opportunities by distance; the further an opportunity is, the less it contributes to accessibility (Hansen, 1959). While more realistic, gravity-based measures require the prediction of a distance decay function, rendering them more difficult to communicate, interpret and analyse across studies.

To account for competition effects, for example among workers competing for jobs, the concept of accessibility has also been extended to include measures of competitive accessibility (Shen, 1998). As cumulative and gravity-based accessibility only measure the "supply side" of opportunities (Geurs and van Wee, 2004; Morris, Dumble, and Wigan,

1979), they assume that no capacity limitations exist. Therefore, when accessibility to jobs is examined through the lens of ordinary cumulative or gravity-based accessibility measures, it is assumed that one job can be filled by an infinite number of workers. To more accurately reflect reality, a demand potential is first computed by determining how many individuals can access each opportunity. Each opportunity is then discounted by this demand potential when calculating accessibility using the cumulative or gravity-based approach, in what is known as a competitive measure of accessibility (Shen, 1998). For example, in a region with 10 jobs and 100 workers that can access these jobs, competitive accessibility would be 0.1.

## 2.2 Equity of Accessibility

Measures of accessibility have often been used to consider the equity of the joint benefits provided by the land use and transportation system (see for example, Delmelle and Casas, 2012; Golub and Martens, 2014; Grengs, 2015; Guzman, Oviedo, and Rivera, 2017). Two different interpretations of equity in accessibility research exist, both founded in the ethical concept of egalitarianism (Foth et al., 2013; van Wee and Geurs, 2011). Horizontal equity requires that all members of society have equal access to all resources. Vertical equity, on the other hand, implies that the more vulnerable groups should be granted more resources. From this point of view, it would be more beneficial to society to increase the accessibility of unemployed young individuals than to increase the accessibility of wealthier individuals (Lucas, van Wee, and Maat, 2016). Yet another approach defines an equitable system as having a minimal gap between transit and car accessibility (Golub and Martens, 2014; Karner and Niemeier, 2013), after which both the horizontal and vertical equity of the distribution of this gap can be measured.

Current literature mostly focuses on examining the vertical equity impacts of transportation projects. To examine this type of equity, socially vulnerable groups first need to be defined. Several studies identify socio-economic groups based solely on income (for example, Fan, Guthrie, and Levinson, 2012; Guzman et al., 2017), whereas other studies also examine race, poverty status, minorities, and housing characteristics (Delmelle and Casas, 2012; Golub and Martens, 2014; Grengs, 2015), or create a social indicator combining several of these measures (Foth et al., 2013). The vertical equity of accessibility can then be investigated by comparing accessibility levels across different populations.

A distinction is often made between equity of opportunity and equity of outcome, the latter relating to the benefits gained from higher levels of opportunity (Delbosc and Currie, 2011; Litman, 2002; van Wee and Geurs, 2011). Transport-related outcomes (or benefits) include, among others, higher educational attendance, new employment opportunities and more frequent health visits. Studies discussing the horizontal and vertical equity of accessibility address equity of opportunity, but refrain from making judgements on the outcome of the process. This chapter attempts to connect the two concepts by considering the link between equity of opportunity, measured by accessibility, and equity of outcome, measured by changes in unemployment and income over time.

## 2.3    Accessibility, Unemployment and Income

To determine the outcomes and subsequent benefits resulting from accessibility and accessibility changes, previous studies have focused on examining the relationship between accessibility to jobs and socio-economic status, mostly concentrating on unemployment duration. Korsu and Wenglenski (2010), using micro-data, demonstrate that low accessibility to jobs is related to high unemployment in Paris, and find that workers living in areas with very low accessibility have a 1.7 percent higher probability of being unemployed for longer than one year compared to workers living in neighbourhoods with medium accessibility. To this end, the authors use a measure of cumulative accessibility, by public transport or car depending on car ownership, specifically considering the employment opportunities of the same socio-professional status as the individuals in question. Andersson, Haltiwanger, Kutzbach, Pollakowski, and Weinberg (2014) investigate low-income workers who were subject to mass layoffs in several US cities, and find that high accessibility to jobs is associated with a reduction in the time spent looking for work. A competitive measure of accessibility to low-income jobs is used for this purpose, taking into account the probability of using car or public transport, and explicitly considering competing job searchers to account for labour market tightness. Tyndall (2015) notes that, after the closure of the R train in Brooklyn due to hurricane Sandy unemployment rates along the line increased considerably, especially for those without a private vehicle, demonstrating that substantial changes in the public transport system affect unemployment. This study did not, however, examine the accessibility impacts of this endogenous shock to the transport system. Blumenberg and Pierce (2014) find that living close to a bus stop highly increases the chances of maintaining consistent employment, while having access to a private automobile has also been shown to be related to increased employment (Blumenberg and Pierce, 2017). Larson (2017) examines the relationship between access to jobs by public transport (broadly defined as the observed transit modal share) and economic opportunity over four decades in four US cities, and concludes that there is a positive relation between transit access and economic opportunity in predominantly white neighbourhoods in Orlando and Minneapolis, while a similar relationship is present in non-white areas in Birmingham.

This emerging body of literature suggests that accessibility to jobs is a potential determinant of unemployment duration. However, little is known about the relationship between unemployment rates and accessibility over time at a more aggregate, metropolitan scale; the literature presented above has not examined how accessibility changes impact longer term unemployment duration and more aggregated unemployment rates. Furthermore, no study has, to our knowledge, examined changes in accessibility and median household income over time. To provide a more holistic view on the relationship between accessibility changes and consequent changes in socio-economic status at an aggregate level, this study attempts to investigate the change in both the unemployment rate and median household income over a ten-year period. This chapter therefore contributes to the literature by presenting a long-term study associating a robust accessibility measure with equity of outcome.

# 3.   DATA AND METHODOLOGY

## 3.1   Study Context

The Greater Toronto and Hamilton Area, the most populous metropolitan region in Canada, housing 5.6 million residents in 2001 and 6.6 million inhabitants in 2011, was chosen to examine the relationship between transit accessibility improvements and changes in income and unemployment. The region is well connected by public transport, and is home to a subway, commuter train system and bus network (Figure 2.1). While the subway only serves the City of Toronto, the bus and train network extend across the entire region. During the ten-year study period, several infrastructure projects altered the public transport network in the area. In 2002, a new subway line, the Sheppard line (the line shown in solid grey below "TORONTO" in Figure 2.1) was opened, serving five new stations in the north of the City of Toronto. Additionally, several new train stations were constructed and new express bus services were introduced. At the same time, transit mode share increased from 20 percent in 2001 to 21 percent in 2011.

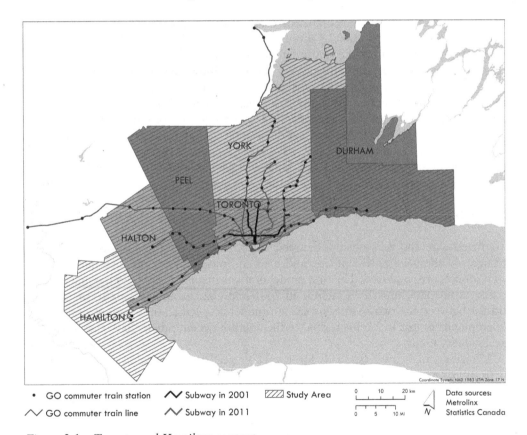

*Figure 2.1   Toronto and Hamilton context*

## 3.2  Data

Three different data sources were used for the analysis. Census and employment data for 2001 and 2011 were obtained from Statistics Canada. This data was enriched by a cumulative accessibility measure for a 45-minute trip by transit in 2011 at the census tract level, derived from GTFS data. The third data source, Metrolinx, provided travel time from 2001 at the traffic analysis zone (TAZ) level, calculated through the EMME travel demand modelling software, for both public transportation and automobile. Additionally, car travel time from 2011 during the AM peak was also supplied by Metrolinx.

A competitive measure of accessibility for 2001 at the TAZ level was first calculated using 2001 travel times and employment. Competitive accessibility is given by:

$$A_m^i = \sum_j \frac{O_j f(t_{ij}^m)}{D_j^m}, \text{ where } D_j^m = \sum_j LF_j f(t_{ij}^m).$$

$A_m^i$ reflects the accessibility at point i for transportation mode m, $O_j$ is the number of opportunities at location j, and $f(t_{ij}^m)$ is 1 when the travel time between locations i and j $(t_{ij}^m)$ is smaller than the set-time limit, and 0 otherwise. $D_j^m$ represents the demand for the opportunities at location j, and is given by the total labour force $(LF_j)$ that can access those opportunities within the set time-limit. To ensure consistency with available data from 2011, and to allow for comparisons, the accessibility measure was calculated for a 45-minute trip limit for public transport, and a 30-minute limit for car, and then projected into 2011 census tract boundaries through a nearest neighbour interpolation (i.e., each 2011 census tract centroid was assigned the accessibility value of the nearest 2001 census tract centroid). These time limits reflect the average commute times in Toronto for both modes (49 and 29 minutes respectively (Statistics Canada, 2010)), in order to capture the opportunities an individual can access in an average trip, while accounting for competition from other residents trying to reach the same opportunities.

## 3.3  Methodology

To investigate the relationship between improvements in transit accessibility and changes in the unemployment rate and median household income, two linear regression models are employed. The first model predicts median household income in 2011, based on median household income in 2001 and changes in accessibility by car and transit between the two years. The second model is specified in a similar manner: the unemployment rate in 2011 is related to the unemployment rate in 2001 and changes in accessibility levels.

As changes in income, especially for low income census tracts, could be related to gentrification, i.e., the upgrading of the socio-economic status of a neighbourhood through local migration (Lyons, 1996), several additional variables are added to the model. Literature on the relation between transit and gentrification usually investigates land and housing values, changes in income, race, car ownership, the number of professionals, and educational attainment to identify gentrifying areas (Grube-Cavers and Patterson, 2015; Kahn, 2007; Pollack, Bluestone, and Billingham, 2011). A neighbourhood is said to be gentrifying if these variables change faster than the average in the metropolitan area. Such

*Table 2.1    Summary statistics*

| Variable | Mean | Standard dev. |
| --- | --- | --- |
| Median Household Income in 2011 ($1,000) | 75.664 | 26.536 |
| Median Household Income in 2001 ($1,000) | 64.534 | 21.558 |
| Unemployment rate in 2011 (%) | 8.7173 | 3.1598 |
| Unemployment rate in 2001 (%) | 5.7868 | 2.4814 |
| Change in competitive accessibility by transit (jobs/worker) | −0.0897 | 1.1893 |
| Change in competitive accessibility by car (jobs/worker) | 0.2422 | 0.2917 |
| Change in percentage of residents with a bachelor's degree or higher (%) | 4.3710 | 4.9699 |
| Percentage of residents that have moved between 2006 and 2011 (%) | 35.131 | 11.480 |

an approach, however, does not account for the movement of people. Some of the changes noted by the literature could, instead of being linked to gentrification, have resulted from an improvement in the conditions of the individuals living in a certain neighbourhood, without the presence of outside forces pushing these residents out; increases in income do not always imply that people were pushed out and wealthier individuals moved in (Freeman, 2005). Also incorporating the percentage of people moving mitigates these disadvantages and acknowledges that in-movers are the driving force behind gentrification (Freeman, 2005). Consequently, the change in the percentage of residents with a bachelor's degree or higher, and the percentage of residents that have moved between 2006 and 2011 are included in the regression model to control for the effects of gentrification, and, more broadly, migration. The summary statistics of the variables used in the two models are shown in Table 2.1.

## 4.    RESULTS AND DISCUSSION

Figure 2.2 shows the spatial distribution of median household income and the unemployment rate in the GTHA in 2001 and 2011. In the top two maps, the darkest colour represents the census tracts with the lowest income, whereas the lightest color represents the least vulnerable neighbourhoods. In both years, the low-income census tracts are centred in a ring around downtown Toronto, although a suburbanization of low income areas has occurred; the neighbourhoods to the north and east of the City of Toronto have become more vulnerable in 2011. The outer suburbs, as well as the CBD of Toronto, house higher income populations in both years. In the bottom map, the lowest unemployment rate is presented in the lightest shading while the highest unemployment rate is shown in the darkest shading. The financial crisis of 2007–2008 radically changed the pattern of unemployment across the region: the unemployment rate skyrocketed between 2001 and 2011 in almost every census tract, especially in the outer suburbs.

The spatial distribution of competitive accessibility by public transport and car in both 2001 and 2011 are shown in Figure 2.3. Transit accessibility was calculated for a maximum travel time of 45 minutes, whereas car accessibility was computed for a 30-minute trip. The two modes display profoundly different spatial patterns, due to significant directionality present in the public transport system. During the morning

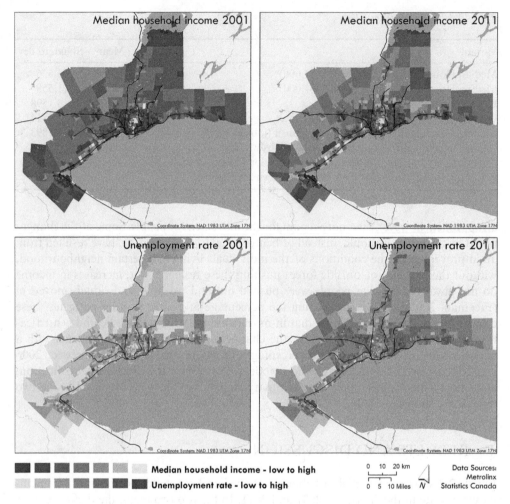

*Figure 2.2    Median household income and unemployment rate in the GTHA in 2001 and 2011*

peak, the GO train network focuses on bringing residents into the Toronto CBD, while the service in the opposite direction is close to non-existent. Suburban job centers are therefore protected from competition by transit: only local residents can access these employment opportunities, resulting in highly competitive accessibility levels. Suburban areas thus exhibit higher competitive accessibility levels than central areas, despite the high proportion of jobs in the CBD, as the potential demand for suburban jobs (number of workers having access to each job) is lower than the potential demand for downtown jobs. Competitive accessibility by transit is thus largely determined by competition effects. By contrast, accessibility by car is mostly influenced by the presence of job opportunities, as directionality is less present in the highway and street networks. Car accessibility is thus highest in downtown Toronto, where the largest amount of job opportunities is present.

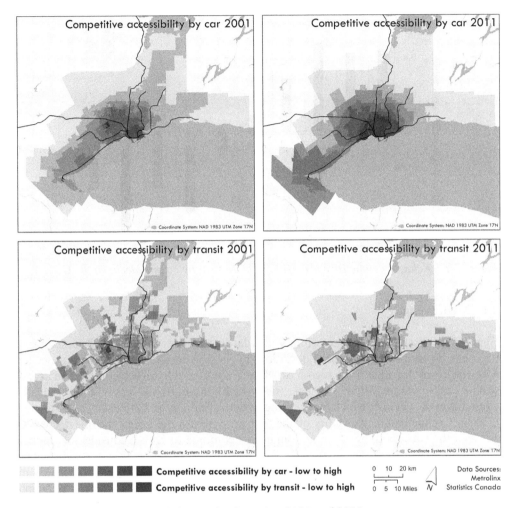

*Figure 2.3   Transit accessibility in the GTHA in 2001 and 2011*

Between 2001 and 2011, accessibility by private automobile rose substantially in Toronto and in the western parts of the region, whereas a small decrease was observed in the eastern census tracts. This increase is likely due to the expansion of the highway 407, especially west of the CBD, allowing individuals residing in the western areas to access a considerably higher number of jobs located in and around the CBD. At the same time, competitive accessibility by transit increased in a few clusters of suburban job centers, and decreased in the rest of the GTHA. This decrease is related to both a suburbanization of jobs and investments made in the GO train network between 2001 and 2011. As jobs moved away from the city centre, accessibility in Toronto's urban core decreased, as people could no longer access these jobs. In addition, the investments made in the GO train network ensured that more people could access jobs in the CBD. Thus, competition for this smaller number of downtown jobs increased, again lowering the competitive accessibility level.

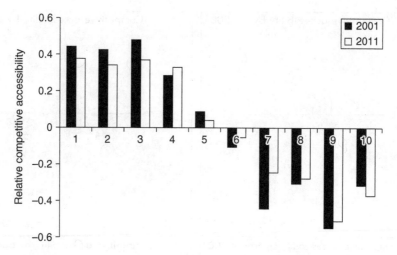

*Figure 2.4   Relative competitive accessibility by transit, by income decile in the GTHA*

### 4.1   Vertical Equity

Figure 2.4 presents transit accessibility standardized values (z-scores – distance from the mean divided by the standard deviation) by income decile. In 2001, the four deciles with the lowest income in the region experience considerably higher competitive accessibility levels by transit than all other groups, highlighting that accessibility is vertically equitable in the GTHA, which is consistent with the findings of Foth et al. (2013) for the GTHA. Competitive accessibility of the four groups with the lowest income decreased between the two years, however, although they continue to have a considerably higher accessibility than the other income deciles. The investments in commuter trains, connecting wealthier neighbourhoods to downtown Toronto, have therefore succeeded in increasing accessibility to employment for high income census tracts, thereby reducing the relative accessibility of low income census tracts This suggests that, while the vertical equity of the transportation and land use system is still high in the GTHA, there is a trend towards decreasing vertical equity and increasing horizontal equity. Note that, as socially vulnerable groups have lower car ownership (Potoglou and Kanaroglou, 2008), this decrease in accessibility can result in substantial negative consequences for the region's most vulnerable populations. To quantify the effects of these accessibility changes on neighbourhood socio-economic status, results of the linear regression models are presented in the next section.

### 4.2   Linear Regression Models

Table 2.2 shows the results of the two linear regression models, with both models showing similar patterns. Only the variables that are statistically significant will be described here. The model predicting median household income in 2011 demonstrates that higher median household income in 2001 is associated with higher median household income in 2011, while the coefficient of 1.12 for this variable suggests that overall income levels

*Table 2.2   Regression results for census tract median household income and unemployment rate in 2011 in the GTHA*

| Variable | Income | | | | Unemployment rate | | | |
|---|---|---|---|---|---|---|---|---|
| | Coefficient | Sig. | Confidence interval[†] | | Coefficient | Sig. | Confidence interval[†] | |
| Constant | 5.11 | *** | 2.071 | 8.15 | 4.7788 | *** | 4.2652 | 5.2925 |
| Median household income in 2001 | 1.121 | *** | 1.093 | 1.149 | – | – | – | – |
| Unemployment rate in 2001 | – | – | – | – | 0.6986 | *** | 0.6362 | 0.761 |
| Change in accessibility by transit | 7.67 | * | 1.276 | 14.065 | −2.5523 | ** | −4.2517 | −0.8529 |
| Change in accessibility by transit • Median household income in 2001 | −0.099 | * | −0.181 | −0.016 | 0.0327 | * | 0.0108 | 0.0546 |
| Change in accessibility by car | 3.37 | *** | 1.49 | 5.249 | −0.5402 | ** | −1.0368 | −0.0436 |
| Change in percentage of residents with a bachelor's degree or higher | 0.664 | *** | 0.554 | 0.775 | −0.093 | *** | −0.1232 | −0.0627 |
| Percentage of residents that have moved between 2006 and 2011 | −0.154 | *** | −0.206 | −0.103 | 0.0116 | | −0.0020 | 0.0252 |
| Adjusted R[2] | 0.8695 | | | | 0.352 | | | |

*Notes:*   Dependent Variables: Median household income in 2011 ($1,000), Unemployment rate in 2011 (%)
\*   95% significance level | \*\* 99% significance level | \*\*\* 99.9% significance level
†   95% confidence interval

rose by 12 percent during the study period, while controlling for all other variables present in the model. Changes in competitive accessibility by transit, and the interaction term between this variable and median household income in 2001, are significantly related to income in 2011. For example, a census tract with a median household income of $40,000 in 2001 is predicted to have an extra increase in income of (7.67 − 0.099\*40) = 3.71 ($3,710) in 2011 per extra unit in competitive accessibility (Table 2.2). A one-unit increase in competitive accessibility occurs when a person can access an extra job that is not accessible to all other residents in the region. The effect of competitive accessibility reverses when income in 2001 is higher than $77,475 (when 7.67 − 0.099\*Income = 0). As higher income populations are more likely to move to less dense areas in search for open space, they tend to migrate to areas without public transport access. As a result, median income decreases in areas where these wealthy groups move out. Increases in competitive accessibility by car are also statistically significant and associated with higher incomes in 2011: a one-unit increase in car accessibility is predicted to increase income by $3,370.

An interaction term between car accessibility and baseline household income in 2001 was also analysed, but was not significant, indicating that the effect of accessibility by car is income-independent.

The remaining statistically significant coefficients highlight that increases in the percentage of residents with a bachelor's degree or higher, and stable neighbourhoods (without many people moving) are related to higher median household incomes in 2011. The significant relationship between income and accessibility by both car and public transport thus highlights that changing equity of opportunity, measured by accessibility, is associated with a changing equity of outcome, measured by income. As the model controls for the migration of highly educated individuals and for percentage of households that moved between 2006 and 2011, the changes in median household income are not only related to gentrification, but also to changes in the income of the residing households.

The second model indicates that higher unemployment rates in 2001 are associated with higher unemployment rates in 2011, suggesting that census tracts with high unemployment rates in 2001 still have higher unemployment in 2011. An extra accessible job by transit that cannot be reached by any other individual (a one-unit increase in transit accessibility) is related to a 2.5 percentage point decrease in unemployment rate for census tracts with a median household income of $0. If median household income in 2001 increases, the effects of changes in transit accessibility lessen and reverse at a median household income of $78,052. By contrast, the change in car accessibility has a uniform effect across income: one extra accessible job by car that cannot be reached by others is linked to a decrease of 0.54 percentage points in unemployment rate. As with the model predicting income, increases in the percentage of residents with a bachelor's degree or higher are significantly associated with lower increases in the unemployment rate. These results are consistent with the findings presented by Tyndall (2015), who found that a substantial change in the provision of public transport (and thus a considerable change in access by transit) was associated with changing unemployment. This suggests that the conclusions by Korsu and Wenglenski (2010) and Andersson et al. (2014) can be extended from unemployment duration at the individual level to aggregated unemployment rates at the neighbourhood scale.

Table 2.3 presents predicted values for median household income and the unemployment rate in 2011 for all income deciles in 2001. The values are predicted for a constant transit accessibility, and for a transit accessibility that increased by one unit during the study period. Median household income in 2011 is greater for all deciles except the two wealthiest groups if accessibility by public transport increased instead of remaining constant. The premium generated by transit accessibility ranges from $3,812 for the lowest income decile to –$13,744 for the highest income decile. One hypothesis for the negative premium observed in the highest income deciles is that wealthier individuals might decide to move away from areas with increased transit accessibility. This is in line with previous research conducted in New Jersey, which found that the construction of a new rail was associated, although not significantly, with a depreciation in property value for houses in high income census tracts near the stations (Chatman, Tulach, and Kim, 2012). This suggests that locations with increased transit accessibility become less desirable for high income individuals. This is likely explained by differing neighbourhood preferences; while low-income individuals might value transit accessibility, high-income individuals, which are more likely to have access to a private vehicle, might place a higher value on residing in

*Table 2.3   Predicted 2011 income and unemployment rates for each income decile in 2001*

| Income decile | Income 2001 | Unemployment rate 2001 | Change in transit accessibility = 0 | | Change in transit accessibility = 1 | |
|---|---|---|---|---|---|---|
| | | | Predicted income 2011 | Predicted unemployment rate 2011 | Predicted income 2011 | Predicted unemployment rate 2011 |
| 1 | 38,967 | 9.7260 | 47,100 | 11.4435 | 50,913 | 10.1655 |
| 2 | 45,353 | 7.5418 | 54,260 | 9.9177 | 57,440 | 8.8484 |
| 3 | 50,835 | 6.5180 | 60,404 | 9.2024 | 63,042 | 8.3124 |
| 4 | 57,487 | 5.8651 | 67,860 | 8.7463 | 69,839 | 8.0738 |
| 5 | 63,125 | 5.6117 | 74,182 | 8.5693 | 75,603 | 8.0812 |
| 6 | 70,204 | 5.0530 | 82,117 | 8.1790 | 82,837 | 7.9223 |
| 7 | 75,605 | 4.6826 | 88,172 | 7.9202 | 88,357 | 7.8402 |
| 8 | 81,954 | 4.6638 | 95,289 | 7.9071 | 94,846 | 8.0347 |
| 9 | 89,749 | 4.1651 | 104,026 | 7.5587 | 102,811 | 7.9411 |
| 10 | 216,308 | 4.0577 | 245,900 | 7.4837 | 232,155 | 12.0046 |

a quiet, less dense neighbourhood. A similar pattern is present in the predicted unemployment rates: the predicted effect of a unit increase in competitive accessibility by transit is –1.28 percentage points for the poorest census tracts, and 4.52 percentage points for the wealthiest decile. Based on these predictions, we can infer that the decreasing vertical equity of transit accessibility (as shown in Figure 2.4) is associated with a widening of the income gap among the census tracts of the GTHA.

## 5.   CONCLUSION

Accessibility to jobs by public transport is a key factor in individuals' quality of life. Results show that accessibility to jobs by public transport is relatively vertically equitable in the Greater Toronto and Hamilton Area, although vertical equity decreased between 2001 and 2011. The census tracts with the lowest income boast the highest accessibility to jobs thanks to their proximity to downtown Toronto and the public transport network, while wealthier groups experience lower accessibility levels.

  This study suggests that, for low and medium income census tracts, increases in transit accessibility are related to higher increases in income. For wealthier census tracts, increases in transit accessibility are associated with decreases in income, potentially due to the migration of high-income populations to less dense neighbourhoods, away from transit. In other words, improvements in transit service, such as a new express bus or rail connection, might bring significant changes to a neighbourhood's structure, namely densification and more mixed use, which might decrease the desirability of living in such areas for some populations. Further research is, however, needed to confirm and understand this relationship. The change in accessibility by car, on the other hand, has a uniform effect across income deciles and is associated with larger income increases. The equity of accessibility to employment opportunities thus plays a key role in determining resulting equity of outcome, stressing the need for methods that can incorporate equity considerations into the evaluation of new transportation projects.

It is important to note that the findings from this study are not conclusive, nor can they determine a causal relationship; more analysis is needed in multiple cities across the globe to further investigate the relationship between accessibility improvements and changes in income and unemployment. Different contexts might be associated with varying housing preferences, for example a preference for central mixed-use and dense neighbourhoods, and accordingly yield different results. While multiple variables related to migration were examined, this study does not fully capture the impacts of population movement between 2001 and 2011. The study controls for changes in the proportion of individuals with a university degree, but does not directly measure the movement of individuals according to their income level. The uncovered relationship could therefore partially be explained by transit accessibility attracting medium income populations, resulting in increases in income for low income areas, and decreases in income for the wealthiest neighbour-hoods. This highlights the need for further research in order to disentangle the complex socio-spatial relationships uncovered in this study. Ideally, future research should employ micro-data to track individuals over time, and use surveys and interviews to shed more light on individual changes in accessibility and socio-economic status.

Future studies should also include the cost of transportation in their analysis and normalize the fares according to income. This would lower the accessibility of the entire population (El-Geneidy et al., 2016), and could reduce accessibility for socially vulnerable groups compared to wealthier groups.

Different types of jobs were not distinguished in the present study, although people cannot access all the different jobs that exist within a city; an individual without a high school diploma will not be able to access the high-wage service-sector jobs that cities offer, regardless of the transport and land use system. Future studies should therefore differentiate low, medium, and high income jobs when comparing accessibility across different groups and different years. The analysis should also take into account the time when different jobs start and incorporate the time aspect in the calculation of accessibility by public transport.

Nevertheless, the results of this study demonstrate a clear association between improvements in accessibility by transit and positive outcomes (measured by changes in income and unemployment) for neighbourhoods with low and medium income. The relationship observed in this study establishes new directions for future research in order to explore the equity of outcome resulting from changing accessibility levels.

## ACKNOWLEDGEMENTS

This research was funded by the Social Sciences and Humanities Research Council of Canada (SSHRC) program. We would like to thank David King, Nicholas Day and Joshua Engel-Yan from Metrolinx for providing the car travel time matrix in 2011. The authors would also like to thank David Levinson and Emily Grisé for their helpful insights.

# REFERENCES

Andersson, F., Haltiwanger, J., Kutzbach, M., Pollakowski, H., and Weinberg, D. (2014). *Job displacement and the duration of joblessness: The role of spatial mismatch*. National Bureau of Economic Research. Cambridge, MA.

Blumenberg, E., and Pierce, G. (2014). A driving factor in mobility? Transportation's role in connecting subsidized housing and employment outcomes in the Moving to Opportunity (MTO) program. *Journal of the American Planning Association, 80*(1), 52–66.

Blumenberg, E., and Pierce, G. (2017). The drive to work: the relationship between transportation access, housing assistance, and employment among participants in the welfare to work voucher program. *Journal of Planning Education and Research, 37*(1), 66–82.

Bocarejo, J., and Oviedo, D. (2012). Transport accessibility and social inequities: a tool for identification of mobility needs and evaluation of transport investments. *Journal of Transport Geography, 24*, 142–154.

Boisjoly, G., and El-Geneidy, A. (2017). How to get there? A critical assessment of accessibility objectives and indicators in metropolitan transportation plans. *Transport Policy*.

Chatman, D., Tulach, N., and Kim, K. (2012). Evaluating the economic impacts of light rail by measuring home appreciation: a first look at New Jersey's river line. *Urban Studies, 49*(3), 467–487.

Delbosc, A., and Currie, G. (2011). Using Lorenz curves to assess public transport equity. *Journal of Transport Geography, 19*(6), 1252–1259, doi:10.1016/j.jtrangeo.2011.02.008.

Delmelle, E., and Casas, I. (2012). Evaluating the spatial equity of bus rapid transit-based accessibility patterns in a developing country: the case of Cali, Colombia. *Transport Policy, 20*, 36–46, doi:10.1016/j.tranpol.2011.12.001.

El-Geneidy, A., Levinson, D., Diab, E., Boisjoly, G., Verbich, D., and Loong, C. (2016). The cost of equity: assessing transit accessibility and social disparity using total travel cost. *Transportation Research Part A, 91*, 302–316.

Fan, Y., Guthrie, A., and Levinson, D. (2012). Impact of light rail implementation on labor market accessibility: a transportation equity perspective. *The Journal of Transport and Land Use, 5*(3), 28–39.

Foth, N., Manaugh, K., and El-Geneidy, A. (2013). Towards equitable transit: examining transit accessibility and social need in Toronto, Canada, 1996–2006. *Journal of Transport Geography, 29*, 1–10.

Freeman, L. (2005). Displacement or succession? Residential mobility in gentrifying neighborhoods. *Urban Affairs Review, 40*(4), 463–491.

Geurs, K., and van Wee, B. (2004). Accessibility evaluation of land-use and transport strategies: review and research directions. *Journal of Transport Geography, 12*(2), 127–140.

Golub, A., and Martens, K. (2014). Using principles of justice to assess the modal equity of regional transportation plans. *Journal of Transport Geography, 41*, 10–20.

Grengs, J. (2015). Nonwork accessibility as a social equity indicator. *International Journal of Sustainable Transportation, 9*(1), 1–14.

Grube-Cavers, A., and Patterson, Z. (2015). Urban rapid rail transit and gentrification in Canadian urban centres: a survival analysis approach. *Urban Studies, 52*(1), 178–194.

Guzman, L., Oviedo, D., and Rivera, C. (2017). Assessing equity in transport accessibility to work and study: the Bogotá region. *Journal of Transport Geography, 58*, 236–246.

Handy, S. (2008). Regional transportation planning in the US: an examination of changes in technical aspects of the planning process in response to changing goals. *Transport Policy, 15*(2), 113–126.

Handy, S., and Niemeier, D. (1997). Measuring accessibility: an exploration of issues and alternatives. *Environment and planning A, 29*(7), 1175–1194.

Hansen, W. (1959). How accessibility shapes land use. *Journal of the American Institute of Planners, 25*(2), 73–76.

Kahn, M. (2007). Gentrification trends in new transit-oriented communities: evidence from 14 cities that expanded and built rail transit systems. *Real Estate Economics, 35*(2), 155–182.

Karner, A., and Niemeier, D. (2013). Civil rights guidance and equity analysis methods for regional transportation plans: a critical review of literature and practice. *Journal of Transport Geography, 33*, 126–134.

Kawabata, M., and Shen, Q. (2007). Commuting inequality between cars and public transit: the case of the San Francisco Bay Area, 1990–2000. *Urban Studies, 44*(9), 1759–1780.

Korsu, E., and Wenglenski, S. (2010). Job accessibility, residential segregation, and risk of long-term unemployment in the Paris region. *Urban Studies, 47*(11), 2279–2324.

Larson, S. (2017). *Social Equity and Public Transit: A Comparative Analysis of Persisting Economic Outcomes and Accountability Indicators*. Denver: University of Colorado.

Litman, T. (2002). Evaluating transportation equity. *World Transport Policy and Practice, 8*(2), 50–65.

Lucas, K., van Wee, B., and Maat, K. (2016). A method to evaluate equitable accessibility: combining ethical theories and accessibility-based approaches. *Transportation, 43*(3), 473–490.

Lyons, M. (1996). Gentrification, socioeconomic change, and the geography of displacement. *Journal of Urban Affairs, 18*(1), 39–62.

Manaugh, K., and El-Geneidy, A. (2012). Who benefits from new transportation infrastructure? Using accessibility measures to evaluate social equity in transit provision. In K. Geurs, K. Krizek, and A. Reggiani (eds), *Accessibility and Transport Planning: Challenges for Europe and North America*. Cheltenham, UK: Edward Elgar.

Mayor of London (2018). Mayor's Transport Strategy. *March 2018*.

Morris, J. M., Dumble, P. L., and Wigan, M. R. (1979). Accessibility indicators for transport planning. *Transportation Research Part A, 13*(2), 91–10.

North Central Texas Council of Governments (2016). Mobility 2040.

NSW Government (2012). NSW Long Term Transport Master Plan.

Paez, A., Mercado, R., Farber, S., Morency, C., and Roorda, M. (2010). Accessibility to health care facilities in Montreal Island: an application of relative accessibility indicators from the perspective of senior and non-senior residents. *International Journal of Health Geographics, 9*(52), 1–15.

Pollack, S., Bluestone, B., and Billingham, C. (2011). *Demographic change, diversity and displacement in newly transit-rich neighborhoods*. Paper presented at the Transportation research board 90th annual meeting.

Potoglou, D., and Kanaroglou, P. (2008). Modelling car ownership in urban areas: a case study of Hamilton, Canada. *Journal of Transport Geography, 16*, 42–54.

Proffitt, D., Bartholomew, K., Ewing, R., and Miller, H. (2015). *Accessibility planning in American metropolitan areas: Are we there yet?* Paper presented at the Transportation Research Board 94th Annual meeting, Washington, D.C.

San Diego Association of Governments (2011). 2050 Regional Transportation Plan.

Shen, Q. (1998). Location characteristics of inner-city neighborhoods and employment accessibility of low-wage workers. *Environment and Planning B: Planning and Design, 25*, 345–365.

Southern California Association of Governments (2016). Regional Transportation Plan 2040.

Stanley, J., and Lucas, K. (2008). Social exclusion: what can public transport offer? *Research in Transportation Economics, 22*(1), 36–40. Retrieved from http://ac.els-cdn.com/S0739885908000103/1-s2.0-S0739885908000 103-main.pdf?_tid=aa219a74-9d1e-11e5-af8f-00000aab0f27&acdnat=1449519253_79a2f9bbd42e1ef58bd61d 7bfcd3de5e.

Statistics Canada (2010). Mode of transportation and average commuting time to get to work in Montréal, Toronto and Vancouver census metropolitan areas. Retrieved from www.statcan.gc.ca/pub/11-008-x/2011002/t/11531/ tblbx-eng.htm.

Tyndall, J. (2015). Waiting for the R train: public transportation and employment. *Urban Studies, 54*(2), 520–537.

van Wee, B., and Geurs, K. (2011). Discussing equity and social exclusion in accessibility evaluations. *European Journal of Transport and Infrastructure Research, 11*(4), 350–367.

Wickstrom, G. (1971). Defining balanced transportation: a question of opprtunity. *Traffic Quarterly, 25*(3), 337–349.

# 3. Reducing social spatial inequity with public transport in Melbourne, Australia
## *Jan Scheurer and Carey Curtis*

## 1. INTRODUCTION

In *The New Urban Crisis*, Richard Florida offers the truism that when it comes to location choices of residential households on different parts of the socio-economic spectrum, 'the rich live where they choose, and the poor live where they can' (Florida, 2017, p.150). Over the past decades, more advantaged groups have re-embraced inner urban living not least because the amenity and diversity of these areas have formed a symbiotic relationship with the emerging knowledge economy where, in many developed cities, the majority of well-paying jobs are found (Newman and Kenworthy, 2015). Residential co-location with such employment hubs generally offers transport users good access to a variety of transport modes for day-to-day travel tasks, from walking and cycling to public transport and the car (both privately owned and shared). The growing concentration of wealthier residents in gentrifying inner-urban areas must thus be understood as aiming for an element of accessibility advantage, or the addition of a greater degree of motility (Kaufmann, 2011; De Vos et al, 2013) to the suite of items constituting socio-economic advantage for this group. Conversely, lower-income households show increasing spatial concentrations in outer suburban areas where walking and cycling conditions are underdeveloped, public transport services fail to meet good standards of useability, and where access to employment by car is tangibly poorer than for inner urban areas.

This chapter builds on the authors' research undertaken in Australia's five largest capital cities (Scheurer et al, 2017), which mapped the spatial patterns of public transport accessibility and socio-economic advantage. Findings for the spatial distribution of socio-economic advantage in relation to public transport accessibility in Melbourne can be considered the closest Australian match to an archetype observed by Florida (2017) in other Anglosphere cities such as New York and London, Boston and Washington DC, San Francisco, Chicago and Toronto. By understanding the associated disparities and broader urban trends, we ask whether future strategic public transport network development can make a meaningful contribution to reducing social-spatial inequity in Melbourne by way of improving accessibility for disadvantaged groups, and if so, what direction it should follow.

## 2. RESEARCH APPROACH

Australian city planning, like other new world cities, has witnessed a change in policy focus over the decades: from post war planning, where individual/household accessibility was to be achieved by planning suburbs and the city to facilitate car-based mobility, to the decades since the 1990s, where planners have shifted to planning the city around ideas of land use–public transport integration (Curtis, 2015). While progress is slow, given long lead times for transport infrastructure and development and also that Australian cities have an urban structure entrenched in car mobility, the investment in public transport can be assessed from an accessibility perspective. This is demonstrated for the major Australian cities drawing using the Spatial Network Analysis for Multimodal Urban Transport Systems (SNAMUTS) tool (Curtis and Scheurer, 2016). It can be seen that the supply of public transport delivers variable accessibility across each metropolitan region and generally favours more centrally located parts of the city over the periphery. This centripetal pattern, much more marked than in European cities since urban areas sprawl over long distances, generally also holds true for car accessibility in relation to jobs, particularly because Australian cities have not developed the major tertiary employment clusters in suburban areas that are common, for example, in many US cities. As shown in investigations on effective job density for commuters (SGSEP, 2015), the number and range of jobs accessible by car consistently remain highest for residents in central areas and lowest at the periphery of Australian agglomerations.

In the following, we will quantify the extent to which more advantaged groups are concentrated in public transport-accessible neighbourhoods, and to which more disadvantaged groups are located away from good public transport access. For this purpose, we superimpose public transport accessibility measures from the SNAMUTS indexes (Curtis and Scheurer, 2016) on the Socio-Economic Indexes for Areas (SEIFA) measures compiled from census data by the Australian Bureau of Statistics (ABS). Our aim is to identify the geographical distribution of statistical areas (SA1) in the highest and lowest average socio-economic status categories (SEIFA quintiles) in relation to public transport accessibility, and to construct a narrative about the opportunities and constraints governing patterns of household location.

The SEIFA have been compiled from ABS census data at five-year intervals since 1986 (Pink, 2013). The Index of Relative Socio-Economic Advantage and Disadvantage (IRSAD) used here represents one out of four published SEIFA indexes and classifies SA1 in relative terms on the basis of a weighted average of 25 separate census measures covering income, education, employment, occupation, housing and other variables. Results are expressed along an arbitrary numerical scale that is standardised for a score of 1000 to represent the mean value across the sample, and for a standard deviation of 100 with higher scores indicating greater area-based socio-economic advantage/lower disadvantage and lower scores indicating lower advantage/greater disadvantage. For ease of interpretation, the ABS recommends the representation of SEIFA results in quantile groups rather than absolute values (ibid). Thus the IRSAD scores used here are differentiated by five residential population quintiles.

Two modified SNAMUTS indicators are utilised in this assessment. The residential coverage indicator is a variation of the network coverage indicator used widely in SNAMUTS and other accessibility analyses (Curtis and Scheurer, 2016). It depicts all residents that are located either within an 800-metre radius of a rail station or ferry terminal, or within a 400-metre linear corridor around a tram or bus route that meets the defined minimum service standard.[1] This figure is expressed as a percentage of the total population of the metropolitan area (in the 'average' column), and as a percentage of the metropolitan population that falls into the SEIFA quintile under consideration. Note that the figures differ from the network coverage figures shown in other SNAMUTS publications (such as Curtis and Scheurer, 2016), since the location of jobs is excluded from this count.

The contour catchment index expresses an approximation of the percentage of metropolitan residents and jobs that can be reached from a reference point within a public transport journey of 30 minutes or less. Out of the suite of eight separate SNAMUTS indicators (Curtis and Scheurer, 2016), this index was chosen because its scores are influenced by a broad combination of speed, frequency and network density of public transport as well as the spatial concentration and density of residents and jobs within each contour. Residents and jobs are combined in this measure to generate a proxy for localising frequent trip origins and destinations associated with residences and workplaces; these categories also reflect the reliable availability of geographically detailed land use data in Melbourne and other jurisdictions. While the rigid 30-minute threshold may lead to 'bracket creep' effects on individual results in scenario comparisons, in practice this shortfall is neutralised by expressing average results over a large sample of measurements.

The index is based on the catchment areas of a suite of defined activity nodes relating to the hierarchy of central places in Melbourne. Each SA1 within the residential coverage areas (as defined above) is allocated to one walkable activity node radius (800 metres for rail stations or ferry terminals) or corridor (400 metres either side along bus or tram routes), or in some cases, to two or more overlapping radii/corridors, and carries the same contour catchment score as all other SA1 within the same radius/corridor (or same configuration of overlapping radii/corridors). The figures in Table 3.1 depict the average 30-minute contour catchment score of all SA1 within the residential coverage areas, and the average 30-minute contour catchment score of all SA1 whose SEIFA scores fall within the respective quintile.[2]

## 3.   PUBLIC TRANSPORT ACCESSIBILITY AND SOCIO-ECONOMIC DISPARITY IN MELBOURNE

In Melbourne the most advantaged 20 per cent of the population are characterised by the highest percentage across all quintiles with walking-distance access to public transport (residential network coverage) (Table 3.1). As relative disadvantage increases, walkable

---

[1]   The minimum service standard requires a rail or ferry route to be operated seven days a week, at a frequency of at least every 30 minutes during the inter-peak period (between 10.00 and 15.00) on weekdays. Buses and trams have to be operated at least every 20 minutes during the weekday inter-peak period, and at least every 30 minutes during the day on Saturdays, Sundays and public holidays.

[2]   Note that the average results in this table differ from those in other publications (such as Curtis and Scheurer, 2016) as they only refer to those SA1 within activity node catchments where there is a residential population, and as they determine averages across all SA1 rather than across the sample of activity nodes.

*Table 3.1*    *Residential network coverage and average 30-minute contour catchments (in percentage of metropolitan residents and jobs) for residents in the five SEIFA quintiles (lowest quintile is most disadvantaged) in Melbourne in 2011*

| Indicator | All quintiles | Lowest quintile | 2nd quintile | 3rd quintile | 4th quintile | Highest quintile |
|---|---|---|---|---|---|---|
| Residential coverage (2011) | 46.1% | 41% | 34% | 45% | 50% | 60% |
| Average contour catchment (2011) | 7.4% | 4.5% | 5.1% | 6.9% | 8.4% | 10.1% |

coverage of public transport and average 30-minute contour catchments decline. Only in the lowest quintile does the coverage figure rise slightly in comparison with the second quintile, but it is still below the metropolitan average. A similar progressive pattern can be observed for the percentage of metropolitan activities a public transport user can reach within a journey of 30 minutes or less (see average contour catchment).

Figure 3.1 shows the geographical distribution of the population's socio-economic advantage and disadvantage in relation to public transport coverage and average 30-minute contour catchment size of residential areas in Melbourne. In this analysis only the top and bottom quintiles are shown in order to discern the patterns more clearly.

Conspicuously, for areas with public transport coverage at the minimum standard there is a clear pattern whereby the most advantaged areas concentrate in inner suburbs, compared to the least advantaged areas, which are predominantly located in the outer suburbs. The most advantaged areas are located in the city's inner east and south-east[3] – districts that have been known as relatively wealthy since they were first urbanised. Today, however, significant parts of what were traditional inner-urban working-class districts (such as Fitzroy and Richmond), located immediately north and east of the CBD, can also be found in the highest SEIFA quintile. The high socio-economic status of these areas thus shows traces both of long-standing affluence and of recent inner-urban gentrification. Loader (2013) documents this pattern over a 25-year period showing a record of sizeable concentrations of disadvantaged households in most of Melbourne's inner-ring suburbs as recently as 1986. In contrast, and echoing the findings in Currie (2010), Melbourne's most disadvantaged areas today are concentrated in the western, northern and south eastern outer suburbs.[4] This is where public transport accessibility performance is low, primarily due to distance from central areas (30 km or more). It is also where walkable access to quality public transport from residential neighbourhoods is largely limited to the station catchments of the widely spaced rail corridors (outer suburban rail nodes on neighbouring corridors tend to be located at an orbital distance of at least 10 km from each other). There are cases where pockets of socio-economic advantage are also found at the urban fringe[5]

---

[3]    The municipalities of Boroondara, Stonnington, Port Phillip, Glen Eira and Bayside.
[4]    Wyndham, Melton, Brimbank, Hume, Whittlesea, Dandenong, Casey, Frankston.
[5]    Particularly surrounding the Yarra Valley in the north-east (Manningham, Nillumbik, Maroondah).

*Figure 3.1*   *Spatial distribution of residential population in the highest and lowest*
*SEIFA quintiles, in relation to public transport network coverage and average*
*30-minute contour catchments in metropolitan Melbourne (2011)*

and in recent high-end master-planned estates.[6] In the broader outer eastern corridors[7] there is a clear tendency for advantaged groups to locate outside the walkable station catchments and for disadvantaged groups to locate inside them. This pattern may be a remnant of post-war preferences of advantaged groups for spacious and scenic residential locations at some distance from the (previously urbanised) direct rail station catchments, but does not appear to be replicated elsewhere in metropolitan Melbourne.

Melbourne's socio-economic and accessibility geography thus illustrates a trend for

---

[6]   Such as Sanctuary Lakes and Point Cook in Wyndham (south-west), Laurimar in Whittlesea (north-east) or Berwick Springs in Casey (south east).

[7]   Ringwood to Lilydale and (to a lesser extent) the Ringwood to Belgrave rail branches.

advantaged groups to consolidate in and capitalise on public transport-accessible inner areas, and a trend for disadvantaged groups to concentrate in outer suburban areas (mostly away from scenic waterfronts and river valleys) where public transport access is patchy.

In a detailed analysis of transport disadvantage, social exclusion and well-being across the Melbourne metropolitan area, Delbosc and Currie (2011) also differentiate between inner, outer, fringe and regional areas. They conclude that transport disadvantage expresses itself more acutely with increasing distance from the city centre, as 'spatial gaps' (Currie, 2010) in public transport supply proliferate and the range of activities that can be reached by non-car modes diminishes. This leads to pressures on low-income households in terms of financial burdens and time poverty associated with high car ownership and use, and/ or to forgone opportunities for social and employment participation due to accessibility gaps. An ongoing trend for socially and economically disadvantaged groups to vacate public transport-accessible and walkable/cyclable inner areas due to gentrification effects in favour of more affordable urban fringe locations takes on additional significance in this context. It must be regarded as an entrenchment both of the geographical division of Melbourne along socio-economic lines, and of the variegation of socio-economic inequality experienced by the affected segments of the population.

In these circumstances our interest is whether there is a role for integrated public transport and land use planning to ameliorate the effects of socio-economic inequality. We question whether current urban development trends, investment priorities and allocation of operational resources in Australian cities reflect this role.

In Melbourne, opportunities for a better alignment of urban development to overcome car dependence and reduce socio-economic inequality have been hampered by spatial mismatches between public transport infrastructure and activity centres as the metropolitan fringe underwent ongoing urbanisation (Goodman and Coote, 2007). Further, there is an absence of effective affordable housing policies that could enable a larger proportion of disadvantaged groups to move to, or remain in, inner suburban areas where a greater choice of transport options is available and pressures toward car ownership and use are diminished (Martel et al, 2013).

Looking forward, the current public transport infrastructure and network development strategies for Melbourne (PTV, 2012; IV, 2016) do not appear to address this important issue of socio-economic inequality. New rail infrastructure proposals focus on the provision of additional radial lines through central areas in order to boost capacity for strong growth in forecast demand. In addition there are proposals for the outer extension or electrification of suburban lines to access fringe growth areas. Important as they are to future-proof public transport in a fast-growing metropolitan area, these proposals, aided by methodological bias inherent in conventional project appraisal tools (Hickman and Dean, 2017), primarily represent a response to existing radial, suburb-to-CBD movement patterns. They do not accommodate the expansion of public transport into multi-directional travel markets that are currently dominated by the car, such as work commutes and discretionary trips to inner urban destinations beyond the CBD (Scheurer et al, 2016).

Melbourne's urban growth has gradually shifted from its previous dominance of Greenfield development at the urban fringe towards a greater role for urban intensification in established areas (Scheurer and Woodcock, 2017). However, both forms of urban growth are almost exclusively guided by the commercial objectives of the development industry and largely lack dedicated, place- or project-based instruments to make housing more affordable. In these circumstances, it is unlikely that the accessibility gains achieved by improved public transport infrastructure in either central or outer suburban areas translate into a tangible broadening of residential location choices for more disadvantaged socio-economic groups away from their current strongholds in outer suburban corridors.

## 4.   ALTERNATIVE PUBLIC TRANSPORT FUTURES

While the above statements suggest that current strategies will do little to resolve the issues on socio-economic disparity, an in-depth analysis using the SNAMUTS accessibility tool provides an opportunity to examine alternative public transport futures. Three scenarios are tested (Figures 3.2–3.5). The first scenario, 2026 Trend, is based on the suite of 'committed projects' that have been commenced or announced by government for likely completion by that year. They range from a multibillion additional rail tunnel through the central city to suburban rail extensions, tram network reconfigurations and frequency improvements on rail, tram and bus routes. These proposals are aimed at better serving an increasing population: between 2011 and 2026, Melbourne is expected to grow by 1.4 million inhabitants to 5.4 million.

The second scenario, 2026 Trend plus orbital links, comprises, in addition to the 2026 Trend measures (above), the conversion of the radially-dominated network structure into a more multi-directional pattern. This is achieved by adding tram and high-frequency bus routes to a number of critical orbital corridors in the inner and middle suburbs. These measures are designed to take pressure off the CBD area by allowing more convenient movement paths around it, and to improve public transport mode share and reduce car commuting to and from the increasing number of knowledge employment clusters that are developing beyond the CBD boundary.

The third scenario, 2026 Trend plus Montulla,[8] also contains the 2026 Trend measures and additionally envisages the construction of a 55-km driverless orbital metro line linking the airport with several university-based employment clusters (Latrobe, Deakin and Monash Universities) as well as several suburban concentrations of socially and economically disadvantaged groups (Broadmeadows, Reservoir North, West Heidelberg, Springvale) at a distance of about 20–25 km from central Melbourne. This piece of infrastructure is primarily intended to improve the spatial and functional integration of what are promoted by the state planners as nationally significant knowledge employment centres outside the CBD, and their accessibility for employees from the metropolitan region.

Table 3.2 illustrates how the two SNAMUTS measures of residential coverage and average contour catchment (used above in relation to current accessibility) are likely to evolve under the assumptions of these three future scenarios.

Due to its greater focus on generating new public transport access in previously underserviced areas particularly in outer suburbs, the incremental increase in residential

---

[8]   The name 'Montulla' is an amalgam of the largest tertiary employment cluster outside the CBD around Monash University, and Melbourne's airport at Tullamarine.

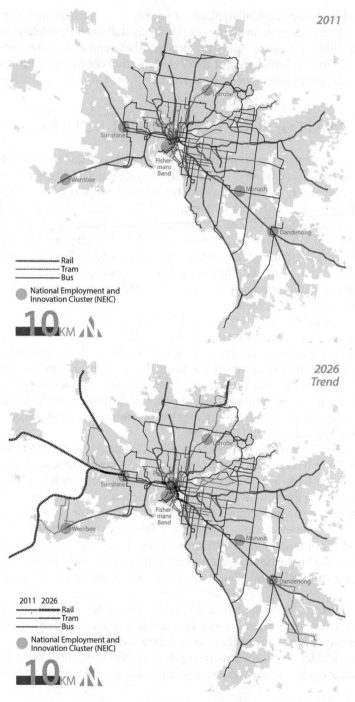

*Figures 3.2–3.5    Melbourne's 2011 public transport network (at the SNAMUTS minimum*
*service standards) and proposed improvements in the 2026 Trend, 2026*
*Trend plus inner orbital links and 2026 Trend plus Montulla scenarios*

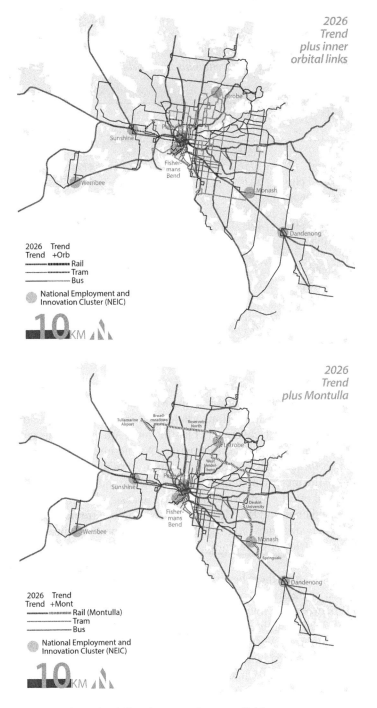

*Figures 3.2–3.5* (continued – full colour versions available at www.snamuts.com)

*Table 3.2    Residential network coverage and average 30-minute contour catchments (in percentage of metropolitan residents and jobs) for residents in the five SEIFA quintiles (lowest quintile is most disadvantaged) in Melbourne in 2011, and in the 2026 Trend, 2026 Trend plus inner orbital links and 2026 plus Montulla scenarios*

| Indicator | Scenario | All quintiles | Lowest quintile | 2nd quintile | 3rd quintile | 4th quintile | Highest quintile |
|---|---|---|---|---|---|---|---|
| Residential network coverage | 2011 | 46.1% | 41% | 34% | 45% | 50% | 60% |
| | 2026 Trend | 49.0% | 47% | 38% | 47% | 52% | 61% |
| | 2026 Trend plus inner orbital links | 50.6% | 48% | 39% | 49% | 54% | 62% |
| | 2026 Trend plus Montulla | 49.3% | 47% | 38% | 48% | 53% | 61% |
| Average contour catchment | 2011 | 7.4% | 4.5% | 5.1% | 6.9% | 8.4% | 10.1% |
| | 2026 Trend | 8.7% | 5.7% | 6.1% | 8.1% | 10.2% | 11.6% |
| | 2026 Trend plus inner orbital links | 10.3% | 6.6% | 7.2% | 9.7% | 12.0% | 13.8% |
| | 2026 Trend plus Montulla | 9.7% | 6.7% | 6.9% | 8.8% | 10.7% | 12.2% |

network coverage is significantly larger in the 2026 Trend scenario over 2011 than after the addition of either inner orbital links or the Montulla line to the 2026 Trend scenario (many of the associated lines or stations are located in areas where existing radial lines already provide geographical coverage). On the more qualitative measure of average contour catchments, a different picture emerges. As the inner orbital routes are added, the relative growth in activities accessible within a 30-minute public transport journey more than doubles the increment achieved in the 2026 Trend scenario when compared to 2011. The additional effect of the Montulla line is also significant. In other words, while both the inner orbital links and the Montulla line add only marginally to the geographical expansion of the network, they add significantly to its performance and thus generate numerous additional travel opportunities for existing and prospective public transport users.

Table 3.2 also shows how these benefits are distributed across different socio-economic groups. There is a regressive effect on the endowment measure of network coverage, in that the gap between the lowest and highest SEIFA quintile is expected to narrow between 2011 and 2026 in all three scenarios. However, despite the growth in coverage, the overall ranking of quintiles in this measure remains intact: the most socio-economically advantaged neighbourhoods remain the most likely to enjoy access to public transport at the SNAMUTS standard, while the most disadvantaged neighbourhoods remain the second least likely to do so. To close this gap further, an ongoing effort is required beyond 2026. This would require public transport services with better frequencies and longer operational spans to penetrate into socio-economically disadvantaged areas in Melbourne's middle and outer suburbs. While these are both objectives of current government policy (IV, 2016), they rely on the deployment of large numbers of buses into low-density areas, where they are likely to only recover a minor portion of their operating costs. Such a policy, in prioritising the allocation of finite operational resources to the goal of geographically accessing a greater share of the population, may work to the detriment of improving routes or access to areas where the potential for patronage gains is highest, such as those suggested in the inner orbital links and Montulla scenario (Walker, 2012).

The average contour catchment measure, in contrast, appears to evolve progressively over the SEIFA quintiles with the infrastructure and service initiatives proposed. This means that existing disparities in public transport accessibility performance between socio-economic groups are further entrenched. The residential areas of the two most advantaged SEIFA quintiles served at the SNAMUTS standard enjoy the highest rate of increase in activities accessible within 30 minutes, while the two least advantaged quintiles experience the lowest rate. This is the case for both the committed projects in the 2026 Trend scenario and the additional proposals around orbital links (though the inner orbital routes conspicuously produce a wider gap between average contour catchments for the most advantaged and most disadvantaged SEIFA quintiles than either the Trend or the Montulla scenario). This is true despite the suites of measures in each scenario following quite different (though complementary) policy goals, and points to a funda-mental dilemma: can public transport network development on its own make a sufficient contribution to overcoming socio-spatial disparities in metropolitan Melbourne, or does it require a multi-sector approach whose coincidence is critical to tackle the problem?

## 5.  DISCUSSION AND CONCLUSION

In this chapter we set out to understand the patterns of public transport accessibility by socio-economic groups. Using Melbourne as our case for analysis we have shown that broadly the most advantaged socio-economic groups are located in inner suburbs where they also benefit from the best levels of public transport accessibility. Such accessibility not only gives them a choice of transport modes, but also provides them with greater accessibility to opportunities (of work, education, shopping and leisure activities) than less advantaged groups. Conversely, those with the least socio-economic advantage tend to locate in the middle and outer suburbs, where public transport access to the full range of metropolitan opportunities is far more limited. This not only reduces the transport choices of these groups, but it also disadvantages them in terms or social and economic participation. It should be noted that improving transport access to employment, while providing part of the solution, does not mean that the jobs are suitable for all. To achieve this, there needs to be greater policy intervention through such means as widening access to education, improving skill levels and so on.

Our analysis, using an accessibility tool to model future public transport investment scenarios, sought to query how this investment could assist the least advantaged groups and so afford them greater social inclusion. We modelled three scenarios for 2026, one comprising government committed and proposed projects, the other two taking these projects and looking also for opportunities to improve the network and multi-directional travel. Overall, all three scenarios succeeded only modestly in improving public transport accessibility for the most disadvantaged groups.

Two key issues must be noted. First, the timeframe to 2026 is not that far away and highlights the need for greater efforts to be made for long-term futures planning if any impact on social disparity is the be addressed. Second, in geographical terms Melbourne, like other Australian metropolitan areas, has a large physical footprint (spanning 70–80 km both east to west and north to south). This is a city whose dominant urban growth period occurred in step with the aspirations for mobility by car. Since 1945, transport investment has concentrated on expanding the road network rather than on serving this growth by public transport. Any desire to switch this balance to favour public transport accessibility will be a considerable challenge even if investment priorities change drastically in favour of public transport in the future.

As we show in our analysis, on the one hand it is geometrically inevitable that the catchments of travel contours increase with greater geographical centrality of their reference point in relation to the overall settlement area. Thus in a city like Melbourne where the more advantaged groups hold and/or recolonise the majority of centrally located neighbourhoods, while the more disadvantaged groups have few options but to occupy the fringes of the metropolitan area, accessibility performance of the public transport network must necessarily grow and decline with socio-economic status. To effectively counter this trend would require considerable investment in dedicated public transport infrastructure – perhaps an expansive network of many Montulla-style driverless metro lines, linking the outer suburbs where lower socio-economic groups concentrate, could make it a difference. The magnitude of such a task, however, highlights the effect of historical path dependence where the issue of superior public transport access in post-1945 urban areas has long remained unaddressed. This shortfall is now extremely costly to resolve – not only from an infrastructure perspective, but also from a social perspective.

On the other hand, the current distributional trend of socio-economic groups to residential locations across Melbourne should not be understood as immutable, or as impervious to policy intervention. There is a paucity of effective strategies to enable more affordable housing in areas with superior public transport accessibility in Melbourne (and across Australian cities in general). Greater ambition in this field would offer a feasible pathway for governments not just to enable greater participation in social and employment activities for disadvantaged groups, but also to maintain or rebuild a greater social mix in existing neighbourhoods as a policy of future-proofing the community against the divisive effects of a housing market left solely or predominantly to commercial forces. A long house price boom has prevailed in Australian cities, especially Sydney and Melbourne, for nearly two decades and has contributed to the socio-spatial disparities investigated in this chapter. There is a broad variety of opinions as to how and when this boom will come to an end, and what housing market conditions will characterise its aftermath (Henderson and Mountain, 2017). But relief from the pressures of rapid property price gains may act as an opportunity for housing policies with a greater focus on the public interest, including the ability of the most disadvantaged members of society to live in areas where they can base their daily movement around high-quality public transport rather than the car.

It is clear that investment in public transport alone will not address the differences in accessibility to opportunity between different social groups. This is not a signal to do nothing, but rather a call to do more to address the imbalance in infrastructure expenditure on public transport accessibility compared to car accessibility, and a call for longer term transport planning framed around clear social inclusion goals. In addition to transport investment, there is an urgent need to address the land use dimension of accessibility. This requires that there are effective housing policies to ensure housing supply for those least advantaged in our society, providing the choice to live in areas where travel by public transport is convenient and attractive. It also suggests a need to ensure a more equitable distribution of jobs and services within closer reach of residents in middle and outer suburbs.

## ACKNOWLEDGEMENTS

SNAMUTS research in Australian cities was made possible through ARC Discovery Grant DP110104884, 'Spatial Network Analysis for Multimodal Urban Transport Systems: A Planning Decision Support Tool', and through collaborations with local and state government agencies in Western Australia and Victoria.

## REFERENCES

Currie, G. (2010) Quantifying Spatial Gaps in Public Transport Supply Based on Social Needs. *Journal of Transport Geography 18*, 31–41.

Curtis, C. (2015) Public Transport Orientated Development and Network Effects, Chapter 9 in Hickman, R., Givoni M., Bonilla, D. and Banister D. (eds) *Handbook on Transport and Development*. Edward Elgar: Cheltenham, UK.

Curtis, C., and Scheurer, J. (2016) *Planning for Public Transport Accessibility. An International Sourcebook*. Routledge: Oxon, UK.

De Vos, J., Schwanen, T., Van Acker, V., and Witlox, F. (2013) Travel and Subjective Wellbeing: A Focus on Findings, Methods and Future Research Needs. *Transport Reviews 33*(4), 421–442.

Delbosc, A., and Currie, G. (2011) The Spatial Context of Transport Disadvantage, Social Exclusion and Wellbeing. *Journal of Transport Geography 19*, 1130–1137.

Florida, R. (2017) *The New Urban Crisis. How Our Cities are Increasing Inequality, Deepening Segregation, and Failing the Middle Class – and What We can Do About It*. Basic Books: New York (NY), USA.

Goodman, R., and Coote, M. (2007) Sustainable Urban Form and the Shopping Centre: An Investigation of Activity Centres in Melbourne's Growth Areas. *Urban Policy and Research 25*(1), 39–61.

Henderson, J., and Mountain, W. (2017) Four Ways an Australian Housing Bubble Could Burst. *The Conversation*, 1 May, available online at https://theconversation.com/four-ways-an-australian-housing-bubble-could-burst-76505.

Hickman, R., and Dean, M. (2017) Incomplete Cost – Incomplete Benefit Analysis in Transport Appraisal. *Transport Reviews*, DOI: 10.1080/01441647.2017.1407377.

[IV] Infrastructure Victoria (2016) *Victoria's 30-Year Infrastructure Strategy*. State of Victoria, December 2016, available online at www.infrastructurevictoria.com.au.

Kaufmann, V. (2011) *Rethinking the City: Urban Dynamics and Motility*. EPFL Press: Lausanne, Switzerland.

Loader, C. (2013) Visualising the Changing Socio-Economic Landscape of Melbourne. *Charting Transport*, available online at www.chartingtransport.com/2013/09/29/visualising-the-changing-socio-economic-landscape-of-melbourne/.

Martel, A., Whitzman, C., Fincher, R., Lawther, P., Woodcock, I., and Tucker, D. (2013) Getting to Yes: Overcoming barriers to affordable family friendly housing in inner Melbourne. *6th State of Australian Cities Conference (SOAC)*, Sydney, November 2013.

Newman, P., and Kenworthy, J. (2015) *The End of Automobile Dependence. How Cities are Moving Beyond Car-Based Planning*. Island Press: Washington (DC), USA.

Pink, B. (2013) *Socio-Economic Indexes for Areas (SEIFA), 2011*. Technical Paper, Australian Bureau for Statistics, available online at www.abs.gov.au.

[PTV] Public Transport Victoria (2012) *Network Development Plan – Metropolitan Rail*. State of Victoria, December 2012, available online at www.ptv.vic.gov.au.

Scheurer, J., and Woodcock, I. (2017) Trams and Politics in Melbourne: Managing Complex Adaptations. *8th State of Australian Cities Conference (SOAC)*, Adelaide, 28–30 November.

Scheurer, J., Curtis, C., and McLeod, S. (2016) Making Melbourne's public transport network multi-directional: Can the associated accessibility boost mobilise latent potential for ridership and city-building? *38th Australasian Transport Research Forum (ATRF)*, Melbourne, November 2016.

Scheurer, J., Curtis, C., and McLeod, S. (2017) Spatial Accessibility of Public Transport in Australian Cities: Does It Relieve or Entrench Social and Economic Inequality? *Journal of Transport and Land Use 10*(1), 911–930.

SGS Economics and Planning (2015) Effective Job Density: Comparing our Cities and Regions. Available online at www.sgsep.com.au/publications/effective-job-density-comparing-our-cities-and-regions.

Walker, J. (2012) *Human Transit: How Clearer Thinking About Public Transit Can Enrich Our Communities and Our Lives.* Island Press: Washington (DC).

# 4. Exploring the travel mode choice of rail transit with geographically weighted regression: evidence from Chongqing
*Lixun Liu*

## 1. INTRODUCTION

China's cities are still growing fast, with increasing population, and areas which previously had poor transport supply open to development. The Chinese government recognises that the positive externalities from rail transit development outweigh the huge investment and subsidies needed to maintain the systems. With severe traffic congestion in large Chinese cites, the government hopes that rail transit systems can provide the capacity to meet the ever-rising transport demands of the increasing urban population. Moreover, it is widely recognised that the deteriorating environment in Chinese cities, especially the level of air pollution, is partly contributed by vehicle emissions, which relates closely to the rapidly increasing use of automobiles. The government has felt unprecedented urgency to encourage the population to switch to rail transit from their private cars. All of these constitute the motives of the government to promote rail transit development, and are considered even more important than the economic stimulus the investments can be expected to bring to the cities.

In 2012, the Chinese central government announced a stimulus of about ¥800 billion (bn) CNY (Chinese Yuan Renminbi; about USD $127 bn), to be used over the next three to eight years for building twenty-five subways and elevated rail lines across China, with the aim of increasing mobility for the population in a rapidly urbanising nation. By 2014, twenty-two cities had begun operating eighty-three rail transit lines in China. The vast majority of these lines were newly built since 2000 (China Research and Intelligence Co. Ltd., 2015; Cao and Pan, 2016). The requirement to ensure public transport has a high mode share in Chinese cities requires us to understand what factors lead to public transport usage.

There are two key concerns within the literature regarding transit investment and the availability of public (rail) transit systems, these being: (a) whether they influence people's transportation mode choice; and (b) whether usage patterns are distributed evenly across space and among different socio-economic groups (Geurs et al., 2009; Lucas, 2012; Schwanen et al., 2015). These issues can be disentangled at two levels. First, we can ask what factors explain the variation in people's choice as to whether they use rail as their mode of transit? Second, does the relationship between transit mode choice and other influential variables vary significantly over space?

The objective of this chapter is to contribute to a more substantive understanding of why people choose rail transit as a mode of travel: studying factors that vary across space and population cohorts within the city; and exploring whether inequity issues arise from the socio-spatial distribution of benefit from new transit development. The issues are explored first at the level of the whole system, by employing a logistic regression model to explore which variables have an influence on transport choice. The effects of spatial heterogeneity are then assessed, by introducing a geographically weighted regression (GWR) model. This is utilised to reveal the spatial variation in parameter estimates of the global model, as a reflection of what is unique about individual places. Therefore, it helps to more deeply examine the causes of the variation.

## 2.    LITERATURE REVIEW

Many studies employ multivariate statistical analyses to explore the interrelationships among variables that may predict people's public transport use (Messenger and Ewing, 1996; Kuby et al., 2004; Cervero, 2006; Cervero et al., 2010; Taylor et al., 2009; Souche, 2010; Pan et al., 2009, 2013). The conventional multivariate regression produces a global predictive model of these relationships. However, at a further level, we also need to acknowledge that the relationships among the independent and dependent variables vary over space. That is to say, statistical models that incorporate spatial data may exhibit spatial non-stationary factors, and this is a reflection of what is unique about individual places. When taking into consideration the spatial non-stationary data of a model, the research questions should also be developed further. For example, does the relationship between transit mode choice and other influential variables vary significantly over space? Then, how do we explain the spatial non-stationary factors in this context? To account for this, spatially-weighted statistical models need to be used, to account for the spatial variation in model parameter estimates (Fotheringham et al., 2003).

There has been previous research on the impact of socio-economic characteristics on people's 'travel mode shift' in response to a newly built mass rail transit line or other rail transit network (Jones, 2015). The critical factors influencing travel mode shift were those relating to income, car ownership, education level, age, perceptions, and residential status (e.g. newcomers vs. established residents). It was found that, compared to the established residents, the newcomers in the Jubilee Line Extension (JLE) impacted areas were more likely to be: younger, white, employed, highly qualified, earn much higher incomes, car owners, make more use of the Underground, and be less likely to use buses or walk. The newcomers had made a significant shift in the pattern of destinations visited — travelling for work, shopping, leisure or social activities. However, the established residents living in the area made relatively limited use of the JLE, and there was minimal evidence of any change to their travel patterns (Butler, 2007; Gatersleben et al., 2007). It is argued that most often people choose bus travel because of the cheaper fare, and that rail transport is the mode of choice for a relatively affluent population (Gwilliam, 2002, 2003).

Many studies employ multivariate statistical analyses to explore the interrelationships among variables that may predict people's public transport use. Global models based on multiple regression analysis (Messenger and Ewing, 1996; Kuby et al., 2004; Cervero, 2006; Cervero et al., 2010; Taylor et al., 2009; Souche, 2010; Pan et al., 2009, 2013) are a complementary approach to estimating transit use-related variables as a function of station environment and transit service features. These predictor variables can reveal the impact of urban planning on transit use, which are particularly relevant in transit oriented development (Cardozo et al., 2012).

However, the main difficulty with global models is the means by which they handle spatial data. The issue of spatial dependency in a global model is an important concern. The inherently spatial nature of data sets in global models potentially leads to biased estimates and unreliable test statistics (Du and Mulley, 2006). In response to these problems, local spatial analytical methods, such as GWR have been developed to address the potential spatial dependency and model spatial heterogeneity (Higgins and Kanaroglou, 2016). Thus in this study it was decided that GWR was the best approach to model the relationship between the dependent and independent variables over space.

## 3.   DATA AND METHOD

The city of Chongqing (重庆) is used as the case study for this chapter. It is located on the upper Yangtze River (长江), in the region of Southwest China (西南) (Figure 4.1). As of the 2014 Census, the main urban area has a residential population of 8.2 million. Although Chongqing's main urban area only spans 5,473 km², its administrative area is more comparable to a province: it spans over 80,000 km², much of which is rural.

The old city centre in Chongqing is located at the junction of the two rivers. With the development of the airport in the early 1990s, development has been witnessed at astonishing speed, turning the previous farmlands on the north of the river into a prosperous new city centre within just 20 years (Figure 4.2).

Currently in Chongqing, four lines of the public transit Metro network are in operation (Lines 1, 2, 3 and 6), with a total length of 202 km. The first line was opened in 2004. Three new lines were added — two in 2011 and one in 2012 (Figure 4.2), and there is now an extensive Metro network. According to the Municipal Government's plan, by 2020, the public transit network will consist of six radial lines and one circular line, with a total length of 480 km. This compares to 402 km on the London Underground network (2013).

The association between people's travel-related variables and socio-economic characteristics, and choice of rail transit for travel, was modelled using data from a citywide travel survey (Chongqing urban household travel survey 2014), which took place three years into the operation of Lines 1, 3 and 6. This survey sampled households in the twenty-five transport zones. The sample size of each zone was based on its population size. The whole survey contained a sample of 80,000 persons, in 28,000 households, in the main city region (representing a one per cent sampling of the total population).

For this study, data for the central city impacted zones were extracted for analysis from four central transport zones — yielding a dataset of 5,111 persons. Next, data from people below 18 years of age were excluded, in order to focus the analysis on people's commuting patterns. Thus, a final dataset amounting to 3,642 persons was used for the analysis in this chapter. The following logistic regression and GWR analysis were carried out on this sample.

The following research questions are asked:

1.  What factors explain the variation in people's choice as to whether they use rail as their mode of transit?
2.  Does the relationship between transit mode choice and other influential variables vary significantly over space? Then, how do we explain the spatial non-stationary data in this context?

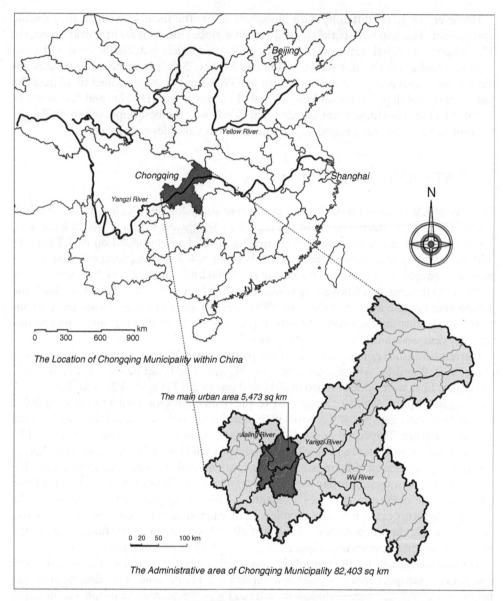

*Figure 4.1   Location of Chongqing municipality within China and the administrative area of Chongqing municipality*

In answering the first research question, the aim was to explore what factors influence people choosing rail transit; that is to say, what factors significantly differentiate those people who choose rail transit from those people who choose other travel modes. Binomial logistic regression was first employed to explore the relationship between the choice of travel mode and a number of explanatory variables.

Following this, GWR was then used to explore the spatial non-stationarity data in

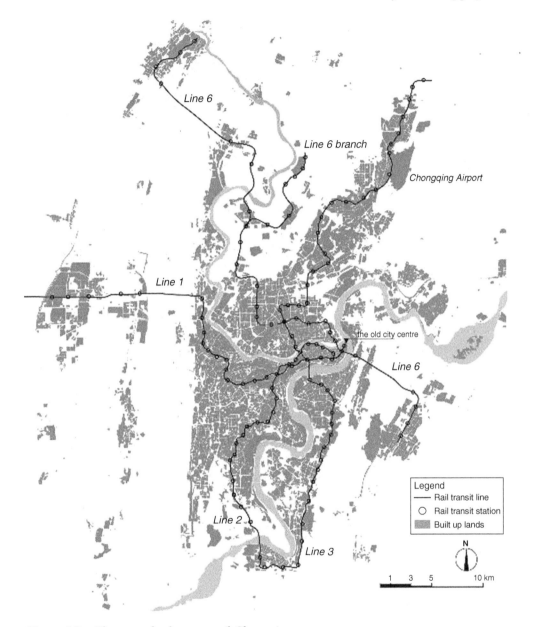

*Figure 4.2   The central urban area of Chongqing*

the global logistic regression model. GWR is utilised to reveal the spatial variation in model parameter estimates, as a reflection of what is unique about individual places. The GWR model is incorporated into the regression process, allowing the inclusion of spatial characteristics within the existing regression model (Du and Mulley, 2006). Therefore, it helps to more deeply explain the cause of the variation, and to better address the research questions.

*Table 4.1    Percentage of transit use in different travel distance categories grouped by region*

| Travel distance categories | | Travel mode | | |
| --- | --- | --- | --- | --- |
| | | Rail transit | Other travel modes | Sum |
| Old city region | 0–5km | 94 | 1039 | 1133 |
| | | 8.30% | 91.70% | 100.00% |
| | 5–10km | 142 | 398 | 540 |
| | | 26.30% | 73.70% | 100.00% |
| | 10–20km | 61 | 134 | 195 |
| | | 31.28% | 68.72% | 100.00% |
| | above 20km | 22 | 44 | 66 |
| | | 33.33% | 66.67% | 100.00% |
| New city region | 0–5km | 31 | 898 | 929 |
| | | 3.34% | 96.66% | 100.00% |
| | 5–10km | 38 | 410 | 448 |
| | | 8.48% | 91.52% | 100.00% |
| | 10–20km | 26 | 211 | 237 |
| | | 10.97% | 89.03% | 100.00% |
| | above 20km | 14 | 80 | 94 |
| | | 14.89% | 85.11% | 100.00% |
| Sum | | 428 | 3214 | 3642 |

*Source:*   Citywide household panel travel survey 2014.

A cross-tabulation of travel distance and travel modes in the city, by old and new city regions is shown in Table 4.1. Within both the old city and the new city, the longer the distance people travel, the higher the percentage of transit use there is. For example, the percentage of transit use in the old city is 8.3, 26.3, 31.3 and 33.3 per cent for the travel distances of 0–5 km, 5–10 km, 10–20 km and above 20 km, respectively. The largest increase in rail transit mode is between the categories of 0–5 km and 5–10 km (in the old city region), with the percentage increasing from 8.3 to 26.3 per cent. A similar pattern is seen for the data from the new city. For example, 26.3 per cent of people in the old city region who travelled 5–10 km chose rail transit as their travel mode, compared to only 8.5 per cent of people who travelled in the same category of distance in the new city region. However, whilst the data in Table 4.1 suggests that rail transit may have a greater impact in the old city than in the new city region (and may be facilitating people's longer trips), the GWR method was also then used to explore this spatial distribution in more detail.

## 4.   RESULTS

### 4.1   Global Model

The global model was used to explore the relationship between a combination of explanatory (independent) variables (on the right side of Equation 1.), and the choice of rail

*Table 4.2  Coefficients of the binary logistical regression model with significant variables*

| | b | Std. Error | Wald z-statistic | Sig. | exp(b) | 95% confidence intervals for Exp(b) | |
|---|---|---|---|---|---|---|---|
| | | | | | | Lower | Upper |
| Constant | 0.316 | 0.219 | 1.442 | 0.149 | 1.372 | 0.894 | 2.112 |
| Commuting travel distance | 0.082 | 0.007 | 10.990 | 0.000 | 1.085 | 1.069 | 1.101 |
| Distance to the nearest transit station | −0.002 | 0.000 | −10.319 | 0.000 | 0.998 | 0.998 | 0.998 |
| Age | −0.039 | 0.005 | −8.049 | 0.000 | 0.962 | 0.953 | 0.971 |
| Car owner | −1.098 | 0.146 | −7.540 | 0.000 | 0.334 | 0.249 | 0.441 |

transit use, or other measures of transport (on the left side of Equation 1.), which was the dependent (response) variable. Travel mode choice was the dependent variable in the model. Independent variables included travel distance, distance to nearest transit station, age and car ownership.

Travel mode (all other travel modes, 0; rail transit user, 1) ~  (1)
Travel Distance + Distance to the nearest transit station + Age
+ Household car ownership (no car, 0; car owner, 1)

$$\chi^2 = 37.809$$
$$df = 8$$
$$AIC = 2236$$

This gave a p-value < .000, which indicated that this model was a good fit of the data. The values of the coefficients of this modified model are shown in Table 4.2.

In summary, the results of the two binary logistic models show four variables, travel distance, distance to transit stations, age and car ownership, are significant in predicting people's choice of rail transit as their travel mode (p < .000). When travel distance increases, the probability of choosing transit decreases. In contrast, when distance to a transit station and age increase, the probability of choosing transit decreases. If the resident is a car owner, they are less likely to choose transit.

## 4.2  Geographic Weighted Regression Analysis

A general GWR model was carried out in R software. Dependent and independent variables are the same as in Equation 1. The results of distributions of coefficients in the GWR model are explained below.

### 4.2.1  The coefficient of 'travel distance'
The spatial distribution of the coefficient of 'travel distance' in predicting travel model choice of rail transit in GWR was studied (Figure 4.3). In the global model, the coefficient

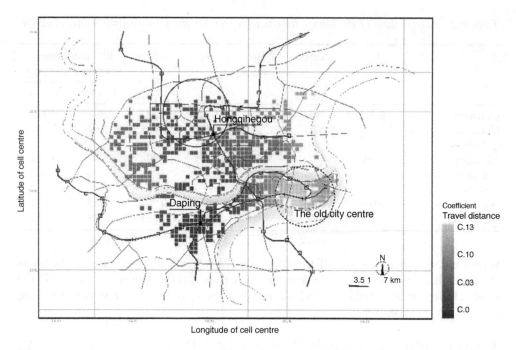

Longitude of cell centre

*Note:* The coefficient represents the change of logit of the outcome variable (travel mode choice) associated with a 1 km change in travel distance. The lightest shading indicates a higher (more positive) value of coefficient than the darker shading.

*Figure 4.3   Coefficient (b in Table 4.2) of the independent variable travel distance in predicting choice of rail transit as mode of travel*

is found to be significantly positive, which means that the longer the distance an individual travels, the more likely they are to choose rail transit as their daily travel mode.

In the GWR model, there is a contrast between the east part and west part of the old city area (the whole peninsula shown in Figure 4.3. The contribution of travel distance to the choice of rail transit as mode of travel is most significant in the old city centre and its adjacent area (dashed circle with grid units of the lightest shading). In contrast, it has the smallest contribution in the regeneration area, Daping, in the old city (grid units of the darkest shading). As shown in Figure 4.3, both areas have very good access to rail transit, given the location of the transit lines. The question, therefore, is why does one unit change in travel distance have a much greater influence on people's choice of rail transit in the old city centre than in Daping, which is just west of the old city centre? How and why does this locational difference occur?

For the relationship between use of rail transit and distance of commute: in the redevelopment area of Daping, the distance of commute has less of an influence on the probability of using transit than it does in the old city centre. Taking into consideration the undergoing mass redevelopment in Daping, a number of wealthy people moved into the newly built communities in that area. At the same time, a lot of rural migrant workers came into that area due to the cheap rent in the remaining dilapidated residential buildings there. Furthermore, there are particularly convenient bus services in that area compared to other parts of the old city (since it's a transport node). For the new higher income residents, they may have the privilege of car ownership. For the majority of established residents and migrant workers, who earn lower incomes, they may rather choose buses, with cheaper ticket fares, if they travelled longer distances. Therefore, the range of other travel mode choices for both the wealthier people and the less well-off groups may explain why longer travel trips in Daping don't have such an influence on the probability of using rail transit as in the old city.

In the north of the prosperous new city region (in an area similar to Daping), which is recently developed with new luxury communities, the coefficient is also much lower than that of the old city centre, as shown by a concentration of dark shaded grid units (solid black circle in Figure 4.3). In that area, travelling a longer distance therefore has less influence on residents' choice of rail transit as their travel mode. The lower coefficient is partly due to there being only sparse transit provision in some areas. But even around the transit stations in that area, the coefficient is still found to be quite low. A possible explanation is that the north part of the new city region has a concentration of established residents and newcomers, who are more likely to have access to private cars, which makes longer distance trips have less impact on choice of transit mode than in the old city centre. Therefore, in the new city region, travelling longer distance doesn't persuade residents to make the switch to rail transit as it does in the old city centre.

### 4.2.2 The coefficient of 'car ownership'

The coefficient value of the independent variable 'household car ownership' in predicting travel mode choice of rail transit was studied (Figure 4.4). In the global model of binary logistic regression, the coefficient is found to be significantly negative, which indicates that if an individual owns a car in their household, they are less likely to choose rail transit as their daily travel mode. The locations of less negative coefficient form a belt of lightly shaded running from the northwest of the new city region to the neck of the Yuzhong peninsular, at Liziba and Eling. This may indicate that the influence of car ownership on people's travel choice of transit is not as modifiable as other areas in the central city region.

Of particular note, is that this variable's contribution to the choice of rail transit is the most negative in the old city centre (dashed circle in Figure 4.4). This suggests that car ownership plays a more influential role in differentiating a person's choice of travel mode in the old city centre, than in other areas, and makes the person less likely to choose rail transit as their daily mode of travel.

The reason for this finding is likely to be that in the old city centre there is quite an inconvenient public transport service because of the mountain topography. People often have to walk a long distance either up or down in order to get to the nearest bus station, and this is even more of a problem when getting to a rail transit station. Although driving a car is also quite inconvenient up and down the steep slopes in the old city centre, people still have a strong desire to possess their own cars. Once they own a car, they may not bother to walk a long way to the station. By comparison, in the whole new city region the topography is quite flat, and here the results indicate that owning a car is not as decisive in people's choice of transit as in the old city centre. This is despite a high level of car ownership in the new city area. It is in the old city that owning a car makes it the least likely for those car users to switch to rail transit use.

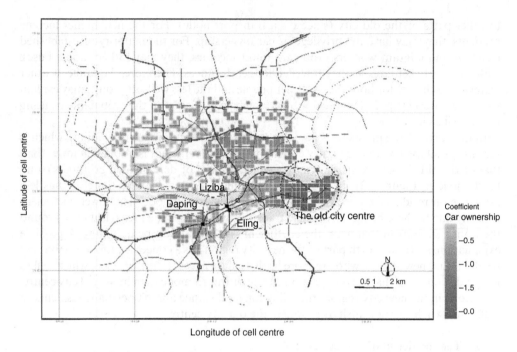

Longitude of cell centre

*Note:*   Presented as in Figure 4.3, but for a one unit change in the categorical variable 'car ownership'. Values are negative, with light shading indicating a value closer to zero, and dark shading indicating the most negative values.

*Figure 4.4    Coefficient of the independent variable car ownership in predicting choice of rail transit as mode of travel*

## 5.   CONCLUSIONS

As indicated in study of the JLE in London, it is generally newcomers who have benefited from the travel convenience that the JLE has provided, and facilitate their work and life in the city centre by taking the JLE. In contrast, the established residents have only enjoyed limited benefits from the new metro investment. There is no sign that they have expanded their travel patterns for work, entertainment, or activities in response to this metro line (Lane et al., 2004). However, the result of the analysis in Chongqing demonstrates that the rail transit system plays a more important role in facilitating the travel of established residents in the areas that haven't experienced dynamic trends of regeneration. It is in these areas that poor, established residents, rural migrants and those without a car are likely to be confined to their local area if there is insufficient supply of public transport. The situation is exacerbated by the interaction with their socio-economic conditions, which potentially results in expanding social segregation.

The result of the GWR model indicates that travelling a longer commuting distance has more of an influence on people choosing rail transit in the old city centre of Chongqing (than other parts of the city). It is probably safe to make the inference that rail transit is the most effective in facilitating longer travel distance in the old city centre. Compared to other parts of the city, in the old city centre there is generally a very inconvenient public transport service, due to the steep mountain topography. Few redevelopments are happening in the older, more traditional areas. There are a number of communities where a high level of established residents and rural migrants (with relatively low incomes) are concentrated, without access to private cars and also with limited access to other public transport facilities. Thus, the rail transit provision in that area promotes the distribution of transport benefits to the relatively deprived population there. These results emphasise the importance of providing rapid rail transit systems especially in the more deprived, old city areas. Car owners in the old city centre are also the least likely to choose rail transit as their travel mode. This, to some extent, reveals the polarisation between the car owners and people with no access to cars in the old city centre. All of these issues call for concern, as they are potential factors that may exclude a certain group of the population from the equal benefit distribution of public transport investment.

To a large extent, we have seen that much of the assumed developmental impact is related to the surrounding planning strategy, and is far from an 'automatic' impact from the transit investment. In a given area of the city, transit provision is only part of a package of planning strategies to boost development, along with other associated planning policies. Integration of land development and public transport planning is critical to enable areas to take maximum advantage of transport provision. The spatial variations in development underline the importance of delivering a policy package. In the package, rail transit development should be combined with urban development strategies, especially supplementary policies (e.g. support with land release procedures, tax concessions and grants for developers) and planning interventions, in order to best achieve the desired result.

If a planning strategy is well formulated, and much of the development is planned and implemented, then the developmental impact of transit investment can be large. Therefore, perhaps developing a 'package' of policy measures is more critical than estimating the impacts of transit investment, which are often quite indirect. This has interesting implications for project appraisal, as often funding is given to the projects where there are assumed high developmental benefits (indirect benefits), alongside high 'user' benefits (direct benefits). Feitelson and Rotem-Mindali (2015) remind us that it is the package of measures that are important; that the emphasis should be on identifying the synergetic measures that will lead to the desired impacts on the neighbourhood and city. Hence, we should seek to conceive and agree how we would like the city to develop, and to plan the transit investment and the urban form and layout accordingly to help facilitate this. It is the integration of transport investment and planning strategies, the macro and city economy, the associated traffic demand management strategy, the wider provision of amenities and facilities, and education and training, which shape the nature of development change.

# REFERENCES

Butler, T. (2007) Re-urbanizing London Docklands: gentrification, suburbanization or new urbanism? *International Journal of Urban and Regional Research*, 31, 759–781.
Cao, X. and Pan, Q. (2016) Rapid transit and land development in a diverse world. *Transport Policy*, 51, 1–3.

Cardozo, O., Garc A-Palomares, J. and Gutierrez, J. (2012) Application of geographically weighted regression to the direct forecasting of transit ridership at station-level. *Applied Geography*, 34, 548–558.

Cervero, R. (2006) Alternative approaches to modeling the travel-demand impacts of smart growth. *Journal of the American Planning Association*, 72, 285–295.

Cervero, R., Murakami, J. and Miller, M. (2010) Direct ridership model of bus rapid transit in Los Angeles County, California. *Transportation Research Record: Journal of the Transportation Research Board*, 1–7.

China Research and Intelligence Co. Ltd. (2015) Research Report on China's Urban Rail Transit Industry, 2010–2020. China Research and Intelligence Co. Ltd.

Du, H. and Mulley, C. (2006) Relationship between transport accessibility and land value: local model approach with geographically weighted regression. *Transportation Research Record: Journal of the Transportation Research Board*, 197–205.

Feitelson, E. and Rotem-Mindali, O. (2015) Spatial implications of public transport investments in metropolitan areas: some empirical evidence regarding light rail and bus rapid transit. In: Hickman, R., Givoni, M., Bonilla, D. and Banister, D. (eds) *Handbook on Transport and Development*. Cheltenham: Edward Elgar.

Fotheringham, A., Brunsdon, C. and Charlton, M. (2003) *Geographically Weighted Regression: The Analysis of Spatially Varying Relationships*. Chichester: John Wiley & Sons.

Gatersleben, B., Clark, C., Reeve, A. and Uzzell, D. (2007) The impact of a new transport link on residential communities. *Journal of Environmental Psychology*, 27, 145–153.

Geurs, K., Boon, W. and Van Wee, B. (2009) Social impacts of transport: literature review and the state of the practice of transport appraisal in the Netherlands and the United Kingdom. *Transport Reviews*, 29, 69–90.

Gwilliam, K. (2002) *Cities on the Move: A World Bank Urban Transport Strategy Review*. Washington DC: World Bank Publications.

Gwilliam, K. (2003) Urban transport in developing countries. *Transport Reviews*, 23, 197–216.

Higgins, C. and Kanaroglou, P. (2016) Forty years of modelling rapid transit's land value uplift in North America: moving beyond the tip of the iceberg. *Transport Reviews*, 36, 610–634.

Jones, P. (2015) Assessing the wider impacts of the Jubilee Line Extension in East London. In: Hickman, R., Givoni, M., Bonilla, D. and Banister, D. (eds) *Handbook on Transport and Development*. Cheltenham: Edward Elgar.

Kuby, M., Barranda, A. and Upchurch, C. (2004) Factors influencing light-rail station boardings in the United States. *Transportation Research Part A: Policy and Practice*, 38, 223–247.

Lane, R., Powell, T., Eyers, T., Paris, J., Lucas, K. and Jones, P. (2004) JLE Summary Report: Final Report. London: University of Westminster for Transport for London and the Department for Transport.

Lucas, K. (2012) Transport and social exclusion: where are we now? *Transport Policy*, 20, 105–113.

Messenger, T. and Ewing, R. (1996) Transit-oriented development in the sun belt. *Transportation Research Record: Journal of the Transportation Research Board*, 145–153.

Pan, H., Shen, Q. and Zhang, M. (2009) Influence of urban form on travel behaviour in four neighbourhoods of Shanghai. *Urban Studies*, 46, 275–294.

Pan, H., Shen, Q. and Zhao, T. (2013) Travel and car ownership of residents near new suburban metro stations in Shanghai, China. *Transportation Research Record: Journal of the Transportation Research Board*, 2394, 63–69.

Schwanen, T., Lucas, K., Akyelken, N., Solsona, D., Carrasco, J.-A. and Neutens, T. (2015) Rethinking the links between social exclusion and transport disadvantage through the lens of social capital. *Transportation Research Part A: Policy and Practice*, 74, 123–135.

Souche, S. (2010) Measuring the structural determinants of urban travel demand. *Transport Policy*, 17, 127–134.

Taylor, B., Miller, D., Iseki, H. and Fink, C. (2009) Nature and/or nurture? Analyzing the determinants of transit ridership across US urbanized areas. *Transportation Research Part A: Policy and Practice*, 43, 60–77.

# 5. Considering the impact of HSR on China's East Coast region

*Qiyan Wu, Anthony Perl, Jingwei Sun, Taotao Deng and Haoyu Hu*

## 1. INTRODUCTION: HSR AND ITS IMPACT ON REGIONAL DEVELOPMENT

Compared with conventional railways, High Speed Rail (HSR) has created a new brand of surface transportation since the first "bullet trains" began operating in Japan in 1964. The effects of this transformation spread from Asia to Europe in the 1990s, with the adoption of HSR in France and Germany. Today, there is growing evidence that HSR deployment creates a differential impact on the regional economy depending on the scale of the infrastructure and the associated development initiatives around HSR station nodes (Javier et al., 1996).

Certainly, by increasing the speed of intercity passenger mobility to a velocity between that of the automobile and aircraft, HSR has enabled new travel patterns, such as frequent commuting to and from large cities that have become closer to their hinterland and to other large cities within HSR networks that contribute to a "shrinking world" (Harvey, 1989). HSR has thus enhanced primate cities' capacity to attract more of the mobile rich "floating" population that spans the globe, and has facilitated a recent wave of urbanization that has reversed the tendency of population loss in big cities (Javier, 2001). In some regions of Europe, HSR has alleviated regional economic disparity and narrowed the development gap between the core and peripheral areas through its significant "siphoning effect" (Gutiérrez, 2001). But at the same time, there has been evidence within HSR networks that towns and cities not served by stations have lost population to cities and towns that are directly connected to the network (Levinson, 2012; Kim, 2000; Nakamura and Ueda, 1989; Sands, 1993; Vickerman, 2015).

It appears that HSR has played a part in the wave of selective (re)urbanization globally and that such trends are evident in Asia. For example, Nakamura and Ueda (1989) found some cities in Japan with a Shinkansen station had higher population growth than the national average, while no prefecture that was lacking access to the Shinkansen network grew faster than the national average between 1980 and 1985. Wang et al. (2012) echo that the enhanced accessibility of HSR in China has rescaled the tourism hinterland through a redistribution of urban migrants now using HSR to visit their regions of origin. This pattern and characteristics of selective population (re)urbanization call for further analysis to consider whether the scale and configuration of the HSR infrastructure have a differential effect on China's intercity travel.

Our initial effort to examine this transformation (Wu, Perl and Sun, 2016) highlighted the correlation between three distinct configurations of HSR operation with regional economic development changes in their service areas. Corridor Mode HSR operation

(CM) resembles Japan's pioneering Shinkansen by offering frequent HSR service between megacities along a linear corridor. Monocentric-Radial Mode HSR development (MRM) approximates the French model of network expansion with multiple HSR routes converging on a single political and financial hub. Multicore-Network Mode (MNM) HSR development compares with metropolitan transit networks within major cities like London, New York, or Tokyo. These three operational configurations are all growing into major mobility avenues across China. Their influence on urban and regional development offers an unprecedented opportunity to compare the social and spatial impacts of this mobility within a single nation.

This new wave of mobility is certainly influencing urbanization across China where HSR has further distinguished the economic development both within city areas and between regions. At the turn of new millennium, HSR was demonstrated to have a markedly asymmetrical impact on interregional economic potential and daily accessibility of the space between Madrid, Barcelona, and the French border based on the presence or absence of HSR mobility options in different communities (Gutiérrez, 2001). Scholarship on the early impacts of Spain's HSR network development revealed the consequence of differential accessibility between regions, rather than within regions (Bruinsma and Rietveld, 1993; Spiekermann and Wegener, 1996; Gutiérrez et al., 1996). More recently, HSR research in Europe and China has demonstrated that the availability of HSR services contributes to business location as well as influencing the development of tourism. Willigers and Van Wee (2011) noted that HSR improved the attractiveness of a location for offices within regions. Wang et al. (2012) also revealed that the enhanced accessibility brought about by an HSR network had salient impact on redistribution of tourist markets and strengthened interregional market competition in China. Undoubtedly, due to the enhanced accessibility of nodes within an HSR network, a few primary national or even regional cities were empowered to absorb more population, financial capital and resources from their enlarged hinterland (Levinson, 2012). Thus, the development of HSR may result in an increase in spatial imbalance and lead to more serious regional polarization through selective urbanization in undeveloped areas and differential re-urbanization in developed areas (Monzón et al., 2013).

## 2.    THE DEVELOPMENT OF CHINA'S HSR NETWORK

### 2.1    Investment and Construction Modes of HSR in China

HSR acts not only as an economic catalyst to both state and local governments, but also as an instrument of technological innovation at the national scale (Sun, 2015). Construction of China's HSR network provided an intentional stimulus to the labor market, to steel manufacturing and to other construction industries following the 2008 global financial crisis while also reshaping the development trajectory of other intercity transport modes in China, such as airlines (Fu et al., 2012). For example, the GDP contribution of the HSR industry was estimated to be 400 billion RMB in 2015, spread among fixed assets such as railway bridges, tunnels, and stations at about 50 per cent, infrastructure construction at 35 per cent, and the manufacture of rolling stock at 15 per cent (China Railway Construction Corporation Limited, 2015). After the world economic recession in 2008,

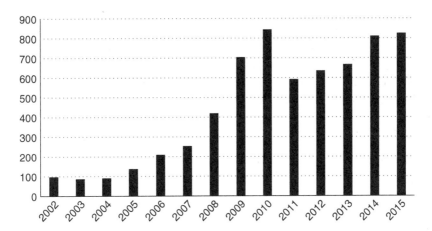

*Figure 5.1    Investment of HSR in China (billion RMB)*[1]

China's direct fixed-asset investment of HSR reached 843 billion RMB (125 billion US dollars) in 2010, over eight times the investment made in 2002 and amounting to three per cent of total investment across China in 2010 (Figure 5.1) Thus, China's unprecedented wave of HSR development caused a distinct change in economic growth, whose consequences can be more fully understood through analysis in a scalar geographical setting.

HSR has brought higher fares and a market shift in railway travel compared to the conventional train services that it has replaced, with attendant impact on economic activities. HSR has also stimulated the transport sector of the economy, from railway manufacturing to logistics. In terms of indirect influence, finance, business, tourism, real estate, and other service sector components have also been stimulated, because HSR accelerates the speed at which capital and people circulate throughout China. China's passenger railway network approached a tipping point during the 2015 spring holiday peak travel season, with total HSR ridership on for the holiday period exceeding that on the conventional rail network for the first time (Xinhua Net, 2015).[2] This suggests that HSR may come to eclipse conventional rail as China's main mode of intercity public transportation sooner or later. The data we have collected on the early effects of this mobility shift to HSR suggests that the social and spatial impacts will be significant.

China's HSR network has been built through a mix of new-construction and hybrid-construction, which blends some newly built HSR with upgraded conventional railway infrastructure. Construction modes clearly differed across regions. In the rapidly growing Yangtze Delta, a strong economy and reliable fiscal capacity of local governments favored a robust infrastructure expansion. Thus, the HSR's infrastructure was mostly new-built, including the Nanjing-Shanghai, Hangzhou-Shanghai, Nanjing-Hangzhou routes. In contrast to these new HSR lines, some routes are served by hybrid construction with a mix of remodeled conventional railway and new HSR infrastructure, such as the networks of the Greater Beijing area, the Greater Wuhan area, and the Harbin–Dalian corridor.

---

[1]   http://www.china-railway.com.cn/.
[2]   http://www.chinanews.com/sh/2015/02-04/7035728.shtml.

Undeniably, the rapid development of HSR in China has changed transportation options significantly. In reality, HSR is becoming the first choice in many of China's intercity passenger transportation markets. The volume of rail passenger transportation has increased sharply from to 961.2 billion person-kilometres in 2011 to 1160.5 billion person-kilometres in 2014, almost equaling highway travel volumes (National Bureau of Statistics of PRC, 2015).

## 2.2    Development of HSR Network on China's East Coast

Four urban clusters in China's east coast region were selected for analysis, which are the Harbin–Dalian Corridor, the Greater Beijing Area, the Yangtze Delta, and the Greater Wuhan Area. The study area includes seven HSR lines (Figure 5.2).

Since China's major cities are now well connected via HSR, travel patterns across China have changed accordingly. Taking the Yangtze Delta as an example, the density of HSR, which here refers to the length of HSR lines per unit area, reached 18.6 km/km², exceeding

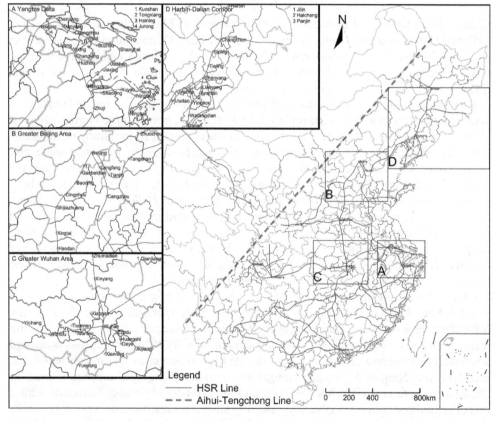

*Note:*
①Harbin–Dalian; ②Qinhuangdao–Shenyang; ③Beijing–Guangzhou; ④Beijing–Shanghai; ⑤Shanghai–Wuhan; ⑥Nanjing–Hangzhou; ⑦Shanghai–Hangzhou.

*Figure 5.2    Chinese HSR network segments under analysis*

*Table 5.1   Development of HSR on China's East Coast in 2017*

|  | Density of HSR (km/km$^2$) | Length of HSR (km) |
| --- | --- | --- |
| Yangtze Delta (MNM) | 18.6 | 1,465 |
| Greater Beijing Area (MNM) | 9.8 | 1,321 |
| Harbin–Dalian Corridor (CM) | 9.1 | 1,796 |
| Greater Wuhan Area (MRM) | 5.7 | 1,103 |

that of all other areas (Table 5.1) in 2017. The high density of HSR and fast travel between cities are reshaping the form of integration in urban regions into a networked complex of city nodes.

## 3.   DATA AND METHODOLOGY

### 3.1   Data

Data for this analysis is drawn from the county based social statistics and geo-referenced data of China, including economy and population data of four urban clusters. We have also obtained origin–destination data in the Yangtze Delta, passenger data in Jiangsu and Shanghai, and field survey data of HSR passengers in Kunshan.

In our previous analysis (Wu et. al., 2016), we created a typology of HSR mobility that differentiated among three spatial configurations emerging in China's unprecedented scale of HSR development. These are: Corridor Mode of development (CM), Monocentric-Radial Mode of development (MRM) to Multicore-Network Mode (MNM) of development. These operational configurations were summarised above. We then applied the geo-referenced data, and considered the potential for spatial integration from HSR by dividing the area of HSR effects on mobility within each configuration into three sub-areas, following Vickerman (2015). This yielded two data subsets:

- Daily Commute Field (DCF), one hour's travel time, or core area of HSR impact on daily travel for work or business.
- Non-core area of HSR impact, which could be further divided into: the territory between the DCF and two hours' maximal commute field (or 300 km distance) and peripheral area of HSR impact, and the territory between two hours' maximal commute field (300 km distance) and three hours' commute field (500 km distance).

### 3.2   Methodology

Accessibility assessment of HSR network was highlighted to reveal the impact of HSR on local society accordingly. Based on Monzón et. al. (2013), the accessibility effects of HSR could be effectively captured through two indices, namely the efficiency and equity impact compared with conventional rail accessibility. The accessibility of each city within the HSR network refers to the reciprocal of weighted average time needed to travel to other cities in this region. The formulation is as follows:

$$A_i = \frac{\sum_j P_j}{\sum_j P_j \cdot I_{ij}}$$

For each origin i, its accessibility ($A_i$)b to destinations j is calculated. $P_j$ is a variable referring to the size of each destination, indicated through either population or gross domestic product (GDP) and ($I_{ij}$) is the generalized travel time using the network.

The formulation for the travel time is as follows:

$$I_{ij} = TT_R(i, E_i) + TT_F(E_i + E_j) + TT_R(E_j, j)$$

The equation takes into account the travel time by road from the origin to the nearest HSR station ($TT_R(i, E_i)$), the travel time by railway ($TT_R(E_i, E_j)$) and the travel time by road[3] from the station nearest the destination to the destination itself ($TT_F(E_j, E_j)$).

In some cases, the local travel time to access HSR or to reach a destination after detraining can take longer than the HSR journey itself. This is partly because of the large size of Chinese municipalities, which often results in extended commuting time between a HSR station and the origin or destination of travel. For example, Nanjing (6,597 km²) is four times the size of London, England (1,577 km²). Road access and egress times would thus tend to be similarly lengthy for journeys by air, and for trips made entirely by automobile. Line haul HSR thus remains the fastest way of commuting between most of China's cities.

Then, efficiency refers to the change of accessibility on interconnections and the resulting patterns of network usage and performance which is benefited by a new transport infrastructure (Román et. al. 2010). Meanwhile, when concerning the impact of new-born HSR on social-spatial justice (Bröcker et. al. 2010), equity impacts refer to the corresponding changes of transport infrastructure investments in the distribution of accessibility:

**Measuring efficiency:**

$$AC_i = \frac{A_{i0} - A_{is}}{A_{i0}} * 100$$

For each origin i, its accessibility change in percentage ($AC_i$) is calculated. $A_{i0}$ is the indicator value in the do-nothing scenario, and $A_{is}$ is the indicator in the project scenario.

**Measuring equity:**

$$CV = \frac{\sigma^P}{\frac{\sum A_i \cdot P_i}{\sum P_i}}$$

---

[3]  Both public transport and private car could resolve door to door accessibility. Actually, in most metropolitans, underground or metro is used as the main tool of transport connection. Taking Beijing South Station as an example, half of the HSR passengers take metro to exit the station and 46.4 per cent take metro to enter the station. But in medium sized and small cities where there is no metro, buses or private cars are preferred.

CV is the coefficient of variation and σ is the standard deviation of accessibility values Ai, weighted by the population Pi.

Finally, we analyzed the different cities' GDP increase, population growth and economic restructuring (especially, tertiary industry development) of both core and non-core areas in our three data subsets. 2010 was set as the base year to assess economic growth, since most HSR lines in the four urban clusters entered service around this year, e.g., the Shanghai–Nanjing HSR line serving the Yangtze Delta opened in 2010, and the Beijing–Shanghai HSR line serving the Greater Beijing Area opened in 2011.

## 4.   EVOLUTION OF HSR NETWORK AND ITS IMPACT ON ACCESSIBILITY AND TRAVEL MODE CHOICE

In order to appreciate the various effects of HSR on China's urban dynamism, we begin by examining the direct impact on accessibility and travel mode choice. We assume that HSR will have a causal effect on urban expansion and development, although not necessarily an exclusive one. In Asia, it has been uncommon for HSR to follow urban expansion and economic development. Instead, HSR infrastructure has contributed to the economic development of most urban spaces where it has been introduced, and such influence is certainly operative in China. Designing the layout of China's HSR network has been a national strategic planning responsibility. In fact, local governments have very limited bargaining power to influence the HSR network's layout. The Ministry of Railways (whose HSR responsibilities were later transferred to the China Railway Corporation) has been the major decision maker on the configuration of China's HSR network. There have been two main considerations in planning the HSR network. First, HSR's first priority was to serve provincial-level capital cities in order to facilitate their economic development. Secondly, whether or not small and medium-sized cities would be served by HSR depended on whether these cities were located close to the HSR routes linking the provincial capitals (Qin, 2016).

### 4.1   Accessibility Changes and Their Impact on Efficiency and Equity

After analyzing HSR network effects using the methodology developed by Monzón et al., (2013), the accessibility changes and efficiency and equity impacts among the four HSR network zones are presented in Table 5.1 and discussed below.

**(1)   Efficiency change**
It is clear that HSR has enhanced the aggregate accessibility of urban areas in China's four largest and most economically dynamic urban regions. Each HSR network configuration has reduced the travel time between the cities that it serves. Nevertheless, a disparity in this impact also becomes apparent. Cities that gain intercity rail connections for the first time through the HSR network have higher accessibility enhancement than cities which gained HSR access alongside conventional rail services in new-build HSR areas. For example, the accessibility value of Huzhou, a city of 748,471 population located 140 km west of Shanghai, increased by over 200 per cent, because it had not been previously served by intercity rail links from the conventional railway system before (Figures 5.3 and 5.4).

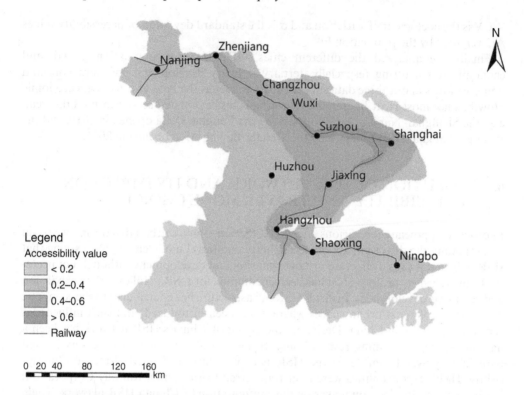

*Figure 5.3    Accessibility values of Yangtze Delta's conventional railway network*

Given the high speed of travel, the time compression effect on central cities, such as Shanghai, Wuhan, Beijing and Shenyang, have grown much larger than before HSR was built, thus accelerating the development of mega-urban clusters that are centered on these urban nodes (Figures 5.5–5.8). For example, the rapid expansion of HSR-based commuting from Beijing has swallowed up the cities of Langfang (530,840 population), Gaobeidian (274,853 population), Zhuozhou (260,493 population) in Hebei province, and even Tianjin (9,562,255 population) into a newly emerging mega commuting cluster, thus creating the U-shaped super city illustrated in Figure 5.6.

**(2)   Equity change and increasing interregional differentiation**
Equity change (EC) refers to the differentiated accessibility of regions, cities or people when the supply of mobility changed following the addition of transport infrastructure (Monzón et al., 2013). Normally, EC in transportation may highlight the spatial imbalance arising from changes in the distribution of accessibility across a particular HSR network configuration. The higher the EC index reading, the greater the degree of inequality resulting from HSR development. Comparing the equity change between conventional rail infrastructure and HSR infrastructure, the EC index values demonstrate that HSR may have a paradoxical impact on regional economy (Table 5.2).

Among the four regional HSR networks, the most equal accessibility distribution is found within the Yangtze Delta, where the EC index is 0.29, much lower than other areas

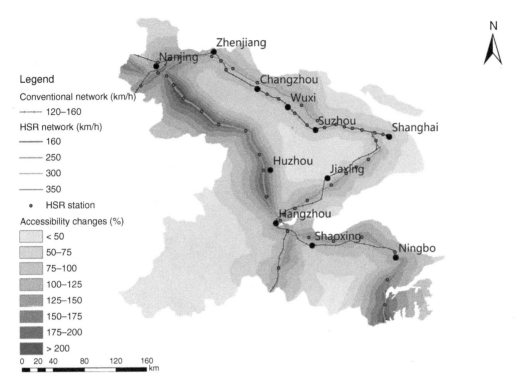

*Figure 5.4   Efficiency changes from HSR network versus conventional railways in the Yangtze Delta*

profiled in Table 5.2. This result suggests that HSR in the Yangtze Delta area could be playing an important role to advance the integration between peripheries and core areas by reducing the commute time for travel within each urban node to its downtown core while also facilitating resettlement by making possible work trips from previously remote suburbs. At the other extreme, the EC index for the Greater Beijing Area is 0.67, which is the highest of our four areas. It indicates that accessibility improvement is concentrated in core areas and the mobility in peripheries remains limited. Considering that Yangtze Delta is a more balanced and developed area while Greater Beijing remains polarized in the mobility effects following HSR, we can conclude that HSR network development can impact the previous spatial structures in different ways.

Furthermore, the emergence of HSR in developed areas has been restructuring the hierarchy-based, networked urban system that was created during China's centrally planned era, when the social economy was tightly controlled by central planners in the national government. (Ma, 2005) Tightly controlled urban development has been replaced with a wider range of spatial dynamics, enabled by a transportation network aligned with a market based economy and featuring more inter-connected accessibility as shown in Figure 5.8. For instance, Kunshan, a city with a population of 1,118,617 near Shanghai, which was a satellite of Suzhou, is now directly connected to Shanghai by HSR. Therefore, the case of the Yangtze Delta revealed the previous state-formatted travel

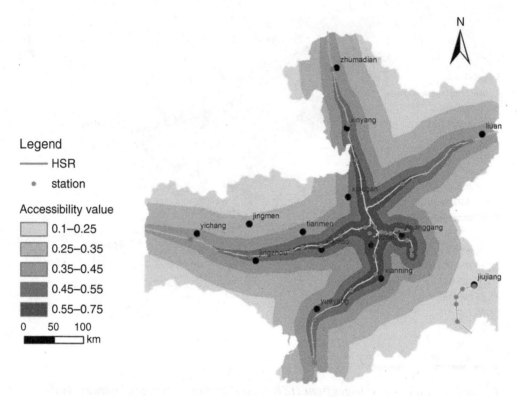

*Figure 5.5    Accessibility impacts of HSR in the Greater Wuhan Area*

hierarchy pattern designed during the centrally planned era has been rapidly replaced by a market led multi-core mobility configuration that extends well beyond Shanghai. For instance, the Yangtze Delta area had the highest accessibility value (Figure 5.8) and lowest equity change among the HSR development areas that we have examined (Table 5.2).

However, the Yangtze Delta's highly integrated mobility from HSR can be contrasted with a greater degree of polarization following HSR's introduction to the greater Beijing area, the greater Wuhan area, and the Harbin–Dalian Corridor, as illustrated in Figures 5.5–5.7. Here, the highest accessibility value areas can be found concentrated in Beijing (Figure 5.6), Wuhan (Figure 5.5) and Shenyang (Figure 5.7) respectively. Taking Greater Beijing as an example, while the EC index approached 0.67 in past years, the most accessible area in this supercity can be found along the corridor between Beijing and Tianjin. Consequentially, most of the mid- and smaller-sized cities in the region have become relatively less accessible, although the accessibility of some intermediate cities, such as Shijiazhuang, did improve somewhat.

Generally speaking, HSR development not only enhances transport accessibility, but also exerts an uneven influence on regional efficiency and equity. These disparate influences vary across China's regions, and may reflect the different effects of HSR network configuration on regional social-spatial structure and social-economic activities. These disparities should be more fully examined in future research.

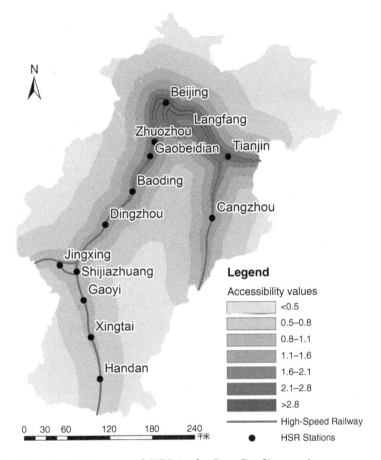

*Figure 5.6    Accessibility impacts of HSR in the Jing-Jin-Ji supercity*

## 4.2    Travel Shifts and Their Implications for Regional Development

### Influence of HSR on China's fast-growing domestic transport

While China has been expanding all of its domestic transport capacity, including express-ways and civil aviation, HSR has demonstrated its superior attributes in: (1) schedule reliability; (2) reducing actual travel time; (3) passenger comfort and travel experience; (4) low carbon emissions. Thus, high-speed train travel has come to dominate China's middle to longer distance travel between 200 km and 1,000 km.

Because of HSR's superior performance attributes, railways are exerting a significant influence effect on China's internal transportation development, for instance by dampening the growth of domestic civil aviation (Fu et al., 2012). Such formative effects on inter-city transportation, as illustrated in Table 5.3, can be expected to have significant effects on regional restructuring.

In fact, the increasing rate of rail travel was mainly contributed by HSR, because there has been no expansion of conventional rail passenger services since the mid-2000s in most areas of China.

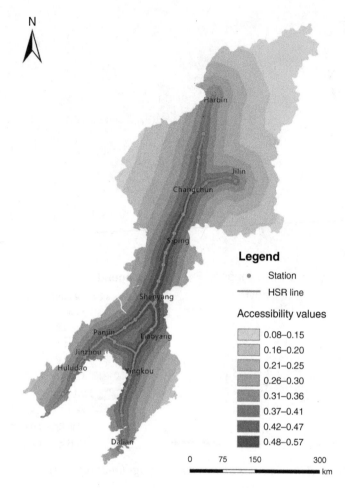

*Figure 5.7   Accessibility impacts of HSR in the Harbin–Dalian corridor*

## 4.3   New Commuting Patterns Facilitated by HSR

### (1) Expansion of daily commute field

Taking the Yangtze Delta as an example, HSR's spatio-temporal compression of travel (Harvey, 1989; Kirsch, 1995) has intensified regional mobility. The travel time between cities, e.g. Kunshan and Nanjing in the Yangtze Delta, Jilin and Dalin in the Harbin–Dalian Corridor, Jinzhou and Wuhan in the Greater Wuhan Area, and Gaobeidian and Beijing in the Greater Beijing Area, has been significantly reduced, so more cities are absorbed into the Daily Commute Field (DCF) of major centers, such as Beijing, Shanghai and Wuhan. Such commuting by HSR enables the integration of business and culture that expands the city-region to the scale of a supercity.

Before HSR, the DCF of Shanghai was restricted to adjacent cities like Suzhou and Jiaxing, which were within one hour's travel time via conventional railway or highway. After HSR was inaugurated in 2011, the DCF expanded to include most of the Yangtze

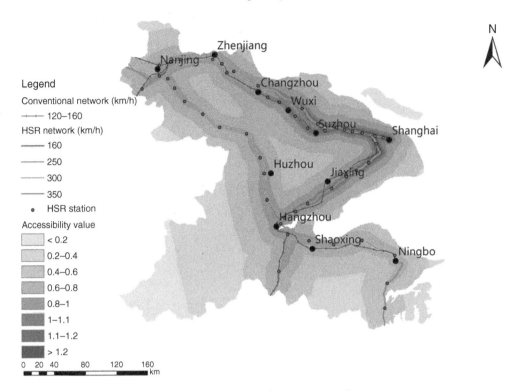

*Figure 5.8 Accessibility impacts of HSR in the Yangtze Delta*

*Table 5.2 Equity impacts of HSR*

|  | Yangtze Delta | Harbin–Dalian corridor | Greater Wuhan area | Greater Beijing area |
|---|---|---|---|---|
| Equity change of HSR scenario | 0.29 | 0.32 | 0.45 | 0.67 |
| Accessibility range of HSR scenario | 0.2–1.23 | 0.08–0.57 | 0.17–0.7 | 0.32–3.5 |
| Most accessible city in network | Shanghai | Shenyang | Wuhan | Beijing |

Delta, extending as far as Danyang and Hangzhou. The frequency of HSR service, e.g. more than 100 one-way trains per day, greatly facilitates commuting activities inside DCF, encouraging the integration of urban commerce and social networks, while the annual intercity passenger travel by all modes is increasing, and among all transport modes, the annual growth of rail passengers is the fastest. In fact, between 2010 and 2014, the annual growth in rail passengers commuting from Shanghai reached 10.8 per cent, leading the growth in other intra-regional transport modes.

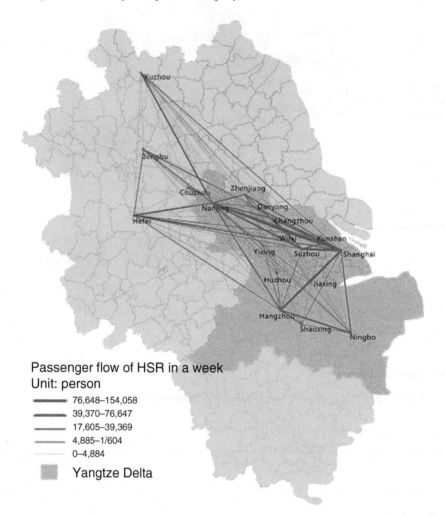

Passenger flow of HSR in a week
Unit: person

76,648–154,058
39,370–76,647
17,605–39,369
4,885–1/604
0–4,884

Yangtze Delta

*Figure 5.9    HSR weekly travel volumes across the Yangtze Delta in 2014*

**(2)   Analysis of travel patterns in Yangtze Delta region**

Origin–destination travel data for the Yangtze Delta also provides evidence on the ways that HSR is facilitating regional expansion to the scale of a supercity (Figure 5.8). The trips made between major centers like Shanghai, Nanjing, Hangzhou and Suzhou, account for 38.3 per cent of total travel across the region. Cities within the DCF of Shanghai, including Changzhou, Wuxi, and Kunshan, reveal traffic flows centered on Shanghai as their primary destination, while for cities beyond Shanghai's DCF, like Zhenjiang and Danyang, Nanjing becomes the primary destination. This reveals a multi-core network that links multiple nodes across the supercity as shown in Table 5.5 below.

As we have shown, rail destinations had been strictly arranged in a hierarchical system during the era of the centrally planned economy; subsequently, travel behaviors in China have been reshaped as the rail hierarchy was reconfigured. However, the rapid

*Table 5.3   Modal share of passenger-kilometers in Jiangsu Province (%)*

|      | Rail (incl. HSR km.) | Road  | Marine | Air  |
|------|----------------------|-------|--------|------|
| 2005 | 20.08                | 77.58 | 0.01   | 2.33 |
| 2006 | 19.60                | 77.74 | 0.01   | 2.65 |
| 2007 | 19.41                | 77.76 | 0.02   | 2.81 |
| 2008 | 18.07                | 79.32 | 0.02   | 2.59 |
| 2009 | 21.87                | 74.33 | 0.09   | 3.71 |
| 2010 | 21.88                | 74.60 | 0.09   | 3.37 |
| 2011 | 22.39                | 73.53 | 0.08   | 3.99 |
| 2012 | 22.89                | 72.75 | 0.07   | 4.29 |
| 2013 | 34.86                | 58.39 | 0.27   | 6.48 |
| 2014 | 38.02                | 54.95 | 0.20   | 6.84 |
| 2015 | 39.17                | 53.31 | 0.17   | 7.35 |

*Table 5.4   Annual intercity passenger travel from Shanghai within Yangtze Delta (unit: 10,000 persons)*

| Year | Total pax | Transport mode | | | | Annual growth in total pax | Annual growth in Rail pax |
|------|-----------|------|---------|--------|------|------|------|
|      |           | Rail | Highway | Marine | Air  |      |      |
| 2005 | 9,487     | 4313 | 2468    | 62     | 2080 |      |      |
| 2006 | 9,619     | 4458 | 2784    | 68     | 2309 | 1.4% | 3.4% |
| 2007 | 10,371    | 4795 | 2872    | 95     | 2609 | 7.8% | 7.6% |
| 2008 | 10,927    | 5343 | 2934    | 89     | 2565 | 5.4% | 11.4% |
| 2009 | 11,136    | 5161 | 2995    | 90     | 2890 | 1.9% | −3.4% |
| 2010 | 13,456    | 6095 | 3634    | 85     | 3642 | 20.8% | 18.1% |
| 2011 | 13,519    | 6198 | 3477    | 78     | 3766 | 0.5% | 1.7% |
| 2012 | 14,547    | 6758 | 3748    | 66     | 3974 | 7.6% | 9.0% |
| 2013 | 15,933    | 7972 | 3720    | 68     | 4173 | 9.5% | 18.0% |
| 2014 | 17,560    | 9194 | 3754    | 90     | 4522 | 10.2% | 15.3% |

development of high speed rail has reshaped the use of the intercity rail system into a means of frequent travel in mega-urban regions. Taking the Yangtze Delta area as an example, the vertical hierarchy of these nodes that was imposed during the centrally planned era is being flattened and simplified into two spheres. Cities in the top level, consisting of Shanghai, Suzhou, Nanjing and Hangzhou, become the primary destination of the HSR network and represent the largest OD volumes over 100,000 per week. Meanwhile, cities in the second level, such as Kunshan, Wuxi, Changhzou, etc., each associate with a first-level city as their primary destination and present an OD volume of less than 100,000 per week. Since this OD data was collected in 2014, in which the Shanghai–Nanjing and Shanghai–Hangzhou HSR line have operated for four years and Nanjing–Hangzhou HSR line has operated over one year. Thus, the travel flow in 2014 was assumed to be stable and the travel patterns being revealed are seen to be reliable.

*Table 5.5    HSR connection of urban nodes across the Yangtze Delta*

| Urban node | Travel patterns | | | Travel pattern |
|---|---|---|---|---|
| | Primary destination | Secondary destination | Tertiary destinations | |
| Nanjing | Shanghai | Suzhou | Wuxi > Changzhou > Zhenjiang> Danyang > Kunshan | Nanjing travel flows past nearby city of Zhenjiang, moving to Suzhou as a secondary destination and Shanghai as a primary center. |
| Zhenjiang | Nanjing | Shanghai | Changzhou> Suzhou > Wuxi> Danyang > Kunshan | Primary flow remains to Nanjing. |
| Danyang | Nanjing | Shanghai | Zhenjiang > Changzhou > Suzhou >Wuxi > Kunshan | Danyang is inclined to Nanjing, but the influences of Shanghai and Nanjing are nearly balanced. |
| Changzhou | Shanghai | Nanjing | Wuxi > Suzhou > Zhenjiang > Danyang > Kunshan | Changzhou is slightly inclined to Shanghai, but the influences of Shanghai and Nanjing are nearly balanced. |
| Wuxi | Shanghai | Suzhou | Nanjing > Changzhou > Kunshan > Zhenjiang > Danyang | Wuxi and Suzhou are comparable cities in economic and social development, but Suzhou is more closely linked to Shanghai and thus has a mobility advantage over Wuxi. |
| Suzhou | Shanghai | Nanjing | Wuxi > Kunshan > Changzhou > Zhenjiang > Danyang | |
| Kunshan | Shanghai | Suzhou | Nanjing > Wuxi > Changzhou > Zhenjiang > Danyang | Although Kunshan is located in Jiangsu province HSR mobility facilitates closer ties with Shanghai. |
| Shanghai | Suzhou | Nanjing | Wuxi > Changzhou > Kunshan > Zhenjiang > Danyang | Shanghai shows modest travel flows to Suzhou and Nanjing, compared to the flows from these cities to Shanghai. |

## 5.    RESHAPING SPATIAL STRUCTURE AND URBAN HIERARCHY UNDER THE INTERREGIONAL IMPACT OF HSR

The uneven expansion of accessibility across these regions may accelerate or retard the circulation of people, and thus indirectly catalyze or constrain economic development accordingly. Then, it is hypothesized that while China's transportation network and social economy is changing, the national spatial structure and urban hierarchy is being reshaped.

## 5.1   Regional Restructuring and the Emerging Supercity

HSR can be a catalyst for regional restructuring along both horizontal and vertical dimensions (Pol, 2003). Along the horizontal dimension, HSR rescales the social economy and re-organizes the division of labor. For an example, due to the fast and frequent commuting between Kunshan and Shanghai, the housing around Kunshan South Station was increasingly favored by Shanghai employers. When we conducted random interviews of local real estate agents and commuters in 2016 at Kunshan and Shanghai HSR stations, it became apparent that the transformation of the local real estate market *"did happen"* while *"more commuters* [like me] *have adopted and then adapted the lifestyle* [of working in Shanghai's downtown area and living in Kunshan]. . .[commuting between Kunshan and downtown Shanghai is] *convenient and* [housing in Kunshan is] *affordable"*. Furthermore, on the vertical dimension, HSR reshaped the relative ranking of economic activity among urban centers, for instance economic scale and population accordingly. Therefore, Table 5.5 revealed the tendency of HSR to accelerate the integration of a regional economy and encourage spreading of urban life through the de-concentration and extension of urban economic activity into secondary nodes.

**Horizontal restructuring: enlarging the scale of social economy in the Yangtze Delta by intensifying the regional division of labor**
The Daily Commuting Field (DCF) has expanded to cover the full territorial scale of the Yangtze Delta's regional social economy. HSR enhances the mutual relationship between economic organizations and agents within DCF. These relationships are intensifying, irrespective of prior administrative and political boundaries. Thus, HSR's effects in a multi-core network may erode the prior bureaucratically based hierarchical administrative structures established under central planning and replace them with a market driven networked structure (Provan and Kenis, 2008; Graham and Marvin, 2001).

In the Yangtze Delta area, there is emerging evidence of a phenomenon of growth convergence throughout Shanghai's DCF (Berthelemy and Varoudakis, 1996). These towns or cities subsumed within this DCF have experienced a similar growth rate between 2010 and 2014 of around 10 per cent. For cities outside the DCF of Shanghai, like Jurong, Zhenjiang, and Nanjing, the annual GDP increases have been even higher. Non-agricultural industry inside the DCF is being centrifugally diffused from the center of Shanghai. The growth rate of secondary industry, such as manufacture, mining, energy and construction industry inside the DCF between 2010 and 2012 is below 16 per cent, whereas in urban centers outside Shanghai's DCF, including Nanjing, Changxin and Zhuji, industrial growth has been greater than 16 per cent. These trends are illustrated in Figures 5.10 and 5.11 below.

Although the correlation between HSR and secondary industry does not mean that HSR is the primary cause of industrial decentralization, we find some evidence that HSR allows entrepreneurs to locate their factories in a wider area. For example, many entrepreneurs transfer their factories from Shanghai to other cities outside Shanghai's DCF, and their engineers commute from factories and headquarters through HSR.

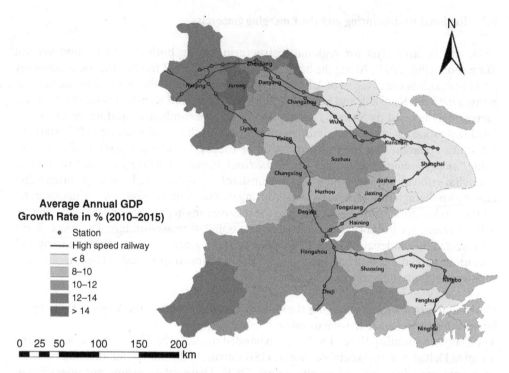

*Figure 5.10    Average annual GDP growth in the Yangtze Delta from 2010 to 2015*

**Fading of traditional administrative boundaries**

As a result of the frequent commuting enabled by HSR, adjacent cities and towns in the DCF are gradually being absorbed into the primate city. This integration works to dissolve the former multi-level administrative boundaries, reshaping the urban form into an edge city configuration (Garreau, 1992), relying on HSR as illustrated in Figure 5.12. For the largest HSR nodes like Shanghai and Beijing, the urban residential function has extended well beyond the city's administrative boundary, with commuter residential settlements developed in adjacent cities and towns like Kunshan, Jiading and Langfang. A percentage of the population purchases housing in adjacent cities and towns, works in central cities and commutes via HSR. From our field survey conducted in 2016,[4] about 80 per cent of HSR passengers from Kunshan South Station to Shanghai at 7:11 a.m., and 33 per cent at 7:35 a.m. and 7:41 a.m. identified themselves as daily commuters. China Railways now accepts Banking Expresspay cards for fare payment, which facilitates daily commuting more than traditional fare media.

**How the supercity is emerging as China's largest unit of spatial organization**

As HSR extends access to China's largest cities by expanding daily commuting mobility on a regional scale, the supercity will surpass the metropolis to become the largest urban

---

[4]    We conducted a field survey in Kunshan from February 27 to March 4 in 2016. Passengers from the entrance and exit were all calculated and some were interviewed stochastically.

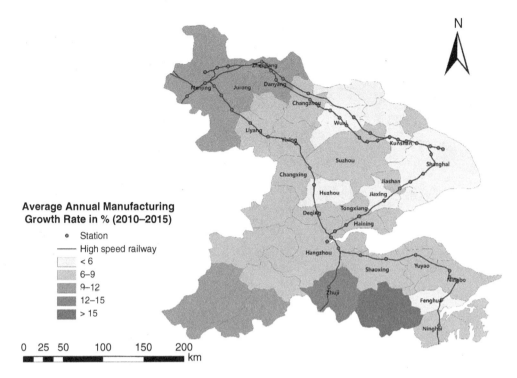

*Figure 5.11   Average annual growth rate of secondary industry of the Yangtze Delta from 2010 to 2015*

territory unit of spatial integration yet known to civilization. The metropolitan division of labor, which used to be expressed as a multi-layered hierarchy and provides a concrete example of this old mode of labor organization, is increasingly being reshaped into a new configuration which transcends the conventional mode of the metropolis. Taking Beijing as an example, residential settlement, manufacturing, recreation and other non-agriculture industries are becoming centrifugally diffused since HSR emerged. According to a survey of companies taken in February 2015, 49 manufacturing firms will move out of Beijing and relocate to nearby cities (Beijing Municipal Bureau of Statistics, 2015).

## 5.2   Vertical Restructuring: The Re-Organization of Socio-Economic Activity

### The expanded orbit of central cities through greater linkage with peripheral cities and towns

HSR neither creates new economic resources, in itself, nor does it generate new opportunities by itself. However, HSR does restructure and redistribute existing production factors quite considerably (Chen, 2012; Levinson, 2012; Dura-Guimera, 2003). The enhanced mobility has a siphoning effect throughout the HSR network, pumping population, resources and capital into central cities. Taking the Harbin to Dalian corridor as an example, HSR accelerates the polarization of major cities along the corridor, such as Shenyang,

*Figure 5.12    The ephemeral boundary between Shanghai and Kunshan*

Harbin and Changchun as illustrated in Figure 5.13. The average annual growth rate of residential population from 2010 to 2015 is 0.76 per cent and 0.19 per cent respectively, in excess of the regional average growth –0.21 per cent. As a matter of fact, the whole of Northeast China has been confronting recession since 2000s. This area is experiencing demographic aging and outflow of population, leading to economic stagnation. Many mid-sized and smaller cities along the corridor experienced population loss after HSR service commenced. Sixty-three point six per cent of cities under one million population reduced in size between 2010 and 2015.

**HSR's effect on supercities**
Further, as HSR enlarges the diameter of the daily commuting field, the integration effect fosters the evolution of China's supercities. With respect to spatial features, the scale of the HSR-based supercity surpasses any single big metropolitan region in GDP, population and area. Moreover, the spatial organization of production of each city will also be reconstructed to enable their integration into a supercity (Berry and Okulicz-Kozaryn, 2012; Schafran, 2014). For instance, the municipalities of supercities, such as Beijing, Nanjing, Hangzhou, Wuhan etc., accelerated the development of one-hour-commute planning, fast rail system and enhanced the mass traffic capacity in

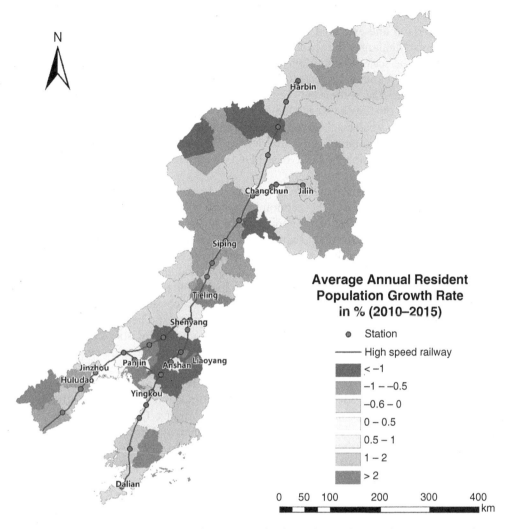

*Figure 5.13* *Average annual population growth along the Harbin–Dalian HSR corridor (2010–2015)*

region to qualify as the national urban centers, which benefited from HSR in regional integration.[5]

However, China's urban development trajectories depend on mobility effects that may differ with HSR network configuration. The Multicore Network Mode (MNM) of HSR development provides the greatest mobility contributions to supercity formation, taking advantage of the stimulus that HSR mobility gives to socio-economic development. For Monocentric Radial Mode and Corridor Mode of development, there is less evidence of supercity formation.

---

[5] http://politics.people.com.cn/n1/2017/0221/c1001-29095124.html.

The emergence of supercities within China's MNM development occurs through the enlarged hinterland and extended influence of primary cities like Beijing and Shanghai. Since HSR greatly enlarges the scope and intensifies the degree of radiation effect from the central city, the scale of hinterland is extended beyond the metropolis to the larger scope of the DCF. Shanghai has been the first choice for HSR travel from cities within its DCF. The passenger flow volume between Shanghai and Danyang, a peripheral city in the DCF, has exceeded the flow between Danyang and its prefecture-level city of Zhenajiang. Commuting frequency can be observed from the passenger growth that was noted in Table 5.4. Therefore, China's ongoing supercity development will most likely extend to cover the territory made accessible by HSR-based DCF in a multicore network that includes a very large urban center.

The emergence of supercities also relies on the restructuring of labor inside the urban region. As mentioned above, the economic growth within DCF appears to deepen the division of labor among urban nodes within the supercity. The urban function is decentralized from the traditional urban core and re-distributed among nodes across the supercity. Currently, within the Yangtze Delta supercity, Suzhou has taken on a greater function in finance and business management; Chagnzhou has become a growing center for medical services; and Kunshan shares with Shanghai the role of hosting meetings and exhibitions, at the same time as it has become a bedroom community for those working in Shanghai. In the Greater Beijing supercity, manufacturing and heavy industry has been dispersed from Beijing to other nodes; Tianjin has become the logistics hub, as well as a bedroom community; and several satellite cities like Langfang have emerged as additional bedroom communities.

HSR has also stimulated tourism within the supercity because of shorter travel time between business and residential locations and cultural and recreational attractions. Suzhou, Kunshan, Hangzhou and other nodes in the Yangtze Delta, for example, have become the weekly destinations of visitors from Shanghai, and from other nodes within the multicore network. During the Qingming festival, from April 2 to April 4 in 2016, daily passenger flow reached about two million, an increase of 9.8 per cent on the previous year (China Radio, 2016).

However, the development effects of China's HSR in Monocentric Radial Mode and Corridor Mode are still evolving. The hinterland of central city in MRM will expand to adjacent cities, which helps metropolitan formation. However, since the accessibility of MRM is highly centrifugal, the development of peripheral cities could be restricted by the polarization effect of the central city. Thus, the spatial organization of production is less likely to restructure than in the supercity. Economic activity and population will tend to concentrate at the center of this network. Corridor Mode regional development effects may be more adversarial. Due to the small hinterland scale and poor socio-economic development between major nodes along a corridor, there tends to be fierce competition among cities and towns in region for mobile capital and population migration (Cox, 1995), which reduces the chance for cities along the corridor to develop symbiotically.

## 6. CONCLUSIONS

It is clear that Chinese population and economic activity data reveal that regions served by HSR exhibit different development patterns that can be associated with the three modes of HSR service. While HSR is positively correlated with economic growth in all three configurations (CM, MRM, and MCM) population growth is more varied in the MRM and MCM configurations. This suggests that HSR commuting reduces the attraction of living in the larger Chinese cities for certain segments of the population by facilitating commuter travel to and from the central hub (MRM) and across the supercity region (MCM) allowing some segments of residential location and employment activity to attenuate on a scale not previously seen within a single metropolitan region. The chapter concludes by considering the implication of such innovative development patterns for China's urban future.

Furthermore, the uneven expansion of accessibility across these regions may accelerate or retard the circulation of people and thus either indirectly catalyze, or constrain economic development. Then, while China's transportation network and social economy is changing, the national spatial structure and urban hierarchy is being reshaped. However, the impact of HSR on urban and regional integration differed. For instance, HSR enhanced the integration of the Yangtze delta area, and even restructured it as a complex of node cities, while HSR may polarize the urban and regional society in Jing Jin-Ji supercity and the Harbin–Dalian HSR corridor.

Nevertheless, HSR inevitably catalyzes social inequality at urban and regional scales. In fact, HSR has not only accelerated the uneven economy in regions, but also enlarged the gap within local residents and urban commuters. For instance, because HSR enlarged the DCF, it then catalyzed the local real estate market and made housing unaffordable for lower income residents, while commuters displaced these lower income dwellers around many HSR stations.

To date, HSR has shown more potential to influence the impact of subsequent regional development than the reverse, where regions without HSR have developed quickly and then attracted the installation of this new mobility infrastructure. That is the reason why Chinese local governments have been eager to create incentive strategies to accelerate the local social-economy development trends that began to emerge following the creation of accessibility by HSR. Thus, one policy implication of China's HSR development suggests that other countries should consider HSR mobility as offering a contribution to their local economic development potential, with the effects differing based upon the network configuration that is pursued.

## ACKNOWLEDGEMENTS

We thank the team work of Gao Li, Wu Jinye, Zhang Yaqian and You Weilun on data collection and calculation. This research was supported by National Natural Science Foundation of China (No. 41271176; 41671155).

# REFERENCES

Angel, S. and Hyman, G. (1976). *Urban Fields: A Geometry of Movement for Regional Science*. London, UK: Pion.

Beijing Municipal Bureau of Statistics (2015). Marked success of industrial re-distribution of Beijing, September, 18, available at: http://www.beijing.gov.cn/tzbj/jjsj/fx/t1403455.htm. Accessed November 25, 2015.

Berry, B. J. (1968). Interdependency of spatial structure and spatial behavior: a general field theory formulation. *Papers in Regional Science*, 21(1), 205–227.

Berthelemy, J. C. and Varoudakis, A. (1996). Economic growth, convergence clubs, and the role of financial development. *Oxford Economic Papers*, 48(2), 300–328.

Bröcker, J., Korzhenevych, A. and Schürmann, C. (2010). Assessing spatial equity and efficiency impacts of transport infrastructure projects. *Transportation Research Part B: Methodological*, 44(7), 795–811.

Bruinsma, F. and Rietveld, P. (1993). Urban agglomerations in European infrastructure networks. *Urban Studies*, 30(6), 919–934.

Chen, C-L. (2012). Reshaping Chinese space-economy through high-speed trains: opportunities and challenges. *Journal of Transport Geography*, 22, 312–316.

China Radio (2016). The announcement of railway transportation schedule during Qingming Festival, March 18, available at: http://news.cnr.cn/native/city/20160318/t20160318_521647868.shtml. Accessed September 8, 2016.

China Railway Construction Corporation Limited (2015). The GDP of China HSR industry is anticipated to exceed 400 billion RMB, January 27, available at: http://www.crcc.cn/g705/s1743/t48811.aspx. Accessed November 25, 2015.

Cox, K. (1995). Globalisation, competition and the politics of local economic development. *Urban Studies*, 32(2), 213–224.

Delaplacea, M., Pagliarab, F. and Aguilérac, A. (2014, April). High-speed Rail Station, Service Innovations and Temporary Office Space for Mobile Workers A Comparison France/Italy. In, Transport Research Arena (TRA) 5th Conference: Transport Solutions from Research to Deployment.

Dura-Guimera, A. (2003). Population deconcentration and social restructuring in Barcelona, a European Mediterranean city. *Cities*, 20(6), 387–394.

Friedmann, J. and Miller, J. (1965). The urban field. *Journal of the American Institute of Planners*, 31(4), 312–320.

Fu, X., Zhang, A. and Lei, Z. (2012). Will China's airline industry survive the entry of high-speed rail? *Research in Transportation Economics*, 35(1), 13–25.

Garreau, J. (1992). *Edge City: Life on the New Frontier*. New York: Anchor Books.

Graham, S. and Marvin, S. (2001). *Splintering Urbanism: Networked Infrastructures, Technological Mobilities and the Urban Condition*. Psychology Press.

Guérois, M. and Pumain, D. (2008). Built-up encroachment and the urban field: a comparison of forty European cities. *Environment and Planning A*, 40(9), 2186.

Gutiérrez, J. (2001). Location, economic potential and daily accessibility: an analysis of the accessibility impact of the high-speed line Madrid–Barcelona–French border. *Journal of Transport Geography*, 9(4), 229–242.

Gutiérrez, J., Gonzalez, R. and Gomez, G. (1996). The European high-speed train network: predicted effects on accessibility patterns. *Journal of Transport Geography*, 4(4), 227–238.

Harvey, D. (1989). *The Conditions of Postmodernity: An Enquiry into the Origins of Cultural Change*. New York, NY: Blackwell.

Kim, K. (2000). High-speed rail developments and spatial restructuring: a case study of the Capital region in South Korea. *Cities*, 17(4), 251–262.

Kirsch, S. (1995). The incredible shrinking world? Technology and the production of space. *Environment and Planning D*, 13(3), 529.

Levinson, D. M. (2012). Accessibility impacts of high-speed rail. *Journal of Transport Geography*, 22, 288–291.

Lewin, K. (1951). *Field Theory in Social Science: Selected Theoretical Papers*. New York, NY: Harper.

Ma, L. (2005). Urban administrative restructuring, changing scale relations and local economic development in China. *Political Geography*, 24(4), 477–497.

Monzón, A., Ortega, E. and López, E. (2013). Efficiency and spatial equity impacts of high-speed rail extensions in urban areas. *Cities*, 30, 18–30.

Plane, D. (1981). The geography of urban commuting fields. *Professional Geographer*, 33, 182–188.

Provan, K. and Kenis, P. (2008). Modes of network governance: structure, management, and effectiveness. *Journal of Public Administration Research and Theory*, 18(2), 229–252.

Qin, Y. (2016). "No county left behind?" The distributional impact of high-speed rail upgrades in China. *Journal of Economic Geography*, 4, 1–32.

Román, C., Espino, R. and Martín, J. (2010). Analyzing competition between the high speed train and alternative modes. The case of the Madrid-Zaragoza-Barcelona corridor. *Journal of Choice Modelling*, 3(1), 84–108.

Sands, B. (1993). The development effects of high-speed rail stations and implications for California. *Built Environment* (1978), 257–284.

Schafran, A. (2014). Rethinking mega-regions: sub-regional politics in a fragmented metropolis. *Regional Studies*, 48(4), 587–602.

Spiekermann, K. and Wegener, M. (1996). Trans-European networks and unequal accessibility in Europe. *European Journal of Regional Development*, 4(96), 35–42.

Stabler, J. and Olfert, M. (1996). Spatial labor markets and the rural labor force. *Growth and Change*, 27, 206–230.

Vickerman, R. (2015). High-speed rail and regional development: the case of intermediate stations. *Journal of Transport Geography*, 42, 157–165.

Wang, X., Huang, S., Zou, T. and Yan, H. (2012). Effects of the high speed rail network on China's regional tourism development. *Tourism Management Perspectives*, 1, 34–38.

Willigers, J. and Van Wee, B. (2011). High-speed rail and office location choices. A stated choice experiment for the Netherlands. *Journal of Transport Geography*, 19(4), 745–754.

Wu, Q., Perl, A. and Sun, J. (2016). Bigger and Different: Understanding the role of high-speed rail as a development catalyst in China's emerging supercities. The Transportation Research Board (TRB) 95th Annual. Washington, D.C, January.

Wuhan Morning Paper (2015). Sixty per cent of Wuhan population takes HSR as commuting tools, March 16, available at: www.cnhan.com/html/whcb/2015/whcb_0316/94699.html. Accessed November 25, 2015.

Xinhua Net (2015). Focusing on the transportation change during Spring Festival: from population flow to data flow, January 27, available at: news.xinhuanet.com/fortune/2015-02/04/c_1114255901.htm. Accessed November 25, 2015.

# 6. Automobile peripheries: travel to school in suburban London through the lens of social practice
*Emilia Smeds*

## 1. INTRODUCTION

School travel is a core feature of everyday mobility in contemporary society – a journey to be achieved twice a day by children and their accompanying parents – yet an often-overlooked transport policy issue. The continued increase in the proportion of children being driven to school in the United Kingdom, instead of using public transport, walking or cycling, has significant impacts on congestion and transport emissions, however the equity dimensions of this modal shift are rarely discussed. This chapter aims to contribute to the literature on travel to school, drawing on social practice theory, sociology of mobility and time geography, to offer insights to inform UK travel to school policy.

The chapter begins with an overview of trends relating to travel to school in Great Britain and recent policy responses, followed by a section outlining the conceptual framework and research design employed. Research findings on three competing practices for travelling to school (walking, cycling and driving) are then presented, using journeys to two case study schools, along with data on the bundling of travel to school and travel to work and space-time constraints faced by parents. The two case study schools are then compared for further nuance. The fifth section discusses how the nature of spatially uneven and predominately 'soft' transport investment reproduced the dominance of driving to school compared to walking and cycling in the case study areas. The concluding section offers some brief reflections on what social practice theory has to offer thinking about social equity and transport.

## 2. TRENDS IN TRAVEL TO SCHOOL IN THE UK

In recent decades, dramatic changes have occurred with respect to travel to school in the United Kingdom. Data on modal shares for journeys to school in Great Britain for children aged 5–10 can be found in the National Travel Survey (DfT 2013) and Pooley et al. (2005). National statistics show a continuous decline in the proportion of children walking to school, from 73.5 per cent of children in 1975–1976 to 47 per cent in 2012. Simultaneously, there has been a continuous increase in the percentage of children travelling to school by car (i.e. being driven): from 15 per cent in 1975–1976 to 44 per cent in 2012. In 2012, walking thus remained the dominant mode for travel to school by a narrow margin, while driving has increased steadily. Cycling has been marginal throughout this period, oscillating between 1.5 per cent modal share in 1975–1976 and 2 per cent in 2012.

Furthermore, longitudinal studies document that since 1971, there has been a dramatic decline in children's independent mobility in the UK (Hillman et al. 1990). A study of five UK primary schools showed that from 1971 to 1990, the percentage of seven- and eight-year-old children allowed to travel to school without adult supervision declined from 80 to 9 per cent (Shaw et al. 2012). In 2012, only 4 per cent of journeys to school by children aged 5–10 in Great Britain were made independently (DfT 2013). The average distance for journeys to school for the same age group increased from 1 mile in 1975 to 1.8 miles in 2012 (Pooley et al. 2005; DfT 2013), which is likely to be the outcome of a complex set of changes including greater freedom for families to choose which school their children attend (referred to as 'school choice').

A large body of behaviour change policy trying to encourage 'active' travel to school (walking and cycling) and counter the increase in driving has emerged in the UK. 'Attitudinal' theories of behaviour change by individuals (Ajzen 1991; Bamberg and Schmidt 2003; Triandis 1977) have become popular in a range of policy domains in the UK (Jones et al. 2013). The policy prescriptions offered by these theories point to the need to influence attitudes and 'break' habit. This approach was reflected in the UK Department for Transport's 'Smarter Choices' programme of 'soft' transport policy measures aiming at informing individual choices (Cairns et al. 2004), and as part of this, a national 'Travelling to School Initiative' (TTSI) aimed at decreasing car use and increasing active travel through School Travel Plans (a plan produced by the school with a set of mainly behaviour change measures) and School Travel Advisers (DfT 2003). Despite evidence suggesting that School Travel Plans had supported substantial modal shift in certain cases, between 2003 and 2010 TTSI had 'not had a significant impact on average mode share figures, at an aggregate level' (Atkins 2010: 7). The impact of travel to school policy has thus been limited to date.

## 3. RESEARCH FRAMEWORK AND DESIGN

The objective of the research presented here is to investigate the utility of social practice theory (Shove et al. 2012), as a major theoretical development, in providing an alternative understanding of travel to school. Attitudinal theories of travel behaviour have come under increasing criticism (Schwanen and Lucas 2011; Schwanen et al. 2012) and the overall empirical evidence regarding the effectiveness of soft measures is mixed (Möser and Bamberg 2008). In a critique, Shove (2010: 1274) has argued that attitudinal theories adopt a so-called 'ABC' framework: an account of social change 'thought to depend on values and attitudes (the A), which are believed to drive the kinds of behaviour (the B) that individuals choose [C] to adopt'. The C is central here, indicating an assumption that travel behaviour is an outcome of conscious and free individual choice. Shove (2010) argues that 'ABC' theories fundamentally misrepresent the nature of social change by focusing on individual attitudes and behaviour, and are thus ill-equipped to engender a transition to sustainable mobility. Considering the trends in travel to school and the limited success of public policies in addressing these, the argument put forward by Shove (2010) – that a new approach to understanding 'what people do' is needed to inform policy-making – is of great relevance.

## 3.1   Conceptual Framework

The majority of the literature on travel to school focuses on 'modal choice', analysing objective variables (e.g. distance, urban form) and/or attitudes as uncovered through survey research (Stewart 2011, McMillan 2005). Although most of the literature is not explicitly grounded in a particular theory of behaviour, there is an implicit adoption of the 'ABC' framework in the focus on individual behaviour and choice.

Social practice theory adopts 'social practices' as the basic unit of analysis, rather than 'behaviour' or the 'individual', acknowledging that we live largely 'by default', and thus 'what people do is never reducible to attitudes or choices, or indeed to anything simply individual' (Watson 2012: 2). A social practice can be defined as 'a routinized type of behaviour which consists of several elements, interconnected to one other' (Reckwitz 2002: 249), and in the model developed by Shove et al. (2012) there are three types of elements that make up a practice: materials (e.g. infrastructure, tools, physical bodies), competences (e.g. skills, know-how) and meanings (e.g. symbolic meanings, ideas and aspirations). Enactment of a practice is only possible when the three elements are 'actively integrated': where the distribution of required competences, access to materials needed, and prevalence of the practice as a meaningful part of daily life overlap. Applying social practice theory to travel understands the activity of travelling by different modes as practices competing for the finite time of the practitioner, finite space in cities and on the road network, finite investment, as well as within discourses of safety and health (Watson 2012). Within the automobility system (Urry 2004), this competition occurs in a context where non-car modes and practices are subordinated and the conditions for their enactment are undermined by the dominance of the car. Practices change when the elements constituting them change. 'Persistence' of practices is dependent on the 'recruitment' of practitioners willing to perform them (e.g. walking to school becomes routinised practice for a family), whereas 'defection' from practices could be understood as an instance when the practice is 'abandoned' (e.g. family stops driving). Different practices also link together to form 'bundles': 'loose-knit patterns based on the co-location and co-existence of practices' (Shove et al. 2012: 82).

Assembling a conceptual framework for understanding travel to school in suburban London from the perspective of social practice involved two broad elements. Firstly, the 'three elements' model developed by Shove et al. (2012) was used to structure data collection and analysis with respect to three practices: driving, walking and cycling to school, and the concept of 'bundling' of different practices was also explored. Secondly, these practice theory concepts were contextualised through a literature review on driving, walking and cycling to school and the mobility of suburban families more broadly, from scholarly perspectives including time geography, activity-based approaches to travel behaviour and sociology of mobilities. This second set of literature is discussed along with research findings in Section 4.

## 3.2   Research Design

Social practice theory has been applied in diverse ways. As per Shove et al. (2012: 4), a practice exists simultaneously both as 'performance' and 'entity': it is performed through individual instances of 'doing', but also exists as an entity as 'something that exists between and beyond specific moments of enactment'. Shove et al. are primarily concerned with 'practices-as-entities' and the trajectories of these over time (including the history of different practices). Others have applied practice theories to understand more localised instances of practice (Barr et al. 2011; Hargreaves 2011), however Shove et al. (2012) are somewhat critical of applications that understand particular practices only as 'situated moments of performance'.

This research focused on understanding travel to school journeys in the particular context of two primary schools located in suburban West London. This chapter draws on observational field visits and semi-structured interviews with 19 parents, conducted in July 2014, to develop an understanding of walking, cycling and driving to school. As such, these practices were explored in the form they took in a particular place and time – as a microcosm of school travel in the UK – thus adopting an approach that was more localised and less historical than that of Shove et al (2012), while keeping the focus on practices-as-entities. The literature on travel to school behaviour for primary school children assumes that parents dominate decision-making regarding school travel, which is supported by ethnographic studies (Barker 2003), and thus the research focused on understanding competing practices for travelling to school from the point of view of parents of children attending the case study schools. Six semi-structured interviews were also conducted with professionals from organisations involved with travel to school policy locally or nationally.

## 4. FINDINGS: COMPETING PRACTICES FOR TRAVEL TO SCHOOL

Research findings are generated from an analysis of three competing practices for travelling to school: driving, walking and cycling, as well as the bundling of other everyday practices with travel to school. A comparison of the two case study schools is included at the end of the section.

### 4.1 Case Study Characteristics

Both of the case study primary schools are situated in the London Borough of Ealing, located in West London. Both of the schools are state-funded, and actively promote active travel to school in line with national and Ealing policy. The first school was a faith (religious) school and the second a 'community state school'. The schools are situated in a suburban context of a relatively car-dominated urban realm, surrounded by major roads and poorly served by public transport. The location of the schools and nearest London Underground stations are displayed in Figure 6.1 below. An official metric called PTAL (Public Transport Access Level) is used in London to assess the accessibility of locations, calculated on the basis of distance to public transport stops and service frequencies (TfL 2018). The community school is located within a residential neighbourhood, 10 minutes by foot from the nearest Underground station (Hanger Lane), yet still has a poor overall PTAL score (2 out of 6). The faith school is located in a less dense residential area at the Western edge of the London Borough of Ealing, approximately 40 minutes by foot to the closest Underground station (Northolt) and with a very poor PTAL Score (1b out of 6).

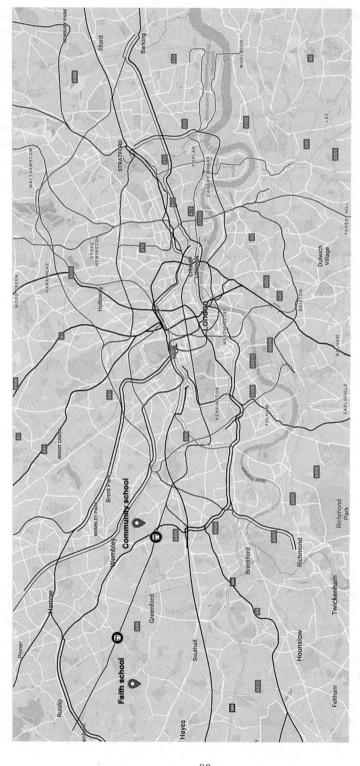

*Source:* Map data © 2018 Google, markers added by author.

*Figure 6.1 Location of case study schools and the nearest underground stations (Hanger Lane, Northolt) within wider London*

## 4.2   Comparing Elements of Walking, Cycling and Driving

Of the three competing practices, cycling was marginal, with 3 and 1 per cent of pupils cycling to respective schools based on 2012/13 data (TfL 2013b). Cycling was perceived as 'fun' but was not a normalised mode of travel to school, seen to be too dangerous for children (meanings), with lack of segregated cycling infrastructure (materials) and cycling skills (competences) cited. Competences did not appear to be significant for walking and driving to school, as skills in relation to these practices were relatively universal. Competition was thus predominately between walking and cycling to school, with respect to meanings and materials.

Parents at both schools associated walking to school with positive meanings: walking was perceived as 'normal', especially for those living near school for whom walking 'made sense'. Other positive meanings included health and fitness benefits for both child and parent, as well as 'good parenting' in some cases, supporting the findings of previous work on travel to school (Collins et al. 2009; Zuniga 2012). There was thus no significant evidence of what 'ABC' perspectives would term 'attitudinal barriers' to walking to school. However, despite such positive meanings, interviews also pointed to strong fear of traffic among many parents who walked their children to school, with reports of 'close misses' and erratic driving behaviour. Jacobsen et al. (2009) have argued that studies of active travel behaviour that focus on attitudes often miss the simple but robust influence of high traffic levels on discouraging walking and cycling. The fear of traffic felt by parents in relation to travel to school has been highlighted in the literature, for example by McLaren and Parusel (2012), who document how this causes parents to 'chauffeur' their children, or makes walking an unpleasant experience of 'parental traffic safeguarding'. In line with this, parents described engaging in safeguarding of children from traffic and the intensely stressful experience that this made the walking journey. Previous studies have found that the most common reasons for driving to school cited by parents are poor road safety and poor pedestrian infrastructure (Lang et al. 2011). This was also supported by the findings. Pedestrian infrastructure deemed acceptable and safe was a key lacking material to enable recruitment to walking as a practice, with specific features such as quality of lighting, paving and unpleasant underpasses mentioned:

> *[The walk to school] is stressful, noisy, no traffic lights to cross the road up there. . . It's all a little bit scary. (Interviewee 3, community school)*

Thus, despite most parents having walked to school as children, and the positive meanings associated with walking, many parents felt pedestrian infrastructure was lacking:

> *I would love that the kids grew up like I grew up. . . I walked to school. . . We all walked, you don't drive. I want to encourage my children to walk, but there is no place. . . the roads are horrible to walk on. They are so wobbly. We can't even walk without tripping. (Interviewee 2, faith school)*

Interview data thus revealed how the lack of materials in turn shaped meanings associated with walking and cycling to school – with inadequate infrastructure resulting in active travel being perceived as unsafe and stressful – thus illustrating how materials and meanings were linked as elements of walking as a practice. Visits to the case study areas allowed for validation of parents' perceptions of poor quality active travel infrastructure and highway-dominated urban realm with high traffic volumes and speeds. Walking was thus associated with both positive and negative meanings, but materials for walking were perceived as lacking.

Driving to school was also associated with both positive and negative meanings. There was no social norm against driving at either school, and some parents held positive associations, with interview responses supporting the findings of previous studies on affective dimensions of car use (Sheller 2004) such as providing a space for 'personal' slow-time in the context of busy lifestyles (Freudendal-Pedersen 2009) and 'mothering' in the sense of family 'quality time' (Maxwell 2001; Barker 2009). Most negative meanings associated with driving were related to parking and congestion as materials. Parking space and an extensive road network were important materials that allowed for driving to school to be faster in terms of travel time. The issue of limited parking surrounding schools and the associated battles of parent drivers was a much discussed issue, which had led to four instances of defection, i.e. families abandoning driving. Congestion was another issue, with the road network in some cases no longer offering advantages in terms of travel time. Meanings and materials as elements of driving to school thus showed some signs of weakening.

In summary, both walking and driving were associated with positive and negative meanings. Negative meanings were largely shaped by the perception of inadequate materials, rather than 'attitudinal' in the sense of norms or beliefs associated with either practice. Findings clearly illustrate how walking and cycling to school were undermined as practices in the context of car-dominated urban form, yet driving and automobility was also marked by some 'cracks'. Across interviewees and in the case of both schools, findings suggested that meanings (and competences) were not central to recruitment, persistence and defection in relation to travel to school practices and thus not central to determining the prevalence of each practice – instead, materials took centre stage.

## 4.3  Bundling and Space-Time Constraints

The research explored the extent to which practices of travelling to school were bundled with other practices of everyday life. Pooley et al. (2005: 52) have argued that the main change that has affected many British children's journey to school is the 'increasingly complex lives led by their parents and other family members . . . many journeys to school are bound up with other activities and this affects both the nature of the journey and the mode of transport'. Travel to school must thus be considered as potentially linked to journeys to other activities through 'trip-chaining'. Trip-chaining is a well-established concept within activity-based approaches to travel behaviour (Jones et al. 1983), which Watson (2012: 5) points out is related to the concept of bundling in social practice theory, sharing a concern with 'spatial and temporal bundling of travel as a means to accomplishing particular activities'.

The vignette below (Box 1) describing the lived reality of one parent, illustrates bundling of practices, trip-chaining and the importance of understanding travel to school in the context of the broader mobility of parents and families. This data points to the extent to which some parents felt their choices relating to travel to school were limited, in contrast to the tenets of 'ABC' theories of behaviour.

Jessica's story illustrates how the practices of travel to school and work can be bundled.

---

**BOX 1  VIGNETTE DESCRIBING BUNDLING AND SPACE-TIME CONSTRAINTS FOR ONE FAMILY  (BASED ON INTERVIEW DATA)**

*Jessica, mother of a child attending the faith school*

Jessica is employed part-time, with one car in the family. She considers her travel routines quite a bit. She is concerned with road safety and air quality in the area, and is not predisposed towards driving:

> 'I like walking, I've always walked. I don't ... particularly like driving. If we don't have to use the car, we won't.'

Jessica commutes to work by car when she needs to bring the children to school, because if she didn't, she would not make it on time to pick up the children from school at 2.50pm – she couldn't risk taking public transport and not getting there on time. Jessica used to work four-hour days, so she walked to school, then to Northolt station, and got two buses to work. This would work in the mornings, but going home she would have to leave 45 minutes early to ensure she could get on the train and buses, which would be infrequent during the day.

> 'So, I started driving in [to school], purely so I could keep to work commitments and give them the hours I'd told them I would work, and then to be able to get the kids on time, without worrying.'

Jessica thus can't travel by the mode she would prefer: walking, and feels that she and other parents are dependent on their cars to cope with daily routines, and may thus face limited choice:

> 'When you're working, you've got to do the huge shop as well ... So many kids have so many extra activities after school. If you have two kids, or even three ... You need the car to get around. It's not possible to walk ... I think a lot of parents have that ... in an ideal world it would be nice if everyone could walk to school, start a bit later, there would be trains and buses for us all to get on in time to get to work.'

---

In time geography, accessibility is understood as restricted by space-time constraints (Hägerstrand 1970), with a 'fixity constraint' resulting from the binding of activities to specific places and clock times. For parents juggling employment and caring, existing research has argued space-time constraints are generated by 'fixed times' such as school and working hours, by the spatial distribution of housing, employment and schools (Schwanen and de Jong 2008), and by public transport provision (Jarvis 2005). Jessica's case lends support to these findings: the bundling of practices is shaped by working hours and school hours as 'fixed times'.

National UK statistics indicate that only 8 per cent of journeys to school were followed by journeys to work (DfT 2013). Beyond the vignette above, travel to work was mentioned by a further four parents. Although it is not possible to generalise from the population interviewed, the findings point to the fact that for families living in areas with similar public transport provision, the influence of trip-chaining between travel to school and travel to work may be greater than indicated by the 8 per cent National Travel Survey figure. This figure also contrasts with other studies: English case studies have found that

'50% of the trips to school by car were part of a trip to work by the parent' (Mackett 2013: 18), whereas Norwegian and US studies have also found trip-chaining to work to be a significant factor determining travel to school mode trends (Fyhri and Hjorthol 2009; McDonald 2008). Furthermore, the vignette illustrates how other practices, such as shopping and children's extracurricular activities, are also bundled as part of complex everyday travel routines.

It is clear that Jessica's attitudes towards active travel to school are positive, but she perceives that her modal choice is limited. Her defection from walking and recruitment to driving to school is not attributable to attitudes, as would be suggested by current policy framings drawing on 'ABC' theories. Rather, defection from walking was a result of inadequate provision of public transport (reliability and frequency of services), which in turn determined the particular space-time constraints that Jessica had to face. Materials were again important here in explaining the prevalence of driving. The vignette thus illustrates the consequences that poor public transport accessibility can have on travel school – in this case to the faith school studied. The differences between the two cases are discussed in the next section.

## 4.4    Comparing Accessibility, Sprawl and Distances Travelled to School

As discussed so far, findings pointed to the central role of materials in shaping the competition between practices for travelling to school, and the role of bundling and space-time constraints. A comparison between the two schools is made here to describe how these factors varied between schools, analysing how differences in accessibility, sprawl and distances travelled to school may explain diverging modal splits, displayed in Table 6.1 below.

In the year preceding data collection, 56 per cent of pupils attending the faith school travelled to school by wholly or partly by car (park-and-stride referring to parking further from the school followed by a short walk), whereas 29 per cent walked to school. By comparison, 33 per cent of pupils travelled to the community school wholly or partly by car, with approximately half of pupils walking to school. Driving was thus significantly more prevalent in the case of the faith school.

Comparing interview data from the schools suggests that parents at the faith school found trip-chaining of travel to school, work and other everyday activities to be difficult without a car, whereas parents at the community school did not. Variation in public transport infrastructure as a material could partly explain this. As discussed earlier, the faith school location has the second worst PTAL score possible in London (1b). The community school scores higher (2), partly because it is located within a 10 minute walk

Table 6.1    *Modal split for travel to the case study schools in the 2012/13 academic year. Indicative data retrieved from respective School Travel Plans based on pupil 'show of hands'*

| Percentage of pupils travelling to school by different modes, 2012/13 | | | | | | |
|---|---|---|---|---|---|---|
| | Car | Car-share | Park and stride | Cycle | Walk | Other |
| Faith school | 30 | 10 | 16 | 3 | 29 | 12 |
| Community school | 25 | 2 | 6 | 1 | 51 | 15 |

of an Underground station. Parents at the community school indicated that trip-chaining travel to school and work, in combining walking and public transport, was easy for them. Slightly better public transport provision is likely to have played a role in this. Community school parents also seemed to suggest that services could easily be accessed in the immediate neighbourhood, such as shopping and children's extracurricular activities provided at the school. In contrast, the faith school is located in a more peripheral area of seemingly greater sprawl, with children needing to be chauffeured to extracurricular activities. Space-time constraints thus vary considerably between families, which may partly explain the differing modal splits between schools.

The difference in modal split is possibly also attributable to distances travelled to school (by pupils from their home): in 2014, the mean distance travelled was 1.45 km for the faith school, compared to a mean of 1 km for the community school (GLA 2018). Faith schools tend to have wider 'catchment areas' (the area in which pupils live) compared to other state schools. Existing research has found that distance is significantly correlated with the prevalence of active travel to school (McDonald and Aalborg 2009), and thus the difference in mean distance could play a role in the faith school having a lower mode share for walking. However, the difference in mean distances and consequent travel times (20–30 minutes, assuming a walking pace of 3 km per hour) between the two schools is not too significant. Distances perceived to be 'too long' for walking to school should, however, be examined in the context of how much time is available for travel. The argument made in this chapter is that distance must be understood in relation to trip-chaining and space-time constraints, rather than as an 'isolated' variable determining modal choice for travel to school.

## 5.   DISCUSSION: TRANSPORT INVESTMENT AND TRAVEL TO SCHOOL

The research discussed in this chapter aims to understand travel to school through the lens of social practice theory, but the findings on suburban mobility also offer plenty of insights for thinking about the impacts of transport investment across space.

Firstly, the findings point to the spatial unevenness of public transport investment in London and the implications for travel to school. Findings regarding space-time constraints and bundled practices of suburban families' mobility show how a lack of investment in public transport provision for peripheral urban areas can cause families to be locked in to car-dependency for everyday activities and thus also to be likely to drive children to school, rather than walk or cycle. Although there was some variation between schools, PTAL scores were very poor in both cases. PTAL scores across London (TfL 2018) reveal how accessibility declines on a steady gradient as one moves outward from Central London, and in the large areas falling between radial Underground lines. Accessibility of suburban areas and orbital connectivity, which could alleviate the space-time constraints faced by suburban families, do not appear to be priorities for public transport investment. These case studies illustrate that in London, like in many other cities globally, automobility can continue to be reproduced in suburban areas despite investment in city centre connectivity.

Secondly, the volume and type of investment that could encourage walking and cycling to school is also uneven across London, varying by local authority (borough).

The funds available and prioritised for local improvements to active travel infrastructure vary between local authorities in the UK, with a mix of internal funds and funds secured through a 'bidding process' administered by the Department for Transport. Significant volumes of funding for walking and cycling infrastructure is thus only available in the areas who manage to 'win' such funding.

'Hard' measures, such as new infrastructure, are typically much more expensive to implement than 'soft' measures such as behaviour change campaigns. The Ealing Borough School Travel Advisor, who oversees policy for the case study schools, argued that much more funding is needed and would ideally be available for 'hard' measures. In the context of fiscal austerity and dramatic reductions to local authority budgets year-on-year across the UK, there is a risk that the volume of funding available will cause overall investment to focus on implementation of 'soft' rather than 'hard' measures. Research findings pointed to how recruitment to walking and cycling is hampered by a lack of materials: active travel infrastructure that is perceived by parents of schoolchildren as safe and convenient to use for travelling to school. A focus on 'soft' measures is thus problematic, as evidenced by the limited impact of this approach to national travel to school policy so far. A policy prescription that could arguably be derived from the 'three elements model' of social practice theory (Shove et al. 2012) is that a change in practice is unlikely to be achieved just through 'soft' measures that address meanings, and must be combined with 'hard' measures that would improve materials for walking and cycling.

Overall, then, it could be argued that the prevalence of travel to school practices in the case study areas are partly produced as a result of spatially uneven transport investment. Findings illustrate how the structure – spatial location, volume and type – of transport investment resulted in access to everyday activities, including travel to school, only being possible by car for some families. It is questionable whether current investment by the UK Government and local authorities will counter the increasing prevalence of driving and declining prevalence of walking to school. Many families in the case study areas faced limited modal choice and some could be argued to effectively be coerced into car-dependency, seemingly lacking freedom to determine their own lifestyles. For other families, walking or cycling to school was the prevalent practice, however, the journey experience was associated with negative meanings such as fear and stress due to the nature of infrastructure and urban form. Families thus enjoy unequal opportunities for engaging in sustainable and healthy mobility practices, and the associated benefits for physical and mental well-being. If this is the case in London, it is also likely to be the case elsewhere in the UK, where materials and meanings for active travel to school are even less prevalent.

Having said this, the research also points to the fact that 'transport investment' was only one factor shaping travel to school. The case study comparison points to the role of spatial planning (location of homes, schools and services in relation to each other) in determining space-time constraints and bundling as part of everyday mobility of suburban families. Addressing this requires planning that ensures the spatial distribution of activities is such that it is possible to organise everyday life using non-car modes. The role of working and school hours as 'fixed times', as well as the impact of 'school choice' policy on distances travelled to school, were also very important. The findings thus points to the value of the theoretical lenses employed in this research in rethinking the scope of 'transport' policy.

## 6.   CONCLUSION: SOCIAL PRACTICES AND SOCIAL EQUITY

Against the backdrop of the limited impact of UK travel to school policy to date, alternative theoretical lenses to understand travel behaviour are needed. The research findings presented here provide an illustration of the value of understanding travel to school in novel ways, and that employing social practice theory can highlight critical as well as overlooked points of policy intervention.

To conclude, it seems appropriate to reflect on what social practice theory may have to offer in thinking about the relationship between transport and social equity. As demonstrated in this chapter, the application of the 'three elements' model of social practices developed by Shove et al. (2012) to analyse practices within a specific case study context can offer a more holistic perspective on the uneven and unequal opportunities for practising mobility, which is arguably more true to people's lived realities compared to an 'ABC' lens that focuses on attitudes and individual choice. Shove et al. (2012: 164) have pointed out that 'the ABC [framework] is a political and not just a theoretical position in that it locates both the problem and the response as a matter of individual behaviour' and downplays 'the extent to which the state sustains unsustainable . . . conventions and ways of life, and the extent to which the individual has a hand in structuring options and possibilities'. Through transport investment and spatial planning, the UK state plays a role in structuring the circulation of elements and prevalence of travel to school practices.

Theories of travel behaviour drawn on for policy-making filter down to the type of transport investment that is made, and through this impact people's lives. Social practice theory throws light on the unfairness of policy discourses prevalent in the UK that blame parents for driving to school and focus on promoting 'choice' through behaviour change policies, rather than tackling automobility through better infrastructure and planning. In reality, choice may be limited, as illustrated by suburban mothers' descriptions of minutely orchestrated daily routines coerced by automobility.

The research highlighted two social dimensions of differentiated mobility that were not explored, but could be included in future research as intersecting with the spatial dimension. Firstly, responsibilities for facilitating children's mobility were strongly gendered: the overwhelming majority of parents accompanying children to and from school were women, and thus everyday struggles with travel to school disproportionately affect them. Furthermore, both schools were situated in neighbourhoods that are among the 40 per cent most deprived in the UK, according to 2015 Index of Multiple Deprivation data from the UK government. Future research on travel to school, and mobility in general, would benefit from attention to deprived, peripheral urban areas.

## ACKNOWLEDGEMENTS

Thank you to Elizabeth Shove for comments on a draft version of this chapter.

# REFERENCES

Ajzen, I. (1991). The theory of planned behaviour. *Organizational Behavior and Human Decision Processes*, 50(2), 179–211.

Atkins. (2010). An Evaluation of the 'Travelling to School Initiative' Programme – Final Report, Department for Transport. Available at: www.gov.uk/government/uploads/system/uploads/attachment_data/file/4480/travelling-to-school-final-report.pdf.

Bamberg, S. and Schmidt, P. (2003). Incentives, morality, or habit? Predicting students' car use for university routes with the models of Ajzen, Schwartz and Triandis. *Environment and Behavior*, 35(2), 264–285.

Barker, J. (2003). Passengers or political actors? Children's participation in transport policy and the micro political geographies of the family. *Space and Polity*, 7(2), 135–151.

Barr, S., Shaw, G. and Coles, T. (2011). Sustainable lifestyles: sites, practices, and policy. *Environment and Planning A*, 43(12), 3011–3029.

Cairns, S. et al. (2004). *Smarter Choices – Changing the Way We Travel*, Department for Transport. Available at: www.gov.uk/government/publications/smarter-choices-main-report-about-changing-the-way-we-travel.

Collins, D., Bean, C. and Kearns, R. (2009). 'Mind that child': childhood, traffic and walking in automobilized space. In Conley, J. and McLaren Tigar, A. (eds) *Car Troubles: Critical Studies of Automobility and Auto-Mobility*. London: Routledge, pp. 127–143.

DfT. (2003). *Travelling to School: An Action Plan*, Department for Transport and Department for Education and Skills. Available at: http://webarchive.nationalarchives.gov.uk/20130401151715/www.education.gov.uk/publications/eOrderingDownload/DFES-0520-2003.pdf.

DfT. (2013). *National Travel Survey 2012 – Statistical Release*, Department for Transport. Available at: www.gov.uk/government/uploads/system/uploads/attachment_data/file/243957/nts2012-01.pdf.

Freudendal-Pedersen, M. (2009). *Mobility in Daily Life: Between Freedom and Unfreedom*. London: Routledge.

Fyhri, A. and Hjorthol, R. (2009). Children's independent mobility to school, friends and leisure activities. *Journal of Transport Geography*, 17(5), 377–384.

GLA. (2018). *London Schools Atlas*. London Datastore, Greater London Authority, accessed 20 June 2018 at data.london.gov.uk/dataset/london-schools-atlas.

Hargreaves, T. (2011). Practice-ing behaviour change: applying social practice theory to pro-environmental behaviour change. *Journal of Consumer Culture*, 11(1), 79–99.

Hägerstrand, T. (1970). What about people in regional science? *Papers of the Regional Science Association*, 24, 7–21.

Hillman, M., Adams, J. and Whitelegg, J. (1990). *One False Move . . . A Study of Children's Independent Mobility*. London: Policy Studies Institute Publishing.

Jacobsen, P.L., Racioppi, F. and Rutter, H. (2009). Who owns the roads? How motorised traffic discourages walking and bicycling. *Injury Prevention*, 15(6), 369–373.

Jarvis, H. (2005). Moving to London time: household co-ordination and the infrastructure of everyday life. *Time and Society*, 14(1), 133–154.

Jones, P.M. et al. (1983). *Understanding Travel Behaviour*. Aldershot: Gower.

Jones, R., Pykett, J. and Whitehead, M. (2013). *Changing Behaviours: On the Rise of the Psychological State*. Cheltenham: Edward Elgar.

Lang, D., Collins, D. and Kearns, R. (2011). Understanding modal choice for the trip to school. *Journal of Transport Geography*, 19(4), 509–514.

Mackett, R.L. (2013). Children's travel behaviour and its health implications. *Transport Policy*, 26(C), 66–72.

Maxwell, S. (2001). Negotiations of car use in everyday life. In Miller, D. (ed.) *Car Cultures*. Oxford: Berg.

McDonald, N.C. (2008). Household interactions and children's school travel: the effect of parental work patterns on walking and biking to school. *Journal of Transport Geography*, 16(5), 324–331.

McDonald, N.C. and Aalborg, A.E. (2009). Why parents drive children to school: implications for safe routes to school programs. *Journal of the American Planning Association*, 75(3), 331–342.

McLaren, A.T. and Parusel, S. (2012). Under the radar: parental traffic safeguarding and automobility. *Mobilities*, 7(2), 211–232.

McMillan, T.E. (2005). Urban form and a child's trip to school: the current literature and a framework for future research. *Journal of Planning Literature*, 19(4), 440–456.

Möser, G. and Bamberg, S. (2008). The effectiveness of soft transport policy measures: a critical assessment and meta-analysis of empirical evidence. *Journal of Environmental Psychology*, 28(1), 10–26.

Pooley, C.G., Turnbull, J. and Adams, M. (2005). The journey to school in Britain since the 1940s: continuity and change. *Area*, 37(1), 43–53.

Reckwitz, A. (2002). Toward a theory of social practices: a development in culturalist theorizing. *European Journal of Social Theory*, 5(2), 243–263.

Schwanen, T. and de Jong, T. (2008). Exploring the juggling of responsibilities with space-time accessibility analysis. *Urban Geography*, 29(6), 556–580.

Schwanen, T. and Lucas, K. (2011). Understanding auto motives. In Lucas, K., Blumenberg, E. and Weinberger, R. (eds) *Auto Motives: Understanding Car Use Behaviours*. Emerald Group Publishing Limited, pp. 3–38.

Schwanen, T., Banister, D. and Anable, J. (2012). Rethinking habits and their role in behaviour change: the case of low-carbon mobility. *Journal of Transport Geography*, 24(C), 522–532.

Shaw, B. et al. (2012). *Children's Independent Mobility: A Comparative Study in England and Germany (1971–2010)*, Policy Studies Institute. Available at: www.psi.org.uk/images/CIM_Final_report_v9_3_FINAL.PDF.

Sheller, M. (2004). Automotive emotions: feeling the car. *Theory, Culture and Society*, 21(4–5), 221–242.

Shove, E. (2010). Beyond the ABC: climate change policy and theories of social change. *Environment and Planning A*, 42(6), 1273–1285.

Shove, E., Pantzar, M. and Watson, M. (2012). The dynamics of social practice. In *The Dynamics of Social Practice: Everyday Life and How it Changes*. London: Sage.

Stewart, O. (2011). Findings from research on active transportation to school and implications for safe routes to school programs. *Journal of Planning Literature*, 26(2), 127–150.

TfL. (2018). *WebCAT*. Transport for London, accessed 20 June 2018 at tfl.gov.uk/info-for/urban-planning-and-construction/planning-with-webcat/webcat.

Triandis, H. (1977). *Interpersonal Behaviour*. Monterey, CA: Brookes/Cole.

Urry, J. (2004). The system of automobility. *Theory, Culture and Society*, 21(4–5), 25–39.

Watson, M. (2012). How theories of practice can inform transition to a decarbonised transport system. *Journal of Transport Geography*, 24, 488–496.

Zuniga, K.D. (2012). From barrier elimination to barrier negotiation: a qualitative study of parents' attitudes about active travel for elementary school trips. *Transport Policy*, 20, 75–81.

# 7. The impact of transport connectivity on housing prices in London
*Imogen Thompson*

## 1. INTRODUCTION

Transport has become an enabler for larger purposes in both urban planning and city politics. Used effectively, transport can create spatial opportunity, foster economic prosperity, preserve and enhance the environment, and link communities together. Housing, too, is crucial to the success of cities. It can anchor neighbourhoods and communities, provide residences for the human capital that drives economic expansion, and decrease social inequality.

A link exists between transport and housing development value. However, while long recognised by practitioners, the link has little evidence proving the magnitude of impact and the opportunities that one provides the other. London recognises the value of a strong transport system as a driver of the economy and of housing growth and delivery (London Connectivity Commission, 2012). Yet, both developers and government are (naturally) hesitant to implement major schemes without a firm grasp on the costs, benefits and economic returns that could be realised. By understanding the mutual benefits and value uplift potential of transport connectivity on housing prices, both developers and politicians can obtain an improved understanding of the wider economic benefits of major transport infrastructure projects, and thus make a stronger case for transport schemes across London.

With strategic goals of opening up development corridors and unlocking housing potential, transport is being judged by decision-makers not only on the 'direct' transport benefits they yield, but also on how they help facilitate development, including housing and commercial spaces (Honey, 2015). In order to help promote a more thorough understanding of housing development potential and future transport schemes within London, questions have been asked by major transport authorities (particularly the Department for Transport and Transport for London) as to how best to capture housing price uplift in transport scheme appraisal processes (ibid). This chapter will address those practical questions by exploring the following: Is there a link between transport connectivity and housing values? Is there empirical evidence that can substantiate the belief that transport connectivity is directly linked with housing price uplift within London? If so, what factors are attributable to this uplift?

## 2. DEFINING TRANSPORT CONNECTIVITY

Transport connectivity is a term increasingly used by planners and policy-makers alike. Traditionally, the term 'accessible' has been used to represent the level of access that all demographics have within a transport system (Transport for London, 2015b). However, the traditional concept is generally seen as a single measurement interacting with a specific location. New measures of connectivity are more inclusive, with attention being focused on an entire line – or system – within which a single point interacts (ibid). As such, within this study transport connectivity is defined as the links between multimodal transport modes and the ease of access to them.

There is a movement towards the evaluation of more inclusive and holistic measures of transport connectivity, including appraisal tools such as London's Public Transport Access Levels (PTAL) and the UK's Web-based Connectivity Assessment Toolkit (WebCAT), designed to create a matrix for locational connectivity assessment (ibid). Tools such as WebCAT have demonstrated the recognition of the importance that connectivity plays in transport scheme appraisal and transport planning. As exemplified by the above tools, transport systems are being redefined as more complex systems with multiple interconnected layers (Boyce, 2005). The interactive nature of these layers and the connectivity between them is what defines a successful transport network (PublicWorld, 2012). As such, within this chapter, transport connectivity will be defined as the matrix that makes a place accessible, integrated with other public transport, and desirable to travel to and from.

## 3. THE IMPORTANCE OF LINKING TRANSPORT CONNECTIVITY AND HOUSING PRICES

The appraisal of major infrastructure projects such as transport links have historically been exclusive of housing price increases. Housing uplift has many positive opportunities, including unlocking housing delivery, access to jobs, and funding opportunities for transport projects. As such, understanding the link between transport connectivity and housing prices is imperative to understanding the development potential of London. Housing prices are recognised as a measurement of property demand forecasting and regional development opportunity. Within this study, housing price is defined as the perceived monetary value of a property during its sale (Mathur, 2014). Property transaction value is a simple concept that has a breadth of applicability across multiple industries. Studies have shown that sales prices tend to reflect expectations of future developments; thus, property prices can act as predictors of the long-term benefits of new infrastructure (Andersson, et al., 2010). This demonstrates an important lesson for London and the UK, which is currently calling for an increase in housing development. Historically, while understood as interconnected, both the provision of transport networks and the strategic location of new residential development have generally remained mutually exclusive in UK policy frameworks, which has led to a loss of development potential in areas with strong transport links, and vice versa (Headicar, 2015).

Previous empirical studies have been conducted using North American and Asian case studies, with multiple types of transit analysed (such as high-speed rail or light rail networks). The San Francisco BART system has been widely studied since the 1970s, focusing on the proximity of property to rail stations as a determinant of housing price (Davis, 1970; Dornbusch, 1975; Lee, 1973). As well, studies have shown that anticipation of transport scheme implementation (the 'anticipatory effect') can lead to housing price increases in localised areas that are proximal to proposed transport stations, even before completion (generally, once it is officially approved by local authorities) (Bae, et al., 2003). This can add value to housing prices in anticipation of the increased value that transport will add to the area. The Washington D.C. Metro has been studied as an example of the anticipatory effect, analysing both the proximity to stations and the anticipatory impact of planning approval on property pricing (Damm, et al., 1980). Other studies have analysed the anticipatory effect from transport improvements in Chicago (McDonald and Osuji, 1995), Toronto rail line proximities (Dewees, 1976), and New York's transit access (Anas and Armstrong, 1993).

Despite the number of studies conducted, mixed results and limitations have surfaced. While the majority of studies have found that rail stations have positive impacts on property values within a particular range, there have also been studies that evidence no impact from rail stations, and some that suggest a negative impact based on proximity (Bowes and Ihlandfeldt, 2001). Most of these studies undertake an empirical study of single variables, or focus on a single line. In doing this, the impacts of transport connectivity are lost to the single impact of physical proximity to a station; arguably, a single variable does not represent the necessary transport connectivity that creates demand for a particular system. As well, by not considering the quality of place and the characteristics of the area within which it is stationed, the demand and desirability for a particular station may not be accurate, or may be falsely accounted for (ibid). Overall benefits of transport connectivity cannot be accurately measured simply by the proximity to a station, but by the total connectivity of a line and/or system. If an individual home was located adjacent to a station, it would not impact the price unless the property market sees benefits from the line; this would vary in each study, based on behavioural choices of transport uses (van de Kaa, 2010).

## 4.  HEDONIC MODELLING

Hedonic analysis for housing prices and real estate was pioneered in the mid-1960s by Lancaster, who proposed that goods are what are subjectively viewed by a purchaser as suiting of their individual needs (Lancaster, 1966). Premised upon the theory of consumer behaviour in deterministic situations, Lancaster noted that consumer reactions to the variations of quality and commodities associated with goods were important in determining the effect of complementarity (Rosen, 1974).

Within a hedonic function, it is theoretically assumed that all characteristics relevant to the determination of the market price should be included (Butler, 1982). However, this is not possible in practice, due to the extensive list of possible characteristics that could be used. Thus, a hedonic function must be acknowledged as incapable of achieving a 100 percent accurate relationship. Despite the inability to capture all poignant variables, a wide and carefully-selected mixed cohort of variables will generate statistically significant results (Brasington and Hite, 2008). Independently, each selected variable helps to provide a better understanding into the overall effects of transport connectivity on housing price increase, as it helps to extrapolate which factors make a stronger impact within a particular area.

## 5.  CASE STUDIES: JUBILEE LINE EXTENSION AND EAST LONDON LINE

Two London rail case studies are examined: The Jubilee Line Extension (JLE) and the East London Line (ELL) (Figure 7.1). In 1989, a Bill was put before Parliament to extend the existing Jubilee Line from Green Park to Stratford, with a route going through the Docklands and Canary Wharf. While the JLE fell short of traditional cost-benefit appraisal standards, the key planning objectives of the JLE were to increase transport connectivity towards inner East London, and to act as a regeneration catalyst for both commercial and residential opportunities within the Docklands (Omega Centre, 2014). With the Isle of Dogs planned as the newest central business district (CBD) of London, existing access via transport was limited, but the potential for economic growth was recognised as promising. The JLE was considered the opportunity needed to spur both commercial and residential development in East London, thus gaining approval despite a poor cost-benefit analysis (Mitchell, 2003).

Few studies have been undertaken to quantify the direct impacts of increased connectivity along the line. Using the JLE as a case study provides an empirical understanding of the impact of the transport link on property values within station catchment areas, and enables an analysis of the impacts of station development and interconnectivity on housing prices in London. For the purpose of this study, the JLE will be considered as the entire line including the extended section. This will better illuminate the impact of independent transport variables on housing prices given a range of characteristics, including new stations, brownfield sites, and varying locational characteristics.

The ELL has existed in its current state since 2010, as part of the London Overground. Prior to being refurbished in 2007, the ELL was the second shortest line in the Transport for London system, with a length of 9 kilometres, infrequent service, and minimal transport interconnectivity. In 2010, the newly refurbished section of the ELL saw several major changes. It underwent a phased extension along previous National Rail-owned routes, in order to create a network branch of 21 stations from Highbury and Islington to Croydon (National Rail, 2014). The line was marked as a London Overground line and added to the London Underground map (Guo, 2011; Saxton, 2013).

The refurbishment of the ELL created a rail corridor that became more integrated with the rest of the transport network in London (Transport for London, 2014a). As this did not happen until 2010, there is a strong availability of data both before and after the project delivery. This case study therefore demonstrates results for significant moments within a project's timeline: specifically, the time periods before scheme approval and after implementation. As well, similar to the JLE, the ELL was seen as an opportunity to increase transport connectivity, in particular in South London, and was hoped to spark development opportunities. Thus, the ELL is a comparative example to the JLE, sharing similar goals but with highly different characteristics.

## 6.  RATIONALE OF VARIABLE SELECTION

While studies and tools exist to understand the overall levels of connectivity within an area of London, variables are rarely explored together. This is in part due to the multitude

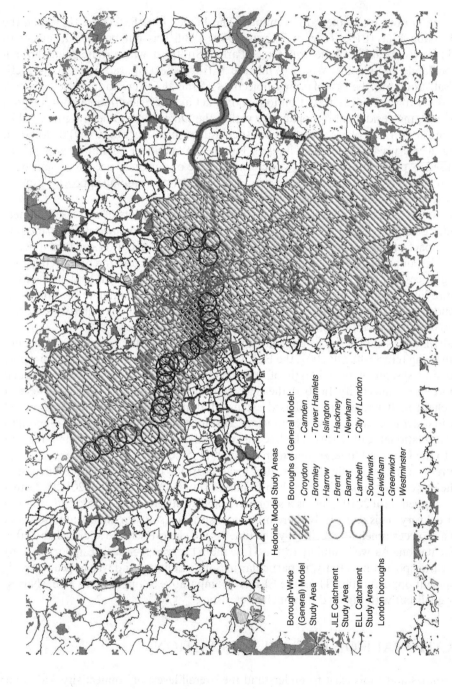

Hedonic Model Study Areas

Borough-Wide
(General) Model
Study Area

JLE Catchment
Study Area

ELL Catchment
Study Area

London boroughs

Boroughs of General Model:

- Croydon        - Camden
- Bromley        - Tower Hamlets
- Harrow         - Islington
- Brent          - Hackney
- Barnet         - Newham
- Lambeth        - City of London
- Southwark
- Lewisham
- Greenwich
- Westminster

*Figure 7.1    Spatial representation of the three hedonic model study areas*

of variables that could qualify as a factor in overall transport connectivity. Multiple transport variables were looked at to determine which are considered most important from a transport scheme appraisal perspective, as well as from locational characteristics. The data used within this study has been selected using precedents from previous studies, in order to obtain the strongest possible collinearity of variables. The selected variables that have been analysed fall under three categories of transport connectivity:

- transport link proximity;
- transport system connectivity; and,
- timing of implementation.

### 6.1 Transport Link Proximity

Proximity to transport has been recognised as an influential variable on property pricing, and thus a primary determinant of analysis of properties within the last 20 years. In particular, studies have shown that catchment areas surrounding transit stations have strong correlations with property prices (Bae, et al., 2003; Cervero and Landis, 1993). As well, transport planning practitioners have identified that proximity to a station plays a large role in transport behaviour and choices, thus affecting the impact of a station on the transit-specific desirability of a property (Zhang, et al., 2014). Using the guidance parameters of WebCAT and PTAL, variables were calculated based on TfL practitioner standards, creating a strong database framework that is specific to current London practitioner standards (Transport for London, 2015b).

### 6.2 Transport System Connectivity

Transport system connectivity in London is highly dependent on the locality and borough in which it is being evaluated. Each borough is subject to its own local authority, and consequently operates independently from neighbouring areas. The profile of each borough in London is different from that of its neighbour: poverty rates, economic activity, population density, and quality of place are but a few of the varying statistics found across the boroughs. Transport connectivity also varies within these regions. Due to the locational differences, the individual boroughs of London are important differentiators between results, as well as a control group that accounts for locational impacts. With a hedonic residential price model, it is seen as necessary to control for location, as the spatial structure of markets and surrounding area characteristics is crucial in explaining differing property transaction values (Bitter, et al., 2007).

### 6.3 Timing of Transport Link Implementation

Timing has been identified as a factor that can impact housing prices surrounding a transport line. As such, the anticipatory effect has been analysed as a factor of housing price increases (McDonald and Osuji, 1995). The ELL model undertakes a different approach than the control or JLE model to timing, focusing on three periods of time: pre-announcement of the line, post-approval of the line, and post-completion of the line. This provides empirical evidence on the anticipatory effect of transport connectivity in

London. The timing of the JLE model was unable to analyse the anticipatory effect, due to its approval dates and completion dates preceding 2001.

## 7.   RESULTS

The results of this study are obtained from an exploratory hedonic data analysis. Three Ordinary Least Squares (OLS) stepwise regressions, using R software, were used to tabulate and run the database. The final dataset includes 28 variables across 3 models. Minimal housing-specific characteristics were available for inclusion, due to the private nature of real estate databases. Future work on this study could attempt to include more detailed housing characteristics.

The three models held adjusted R-squared values of 0.5534, 0.4816, and 0.5341 respectively, demonstrating an acceptable level of reliability within this study. The current study has a limited scope and dataset compared to a prolonged study ranging over a longer time period. As such, future studies could be added to help raise the adjusted R-squared value.

## 8.   ANALYSIS OF THE RESULTS OF TRANSPORT CONNECTIVITY ON HOUSING PRICES

### 8.1   Results of Borough-Wide Model

The borough-wide model results (Table 7.1) uncovered several major trends. A strong positive correlation exists between housing price increases and the proximity to London Underground ('underground') stations. While the London Overground ('overground') access is also positively correlated, the underground correlates at a significantly higher level. Contrary to the underground and overground positive correlations, more bus stops within a walking catchment area results in a negative correlation of –0.039, and National Rail ('NR') connections stand at –0.0604.

### 8.2   Results of JLE Model

In the JLE model (Table 7.2), proximity to both motorways and B-type roads (also known as arterial roads and local streets respectively) have shown negative impacts on housing value increases. However, proximity to A-type roads (high streets and high roads) had a positive correlative value, and could suggest several scenarios that have impacted property value increases.

Results in the borough-wide control model showed that proximity to brownfield sites saw a positive correlation between transport connections and housing prices. In the JLE model, an even stronger positive correlation exists, with a value of 0.0156.

### 8.3   Results of ELL Model

An analysis of ELL anticipatory effects was possible due to the more recent implementation of the line. The JLE model was unable to have the same analysis completed, as the

*Table 7.1   Borough-wide model*

| GENERAL | | | | |
|---|---|---|---|---|

**Residuals:**

| Min | 1Q | Median | 3Q | Max |
|---|---|---|---|---|
| −4.0183 | −0.2021 | −0.0069 | 0.1989 | 2.9624 |

**Coefficients:**

| | Estimate | Std. Error | t value | Pr(.|t|) | |
|---|---|---|---|---|---|
| (Intercept) | 13.2058347 | 0.0122190 | 1080.766 | <2e-16 | *** |
| DateSoldy2002 | 0.1580194 | 0.0017227 | 91.729 | <2e-16 | *** |
| DateSoldy2003 | 0.2639931 | 0.0017900 | 147.479 | <2e-16 | *** |
| DateSoldy2004 | 0.3406574 | 0.0017645 | 193.065 | <2e-16 | *** |
| DateSoldy2005 | 0.3798021 | 0.0018334 | 207.161 | <2e-16 | *** |
| DateSoldy2006 | 0.4421936 | 0.0017400 | 254.136 | <2e-16 | *** |
| DateSoldy2007 | 0.5520271 | 0.0017742 | 311.142 | <2e-16 | *** |
| DateSoldy2008 | 0.5480643 | 0.0021787 | 251.557 | <2e-16 | *** |
| DateSoldy2009 | 0.4792293 | 0.0022527 | 212.732 | <2e-16 | *** |
| DateSoldy2010 | 0.5569434 | 0.0021402 | 260.232 | <2e-16 | *** |
| DateSoldy2011 | 0.5663188 | 0.0021768 | 260.157 | <2e-16 | *** |
| DateSoldy2012 | 0.6044584 | 0.0021672 | 278.908 | <2e-16 | *** |
| DateSoldy2013 | 0.6773969 | 0.0020829 | 325.214 | <2e-16 | *** |
| DateSoldy2014 | 0.7910708 | 0.0020848 | 379.454 | <2e-16 | *** |
| IsNewTrue | 0.1746619 | 0.0013588 | 128.539 | <2e-16 | *** |
| IsHouseTrue | 0.2237333 | 0.0013199 | 169.505 | <2e-16 | *** |
| DurationTrue | 0.3732528 | 0.0010013 | 372.768 | <2e-16 | *** |
| log(WalkDistanceBusStops) | −0.0390994 | 0.0011431 | −34.204 | <2e-16 | *** |
| log(WalkDistanceNationalRail) | −0.0604599 | 0.0009029 | −66.964 | <2e-16 | *** |
| log(WalkDistanceOverground) | 0.0636455 | 0.0015625 | 40.733 | <2e-16 | *** |
| log(WalkDistanceUnderground) | 0.1006224 | 0.0009826 | 102.401 | <2e-16 | *** |
| log(ProximityToARoad) | 0.0142510 | 0.0003976 | 35.846 | <2e-16 | *** |
| log(ProximityToBRoad) | −0.0126249 | 0.0003656 | −34.531 | <2e-16 | *** |
| log(ProximityToMotorWay) | −0.0532128 | 0.0006807 | −78.177 | <2e-16 | *** |
| log(ProximityToGreenArea) | −0.0228191 | 0.0004224 | −54.027 | <2e-16 | *** |
| log(ProximityToBrownfield) | 0.0075503 | 0.0003287 | 22.973 | <2e-16 | *** |
| log(ProximityToCAZ) | −0.0534624 | 0.0002600 | −205.653 | <2e-16 | *** |
| log(ProximityToCWZ) | 0.0056721 | 0.0003427 | 16.552 | <2e-16 | *** |
| log(PopulationPerSqKm) | −0.0234715 | 0.0007709 | −30.447 | <2e-16 | *** |
| logit(CrimeRatePer1000) | −0.0024499 | 0.0009749 | −2.513 | 0.012 | * |
| logit(PercentEducationAbove4) | 0.4665239 | 0.0010050 | 464.205 | <2e-16 | *** |

---

Signif. codes: 0 '***' 0.001 '**' 0.01 '*' 0.05 '.' 0.1 ' ' 1

Residual standard error: 0.3417 on 808838 degrees of freedom
Multiple R-squared: 0.5534, Adjusted R-squared: 0.5534
F-statistic: 3.341e+04 on 30 and 808838 DF, p-value: < 2.2e-16

*Table 7.2    JLE model*

|  | JLE |  |  |  |  |
|---|---|---|---|---|---|

**Residuals:**

| Min | 1Q | Median | 3Q | Max |
|---|---|---|---|---|
| −4.0461 | −0.2291 | −0.0073 | 0.2292 | 2.8773 |

**Coefficients: (1 not defined because of singularities)**

|  | Estimate | Std. Error | t value | Pr(>\|t\|) |  |
|---|---|---|---|---|---|
| (Intercept) | 13.9773039 | 0.0212336 | 658.26 | <2e-16 | *** |
| DateSoldy2002 | 0.1411254 | 0.0021351 | 66.10 | <2e-16 | *** |
| DateSoldy2003 | 0.2164258 | 0.0022183 | 97.56 | <2e-16 | *** |
| DateSoldy2004 | 0.2957298 | 0.0021810 | 135.59 | <2e-16 | *** |
| DateSoldy2005 | 0.3376967 | 0.0022569 | 149.63 | <2e-16 | *** |
| DateSoldy2006 | 0.4066293 | 0.0021407 | 189.95 | <2e-16 | *** |
| DateSoldy2007 | 0.5278936 | 0.0022017 | 239.76 | <2e-16 | *** |
| DateSoldy2008 | 0.5307743 | 0.0026393 | 201.10 | <2e-16 | *** |
| DateSoldy2009 | 0.4807999 | 0.0027005 | 178.04 | <2e-16 | *** |
| DateSoldy2010 | 0.5620050 | 0.0025519 | 220.23 | <2e-16 | *** |
| DateSoldy2011 | 0.5842161 | 0.0026290 | 222.22 | <2e-16 | *** |
| DateSoldy2012 | 0.6298648 | 0.0026468 | 237.97 | <2e-16 | *** |
| DateSoldy2013 | 0.7079982 | 0.0025829 | 274.12 | <2e-16 | *** |
| DateSoldy2014 | 0.8090812 | 0.0026295 | 307.69 | <2e-16 | *** |
| IsNewTrue | 0.1531667 | 0.0015437 | 99.22 | <2e-16 | *** |
| IsHouseTrue | 0.1503576 | 0.0020402 | 73.70 | <2e-16 | *** |
| DurationTrue | 0.4030933 | 0.0013945 | 289.05 | <2e-16 | *** |
| log(WalkDistanceBusStops) | 0.0217790 | 0.0016276 | 13.38 | <2e-16 | *** |
| log(WalkDistanceNationalRail) | −0.0909278 | 0.0012559 | −72.40 | <2e-16 | *** |
| log(WalkDistanceOverground) | 0.0560409 | 0.0016888 | 33.18 | <2e-16 | *** |
| log(WalkDistanceOtherUnderground) | 0.3324171 | 0.0096900 | 34.30 | <2e-16 | *** |
| log(ProximityToARoad) | 0.0169467 | 0.0005132 | 33.02 | <2e-16 | *** |
| log(ProximityToBRoad) | −0.0175001 | 0.0004540 | −38.54 | <2e-16 | *** |
| log(ProximityToMotorWay) | −0.0568593 | 0.0010510 | −54.10 | <2e-16 | *** |
| log(ProximityToGreenArea) | −0.0266425 | 0.0005356 | −49.74 | <2e-16 | *** |
| log(ProximityToBrownfield) | 0.0156623 | 0.0003885 | 40.31 | <2e-16 | *** |
| log(ProximityToCAZ) | −0.0504469 | 0.0002515 | −200.58 | <2e-16 | *** |
| log(ProximityToCWZ) | 0.0063877 | 0.0004681 | 13.65 | <2e-16 | *** |
| log(PopulationPerSqKm) | −0.0626640 | 0.0011120 | −56.35 | <2e-16 | *** |
| logit(CrimeRatePer1000) | 0.0291878 | 0.0011135 | 26.21 | <2e-16 | *** |
| logit(PercentEducationAbove4) | 0.4968956 | 0.0012672 | 392.12 | <2e-16 | *** |
| log(X640.960mWalk) | −0.4419589 | 0.0146539 | −30.16 | <2e-16 | *** |
| log(X320.640mWalk) | 0.0368460 | 0.0013018 | 28.30 | <2e-16 | *** |
| log(X0.320mWalk) | 0.0317564 | 0.0017498 | 18.15 | <2e-16 | *** |
| IsNewStationTrue | −0.0664468 | 0.0023747 | −27.98 | <2e-16 | *** |
| IsUpgradedStationTrue | −0.1371564 | 0.0027688 | −49.54 | <2e-16 | *** |
| IsMajorInterchangeTrue | 0.0502467 | 0.0017015 | 29.53 | <2e-16 | *** |
| log(AvgNumTrains) | NA | NA | NA | NA |  |

---

Signif. codes: 0 '***' 0.001 '**' 0.01 '*' 0.05 '.' 0.1 ' ' 1

Residual standard error: 0.386 on 687823 degrees of freedom
Multiple R-squared: 0.4816, Adjusted R-squared: 0.4816
F-statistic: 1.775e+04 on 36 and 687823 DF, p-value: < 2.2e-16

*Table 7.3   ELL model*

| | **ELL** | | | | |
|---|---|---|---|---|---|

**Residuals:**

| Min | 1Q | Median | 3Q | Max |
|---|---|---|---|---|
| −2.59124 | −0.21920 | 0.00506 | 0.22700 | 1.77677 |

**Coefficients: (1 not defined because of singularities)**

| | Estimate | Std. Error | t value | Pr(>|t|) | |
|---|---|---|---|---|---|
| (Intercept) | 13.0072617 | 0.0306637 | 424.191 | <2e-16 | *** |
| Sold2001to2004True | −0.5389976 | 0.0041970 | −128.423 | <2e-16 | *** |
| Sold2005to2009True | −0.1749194 | 0.0015574 | −112.317 | <2e-16 | *** |
| Sold2010to2014True | NA | NA | NA | NA | |
| IsNewTrue | 0.1274471 | 0.0020294 | 62.801 | <2e-16 | *** |
| IsHouseTrue | 0.1470392 | 0.0026786 | 54.894 | <2e-16 | *** |
| DurationTrue | 0.4048844 | 0.0015423 | 262.520 | <2e-16 | *** |
| log(WalkDistanceBusStops) | 0.0440554 | 0.0019266 | 22.867 | <2e-16 | *** |
| log(WalkDistanceNationalRail) | −0.0695540 | 0.0012900 | −53.920 | <2e-16 | *** |
| log(WalkDistanceOverground) | 0.1090697 | 0.0022606 | 48.248 | <2e-16 | *** |
| log(WalkDistanceUnderground) | 0.0534442 | 0.0017454 | 30.620 | <2e-16 | *** |
| log(ProximityToARoad) | 0.0162568 | 0.0006098 | 26.659 | <2e-16 | *** |
| log(ProximityToBRoad) | −0.0053635 | 0.0006076 | −8.827 | <2e-16 | *** |
| log(ProximityToMotorWay) | −0.1412130 | 0.0018915 | −74.656 | <2e-16 | *** |
| log(ProximityToGreenArea) | −0.0215121 | 0.0006389 | −33.672 | <2e-16 | *** |
| log(ProximityToBrownfield) | −0.0016146 | 0.0005154 | −3.133 | 0.00173 | ** |
| log(ProximityToCAZ) | −0.0533958 | 0.0005191 | −102.871 | <2e-16 | *** |
| log(ProximityToCWZ) | 0.0313647 | 0.0012358 | 25.381 | <2e-16 | *** |
| log(PopulationPerSqKm) | 0.0669985 | 0.0016902 | 39.640 | <2e-16 | *** |
| logit(CrimeRatePer1000) | −0.0683457 | 0.0016998 | −40.208 | <2e-16 | *** |
| logit(PercentEducationAbove4) | 0.5001929 | 0.0016244 | 307.918 | <2e-16 | *** |
| log(X640.960mWalk) | −0.0217329 | 0.0022269 | −9.759 | <2e-16 | *** |
| log(X320.640mWalk) | −0.0193457 | 0.0020753 | −9.322 | <2e-16 | *** |
| log(X0.320mWalk) | −0.0210329 | 0.0023010 | −9.141 | <2e-16 | *** |
| IsNewStationTrue | 0.0292104 | 0.0026622 | 10.972 | <2e-16 | *** |
| IsMajorInterchangeTrue | 0.0248142 | 0.0023042 | 10.769 | <2e-16 | *** |
| log(AvgNumTrains) | −0.0482831 | 0.0020826 | −23.184 | <2e-16 | *** |

---

Signif. codes: 0 '***' 0.001 '**' 0.01 '*' 0.05 '.' 0.1 ' ' 1

Residual standard error: 0.3569 on 390604 degrees of freedom
Multiple R-squared: 0.5342, Adjusted R-squared: 0.5341
F-statistic: 1.792e+04 on 25 and 390604 DF, p-value: < 2.2e-16

dates of implementation are unable to correspond to the available data for this study. ELL results (Table 7.3) showed that housing price increases during 2001 to 2004 had a correlation value of –0.3640, and 2010 to 2014 a value proximal to 0.1749: 2005–2009 was used as a benchmark with a value of 0.

Proximity to other transport links within an ELL catchment area resulted in strong correlations. Unlike the JLE case study, the proximity of bus stations shows a positive correlation of 0.0440. As well, the walking distance to an underground station has a positive correlation of 0.0534, and the overground proximity correlates at 0.1090.

Within the ELL model results, a positive correlation exists between both the station typology and station upgrade status, indicating that the accessibility of stations as well as the interconnectivity with other transit modes has played a role in housing price increases within ELL catchment areas. Beyond station improvements, the station typology as a major interchange has a positive correlation with increasing housing prices. Results demonstrate a strong link between intermodal access, such as other rail stations and bus stops. The positive correlation of a station being classified as a major interchange evidences that connectivity between rail transport links increases housing values.

The proximity to Canary Wharf resulted in a positive correlation, while proximity to the CAZ was slightly negative. This result is not unexpected, as Canary Wharf also had a positive impact in the JLE model. However, what differs between the two is that the ELL has a stronger correlation than the JLE, despite the fact that it does not run directly through Canary Wharf (unlike the JLE).

## 9.   SYNTHESIS OF RESULTS AND POLICY IMPLICATIONS

Correlations between London transport connectivity and housing prices have been discovered. The findings that these results suggest tell a story for London decision-makers, as well as for the future of transport investment and development policies. Findings show correlations of variables within the different case study models, as well as three trends that are found across all case studies. Firstly, this study shows that London housing prices increase when transport interconnectivity increases. Second, housing prices notice significant increases in areas with previously low value and under-development when transport links are introduced. Finally, housing proximity to metro rail transport stations plays a significant role in housing prices within London.

In the borough-wide model results, the strong positive correlation exists between housing price increases and the proximity to London Underground and London Overground stations. These results suggest that rail transport is considered the most desirable form of transit within the London boroughs looked at in this study. In the ELL case study, the proximity of bus stops shows a positive correlation of 0.0440, suggesting that the bus is a more common form of interchange from overground routes. Furthermore, the walking distance to an underground station has a positive correlation that is half of that of overground proximity, demonstrating the importance of different types of modes depending on your spatial location in London. The importance of these results is threefold. Firstly, underground connectivity is important in transport connectivity options impacting housing prices (as demonstrated by a positive correlation), but does not have as great an impact as the newer overground when moving away from longstanding underground networks. The strength of the overground and bus correlations is important within the ELL region as well, as above-ground rail and bus are more prevalent than the underground in East and South London (Transport for London, 2014b) – therefore, it shows that a different hierarchy of transport needs is present depending on where one is looking to purchase in London. Were this study to be applied in other cities, it is likely that a different hierarchy of travel needs may emerge, depending on local purchaser behaviours.

Proximity to both motorways and B-type roads (also known as arterial roads and local streets respectively) have shown negative impacts on housing value increases. This is likely due to the movement-oriented nature of these streets – leading to less of the amenities that create mixed-use vibrant neighbourhoods. However, proximity to A-type roads (high streets and high roads) had a positive correlative value, and could suggest several scenarios that have impacted property value increases. According to TfL, a street types matrix classifies particular routes based on 'movement' and 'place', in which A-type roads are considered of moderate-to-high movement corridors and contain a mix of local and city place values (Roads Task Force, 2015). Due to these roads being locations along which retail and jobs will tend to locate, the place-making within the areas creates more desirable areas in which to live and access. As such, housing prices may increase due to the desirability and place-making impact of the London A-type road locality (Bohl and Schwanke, 2002).

Proximity to brownfield sites saw a positive correlation between transport connections and housing prices in both the JLE and ELL models. This evidences a link between transport lines opening up housing opportunities in previously under-developed areas, as well as a consequent housing value increase because of it. In particular, this result demonstrates the housing value implications of the JLE within East London. Formerly used for more industrial purposes, East London areas such as Stratford, Canary Wharf, and Canada Waters have been historically brownfield; the advent of the JLE has been touted as a harbinger of development, and a crucial element of the successful uplift of these areas (Mejia-Dorantes and Lucas, 2014). The positive correlation between housing prices within a JLE catchment area and brownfield sites shows that housing value uplift has been brought about by the increase in transport connectivity within the area, in conjunction with development opportunities and new builds.

Timing of the transport line's implementation has been shown to be an important variable in the link between transport connectivity and housing price increases. The analysis of ELL anticipatory effects was possible due to the more recent implementation of the line. The JLE model was unable to have the same analysis completed, as the dates of implementation are unable to correspond to the available data for this study. Between the years of 2001 to 2015, the ELL was both conceived and implemented, with an announcement and approval date in 2004, construction as of 2007, and the line opening in 2010 (Transport for London Board, 2012). Studies have shown that announcement dates of transport projects have impacted housing prices and land values. For example, light rail systems in Oregon were shown to have no property price increases prior to the announcement of the project, but noticed a 31 percent increase post-announcement within a half mile radius of planned stations, and a 10 percent increase within a mile radius (Knaap, et al., 2001). Other studies have not seen as large an impact due to project announcements, and have also suggested that the uplift in property value due to announcements is location-contextual (Gatzlaff and Smith, 1993). The announcement of the line correlated with a significant increase in housing prices relative to pre-announcement prices, and even further once the line was open. This supports previous studies' findings, and demonstrates the importance of the transport anticipatory effect on London housing prices.

A positive correlation was found between both the station typology and station upgrade status, indicating that the accessibility of stations as well as the interconnectivity with other transit modes has played a role in housing price increases within catchment areas. Demonstrated by the ELL case study, major improvements including station upgrades from old National Rail stations to London Overground stations, as well as the creation of four new stations, played a major role in connecting new areas and better connecting existing ones (Kable Intelligence Limited, 2015). Similarly, the JLE new stations experienced similar impacts. Improved station accessibility, capacity, and situational factors such as weather protection could be implicated in the positive correlation between housing prices. As the station improves, it becomes more desirable as a transport option, thus increasing the perceived 'connectivity' of the line (Steer Davies Gleave, 2011). Beyond station improvements, the station typology as a major interchange has a positive correlation with increasing housing prices. Results demonstrate a strong link between intermodal access, such as other rail stations and bus stops. The positive correlation of a station being classified as a major interchange evidences that connectivity between rail transport links increases housing values.

The proximity to Canary Wharf resulted in a positive correlation in both models, while proximity to the CAZ was slightly negative. However, what differs between the two is that the ELL has a stronger correlation than the JLE, despite the fact that it does not run directly through Canary Wharf (unlike the JLE). The ELL connects with both the JLE and the DLR, which could be a reason for the higher positive correlation: the JLE only connects with the DLR at Canary Wharf, and has no other links that connect directly. Thus, the increased connectivity of the ELL to Canary Wharf evidences the importance of access to multimodal, multi-directional transport connectivity when looking at housing price increases.

## 10.    CONCLUSIONS

There are three major themes that have emerged from this study, which have shown significant positive correlations between transport and housing prices. Transport interconnectivity within London has always been a major goal of transport authorities. However, when looking at transport projects, there has never been an empirical justification of why it is so important beyond transport-specific goals. The results of this study demonstrate that transport interconnectivity – which promotes increased access to transport and better connections between modes – has a direct impact on housing price increases. With positive correlations in all three models for underground and overground links, and positive correlations in both case study models for bus route station access points, evidence shows that increased transport connectivity within London is seen to add value to housing within specified catchment areas. This is important for London transport policy and for future transport-specific business cases, as it demonstrates that increased transport adds monetary value to housing and residential development within a station catchment area. Thus, this study can support business cases for projects such as future major transport infrastructure in London, evidencing the housing uplift benefits of new rail and bus transit provisions.

This study also demonstrates a strong link between London housing price increases and providing transport links into previously under-developed areas. In particular, it evidences the ability of London transport links to unlock areas of opportunity and development, and notes a positive housing price response to this mechanism. Results have shown positive correlations between proximity to Canary Wharf opportunity areas and housing price increases in both the JLE and ELL models, which are significantly higher than that of the control model (also a small positive correlation). Proximity to brownfield sites along the JLE noticed a positive correlation, more than double that of the control model; this matches targets of the JLE to regenerate parts of East London and to encourage development in these areas through transport connectivity. Furthermore, results of the ELL model demonstrate increasing housing prices within catchment areas both during the approval and construction phase, and even higher once the line was opened for use; these catchment zone price increases correspond with proximity to multiple opportunity areas that are featured along the JLE and ELL trajectories.

Finally, an important result of this study demonstrates that certain proximities to stations yield the highest housing price increases. Specifically, proximity within 960 metres has yielded significant positive correlations, evidencing the importance of transport access adding value to housing. When analysed further, both models demonstrated higher correlations to housing prices when housing was located within 320–640 metres, and moderate housing price increase correlations within proximity of 0 to 320 metres. The furthest housing (from 640 to 960 metres) within all catchment areas studied yielded the lowest housing price increases, but saw increases nonetheless. The importance of these results is twofold for London policy-makers. Firstly, this suggests that a behavioural element exists to the value of residential property purchases near transport links: with higher prices attributed to closer proximities to stations, this result suggests that individuals are more likely to purchase housing for higher prices in exchange for increased transport system connectivity. This study thus evidences the value of station proximity and access in London, supporting existing systems such as the PTAL measurement and strengthening business cases for new transport links and improved connectivity. Secondly, this suggests that future development in London can benefit both economically and with housing provision from these proximities, through policies promoting intensification of developments within these bands and within accessible distances to transport stations.

These three lessons create a stronger foundation of evidence on the benefits of transport connectivity within London. By demonstrating there is a link between housing prices and proximity of housing to transport stations, the evidence of housing price uplift can be used to secure funding for transport infrastructure by targeting the increase in housing value. Thus, a stronger evidence base is now available for practitioners to draw from, proving that a link exists between transport connectivity and housing price increases, and consequently better informing policy choices related to both transport and housing provision.

This study set out to analyse whether transport connectivity directly impacted housing price increases within London, seeking to provide empirical hedonic evidence linking the two together, and uncovering key trends via empirical findings, in order to provide lessons for policy-makers. Hedonic empirical results have shown that a correlation does exist between transport connectivity and housing price increases within London. Through a synthesis of results, three trends have emerged with empirical evidence linking them as impactors of housing prices: proximity within station catchment areas, transport links being placed in under-developed areas, and transport interconnectivity within the transport system. This supports multiple studies that have also demonstrated the importance of transport on property transaction prices (Anas and Armstrong, 1993; Bae, et al., 2003;

Damm, et al., 1980). However, this study has attempted to also provide a new focus on transport connectivity as a multi-variable and complex set of factors (contrary to the traditional approach of single variable analysis), and has demonstrated a link between house prices and certain variables that appear more desirable than others to property purchasers. This study will add to the knowledge of practitioners to better evidence proof of the economic and housing benefits that transport connectivity provides (Honey, 2015; Volterra Partners, 2014). This will ultimately aid in strengthening transport appraisal methods and de-risk housing development along London transport corridors.

Although individual variable isolation will require further research to identify weighted impacts, this body of research provides evidence of a link between housing and transport connectivity in London, and refreshes a theory that many practitioners have promoted in planning and policy with little evidence to support it. Thus, this research serves to provide new evidence in what is already recognised by many: that transport connectivity is about an interconnected, complex system that, when planned properly, can have a significant impact on buyer decisions, property prices, and shaping the housing stock and urban fabric.

# REFERENCES

Anas, A. and Armstrong, R. (1993). *Land Value and Transit Access: Modeling the Relationship in the New York Metropolitan Area*. Washington, DC: United States Department of Transport, Federal Transit Administration.

Andersson, D., Shyr, O. and Fu, J. (2010). Does high-speed rail accessibility influence residential property prices? Hedonic estimates from southern Taiwan. *Journal of Transport Geography*, 18(1), 166–174.

Bae, C.-H. C., Jun, M.-J. and Park, H. (2003). The impact of Seoul's subway line 5 on residential property values. *Transport Policy*, 10(2), 85–94.

Berry, M. and Dalton, T. (2004). Housing prices and policy dilemmas: a peculiarly Australian problem? *Urban Policy and Research*, 22(1), 69–91.

Bitter, C., Mulligan, G. and Dall'erba, S. (2007). Incorporating spatial variation in housing attribute prices: a comparision of geographically weighted regression and the spatial expansion method. *Journal of Geographical Systems*, 9(1), 7–27.

Bohl, C. and Schwanke, D. (2002). *Place Making: Developing Town Centres, Main Streets; and Urban Villages*. Washington, DC: Urban Land Institute.

Bowes, D. and Ihlandfeldt, K. (2001). Identifying the impacts of rail transit stations on residential property values. *Journal of Urban Ecnomics*, 50(1), 1–25.

Boyce, D. (2005). Transport systems. In: T. Kim (ed.) *Transport Planning and Engineering*. Oxford: EOLSS Publishers, Section 6.40.2.

Brasington, D. and Hite, D. (2008). A mixed index approach to identifying hedonic price models. *Regional Science and Urban Economics*, 38(3), 271–284.

Butler, R. (1982). The specification of hedonic indexes for urban housing. *Land Economics*, 58(1), 96–108.

Damm, D., Lerman, S., Lerner-Lam, E. and Young, J. (1980). Response of urban real estate values in anticipation of the Washington Metro. *Journal of Transport Economics and Policy*, 38, 315–336.

de Haan, J. and Diewert, E. (2013). Hedonic regression methods. In: OECD (ed.) *Handbook on Residential Property Prices Indices (RPPIs)*. Luxembourg: Eurostat, pp. 50–64.

Dewees, D. (1976). The effect of a subway on residential property values in Toronto. *Journal of Urban Economics*, 3, 357–369.

Dimitriou, H. and Oades, R. (2008). *The Contemporary Treatment of Risk, Uncertainty and Complexity in Decision-Making in Selected Disciplines*. London: Working Paper 2, Omega Centre, University College London.

Enoch, M., Stephen, P. and Ison, S. (2005). A strategic approach to financing public transport through property values. *Public Money and Management*, 25(3), 147–154.

Farber, S. and Yeates, M. (2006). A comparison of localized regression models in a hedonic house price context. *Canadian Journal of Regional Science*, XXIX(3), 405–420.

Gatzlaff, D. and Smith, M. (1993). The impact of the Miami Metrorail on the value of residences near station locations. *Land Economics*, 69(1), 54–66.

Greater London Authority. (2008). *London's Central Busines District: Its Global Importance*. London: Greater London Authority.

Greater London Authority. (2014). *Homes for London: The London Housing Strategy 2014*. London: Greater London Authority.

Guo, Z. (2011). Mind the map! The impact of transit maps on path choice in public transit. *Transport Research Part A: Policy and Practice*, 45(7), 625–639.

Headicar, P. (2015). Homes, jobs and commuting: development location and travel outcomes. In: R. Hickman, M. Givoni, D. Bonilla and D. Banister (eds) *Handbook on Transport and Development*. Cheltenham: Edward Elgar Publishing, pp. 59–72.

Honey, M. (2015). *Crossrail 2: Demand Forecasting for a Major New Rail Line in London*. London: Transport for London.

Knaap, G., Ding, C. and Hopkins, L. (2001). Do plans matter? The effects of light rail plans on land values in station areas. *Journal of Planning Education and Research*, 21(1), 32–39.

Lancaster, K. (1966). A new approach to consumer theory. *Journal of Political Economy*, 74(2), 132–157.

Landis, J., Guhatharkuta, S. and Zhang, M. (1995). *Capitalisation of Transit Investments into Single-Family Home Prices: A Comparitive Analysis of Five California Rail Transit Systems*. Institute of Urban and Regional Development, Berkeley, CA: University of California at Berkeley, Working Paper 619.

Lochl, M. (2007). *Considering Spatial Dependence in Hedonic Rent Price Regression*. Monte Verita, Ascona: Swiss Transport Research Conference.

London Connectivity Commission. (2012). *London, Britain, and the World: Transport Links for Economic Growth*. London: London First.

Mathur, S. (2014). *Innovation in Public Transport Finance: Property Value Capture*. Farnham: Ashgate Publishing.

Mayor of London. (2011). *Opportunity Areas Planning Frameworks*. London: Mayor of London.

McDonald, J. and Osuji, C. (1995). The effect of anticipated transport improvement on residential land values. *Regional Science and Urban Economics*, 25, 261–278.

Mejia-Dorantes, L. and Lucas, K. (2014). Public transport investment and local regeneration: a comparison of London's Jubilee Line Extension and the Madrid Metrosur. *Transport Policy*, 35(1), 241–252.

Mitchell, B. (2003). Chapter one – planning and design, 1990 to 1993. In: *Jubilee Line Extension: from Concept to Completion*. London: Thomas Telford Limited, pp. 10–50.

Miyamoto, M. and Tsubaki, H. (2002). A linear mixed model for the hedonic pricing model. *Applied Stochastic Models in Business and Industry*, 18(3), 259–270.

Niedzielski, M. and Boschmann, E. (2014). Travel time and distance as relative accessibility in the journey to work. *Annals of the Association of American Geographers*, 104(6), 1156–1182.

Paez, A., Long, F. and Farber, S. (2007). Moving window approaches for hedonic price estimation: an empirical comparison of modelling techniques. *Urban Studies*, 45(8), 1565–1581.

PublicWorld. (2012). *What do Good Public Transport Services Look Like?* London: Public World.

Roads Task Force. (2015). *Roads Task Force Progress Report: A Successful First Year*. London: Transport for London.

Rose-Ackerman, S. (2013). Precaution, proportionality, and cost/benefit analysis: false analogies. *European Journal of Risk Regulation*, 4(2), 281–286.

Rosen, S. (1974). Hedonic prices and implicit markets: product differentiation in pure competition. *Journal of Political Economy*, 82(1), 34–56.

Steer Davies Gleave. (2011). *The Value of Station Investment: Research on Regenerative Impacts*. London: Network Rail.

Transport Committee. (2014). *Transcript of Item 6 – Mayor's London Infrastructure Plan 2050*. London: Mayor of London.

Transport for London. (2012). Chapter 2, Part 1: The framework, tools, and processes to build the strategy. In: M. o. London (ed.) *The Vision and Direction for London's Streets and Roads*. London: Transport for London, pp. 78–101.

Transport for London. (2014a). *Fit for the Future: Our Plan for Modernising London Underground, London Overground, Trams, and the DLR*. London: Transport for London.

Transport for London. (2014b). *Travel in London: Report 7*. London: Transport for London.

Transport for London. (2015a). *Crossrail 2: The Strategic Outline Business Case*. London: Transport for London.

Transport for London. (2015b). *Assessing Transport Connectivity in London*. London: Transport for London.

Transport for London Board. (2012). *London Overground Impact Study*. London: Transport for London.

Transport Studies Group. (2004). *JLE Summary Report*. London: University of Westminster.

van de Kaa, E. (2010). Prospect theory and choice behaviour strategies: review and synthesis of concepts from social and transport sciences. *European Journal of Transport and Infrastructure Research*, 10(4), 299–329.

van Geenhuizen, M. (2000). Interconnectivity of transport networks: a conceptual and empirical exploration. *Transport Planning and Technology*, 23(3), 199–213.
Volterra Partners. (2014). *Investing in City Regions: The Case for Long-Term Investment in Transport*. London: Transport for London.
Waddell, P. and Ulfarsson, G. (2003). *Dynamic Simulation of Real Estate Development and Land Prices Within an Integrated Land Use and Transport System*. Washington, DC: 83rd Annual Meeting of the Transport Research Board.
Wheeler, D. and Tiefelsdorf, M. (2005). Multicollinearity and correlation among local regression coefficients in geographically weighed regression. *Journal of Geographical Systems*, 7(2), 161–187.
Zhang, M., Meng, X., Wang, L. and Xu, T. (2014). Transit development shaping urbanization evidence from the housing market in Beijing. *Habitat International*, 44(1), 545–554.

# PART III

# TRANSPORT AND SOCIAL EQUITY IMPACTS

# 8. Equity aspects of transportation in a multi-network world: a societal perspective
*Eran Feitelson*


## 1. INTRODUCTION

Intra-generational equity is one of the three pillars of sustainability. Yet, the question how should equity be assessed is a source for ongoing discussion. Sen (1992) argues that equality should be viewed as the freedom people have to achieve what they value. The capability to do so is affected by spatial patterns, as space affects the ability to access the wide variety of things people value. Hence, transportation, as the set of means that affect accessibility, has a major role in determining intra-generational (in)equality (Hananel and Berechman, 2016).

The effects of transportation on (in)equality are well recognized (Soja, 2010; Levine, 2013). Quite naturally, much of the discussion has focused on those that are underserved by the existing transport systems (Martens, 2017), and on the incorporation of equity aspects in evaluations of new transportation projects (Lucas et al., 2016a). Hence, most of the research on equity facets of transport focuses on a limited set of transportation systems. Yet, the transportation system today is comprised of multiple means operating as part of (partially) inter-connected networks.

Since the early 1990s the investment in transportation infrastructure, and particularly public transport, has increased worldwide. This increase is driven by the perceived contribution of transport infrastructure to economic development, originating with the early work of Aschauer (1989). Skeptical evidence notwithstanding (such as Banister and Berechmen, 2001), transportation investments are widely viewed as an effective anti-recession measure. Moreover, such investments conform to the dominant neo-liberal discourse, as they are seen as facilitating market expansion and thus the geographic mobility of capital (Harvey, 2005). The result has been manifested in the large number of transportation mega-projects undertaken (Flyvberg, Brutelius and Rothengatter, 2003). It could be expected, thus, that the massive investment in public transportation infrastructure will eliminate, or at least substantially reduce, "transport poverty."[1] Yet this does not seem to be the case.

The purpose of this chapter is to ask how should the equity implications of investments in public transport in a multi-modal multi-network world be analyzed, from a broad, societal, perspective. That is, what are the aspects that should be analyzed when trying to assess the societal equity implications of the cumulative investments in the different transport infrastructure. To this end, I begin with a discussion of the equity aspects of transport systems focusing on the attributes that differentiate these effects

---

[1] For the definition and discussion of transport poverty, see Lucas et al. (2016b).

among transport systems, looking at the supra-urban scale.[2] Then, I briefly review the types of trips made in the different modes and the attributes of the travellers making them. On this basis, the direct equity implications of investments in the different modes can be gleaned. However, a full equity analysis should arguably assess not only the direct effects but also the long-term implications. Hence in the third section I discuss the effects of the investments in the different modes in terms of motility and network capital. This analysis points to the need to analyse equity effects not only in terms of accessibility of the transport or access for the poor, but also in terms of the benefits that accrue to the hyper-mobile versus everyone else. On this basis some concluding comments are made regarding the relative equity implications of investments in different transport modes.

## 2.   THE EQUITY ASPECTS OF TRANSPORT NETWORKS

Lucas et al. (2016b) differentiates between mobility poverty and accessibility poverty. Both are a function of the degree to which a transport system can be accessed. Such access is a function of the physical ability to access the system and the pecuniary ability to do so. Hence, the degree to which a transport system advances or digresses equity (eq) is a function of these two factors: physical accessibility (ac) and affordability (af):

$$eq = f (ac, af)$$

The physical access to a transport system is a function of the number of entry points. The number of such entry points is an inverse function of its flexibility (Feitelson and Salomon, 2000). That is, a system that has greater flexibility (F) in terms of the location of its nodes and links tends to have a greater number of possible entry points. Flexibility is largely a function of speed. Faster modes have fewer entry points. This is perhaps most evident in the case of rail where there is an obvious trade-off between access (additional stops) and speed, as each stop imposes an additional cost (Givoni and Rietveld, 2011). Thus, high speed rail, which is among the least flexible systems, has very few entry points in comparison to the slower suburban and the much more flexible road-based systems, which have multiple entry points.

The affordability of a system (i) to users is a function of the cost of use (uci) and the cost of reaching the entry point (cai). Hence, the less flexible a system and the fewer access points there are, the cost of reaching those access points, in terms of both money and time, is likely to be higher. These costs are, in turn, a function of the means available to reach those entry points (ami). The actual cost of access is also affected by the interfaces between the different means (Givoni and Rietveld, 2007). Once arrived at a node, the cost to the user of using a particular system is a function of the cost of providing and operating the system (opci), and the extent to which these costs are subsidized (si).

The equity effect of any particular system is thus a function of its flexibility (and hence

---

[2]   Analyses of equity facets at the intra-city scale, where most trips are short, and walking and cycling (the most equitable means) possibly require a different framework and considerations than presented here, and thus are left for future studies.

*Table 8.1    Attributes of various transport systems*

| Mode (i) | Flexibility ($F_i$) | Cost of access ($ca_i$) | Use cost ($uc_i$) |
|---|---|---|---|
| Roads | Very High | Low/Medium* | Low |
| Buses | High | Low | Low |
| Limited access highways | Medium | Medium | Low/medium** |
| Light rail/metro | Medium/low | Low | Low/medium*** |
| Suburban/regional rail | Low | Medium | Medium*** |
| High speed rail | Very low | High | High |
| Regional airports | Low | High | Medium-high**** |
| Hub airports | Very low | Very high | High |

Notes:    *    Function of the cost of cars and fuel
        **    Function of whether free use or toll road
       ***    Function of extent of subsidies
      ****    Function of extent to which served by low-cost airlines

physical access to it), the means that are needed to get to the entry node, the fixed and operation costs of the system, and the extent to which these are subsidized:

$$eqi = f \,[aci(Fi), \, cai(Fi, \, ami), \, uci(opci, \, si)]$$

Overall, the more flexible a public transport system is, the more access nodes there are, the easier and cheaper it is to access it, and hence the more equitable it is. Similarly, the less fixed cost and lesser operation cost needed to supply the service the more equitable a system is likely to be. That is, the more it is likely to alleviate transport poverty and serve those whose accessibility is limited.

In Table 8.1 these attributes are given for several transport systems in a highly simplified and abstract manner. Still, it is possible to identify on this basis the overall equity implications of the different systems.

As can be gleaned from Table 8.1 there is a wide variance in the equity effects of different systems. The most flexible easily accessed systems are roads and buses. From an equity perspective buses have the advantage of being a public transport service, but given the low cost of cars, and the ability to purchase second-hand cars or to utilize servicized vehicles (from Uber to rental cars) roads can be considered as highly equitable too. Then there is a range of services which are less flexible, but still are highly accessible. These include limited access highways, and regional or suburban rail. At the other end of the scale high speed rail and hub airports are costly to access and use, and are very inflexible. They are the least equitable from our perspective.

## 3.    WHOM DO THE DIFFERENT TRANSPORT SYSTEMS SERVE? A BRIEF REVIEW

The recent studies discussing transport from a justice perspective focus on the accessibility of all population groups to opportunities (e.g. Hananel and Berechman, 2016; Martens,

2017). These are a function of the physical access to (public) transport systems, the pecuniary facets of access to transport opportunities and the attributes of the available transport systems accessed in terms of speed, reliability, safety, convenience and affordability. From an equity perspective the question is thus whose accessibility is improved by the investments in different modes. To this end, analyses of investments in transport systems in a multi-modal world have to ask who are the people and trip types served by the different systems, and whether the supply provided by the combinations of the different systems address the accessibility deficits of different potential users.

The most ubiquitous transport services are those of the private car and bus. The car is the most readily available to those that can afford both purchasing and maintaining a car and are capable of driving or to those using the servicizing services noted above. Buses are the most readily available to those that don't. However, there is a wide difference between the two groups. The car is the mode that reduced the total private cost of travel more than others, from a long-term historical perspective, and has therefore increased the potential opportunities to many, as seen by the increasing commute sheds (Axhausen, 2007). These options are much more constrained for the carless, as bus services seldom come near to the convenience, speed and reliability of the automobile. It is not surprising, therefore, that in societies and cities with high motorization rates, such as in the USA, bus users are typically poorer than the average transport user, carless and either old or young, without the ability to drive (Neff and Pham, 2007). Many are thus captive users. As the investments in roads usually exceed those in buses, the equity outcome, as Cornut and Madre (2017) show for Paris, is that the behaviour of people in the upper three quadrants becomes progressively closer, while the bottom quadrant lags behind.

Bus rapid transit (BRT) may be somewhat of an interim case. These systems have largely been developed in the global south, particularly Latin America. They were developed as low-cost transit systems, and indeed attract a wide ridership in such locales, offering significant benefits to low-income groups (Venter et al., 2018). However, detailed studies within Latin American cities have shown that they may be geared toward the middle class in such cities (Delmelle and Casas, 2012). As similar findings are seen elsewhere, Venter et al. (2018) conclude that such systems may be less progressive than originally lauded, unless planners specifically route the BRT lines to serve weaker neighbourhoods.

In contrast to buses, rail services do cater also to car owners, even in the USA (Neff and Pham, 2007). Actually, in the USA several of the rail systems analyzed in the literature have been shown to cater largely to suburban car-owning middle-class families, tilting investments away from bus systems that largely cater to carless minority groups, due to the political power of potential rail users and the Federal Government's bias toward capital-intensive projects (Li and Wachs, 2004). Thus, while the majority of public transport passenger trips are provided by buses, most of the capital investments are in rail (Garrett and Taylor, 1999). This picture, however, is a function of the local policies. For example, Foth et al. (2013) show that in Toronto rail transit is geared toward socially disadvantaged areas, thereby improving equity. In most cases, however, equity does not seem to be a consideration in the routing of rail systems and the location of stations (Taylor and Morris, 2014). An ongoing study in Israel indicates that the rail system, which is the focus of substantial investment in the past two decades, is geared mainly toward Jewish middle-class towns, providing very limited service to minority and ultra-orthodox communities, which are the communities with the lowest motorization rates and thus the most dependent on public transport (Feitelson, 2017).

Yet, there is a wide variance in rail services, from local and suburban rail, such as those discussed above, to high speed rail (HSR). The differences in services is reflected in the cost of travel and consequently in the attributes of users and types of trips conducted in the different types of services. Suburban and local rail services are widely used by commuters as well as for other trips. As noted above, the extent and attributes of users are largely a function of the layout of the rail system and the accessibility of the train stations. HSR serves a completely different travel market, as it serves long-distance inter-city travel. In doing so HSR competes with "regular" local or regional rail and short distance aviation. Analysis by Givoni and Dobruszkes (2013) of the demand for new HSR services shows that the majority is demand diverted from (conventional) rail services. Thus HSR, by replacing conventional rail, "splits" the demand for rail into the rich that move to HSR and the less rich that stay behind.

Much of today's travel is long-distance (Janzen et al., 2018). In recent decades extensive HSR systems were built in Europe and East Asia to serve long-distance travel. Additional systems are being discussed in North America and the UK. Analyses of the existing and proposed systems indicate that they have a largely polarizing effect (Monzon et al., 2013), and are successful mainly when they serve high-demand corridors (Albalate and Bel, 2012). Consequently, they tend to reinforce existing inequities among regions, rather than ameliorating them (Zhu et al., 2016).

As noted in the previous section, HSR is a largely inflexible systems with few access points, thereby increasing spatial inequality, both within regions and between regions (Feitelson and Salomon, 2000). This can be seen, for example, in Sanchez-Mateos and Givoni's (2011) analysis of the impacts of HSR in Spain and the potential spatial implications of the proposed HS2 line in the UK. Essentially, they show that HSR in Spain led to a re-configuration of relative advantages, with cities that previously were rail nodes losing out to new nodes. In the UK, while the accessibility of certain nodes will improve, the accessibility of many other nodes will deteriorate.

Analyses of HSR users show that they primarily have a high income and travel mainly on business (Li and Schmocker, 2017). This is not surprising, as the cost of using HSR is high, and they substitute mainly for short distance air travel (Albalate and Bel, 2012). So, the use is determined to a large extent by the ability to pay. As business people can write off their travel expenses, either for tax statements (if they own the business) or on company expense accounts, their out-of-pocket travel expense is lower than of private travellers. Moreover, HSR offers high-end comfort, providing business-class cars with a good working environment, and thereby catering to such travellers. HSR thus largely tenders to high-end travellers (Givoni and Dobruszkes, 2013).

A somewhat similar distribution pattern can be seen in the aviation sector. Air travel offers different levels of service to different travel segments. At the top end are largely business travellers who are members of frequent-flyer clubs. Members of this aeromobile class are often members of more than one club (Gossling and Nilsson, 2010). Such membership is conducive to additional travel (Chin, 2002), thereby reproducing aeromobility (Gossling and Nilsson, 2010). The members of these programs tend to be CEOs and owners of businesses. In Chin's (2002) analysis of frequent flyers in Singapore he notes that they also tend to use flag carriers more often that other travellers. They are also the occupants of the first and business classes within the aircrafts, thereby enjoying a substantially better level of service than other passengers, particularly on long-distance flights.

Since de-regulation two general trends can be seen in the aviation industry. The first is the advent of hubbing. That is, the full-service network carriers (FSNC) maintain large hubs within hub and spoke systems. Such hubs provide an advantage to businesses and residents in the cities near them, as they provide a large number of direct flights to a wide variety of destinations. By contrast, for cities which serve only as spokes, hubbing has led to the need of more connections to get to other non-hub destinations. Thus, frequent flyers from central cities that serve as hubs are the main beneficiaries of hubbing, and investment in hub airports.

The second trend has been the increase in numbers and scope of services by low cost carriers (LCC). These carriers often serve secondary airports, where landing slots are readily available. Hence, the advent of LCC has widened the scope of services, mainly to secondary cities, and lowered the cost of flights. These carriers specialize in providing direct no-frills services from secondary airports, thereby extending the range of airports from which passengers can get inexpensive flights. The combination of the two trends implies a bifurcation in the equity effects of airport development. In recent years LCC have extended the number of routes served by them to major airports, competing directly with FSNCs. In Europe the range of routes supplied by LCCs has grown rapidly since 2013 (Berster et al., 2017). However, this increase masks a reduction in the number of flights offered from small airports, as the main potential is seen to be in high-demand routes.

The overall picture in the aviation industry, as described by Berster et al. (2017) for the European case, is thus that there are a limited number of large hub airports that concentrate inter-continental flights, provided largely by FSNC. Concurrently there are a large number of both large and smaller airports catering for short-distance low-cost flights, thereby allowing wider segments of the population to travel by air. Similar developments are also seen elsewhere suggesting that from an equity perspective we are indeed seeing differing trends. Air travel is becoming more readily available to wider segments of society, from a wide set of airports. Concurrently high-end services are supplied to discerning passengers, many of which may not pay the full cost out of their pockets, from a much more limited set of airports.

In Table 8.2, the overall equity implications of the different modes, in terms of use patterns are summarized. The users, however, are not differentiated only by their personal attributes, but also by their activity spaces. Activity spaces are the part of the environment used by travellers for their activities. Yet, as Schonfelder and Axhausen (2003) have found, these are not well related to socio-economic status. Thus, it is hypothesized that they should be related to activity and travel type. In Table 8.2, I therefore hypothesize the type of activity spaces that can be related to the main users of the different modes, based on the discussion in this section. An empirical test of this hypothesis, however, awaits further research.

The picture that emerges from Table 8.2 is that the different modes have wide-ranging implications for the extent of activity spaces. FSNC at hub airports are the focal points in expanding activity spaces of frequent flyers and business travellers to the inter-continental sphere. High speed rail and secondary airports are also instrumental in widening the activity spaces to the international or long-distance intra-national levels. It should be noted,

*Table 8.2   Users and activity spaces by transport system*

| Transport system | Main users | Activity spaces |
| --- | --- | --- |
| Hub airports (FSNC) | Frequent flyers, business travellers, high-medium income | Very wide – international, inter-continental |
| Secondary airports (LCC) | Middle class travellers | Medium – long distance inter-city, short distance flights |
| High speed rail (HSR) | High income and business travellers | Medium and wide – long distance inter-city |
| Regional/local/suburban rail | Commuters, suburbanites | Local – regional |
| Buses | Low income commuters, carless, non-drivers | Local |
| Roads (private or hired car) | Wide variety, some excluded | Local – regional |

however, that while activity spaces are usually analyzed temporally as travel that takes place during the week (Schonfelder and Axhausen, 2003), I take a broader view: travellers who operate regularly at the supra-local level may exhibit a high variance in their travel between weeks – some weeks they may work close to home, while in others they may travel widely. Thus, a test of the aforementioned hypothesis will have to define activity spaces on the basis of yearly or quarterly travel, rather than on a weekly basis. Still, most travellers do not go on long-distance trips on a quarterly or yearly basis, so we can imagine that those who mainly utilize rail might have regional level activity spaces, and those that rely on buses local level activity spaces. These differences may have, however, wide-ranging life-chance implications, to which we now turn.

## 4.   SOCIETAL PERSPECTIVES: SOME INSIGHTS

The equity analyses of transport focus largely on the implications of the provision, or lack thereof, of transport services for the motility (the ability to move freely) and for the accessibility of different population segments. Much of it focuses on the extent to which the weaker strata of society are excluded from opportunities due to inaccessibility (Lucas et al, 2016c). These are undoubtedly important and relevant aspects well worth the increasing attention they have garnered in the past few years. These are also the aspects discussed in the previous sections. However, the societal equity implications of transport go beyond the cross-sectional analyses discussed so far.

Following Shliselberg and Givoni (2018), I argue that the long-term effects of the provision of different transport modes should be analyzed also in terms of the long-term contribution of accessibility and motility to the life prospects of different strata in society, and their ability to fulfill the life course they desire. In particular, these should be discussed in the context of the contribution of the different modes to the formation of network capital. The term "network capital" can conceivably take two forms. The first is the elements of the physical capital which form the transport network (Larsen et al., 2006). The second is the aspect of social capital that makes resources available to people through interpersonal ties (Wellman and Frank, 2000). In this chapter I take the second view, and hence any subsequent reference to network capital refers to this interpretation.

Transport alters the spatiality of social capital. The overall trend is widening the extent of personal ties due to the development in communication and transport technologies. As Axhausen (2007) suggests, while the daily routines of most people remain local, their range of interactions widens. An increasing number of households engage in long-term travel both for social purposes such as retaining familial relations (travelling to weddings, funerals and other family gatherings) and for leisure. However, the physical travel in these cases can be argued to mainly retain existing interpersonal relations (such as in the case of familial or social ties), or to form limited or largely temporal new relations (as is the case in much of the leisure travel). While these are important for the maintenance of social capital and may enhance personal development (Shliselberg and Givoni, 2018), their contribution to the enhancement of social capital is limited. To form new connections that enhance social capital a functional network capital is needed. This is the capital that is formed largely through professional interpersonal linkages. The purpose of business trips, including those for educational purposes, is in many cases to form new interpersonal ties that can enhance the future prospects of those undertaking them.

The academic world is one field where this is the case. The social capital that is formed in conferences and workshops has been shown to enhance research productivity (Gonzalez-Brambila, 2014). However, as any post-doctoral student quickly realises, network capital is important in obtaining academic positions, due to the need for support letters from established researchers that know the candidates, as well as in academic promotion procedures. But the importance of network capital is not limited to academia. The information regarding positions and the evaluation of candidates often runs through interpersonal ties (Elliott and Urry, 2010). Hence, network capital cannot be limited to the immediate support one can get from family and friends, as it is often portrayed (Wellman and Frank, 2000). Rather, network capital should be viewed as an important facet in producing and reproducing inequality, particularly among the privileged (Bourdieu, 1986).

From this perspective, it can be argued that the groups whose life chances are most enhanced by travel are those whose trips are used to enhance social network capital by creating new interpersonal ties. It is not surprising therefore that those that benefit most from travel are the hyper-mobile. These hyper-mobiles, sometimes termed globals or aero-mobiles (Elliot and Urry, 2010) are not only the rich, whose travel is often glamourized (Cohen and Gossling, 2015). Rather, they include a wider stratum, such as young upper mobile academics or members of the creative class, who may not be rich but still need to travel widely to enhance their life chances. Still, the frequency and distance travelled does increase as a function of income, as the willingness to pay (or value of time saved) rises with distance and income (Axhausen et al., 2008). As a result of this relationship between income, distance and frequency of travel, and the likelihood that much of the hyper-mobile class are well-off (or do not pay out of pocket the cost of travel) we do see the provision of high-quality glamourized supply of services, such as that discussed by Cohen and Gossling (2015). This has important implications for the discussion of the distribution effects of the different modes.

If we re-look at the implications of the different modes, this time from a life-chance perspective, we can see that two of the modes are those that mainly serve the hyper-mobile. These are the FSNC operating at the inter-continental level from major hub airports and the HSR. These two modes, which also the show widest spatial inequities (Feitelson and Salomon, 2000), are those that contribute most to the accumulation of network capital. Yet, this capital accumulation occurs mainly within the elites, thereby widening the long-term societal inequities (Elliott and Urry, 2010). These two modes support thus Bourdieu's (1986) argument that the formation of such social capital reproduces inequities.

At the other end, buses and cars (or car-based servicizing) are the modes that determine most people's motility, and thus are the most important in determining the accessibility to opportunities for the majority of the population. Thus, the degree to which these services, as well as additional transit (such as light rail or metro), provides a high level of service to all population groups is the factor that affects more than others the degree to which weak groups will be spatially excluded. In this case, the extent to which a transit system provides equitable service is of particular importance, as it addresses the limitations of the carless, and also provides access to educational opportunities (Kaplan et al., 2014). This latter facet is also important from a long-term perspective, as if students can access a wide variety of educational facilities they have the option of increasing their human capital, thereby also improving their life chances. Mobility, allowed by the accessibility to various transport modes, can thus be viewed as a form of capital (Kaufmann et al., 2004; Shliselberg and Givoni, 2018). Yet, it is doubtful to what extent these modes, as well as rail, enhance network capital.

LCC, both when operating from large airports and when serving smaller under-served markets, and rail widen the activity spaces of wide strata of largely middle-class groups. This is perhaps clearer in the case of rail, which serves commuters and thus enlarges activity spaces as measured in weekly diaries. But if we widen the scope of analyses to include also activity spaces analyzed on the basis of yearly travel the contribution of LCC may become clearer. In both cases these modes widen the opportunity set of households and individuals, and thus enhance their motility. But they are much less likely to reduce social exclusion or transport poverty, as while they are much more readily available than HSR or hubs of FSNC, they still require substantial access and egress time and cost.

In Table 8.3, the societal implications that were briefly noted here are summarized by mode. However, the benefits that accrue also entail external costs – costs that are not borne by users. These may be environmental costs, such as the noise suffered by airport neighbours or pecuniary cost, in the case that the capital cost (or operating cost) of the mode are subsidized by tax payers at large (in contrast to the cases where the cost is ultimately borne by users, even if not directly and not per trip).

On the basis of Table 8.3, I suggest that the most inequitable transport mode is HSR.[3] On the one hand, it caters to high-end travellers, many engaged in building the network capital that distinguishes the new elite from the rest of society (Elliott and Urry, 2010). On the other hand, it is supported by public funds. Several studies have shown that HSR rarely meets cost–benefit criteria, and that only under very exceptional circumstances

---

[3]    The only mode which may exceed the HSR in terms of its contribution to inequality is the corporate jet, which is not discussed in this chapter. The corporate jet exclusively serves the global elite, much more so than the HSR. However, corporate jets are not supported by tax payers' money, unless they utilize airports built by public funds that are not being repaid by users. A discussion of the corporate jet and its contribution to societal inequities is, however, beyond the scope of this chapter.

*Table 8.3   The beneficiaries and costs of transport modes*

| Mode | Who and how benefits | Who pays the external costs |
| --- | --- | --- |
| FSNC (operating hubs) | Business travellers and the hyper-mobile (aeromobile); creating network capital for these groups; employees in hubs | Residents near hub airports (assuming self-financing) |
| LCC (operating from regional airports) | Middle class; residents and businesses in secondary markets; widening activity spaces | Residents near airports; taxpayers if capital cost is subsidized |
| HSR | Business travellers and the hyper-mobile; enhances network capital of users | Residents near rail lines; tax payers; by-passed towns |
| Regional and suburban rail | Commuters (middle class); improves accessibility to opportunities | Residents near rail lines; tax payers (if subsidized) |
| Buses/transit/BRT | Carless; weaker strata of society; improves accessibility to opportunities | Tax payers |
| Cars (private + servicizing) | Wide strata; improves accessibility to opportunities; widens activity spaces | Tax payers (for roads) |

can the exceedingly high capital cost be repaid by users (Sichelschmidt, 1999; de Rus and Nombela, 2007; Proost et al., 2014). Thus, HSR, perhaps more than any other mode, should be considered to be regressive – shifting funds from the general public to the benefit of the better-off who utilize it to increase their relative advantage.

It is true that business-class travel on inter-continental flights of FSNC serves the hyper-mobile even more than HSR. However, the same aircraft also carry tourist class passengers, whose composition is much more diverse, and the airlines are hardly any longer supported by public funds, if at all. Moreover, the multiple (regulated) airport revenues in hub airports are set to cover costs, while encouraging productive efficiency (Adler et al., 2015). Thus, even though the extent to which they cover capital cost varies, they are largely self-financing – that is, users pay most of the cost, if not all of it. Therefore, I suggest that even if they do have a regressive effect it is lesser than that of HSR. Actually, their main regressive effect may pertain to their environmental effects. As I argued elsewhere, when it comes to transport, environmental equity should be analyzed by relating those that benefit from the use of the transport system to the cost borne by those that suffer from its environmental externalities (Feitelson, 2002). Airports, particularly hub airports, have wide-ranging environmental externalities. If these are borne by communities that are typified by local activity spaces, and that rarely use the airport (and are not employed in it), then the mobile lifestyles come at the expense of those less mobile neighbours. This is true to a much lesser extent around regional airports, both because the extent of externalities is smaller and the discrepancy between the attributes of users and those of neighbours may be less pronounced.

A similar rationale pertains to regional and suburban rail. These often serve largely middle-class commuters. Yet, the capital, and in many cases also the operating cost, are often subsidized by the tax payers. They also may have substantial environmental externalities borne by those along the tracks. The equity implications of these rail systems are thus a function of the extent to which users are tax payers, and the comparison of the attributes of users to those of adversely affected neighbourhoods. Thus, the equity aspects of such rail services will differ by line and context. In cases where rail serves wealthy sub-urbs at the expense of poorer less mobile inner-city areas, such as in the cases noted in the USA, rail is regressive. By contrast, where rail serves poor outlying towns passing through wealthier inner core areas, it may be seen as progressive – enhancing the accessibility of the less fortunate at the pecuniary and environmental cost of the better-off middle class.

The most obviously progressive mode is buses. These are often subsidized by tax payers, while serving the carless and below average income households. Thus, from an equity per-spective buses are those that deserve support, more than other modes. But as the bus lobby is often weaker than that of other modes, bus networks and busways receive less support than other modes. Another potentially progressive mode is the servicized autonomous car. Such a car will be able conceivably to serve the carless and those who cannot drive. However, the pecuniary and time costs of such services are yet to be seen. Moreover, it has already been suggested that such services may come primarily at the expense of the bus and may materialize only in the more distant future, after 2040 (Litman, 2018). If this is the case, and using servicized autonomous cars costs more than the bus (which is likely), they may prove to be regressive. At this point, the equity implications of the autonomous car cannot be stated unequivocally as either progressive or regressive. This issue is, however, beyond the scope of this chapter and will merit further research as such cars become operational.

## 5.    CONCLUSIONS

In this chapter I have compared the equity effects of different transport modes, focusing on inter-city or metropolitan-level travel (that is, excluding short trips that can also be taken by non-motorized means). In this comparison, I have included both direct equity effects and indirect long-term societal effects. The expansion of the discussion to include long-term motility and network capital enhancement effects highlighted the importance of analyses that take into account both sides of the socio-economic spectrum.

Low-end modes, such as (second hand) cars and especially buses (including BRT services), are important in widening the activity spaces and opportunities of the weaker strata of society, improving their motility, and thereby potentially reducing inequities. Concurrently, high-end modes, most significantly HSR, mainly serve and enhance the motility and network capital of the hyper-mobile, thereby increasing and re-producing inequities.

If we accept Harvey's (2005) analysis of the neo-liberal enterprise as the calculated shift of resources to the upper classes, then the investments in HSR can be viewed as elements in this enterprise – the gist of which is the widening inequity between the top one per cent and the rest of society. By utilizing frequent flyer clubs of FSNC and HSR to increase their network capital, the hyper-mobile elites improve their life chances vis-à-vis all the rest. Between these two extremes, LCC and regional and commuter rail services can have differential equity implications, the specifics of which are a function of the local circum-stances. They may reduce inequity if they serve the average or below-average taxpayer or increase inequities if they serve the better-off at the pecuniary or environmental expense of weaker strata. These are largely a function of the cost to travellers, and the spatial layout of the rail and airport infrastructure.

This chapter is clearly not definitive. Rather, it has sought to widen the scope of equity analysis – specifically to include the possible inequitable distribution of benefits of high-end services. In particular, this chapter has attempted to highlight the need to explicitly discuss the long-term equity facets of investment in different modes of motility and social capital formation. In doing so it raises several hypotheses, all of which can be further scrutinized in empirical studies.

# ACKNOWLEDGMENTS

An early version of this chapter was presented at the ERSA regional meeting at Timisoara in May 2014. Early discussions and work with Ilan Salomon and research assistance by Charlotte Leis are gratefully acknowledged, as are the helpful comments of the reviewers.

# REFERENCES

Adler, N., Forsyth P., Mueller J., and Miemeier H-M. (2015) An economic assessment of airport incentive regulation. *Transport Policy* 41, 5–15.
Albalate, D. and Bel, G. (2012) High speed rail: lessons for policy makers from experience abroad. *Public Administration Review* 72, 336–349.
Aschauer, D. (1989) Is public expenditure productive? *Journal of Monetary Economics* 23, 177–200.
Axhausen, K. (2007) Activity spaces, biographies, social networks and their welfare gains: some hypotheses and empirical results. *Mobilities* 2, 15–36.
Axhausen, K, Hess, S., Konig, A., Abay, G., Bates, J. and Bierlaire, M. (2008) Income and distance elasticities of values of travel time savings: new Swiss results. *Transport Policy* 173–185.
Banister, D. and Berechman, J. (2001) *Transport Investment and Economic Development*. UCL Press, London.
Berster, P., Gelhausen, M. and Wilken, D. (2017) The second wake of network extensions of low cost carriers in Europe: background and trends, paper presented at the 21st ATRS World Congress, Antwerp, 5–8 July.
Bourdieu, P. (1986) The forms of capital, in: J. Richardson (ed.) *Handbook of Theory of Research for the Sociology of Education*. Greenwood Press, NY.
Chin, A. (2002) Impact of frequent flyer programs on the demand for air travel. *Journal of Air Transportation* 7, 53–86.
Cohen, A. and Gossling, S. (2015) A darker side of hypermobility. *Environment and Planning A* 47, 1661–1679.
Cornut, B. and Madre, J-L. (2017) A longitudinal perspective on car ownership and use in relation to income inequalities in the Paris metropolitan area. *Transport Reviews* 37, 227–244.
Delmelle, E. and Casas, I. (2012) Evaluating the spatial equity of bus rapid transit-based accessibility patterns in a developing country: the case of Cali, Colombia. *Transport Policy* 20, 36–46.
de Rus, G. and Nombela, G. (2007) Is investment in high speed rail socially profitable? *Journal of Transport Economics and Policy* 41, 3–23.
Elliot, A. and Urry, J. (2010) *Mobile Lives*. Routledge, Abingdon.
Feitelson, E. (2002) Introducing environmental equity dimensions into the sustainable transport discourse: Issues and pitfalls. *Transportation Research D* 7, 99–118.
Feitelson, E. (2017) Public transport for whom? The Israeli case. Paper presented at the RBG annual conference, London, 29 August–1 September.
Feitelson, E. and Salomon I. (2000) The Implications of differential network flexibility for spatial structures. *Transportation Research A* 34, 459–479.
Flyvberg, B., Brutelius, N. and Rothengatter, W. (2003) *Megaprojects and Risk: Anatomy of Ambition*. Cambridge University Press, Cambridge.
Foth, N., Manaugh, K. and El-Geneidy, A. (2013) Towards equitable transit: examining transit accessibility and social need in Toronto, Canada, 1996–2006. *Journal of Transport Geography* 29, 1–10.
Garrett, M. and Taylor, B. (1999) Reconsidering social equity in public transit, University of California Transportation Center, UC Berkeley.
Givoni, M. and Dobruszkes, F. (2013) A review of ex-post evidence for mode substitution and induced demand following the introduction of high-speed rail. *Transport Reviews* 33(6), 720–742.

Givoni, M. and Rietveld, P. (2007) The access journey to the railway station and its role in passengers' satisfaction with rail travel. *Transport Policy* 14, 357–365.

Givoni, M. and Rietveld, P. (2011) Access to rail in urban areas – examination of the number of stations, in: K. Button and A. Reggiani (eds) *Transportation and Economic Development Challenges*. Edward Elgar, Cheltenham.

Gonzalez-Brambila, C. (2014) Social capital and academia. *Scientometrics* 101, 1609–1625.

Gossling, S. and Nilsson, J. (2010) Frequent flyer programmes and the reproduction of aeromobility. *Environment and Planning A* 42, 241–252.

Hananel, R. and Berechman, J. (2016) Justice and transportation decision-making: the capabilities approach. *Transport Policy* 49, 78–85.

Harvey, D. (2005) *A Brief History of Neoliberalism*. Oxford University Press, Oxford.

Janzen, M., Vanhoof, M. Smoreda, Z. and Axhausen, K. (2018) Closer to the total? Long distance travel of mobile phone users. *Travel Behavior and Society* 11, 31–42.

Kaplan, S., Popos, D., Prato, C. and Ceder, A. (2014) Using connectivity for measuring equity in transit provision. *Journal of Transportation Geography* 37, 82–92.

Kaufmann, V., Bergman, M. and Joye, D. (2004) Motility: mobility as capital. *International Journal of Urban and Regional Research* 28, 745–756.

Larsen, J., Urry, J. and Axhausen, K. (2006) *Mobilities, Networks, Geographies*. Routledge.

Levine J. (2013) Urban transportation and social equity: transportation-planning paradigms that impede policy reform, in: N. Carmon and S. Fainstein (eds) *Policy, Planning and People: Promoting Justice in Urban Development*. University of Pennsylvania Press, Philadelphia.

Li, J. and Wachs, M. (2004) The effects of federal transit subsidy policy on investment decisions: the case of San Francisco's Geary corridor. *Transportation* 31, 43–67.

Li, Y-T. and Schmocker, J-D. (2017) Adaptation patterns of high-speed rail usage in Taiwan and China. *Transportation* 44, 807–830.

Litman, T. (2018) Autonomous Vehicle Implementation Predictions: Implications for Transport Planning, Victoria Transport Policy Institute.

Lucas, K., van Wee, B. and Maat, K. (2016a) A method to evaluate equitable accessibility: combining ethical theories and accessibility-based approaches. *Transportation* 43, 473–490.

Lucas, K., Mattioli, G., Verlinghieri, E. and Guzman A. (2016b) Transport poverty and its adverse social consequences. *Proceedings of the Institution of Civil Engineers: Transport* 169, 353–365.

Lucas, K., Bates, J., Moore, J. and Carrasco, J. (2016c) Modelling the relationship between travel behaviours and social disadvantage. *Transportation Research Part A: Policy and Practice* 85, 157–173.

Martens, K. (2017) *Transport Justice: Designing Fair Transportation Systems*. Routledge, Abingdon.

Monzon, A., Ortega, E. and Lopez, E. (2013) Efficiency and spatial equity of high-speed rail extensions in urban areas. *Cities* 30, 18–30.

Neff, J. and Pham, L. (2007) A profile of public transportation passenger demographics and travel characteristics in on-board surveys, American Public Transportation Association, Washington, DC.

Proost, S., Dunkerley, F., van der Loo, S., Adler, N., Brocker, J. and Korzhenevych, A. (2014) Do the selected European transport investments pass the cost benefit test? *Transportation* 41, 107–132.

Sanchez-Mateos, H. and Givoni, M. (2011) The accessibility impact of a new high-speed rail line in the UK – a preliminary analysis of winners and losers. *Journal of Transport Geography* 25, 105–114.

Schonfelder, S. and Axhausen, K. (2003) Activity spaces: measures of social exclusion? *Transport Policy* 10, 273–286.

Sen, A. (1992) *Inequality Reexamined*. Harvard University Press.

Shliselberg, R. and Givoni, M. (2018) Motility as a policy objective. *Transport Reviews* 38(3), 279–297.

Sichelschmidt, H. (1999) The EU programme "Trans-European Network" – critical assessment. *Transport Policy* 6, 169–181.

Soja, E. (2010) *Seeking Spatial Justice*. University of Minnesota Press.

Taylor, B. and Morris, E. (2015) Public transportation objectives and rider demographics: are transit's priorities poor public policy? *Transportation* 42, 347–367.

Venter, C., Jennings, G., Hildago, D. and Pineda, A. (2018) The equity impacts of bus rapid transit: a review of the evidence and implications for sustainable transport. *International Journal of Sustainable Transportation* 12, 140–152.

Wellman, B. and Frank, K. (2001) Network capital in a multi-level world: getting support from personal communities, in: N. Lin, R. Burt and K. Cook (eds) *Social Capital: Theory and Research*. Aldin de Gruyter, Chicago.

Zhu, Y., Diao, N. and Fu, G. (2016) The evolution of accessibility surface of China in the high-speed-rail era. *Environment and Planning A* 48, 2108–2111.

# 9. Urban public transport investment and socio-spatial development: the case of the Copenhagen Metro

*Kristian Bothe and Christine Benna Skytt-Larsen*

## 1. INTRODUCTION

It is claimed that investments in urban public transport bring numerous benefits to cities. Investments in public transport can act as an indirect catalyst for the development and redevelopment of urban areas (Mejia-Dorantes and Lucas, 2014; Loo and Cheng, 2010; Gospodini, 2005). Despite a growing interest in recent decades in the wider benefits of investments in urban transport, identifying and assessing their social and distributional impacts has attracted less attention (Jones and Lucas, 2012). While a growing number of studies of the effects on house prices have indicated that local regeneration potentially occurs around new transit stations (Jones, 2015; Mohammad et al., 2013; Agostini and Palmucci, 2008), a broader understanding of these regeneration processes and their social consequences is missing.

Today most transport projects are implemented using cost–benefit analyses that make extensive use of economic costs and focus on the measurable benefits of transport investments. This focus has met with criticism, as it does not consider the potential inequalities of outcomes at the disaggregated level (Hickman and Dean, 2017; Beyazit, 2015; Meijers et al., 2012; Beyazit, 2011; Næss, 2006; Grengs, 2005). In recent years, however, more studies have focused on the relationship between transport accessibility and social mobility for marginalized individuals or social groups (Kenyon, 2015; Bocarejo and Oviedo, 2012; Lucas and Jones, 2012; Lucas, 2012; Power, 2012; Lucas et al., 2009). On the one hand, findings indicate that transport accessibility is an important location parameter for residential moves and that improving it may increase the social mobility of individuals. On the other hand, we also know that mobility opportunities are unevenly distributed among social groups and across urban space and that investments in public transport are not necessarily beneficial for all social groups (see e.g. Hickman and Dean, 2017 or Næss, 2006). Despite these issues having been addressed recently with a renewed theoretical focus on social justice and social equality, few long-term empirical studies have been undertaken to address how public transport investments affect a city's intra-urban socio-economic development. Previous studies have tended to focus either on aggregated spatial urban and regional scales or on the local scale of the everyday life of individual marginalized citizens, leaving aside any deeper multiscale understanding of the regeneration processes of urban public transport investments.

To address some of these shortcomings in the existing literature, this chapter shows how the socio-economic composition of residents in areas served by public transit systems is affected both before and after large-scale investment in public transport. Based on a case study of the establishment of the Copenhagen Metro system in 2002, we ask how the socio-economic characteristics of local metro-served areas developed ten years before and after the opening. We also examine whether the areas developed differently than the rest of the city in these periods and to what extent this sort of development can be explained by the dynamics of moving on the part of the residents of these areas in whether they stay put, move in or move out.

The remainder of the chapter is structured as follows. The next section briefly introduces the methodology used in the case study. The third section describes the case study area and the context of investment in the metro. In the following sections, socio-economic development in the areas served by the Metro is analysed, while the final section discusses and concludes the chapter's findings.

## 2.   DATA AND METHODOLOGY

Assessing the link between socio-spatial development and investments in urban public transport is not a straightforward task. While a piece of transport infrastructure can be seen as a rather static physical structure in an urban milieu, the socio-economic urban structures and development surrounding it are highly dynamic and are shaped by a myriad of influencing factors. The aim of this chapter is not to simplify or underestimate the complexity of these links, but to address a rather simple question: How do areas in close proximity to new transit stations develop socio-economically when a new public transport infrastructure is introduced, and how are the dynamics of moving among residents in these areas affected?

The study is based on detailed register-based data from Statistics Denmark covering all residents aged between 15 and 64 years who lived in Copenhagen from 1992 to 2012. The data are disaggregated, longitudinal and provide detailed information on the socio-economic characteristics of all residents and their moving patterns. The variables of age, income, level of education, employment and area of residence are attached to each individual in the time period of the study. In addressing the relationship between transport investments and socio-economic development, a key issue is the actual spatial scale on which the development is examined. In the literature, the impact distance for residential and commercial development has been widely debated (see e.g. Banister and Thurstain-Goodwin, 2011 or Guerra et al., 2012), but in this case study, the catchment areas are defined as areas within 600 metres' walking distance of the new established metro stations. This walking distance is defined somewhat narrowly, but it is in accordance with the Danish planning principle that guides urban development near transit stations. To analyse socio-economic development, the catchment areas have been aggregated into seven metro-served areas (MSAs) based on each area's local characteristics, housing stock and earlier development. In the analysis Copenhagen is defined as consisting of the municipalities of Copenhagen, Frederiksberg (which is surrounded by Copenhagen) and Taarnby.

To answer the questions posed in this chapter, the data are analysed in two steps. First, the changing socio-economic characteristics of the MSAs is analysed ten years before and after the completion of the Copenhagen Metro using simple descriptive statistical methods, and they are compared with areas not served by the Metro and Copenhagen in general as reference areas. This step is taken in order to examine whether socio-economic changes in the MSAs are specific to these areas compared with other parts of Copenhagen.

Secondly, we zoom in on the socio-economic development in the seven MSAs after the opening in 2002, allocating their respective residents into the three categories of 'stayers', 'in-movers' and 'out-movers' based on their recent moving patterns, similar to the resident typology developed by Hickman and Banister (2015). 'Stayers' are residents who have lived in a local MSA throughout the entire period from five years before the completion of the metro in 2002 and ten years after. In-movers are residents who have moved into an MSA, while out-movers are residents who have moved out between 1997 and 2012. The socio-economic characteristics of these three types of resident are analysed using simple descriptive statistics for all seven MSAs in 2002, 2007 and 2012 based on their moving patterns within the previous five years. Due to the considerable variations in age and life stages between the three types of resident, comparing them directly could produce misleading conclusions. Therefore, the last part of the analysis is based on a subset of residents aged between 30 and 49 in the year of the analysis.

## 3.   CASE STUDY: THE COPENHAGEN METRO

Like most other Western cities, Copenhagen has undergone extensive processes of transformation since the 1970s that have affected both its demographics and its socio-economic characteristics. First, there has been a process of continuous de-industrialization, which included the downsizing or closing of manufacturing firms. Second, there has been a strong outward movement of residents, back-office functions and other service jobs towards suburban locations, leaving the city's tax base near to collapse (Illeris, 1997). Thus, in the early 1990s, Copenhagen had serious financial problems, and as a consequence the national government agreed that large-scale initiatives and investments were needed to revitalize the city's economy and maintain Denmark's international competitiveness. This required a controversial change in Copenhagen's spatial planning policies from a social-democrat welfare-oriented perspective to a neo-liberal entrepreneurial agenda (Andersen and Jørgensen, 1995; Majoor, 2008). A wide range of initiatives were introduced, including neighbourhood programmes aimed at modernizing the city's housing stock, redeveloping the harbour front, building new residential areas, constructing a bridge linking the city to southern Sweden and introducing a Metro system for Copenhagen (Knowles, 2012).

The investment for the Copenhagen Metro received political approval in 1992, and construction started in 1996. The Metro served several purposes. First, it improved the public transport connection between the inner city and Amager, the previously less accessible south-east of Copenhagen, including the airport. Secondly, there was a plan to develop a new modern 310-hectare business and residential district, Ørestad, on a greenfield site in western Amager. The Metro system has 22 stations, of which nine are underground, and it passes through three municipalities. The first phase connecting Ørestad to the inner city opened in 2002, and the second phase connecting the inner city with the western side of the city opened the year after. The last phase connecting the airport opened in 2007.

Figure 9.1 shows the location of the Copenhagen Metro in relation to the existing S-train network and the seven aggregated Metro-served areas chosen for the case study: MSA Frederiksberg, MSA Inner City, MSA Christianshavn, MSA Ørestad, MSA Amagerbro, MSA Amager Strand and MSA Amager East. MSA Inner city includes three local catchment areas for the Metro. This is a classic inner city area consisting mainly of

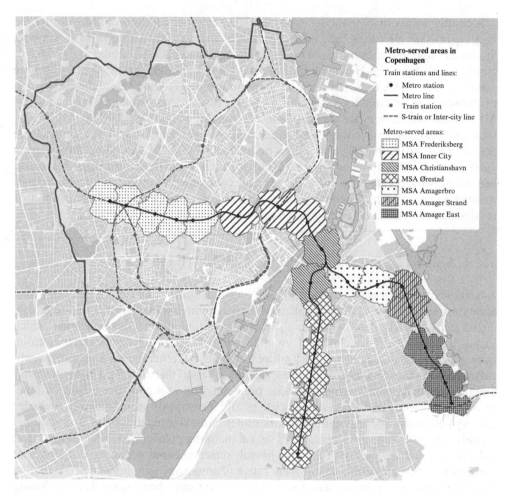

*Figure 9.1   The location of the metro and of metro-served areas in Copenhagen*

privately owned apartments and shopping areas, while both rented and owned apartment buildings and many detached one-family villas characterize the housing stock in the five local catchment areas of MSA Frederiksberg. MSA Christianshavn includes the local catchment areas of both Christianshavn, an old working-class neighbourhood, and Islands Brygge near the harbour front, a former industrial area that has been transformed into a new residential zone and an old working-class neighbourhood that has undergone modernization. The five local catchment areas of MSA Ørestad contain two rather different areas. On the western side of the metro line, new residential and commercial areas have been built in a hitherto unbuilt nature reserve since the opening of the Metro. The eastern side of the Metro line had already been built on before the Metro was introduced, consisting of social housing, one-family villas and allotment houses. MSA Amagerbro is an old borough area of Copenhagen with a housing stock characterized by smaller apartments that were modernized in the 1990s through a publicly funded urban renewal project. MSA Amager Strand is located near the restored urban beach and is characterized by new apartment blocks on former industrial sites and detached one-family villas. Finally, both detached one-family villas and great amounts of social housing characterize the three local catchment areas of MSA Amager East.

## 4. SOCIO ECONOMIC DEVELOPMENT IN METRO- AND NON-METRO-SERVED AREAS 1992–2012

Following decades of depopulation, Copenhagen has experienced large-scale population growth since the mid-1990s. Driven by the re-urbanization of younger families especially, the mean age of the entire population of the city fell by approximately five years from 1992 to 2012. Table 9.1 highlights the aggregate level change in Copenhagen's MSAs and non-MSAs for the working population (aged 15–64 years) ten years before and after the Metro opened in 2002, showing a slightly higher population growth in metro-served areas since that date.

About one quarter of the residents of Copenhagen live within a local Metro catchment area compared to the non-served areas of the city. Figure 9.2 maps Copenhagen's intra-urban population growth in the periods 1992–2002 and 2002–2012. It appears that population growth between the two periods differs significantly. From 1992 to 2002 population growth was widely spread across the city and took place mostly in the older working-class neighbourhoods surrounding the inner city. From 2002 to 2012, population growth was concentrated in fewer areas experiencing larger growth. This was especially the case in the southern part of the inner harbour and in particular areas around some of the Metro stations in the metro-served areas (MSA Frederiksberg, MSA Christianshavn and MSA Amager Strand), where old industrial areas were being transformed to new residential areas. Lastly, significant growth was seen around some of the metro stations in the greenfield residential development of MSA Ørestad.

In Table 9.1, the key socio-economic variables are summarized for Copenhagen's MSAs and non-MSAs respectively. It appears that residents in MSAs on an aggregated level have a slightly higher level of education, lower unemployment rates and higher mean incomes. Although these relative differences can be observed in Table 9.1, it is important to understand whether there is a significant difference between the socio-economic levels in the two areas. To assess this, chi-square tests and t-tests were applied to educational level, unemployment and annual income. All tests showed a significant relationship between the socio-economic variables and their location in all years.[1] By comparing socio-economic

---

[1] Basic significance tests were applied to test the socio-economic levels in the two areas. Chi-square tests were applied for higher education and unemployment and t-tests on annual income, and all tests were performed on the full population of residents (N=400,822 (1992); N= 452,634 (2002); N =502,889 (2012)). The chi-square tests showed a significant association between higher education and residents in MSAs and non-MSAs as a location variable for all years (1992: $\chi^2$=85,93, df=1, p < 0, 001; 2002: $\chi^2$=210,43, df=1, p < 0, 001; 2012: $\chi^2$=417,55, df=1, p < 0, 001) and a significant association between unemployment and residents in MSAs and non-MSAs as a location variable (2002: $\chi^2$=283,95, df=1, p < 0, 001; 2012: $\chi^2$=473,59, df=1, p < 0, 001). The two-tailed test showed that the annual mean income of residents in MSAs and non-MSAs are significant different in all three years (1992: diff= -5,430, t(400,820) = -13.97, p < 0,001; 2002: diff= -8,847, t(452,632) = -15.56, p < 0,001; 2012: diff= -13,050, t(502,887) = -17.82, p < 0,001).

Table 9.1  Socio-economic development in metro- and non-metro-served areas 1992–2012

| | Metro- vs. non-metro served areas | | | Metro-served areas | | | | | | |
|---|---|---|---|---|---|---|---|---|---|---|
| | City of Copenhagen | Metro-served | Non-metro-served | Frederiks-berg | Inner City | Christians-havn | Ørestad | Amager-bro | Amager strand | Amager East |
| **Population (abs.)** | | | | | | | | | | |
| 1992 | **400,822** | **86,728** | **314,094** | 25,359 | 19,139 | 9,455 | 3,936 | 21,615 | 2,189 | 5,035 |
| 2002 | **452,634** | **97,402** | **355,232** | 28,497 | 21,237 | 10,779 | 4,161 | 25,120 | 2,710 | 4,898 |
| 2012 | **502,889** | **112,170** | **390,719** | 32,060 | 23,324 | 12,910 | 7,799 | 27,129 | 3,831 | 5,117 |
| **Population growth (pct.)** | | | | | | | | | | |
| 1992–2002 | *12.93* | *12.31* | *13.10* | *12.37* | *10.96* | *14.00* | *5.72* | *16.22* | *23.80* | *-2.72* |
| 2002–2012 | *11.10* | *15.16* | *9.99* | *12.50* | *9.83* | *19.77* | *87.43* | *8.00* | *41.37* | *4.47* |
| **Mean age** | | | | | | | | | | |
| 1992 | *36.2* | *36.1* | *36.3* | *37.0* | *36.0* | *35.9* | *35.0* | *34.5* | *38.2* | *39.4* |
| 2002 | *36.8* | *36.9* | *36.6* | *37.7* | *37.3* | *36.9* | *36.7* | *34.6* | *39.1* | *40.6* |
| 2012 | *36.7* | *36.5* | *36.7* | *37.2* | *36.4* | *37.0* | *34.9* | *34.9* | *39.5* | *40.3* |
| **Share with higher education (pct.)** | | | | | | | | | | |
| 1992 | *6.31* | *6.99* | *6.13* | *8.67* | *11.06* | *8.32* | *1.78* | *3.38* | *4.70* | *1.12* |
| 2002 | *10.75* | *12.02* | *10.40* | *14.62* | *17.90* | *14.46* | *2.84* | *6.93* | *7.89* | *2.01* |
| 2012 | *16.78* | *18.79* | *16.20* | *20.79* | *24.20* | *23.97* | *14.17* | *13.28* | *20.09* | *4.30* |
| **Unemployment rate (pct.)** | | | | | | | | | | |
| 2002 | *8.75* | *7.31* | *9.15* | *6.75* | *5.77* | *7.44* | *11.14* | *9.75* | *3.96* | *5.98* |
| 2012 | *6.65* | *5.12* | *7.09* | *4.42* | *3.78* | *4.32* | *6.10* | *7.11* | *3.54* | *6.78* |
| **Annual income (in DKK)** | | | | | | | | | | |
| 1992 | **172,670** | **176,916** | **171,486** | 185,193 | 190,583 | 171,697 | 147.456 | 159,087 | 196,950 | 182,318 |
| 2002 | **240,941** | **247,875** | **239,028** | 264,405 | 275,465 | 245,806 | 193,477 | 213,493 | 277,834 | 240,132 |
| 2012 | **315,339** | **325,462** | **312,412** | 335,716 | 363,508 | 342,543 | 308,204 | 274,069 | 398,303 | 292,365 |
| **Growth in annual income (pct.)** | | | | | | | | | | |
| 1992–2002 | *39.54* | *40.11* | *39.39* | *42.77* | *44.54* | *43.16* | *31.21* | *34.20* | *41.07* | *31.71* |
| 2002–2012 | *30.88* | *31.30* | *30.70* | *26.97* | *31.96* | *39.36* | *59.30* | *28.37* | *43.36* | *21.75* |

*Notes:*  All residents aged between 15 to 64 years; Metro-served areas are defined as areas within 600 meters walking distance of a metro station and non-metro-served areas as the rest of Copenhagen higher education is defined as the share of residents with at least a master degree: Unemployment is defined as the share of residents that was unemployed more than six months the given year; Annual mean income is calculated based on all residents personal income before tax

*Source:*  Statistics Denmark.

126

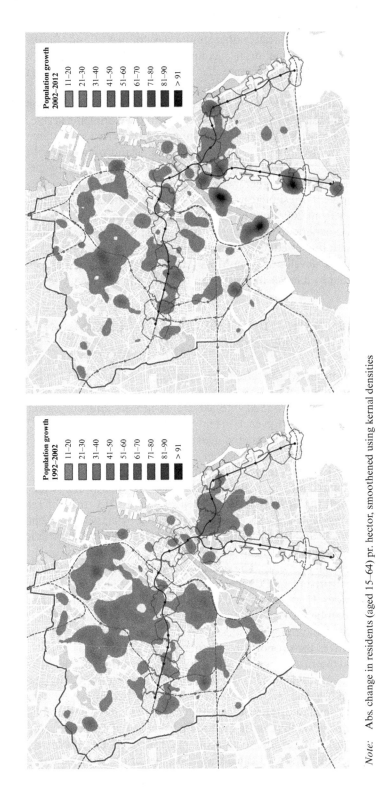

*Note:* Abs. change in residents (aged 15–64) pr. hector, smoothened using kernal densities

*Figure 9.2  Population growth in Copenhagen 1992–2002 and 2002–2012*

development on this aggregated scale, rather similar development trends for the two areas appear during this period. Annual mean incomes and the share of residents with higher education increased in both area categories throughout this period, while the unemployment rate slightly fell.

Addressing the socio-economic composition of residents and their development in the seven MSAs shows that these areas experienced different developments (Table 9.1). First, it appears that MSA Frederiksberg and MSA Inner City experienced different developments compared to the five local MSAs located on the island of Amager. In 1992 and throughout the period, both MSAs had a higher share of residents with higher education, a lower unemployment rate and higher mean income than the Copenhagen mean, still the trends of the development are similar to the development in the city in general. Secondly, Table 9.1 reveals that from 2002 and onwards MSA Christianshavn, MSA Ørestad and MSA Amager Strand experienced larger increases in population, mean income and the share of residents with higher education than the Copenhagen mean. Finally, it appears that the socio-economic development in MSA Amagerbro and especially MSA Amager East was characterized by a lower increase than the Copenhagen mean.

## 5.    SOCIO-ECONOMIC DEVELOPMENT IN LOCAL METRO-SERVED AREAS 2002–2012

The local development in MSAs after the opening is examined in more detail by disaggregating the residents. Based on each individual's moving pattern within the last five years, all residents were grouped into stayers, in-movers and out-movers, and the socio-economic characteristics for each group were examined for 2002, 2007 and 2012 respectively. In doing this, we address the question of whether there are any significant differences between the three types of resident, especially between in-movers and stayers, over the three time periods and between the different local MSAs.

In addressing residential moving patterns, it is important to be aware of the significant age differences between the three types of resident. In Figure 9.3, the differences in age among the types of resident in the local MSAs are shown by classifying them into three age groups (15–29, 30–49 and 50–64). From the figure, it is seen that the variation in age is limited in all MSAs. Most in-movers are 15–29 years old, and the largest group of stayers are the 30–49 and 50–64-year-olds. The age differences between stayers, in-movers and out-movers are not surprising, as Copenhagen has experienced a great inflow of younger people in recent decades. However, these differences show that comparing the three types of resident directly can be misleading. To overcome this, we therefore focus in what follows on the socio-economic characteristics of residents in the middle age group.

Figure 9.4 summarizes the proportion of residents aged between 30 and 49 years with higher education, and the unemployment rates and annual mean incomes in the seven MSAs based on the typology of residents in 2002, 2007 and 2012 respectively. The general trends in the graphs are that a bigger share of the MSA residents had higher education, higher annual mean incomes and lower rates of unemployment over time. These trends follow the overall socio-economic development of the total population of Copenhagen (Table 9.1). Moreover, there is a tendency for the socio-economic characteristics of the in-movers and out-movers to be similar, these two categories being better off socio-economically than

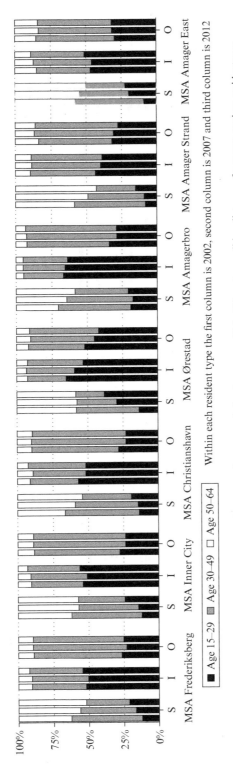

*Note:* All residents aged between 15 to 64 years; Metro served areas are defined as areas within 600 meters walking distance of a metro station; residents are allocated into three resident types based on their moving patterns within the previous five years (S = residents that have lived in the MSA from 1997 and onwards, I = residents who have moved into the MSA, O – residents who have moved out of the MSA)

*Source:* Statistics Denmark.

*Figure 9.3 Stayers, in-movers and out-movers in metro served areas by age group 2002–2012 (pct.)*

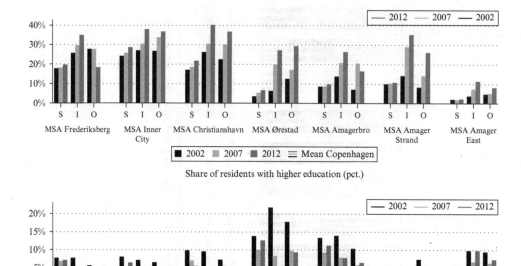

Share of residents with higher education (pct.)

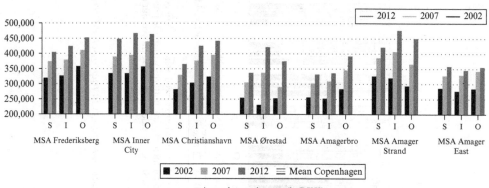

Unemployment rate (pct.)

Annual mean income (in DKK)

*Notes:*  All residents aged between 30 to 49 years; Metro-served areas are defined as areas within 600 meters walking distance of a metro station; residents are allocated into three resident types based on their moving patterns within the previous five year (S = residents that have lived in the MSA from 1997 and onwords, I = residents who have moved into the MSA, O = residents who have moved out of the MSA); higher education is defined as the share of residents with at least a master's degree; unemployment is defined as thr share of residents that was unemployed more than six months the given year; annual mean income is calculated based on all residents personal income before tax

*Source:*  Statistics Denmark.

*Figure 9.4    Socio-economic development in metro-served areas based on resident typology 2002–2012 (30–49 years-old residents)*

the stayers. However, there are great variations in the socio-economic development of the different MSAs and their categories of residents respectively.

All types of resident in MSA Frederiksberg had lower unemployment rates and higher annual mean incomes than the general mean of Copenhagen in the whole period. In 2002 and 2007, the proportion of stayers with a higher education was much lower than among the in-movers and out-movers. In 2012, however, the proportion of residents with a higher education was similar among both the stayers and the out-movers, though still almost seven percent lower than the Copenhagen mean. Nevertheless, the out-moving residents had the highest annual mean incomes of all residents in MSA Frederiksberg in 2012. In MSA Inner City the residents in all three resident groups were better educated, less likely to be unemployed and had higher annual mean incomes than the general mean for the total population of Copenhagen. It is shown that the educational level for both in-movers and out-movers increased much more than for the stayers. However, this is not reflected in mean incomes, in which respect the different categories of residents were similar to a large extent except for the out-movers' incomes in 2007, which were slightly higher than those of the stayers and in-movers. In 1992, the socio-economic profile of all residents in MSA Christianshavn was comparable to the Copenhagen mean, while there was a large growth in income and residents with a higher education between 2002 and 2012 (Table 9.1). Figure 9.4 shows a greater difference between the 30–49-year-old in-movers and stayers with higher education compared to the difference in the case of the other MSAs, and further that it increased over time. A steady decrease in unemployment and an increase in incomes with only small variations between the different types of resident are also shown.

In the remaining local MSAs, Figure 9.4 shows greater differences in the areas' overall socio-economic development as well as for each type of residents. Socio-economic development in MSA Ørestad differs radically from the overall development picture. In 2002, the MSA had a low share of residents with higher education, a high unemployment rate and a slightly lower mean income than the other MSAs and the Copenhagen mean. Figure 9.4 shows that this trend was worsened by the fact that the 30–49-year-old in-movers had a higher rate of unemployment and lower incomes than the stayers. However, this trend changed dramatically as the new residential areas on the western side of the metro line attracted better educated in-movers with lower unemployment rates and higher incomes from 2002 onwards. Thus, socio-economic development in this MSA was highly segregated spatially, as the stayers were the residents living in the already built-up areas on the eastern side. Like MSA Ørestad, MSA Amagerbro also had a low share of residents with higher education, a high unemployment rate and a slightly lower mean income in 2002. In contrast to MSA Ørestad, and despite an increase in 30–49-year-old in-movers with a higher education in the following years, the stayers' and in-movers' mean income levels were similar in all years, whereas the mean incomes of the out-movers were higher.

Compared with the other MSAs, Amager Strand and Amager East differ in three ways: the Metro did not serve these areas before 2007, the mean age was higher in both areas, and the residents experienced dissimilar socio-economic developments. MSA Amager Strand had a high income and low unemployment rate throughout the whole period. The area was characterized by a large growth in population, and the proportion of residents with higher incomes increased significantly from 2002 to 2012, going from below to above average (Table 9.1). Figure 9.4 shows that among the 30–49-year-olds this increase was driven by the in-movers and that the differences in educational level and income between stayers and in-movers grew considerably throughout the period. This is the same pattern that was seen in MSA Ørestad. In contrast, MSA Amager East was characterized by the lowest share of residents with a higher education of all MSAs, and between 1992 and 2012 the growth in incomes was lower than the city average. Unlike all the other MSAs, Figure 9.4 reveals that the differences between the socio-economic profiles of the 30–49-year-olds of all three types of resident were very small despite a small increase in in-movers with a higher education. As the only MSA, the unemployment rate of MSA Amager East increased slightly in the period.

## 6.    CONCLUSIONS

This case study has analysed the socio-economic development of Metro-served areas from five years before to ten years after the introduction of the Copenhagen Metro. It shows that the MSAs' residents tend to have a slightly higher level of education, lower unemployment rates and higher mean incomes compared to residents living in non-MSAs. Despite the small difference in socio-economic status, the two areas experienced similar development paths in the period of the study. Thus, evaluating socio-economic development at an aggregated scale leads us to conclude that introducing the Metro has not had noteworthy socio-economic impacts in Copenhagen. However, addressing socio-economic development on the local scale reveals large differences between the different MSAs. This underlines the fact that the scale of the study is of great importance when studying the impact of large public transport investments on the socio-economic development of urban areas.

The case study also indicates that local pre-conditions and the existing socio-economic composition of residents seem to matter for the developments observed here. In the case of Copenhagen, the Metro line passes through very different neighbourhoods with very different socio-economic characteristics. Frederiksberg, Inner City, and to a large extent Christianshavn, are neighbourhoods that experienced housing modernization and the in-migration of high-income residents from the early 1990s, and thus the MSAs of these areas already had a 'better' socio-economic composition than the remaining MSAs before the Metro was introduced. In the ten years after the establishment of the Metro, the mean incomes and the proportion of residents with a higher education in these MSAs increased close to or more than the city mean.

Developments in the remaining four MSAs have been more diverse. In these areas bringing the Metro to Amager led to relatively greater improvements in public transport accessibility. Despite great variation in the socio-economic composition of the initial residents, two of these MSAs, namely Amagerbro and Ørestad, experienced a large increase in mean incomes and residents with a higher education after the Metro was introduced. This could indicate that in these areas the Metro has worked as a trigger for socio-economic development by opening up hitherto less accessible areas of the city (Knowles and Ferbrache, 2016). On the other hand, socio-economic development in MSAs Amager East and Amager Strand only appears similar to or less positive than the overall development of the city.

Overall, addressing local socio-economic development in the MSAs shows a diverse picture. While some of the development can be explained by differences in local pre-conditions, the existing socio-economic composition of the residents and/or the increased transport accessibility, some of it cannot. This implies that interpretations of the Metro cannot be reduced to its having had a clear and evenly distributed socio-economic impact. It appears that it is not the Metro in itself, nor the improvements in transport accessibility in general, that explain the socio-economic development of the MSAs. Rather, the explanation must be found in the combination of the establishment of the Metro, the local context, the provision of urban amenities, attractive newly built housing and supporting urban policies. This conclusion sustains the arguments of Banister and Berechman (2001) in discussing the wider economic benefits of transport investments and of Batholomew and Ewing (2011) in their discussion about house price effects.

Disaggregating the different types of resident in the MSAs highlights three important aspects to socio-economic development in the period. First, in four of the MSAs the mean incomes of stayers and in-movers were not considerably different nor differed in their change throughout the studied period. However, we do see large and increasing differences in the proportions of staying and in-moving residents with higher education in all MSAs. Secondly, despite a small increase in residents with higher education, the increase in mean incomes among stayers did not proceed very differently than the general development in the city. Thirdly, it appears that generally the socio-economic characteristics of the out-movers were similar to or better than those for the other types of resident. Altogether, this implies that, in the case of Copenhagen, the introduction of the Metro has neither clearly gentrified the areas it serves nor improved the social mobility of the residents in the local MSAs. Nevertheless, small signs of gentrification can be seen in the local MSAs where larger new residential areas are being developed (Ørestad, Amager Strand and Christianshavn). In these areas, we see a large and increasing difference between the socio-economic composition of stayers and in-movers throughout the period. However, as most of the newly built housing is spatially concentrated in these MSAs, this development points to increasing local segregation in these neighbourhoods rather than overall gentrification. The existing housing stock and the amount of newly built housing therefore appear to be significant for local development. This is further underlined by the remarkable similarities between the socio-economic characteristics of the staying and in-moving residents in the other MSAs, where only a small amount of new housing has been built.

Thus, our analysis shows great spatial varieties of socio-economic development. Consequently, the methodological considerations of the spatial perspectives of an analysis of the possible impacts of public transport investments are very important. Future research on the impacts of the Copenhagen Metro could therefore benefit from regression analysis of the general socio-economic development in Copenhagen adding the distance to the Metro as an important variable. Moreover, the quantitative approach to our case study causes some limitations on studying the relationship between public transport investments and social mobility. Thus, this area of research would profit from adding a qualitative approach, i.e. interviews with local residents on whether the new and increased accessibility contributes to new or better opportunities in the labour market. Lastly, as briefly mentioned in the chapter, the housing stock in the different areas of Copenhagen varies a lot. Therefore, greater insight into the different forms of ownership would add a deeper understanding of the processes behind the socio-economic development of the MSAs. This knowledge could also inform practice and policy makers on how to ensure socially equitable results of public transport investments.

In conclusion, this case study shows that addressing the socio-spatial impacts of public transport investments is a complex and methodologically challenging task. Throughout the chapter, we have argued that the socio-economic development of the new MSAs was a highly dynamic process that needs to be understood and examined in relation to a range of influencing factors. In the case of the Copenhagen Metro, scale, local context and the earlier development paths of local areas seem to have been particularly important for socio-economic development.

# REFERENCES

Agostini, C. and Palmucci, G. (2008), The anticipated capitalisation effect of a new metro line on housing prices. *Fiscal Studies*, 29(2), 233–256.

Andersen, H. and Jørgensen, J. (1995), City profile: Copenhagen. *Cities*, 12(1), 13–22.

Banister, D. and Berechman, Y. (2001), Transport investment and the promotion of economic growth. *Journal of Transport Geography*, 9(3), 209–218.

Banister, D. and Thurstain-Goodwin, M. (2011), Quantification of the non-transport benefits resulting from rail investment. *Journal of Transport Geography*, 19(2), 212–223.

Bartholomew, K. and Ewing, R. (2011), Hedonic price effects of pedestrian and transit-oriented development. *Journal of Planning Literature*, 26, 18–34.

Beyazit, E. (2011), Evaluating social justice in transport: lessons to be learned from the capability approach. *Transport Reviews*, 31(1), 117–134.

Beyazit, E. (2015), Are wider economic impacts of transport infrastructures always beneficial? Impacts of the Istanbul Metro on the generation of spatio-economic inequalities. *Journal of Transport Geography*, 45, 12–23.

Bocarejo, J. and Oviedo, D. (2012), Transport accessibility and social inequalities: a tool for identification of mobility needs and evaluation of transport investments. *Journal of Transport Geography*, 24, 142–154.

Gospodini, A. (2005), Urban development, redevelopment and regeneration encouraged by transport infrastructure projects: the case study of 12 European cities. *European Planning Studies*, 13(7), 1083–1111.

Grengs, J. (2005), The abandoned social goals of public transit in the neoliberal city of the USA. *City*, 9(1), 51–66.

Guerra, E., Cervero, R. and Tischler, D. (2012), Half-mile circle. *Transportation Research Record: Journal of the Transportation Research Board*, 2276, 101–109.

Hickman, R. and Banister, D. (2015), New household location and the commute to work: change over time. In R. Hickman, M. Givoni, D. Bonilla and D. Banister (eds) *Handbook on Transport and Development* (pp. 318–333). Cheltenham: Edward Elgar.

Hickman, R. and Dean, M. (2017), Incomplete cost – incomplete benefit analysis in transport appraisal. *Transport Reviews*. Available at: https://doi.org/10.1080/01441647.2017.1407377.

Illeris, S. (1997), The changing location of service activities in the Copenhagen region. *Geografisk Tidsskrift-Danish Journal of Geography*, 1997, 120–142.

Jones, P. (2015), Assessing the wider impacts of the Jubilee Line extension in East London. In R. Hickman, M. Givoni, D. Bonilla and D. Banister (eds) *Handbook on Transport and Development* (pp. 318–333). Cheltenham: Edward Elgar.

Jones, P. and Lucas, K. (2012), The social consequences of transport decision-making: clarifying concepts, synthesizing knowledge and assessing implications. *Journal of Transport Geography*, 21, 4–16.

Kenyon, S. (2015), Development and social policy: the role of transport in social development, in the UK context. In R. Hickman, M. Givoni, D. Bonilla and D. Banister (eds) *Handbook on Transport and Development* (pp. 430–440). Cheltenham: Edward Elgar.

Knowles, R. (2012), Transit-oriented development in Copenhagen, Denmark: from the finger plan to Ørestad. *Journal of Transport Geography*, 22, 251–261.

Knowles, R. and Ferbrache, F. (2016), Evaluation of wider economic impacts of light rail investment on cities. *Journal of Transport Geography*, 54, 430–439.

Loo, B. and Cheng, A. (2010), Are there useful yardsticks of population size and income level for building metro systems? Some worldwide evidence. *Cities*, 27(5), 299–306.

Lucas, K. (2012), Transport and social exclusion: where are we now? *Transport Policy*, 20, 105–113.

Lucas, K. and Jones, P. (2012), Guest editorial. Social impacts and equity issues in transport: an introduction. *Journal of Transport Geography*, 21, 1–3.

Lucas, K., Tyler, S. and Christodoulou, G. (2009), Assessing the 'value' of new transport initiatives in deprived neighbourhoods in the UK. *Transport Policy*, 16, 115–122.

Majoor, S. (2008), Progressive planning ideals in a neo-liberal context: the case of Ørestad Copenhagen. *International Planning Studies*, 13(2), 101–117.

Meijers, E., Hoekstra, J., Leijten, M., Louw, E. and Spaans, M. (2012), Connecting the periphery: distributive effects of new infrastructure. *Journal of Transport Geography*, 22, 187–198.

Mejia-Dorantes, L. and Lucas, K. (2014), Public transport investment and local regeneration: a comparison of London's Jubilee Line Extension and the Madrid Metrosur. *Transport Policy*, 35, 241–252.

Mohammad, S., Graham, D., Melo, P. and Anderson, R. (2013), A meta-analysis of the impact of rail projects on land and property values. *Transportation Research Part A: Policy and Practice*, 50, 158–170.

Næss, P. (2006), Cost-benefit analyses of transport investments. *Journal of Critical Realism*, 5(1), 32–60.

Power, A. (2012), Social inequality, disadvantaged neighbourhoods and transport deprivation: an assessment of the historical influence of housing policies. *Journal of Transport Geography*, 21, 39–48.

# 10. Assessing transport equity through a cumulative accessibility measure and Google Maps: a case study for healthcare in Metro Manila
*Neil Stephen Lopez and Jose Bienvenido Manuel Biona*

## 1.  INTRODUCTION

Decades ago, it was quite common to walk to and from school, to the market, to the hospital – to almost everywhere. It is just possible now, if you don't mind all the pollution and safety risks on the road. Undeniably, motorised transport has mostly become essential. Large-scale urbanisation and sprawl has created a totally new concept and form of the city. Cities are now more spread out, and more families are starting to prefer suburban homes in order to escape from the urban jungle that is the city. Moreover, especially in developing countries, new infrastructure developments have increasingly favoured automobiles (Vasconcellos, 2013). Add to this the poor status and quality of public transport in lower- to middle-income countries, it is definitely a formula for serious implications on transport inequality. Low- to middle-income populations have struggled to cope, if they have not yet been alienated, with these trends in mobility. Coincidentally, the complicated data requirements to analyse this type of situation makes it difficult for scholars in the Global South to perform their tasks well and conduct good quality analysis for their developing countries.

In a similar vein, Sheppard et al. (2013) challenged traditional treatment of transportation studies and proposes a "provincialisation" of such studies. Provincialisation calls for a focus on unique and specific needs of various cities, from developing to developed ones. The argument arises from apparent failure of emulating practices from the Global North to bring prosperity and equality in the Global South. Thus, an increasing significance for independent studies in developing country contexts is present.

The impact of land use and transportation strategies are often evaluated by researchers using accessibility measures, which policy makers can more directly understand. Geurs and van Wee (2004) provide a review of various accessibility measures, and assessed them in terms of usability, data requirements, and communicability. Furthermore, Guagliardo (2004), Wang (2012), and Neutens (2015) each provide their own review of accessibility studies specifically to healthcare services, providing important insights on barriers, methodological comparison, and equity considerations, respectively.

However, as mentioned above, the extent and complexity of data requirements to perform high quality studies make it challenging for scholars in developing countries. At the minimum, a map of services and/or opportunities has to be maintained. Significant computing resources are also necessary. In this chapter, we discuss a methodology to assess transport equity using cumulative accessibility and the Google Maps platform. The cumulative accessibility approach is perhaps the simplest in terms of data requirements, but it provides enough sophistication to be useful to city planners and policymakers.

Neutens et al. (2010) discuss the pros and cons of the approach. Information from the Google Maps platform provides an alternative that researchers with limited resources and access to data can use.

Using publicly available data in Google Maps API, the study performs an accessibility assessment for healthcare services in Metro Manila, Philippines, and then the resulting data is used to perform an equity assessment. The platform has been used in similar studies before, such as in Paez et al. (2013), to develop a web-based accessibility calculator; Santos et al. (2011), to create a decision-support system for vehicle routing; Wang and Xu (2011), to develop an origin-destination travel time matrix; and Luo and Shen (2009), to develop an information system for bike-sharing.

In the wide literature of equity studies, plenty of interpretations have been offered for transportation equity – a significant portion of which, have proposed to associate it with accessibility as a measure, such as in Wang (2012), Neutens (2015) and Okafor (1990). Pereira et al. (2017) performs a theoretical review of key theories in justice (i.e. utilitarianism, libertarianism, intuitionism, Rawl's egalitarianism, and capability approaches) towards formulating a measure for transport equity. In conclusion, it proposes a distributive justice-based conceptualisation of transport equity, with mixed roots from egalitarianism and capability approaches. The distributive justice takes a look at the individual accessibilities of each person, and then equity is maximised by reducing the gap between those with least and most access to desired opportunities or services.

In this case, from a capabilities perspective, the individual accessibility of each person is assumed synonymous to his or her individual "capability," acknowledging individual differences in needs and preferences. For example, a younger person might find the use of a bicycle more helpful than an older person. Similarly, a low-income person may find difficulty availing private modes compared to middle- to high-income persons, significantly affecting their own accessibilities. This interpretation of transport equity shall be adopted in this methodology, albeit with limitations on aggregation of population characteristics. An illustrative case study will be used to demonstrate the use of the methodology in assessing spatial equity of access to healthcare services in Metro Manila, Philippines.

## 2. METHODOLOGY

### 2.1 Accessibility as a Measure of Equity

As discussed in the previous section, accessibility shall be used as a measure of spatial equity in transport. Inspired by the arguments of Pereira et al. (2017) discussed above, the following expression will be used to measure equity (Eq. 1).

$$\text{Equity} = \min(\text{Access}) - \max(\text{Access}) \tag{1}$$

### 2.2 Cumulative Accessibility

There are many forms of measure for accessibility. Generically, they can first be divided into place-based and person-based measures. More traditional measures are place-based, and use static origins and destinations in their analysis. On the other hand, more recent works look into person-based measures which consider the individual time-space constraint of the person, albeit requiring more complex information. In this chapter, we discuss a methodology using a place-based measure called cumulative accessibility. Cumulative accessibility works by counting the number of available services or opportunities within a specified generalised cost, which can be a monetised sum of cost and travel time. Say, with 10 USD and 30 minutes, how many hospitals can you reach from your origin? The expression for cumulative accessibility is shown in Eqs. 2 and 3 below. A simple counting function may be employed to perform the cumulative accessibility calculation in any spreadsheet software, once an origin-destination travel time and distance matrix is available. This matrix will be created using Google Maps, and is discussed in the following section.

$$Accessibility_{ij} = \Sigma_n Facility_{ij} \quad for\ all\ i,j \tag{2}$$

where,

$$Facility_{ij} = \begin{cases} 1,\ GenCost_{ij} \leq travel\ budget \\ 0,\ GenCost_{ij} > travel\ budget \end{cases} \tag{3}$$

where i and j refer to origin zone and mode, respectively; GenCost is a generalised cost function, considering travel time and distance; and travel budget is an assumed value that a person is willing or prepared to spend for travel to a healthcare facility.

## 2.3   Using Google Maps to Create Travel Time and Distance Matrices

The study created its own origin-destination travel time and distance matrices using the Google Maps Application Programming Interface (API) service. The full documentation of the service is available here: https://developers.google.com/maps/documentation/directions.

Using HTML coding, a spreadsheet software was programmed to perform the data inquiries automatically for the user. The calculation for travel times and distances were based on the coordinates of each origin zone and healthcare facility, which were manually obtained from Google Maps prior to creating the matrices. This was an important step because of the user-contributed nature of Google – creating problems such as multiple entry, missing and misspelled places. In the analysis below, 167,552 combined queries for travel times and distances were made. Also, separate travel time and distance matrices were created for both private and public modes. For interested researchers, walking and cycling modes are also available in the Google Maps database for select cities.

## 2.4   Limitations of the Study

Certain limitations to the analysis had to be applied for simplification purposes. First, a certain service had to be selected for assessment, in this case healthcare. Second, an average fare for public transport had to be assumed. To factor in transfers between public modes throughout the trip, an average per kilometre fare was estimated to simplify the calculation procedures. Also, for private transport, the taxi fare system was used to make it more inclusive, since more people have access to taxis than private cars in the city. Finally, the socio-economic considerations were only reflected in terms of travel budget. As discussed above, the population may be ideally divided by age, gender and other individual preferences. The aggregation may be increased in detail as the data becomes available.

## 3.   ILLUSTRATIVE CASE STUDY: HEALTHCARE IN METRO MANILA, PHILIPPINES

The site of the case study is Metro Manila in the Philippines, located in Southeast Asia. Metro Manila lies on a narrow strip of land bordered by a bay to the west, and a lake to the east. It is the capital of the Philippines, the country's centre for business and economics, and a passageway linking the northern and southern regions of the Luzon island. The megacity had a population of 12.8 million in 2015. With an area of approximately 620 sq.km, the city has a population density of about 21,000 persons per sq.km.

The city has a private vehicle ownership rate of 11.5 per cent (JICA–DOTC, 2015). For other private transport options, there are also taxis and ridesharing options (e.g. Uber, Grab). In terms of public transport, there are four rail lines circling the city, with city buses, utility vans, and utility jeepneys (mini-buses) going around fixed routes. The approximate fare per kilometre is 12 Philippines Pesos (PhP) (0.24 USD) for private transport, and two PhP (0.04 USD) for public transport. In terms of income, the minimum wage is approximately 500 PhP (10 USD) per day for non-agricultural jobs. The city is typical of a developing country with rapid urbanisation, increasing vehicle ownership, and, unfortunately, poor public transportation.

For the case study, considered are 154 healthcare facilities, and the city is divided into 272 individual zones. For the purpose of this study, healthcare facilities are limited to all levels of private and government hospitals only, excluding birthing homes, clinics and infirmaries. The official list can be downloaded from the Department of Health (2017). Transport equity to healthcare facilities will be shown in two perspectives: spatial and modal. In assessing spatial equity, the zones will be divided into central and peripheral, to emphasise the premium on accessibility central zones commonly have, and the handicap peripheral zones suffer. As for modal equity, access between and within zones will be analysed.

### 3.1   Spatial Equity

Out of the 272 zones, 102 belong to the central area of the city. Focusing on private modes in the central area (see Figure 10.1), a few zones have the luxury to access 15 different healthcare facilities even with a minimal budget of only 100 PhP, while the maximum is only eight for the peripheral zones (see Table 10.2). Notably, there are certain zones within both central and peripheral areas which have zero access to any healthcare facility, when the budget is only 100 PhP. As the travel budget increases to 300 and 500 PhP, the difference in accessibility gets negligible, with some peripheral zones even having more access than the best central zones (102 versus 99). With 300 PhP, all zones will have access to at least 4 healthcare facilities, which is important if individual preference is valued.

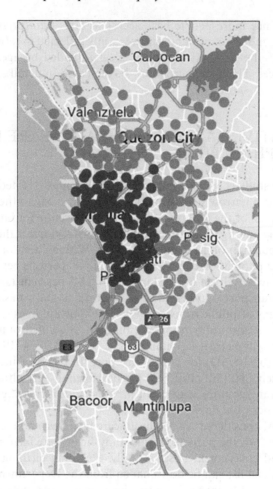

*Note:*   Black dots – central zones; grey dots – peripheral zones

*Figure 10.1   Distribution of zones*

From an equity perspective, the difference in accessibility is only significant for a travel budget of 100 PhP when the comparison is spatial (i.e. between central and peripheral zones). With 100 PhP, coming from the central zone, the average number of healthcare facilities accessible is 4.19, while it is 1.65 from the peripheral zone. Considering that the quality of each facility cannot be the same, and the possibility that not all facilities can provide all services, the difference in accessibility of 2.54 can be a significant equity issue. With higher travel budgets, the average accessibility in both areas rises, reducing equity issues.

### 3.2   Modal Equity

Within the private mode, there is severe inequity with a travel budget of less than 100 PhP, with almost half of all zones appearing to not have access to a single healthcare

*Table 10.1   Cumulative accessibility, private modes*

|  | Cumulative access to healthcare facilities | | |
|---|---|---|---|
|  | *<100 PhP* | *<300 PhP* | *<500 PhP* |
| Maximum | 15 | 99 | 143 |
| 75th quartile | 5 | 74 | 134 |
| Median | 3 | 63 | 123 |
| 25th quartile | 2 | 53 | 114 |
| Minimum | 0 | 27 | 88 |
| **Average** | **4.19** | **62.85** | **122.37** |

*Table 10.2   Cumulative accessibility, public modes*

|  | Cumulative access to healthcare facilities | | |
|---|---|---|---|
|  | *<100 PhP* | *<300 PhP* | *<500 PhP* |
| Maximum | 8 | 102 | 140 |
| 75th quartile | 2 | 61 | 121 |
| Median | 1 | 37 | 107 |
| 25th quartile | 0 | 22 | 80 |
| Minimum | 0 | 4 | 20 |
| **Average** | **1.65** | **41.43** | **98.16** |

*Table 10.3   Inequity, modal perspective*

|  | Inequity, difference between least and most accessibility | | |
|---|---|---|---|
|  | *<100 PhP* | *<300 PhP* | *<500 PhP* |
| Within private modes | –15 | –98 | –95 |
| Within public modes | –95 | –144 | –144 |
| Between modes | 0 | –4 | –59 |

facility. As the budget increases to 300 PhP, the difference in accessibility, and therefore equity, quickly becomes negligible. More so, anyone can conveniently reach any hospital anywhere in Metro Manila with approximately 900 PhP via private modes. Looking at Table 10.3, the inequity increases as the available budget to travel increases. But to be critical about it, it can be argued that it is no longer significant, as the minimum number of accessible healthcare facilities is already within acceptable levels for all zones with 900 PhP on hand. For example, nobody needs access to more than 40 hospitals at a time, but having access to only one hospital can be problematic, and it means that the person would not be able to choose, in case the only hospital available is not of good quality, and if it does not offer the required service. This condition makes the inequity significant for the low budget scenario, but not for the high budget scenario.

Within the public transport mode users, it is alarming to find out that certain zones from the periphery would still have zero access to any hospital even with 900 PhP already. This suggests poor public transport connectivity in those areas. Hickman et al. (2018) share opinions and discourses on the case of poor public transport in Metro Manila. Taking the difference in accessibility between zones, the inequity worsens (see Table 10.3) as the budget increases, because the minimum accessibility remains to be zero in a few peripheral zones. In this case, the increase in inequity should be alarming because the accessibilities of some peripheral zones do not increase no matter how much the budget increases.

Comparing between modes, the public modes have an advantage over the private modes at lower budgets. Via public modes, the best zones can reach 95 hospitals with only 100 PhP, while it is only 15 hospitals via private modes. At higher budgets, the private modes start to become more advantageous, eliminating zero accessibility across the city. Looking at the zones with least access for each mode, the inequity increases between modes as the budget increases. The private mode can significantly reach more hospitals as the budget increases.

### 3.3   Towards an Inclusive Measure for Accessibility

Looking at the differences in accessibility, from a spatial perspective, there is an inequity of 2.54 additional hospitals accessible to central zones, which are not available to peripheral zones. From a modal perspective and considering a low budget (i.e. 100 PhP), within mode, the inequity is 15 hospitals for the private mode and 95 hospitals for the public mode. These are both high, considering that the minimum value is zero – meaning there are places with no access to hospitals with a 100 PhP low budget. This suggests that a few small areas have to be the focus of new transport interventions first, before the quality of transport in areas which are already good to begin with, is further improved. Between modes and considering a moderate budget (i.e. 300 PhP), the inequity is four hospitals when we look at the places with least access for each mode. Again, this inequality can be considered significant since the minimum value for public transport is still zero.

Working towards an inclusive measure for equity, the proposed measure of simply obtaining the difference in access between the least and most can be a good option. This is because the inequity score it provides cannot improve unless the last group with poor accessibility can get attended to. The last two or three zones suffering from poor accessibility will not be lost in aggregation.

Concluding on the case study, the immediate accessibility issues which need to be addressed include: (1) reducing the cost of accessing healthcare from the peripheral zones, and (2) increasing access to public transport from the peripheral zones. With a moderate budget (i.e. 300 PhP), accessibility looks acceptable already for both modes from a map (see Figures 10.2 and 10.3). However, the inequity remains poor due to bad accessibility in a few peripheral zones.

## 4.   CONCLUSION

The chapter discusses a method to assess transport equity using a cumulative accessibility measure and open data from Google Maps. With the need for similar studies in

*Figure 10.2   Cumulative accessibility via private modes, increasing travel budget*

143

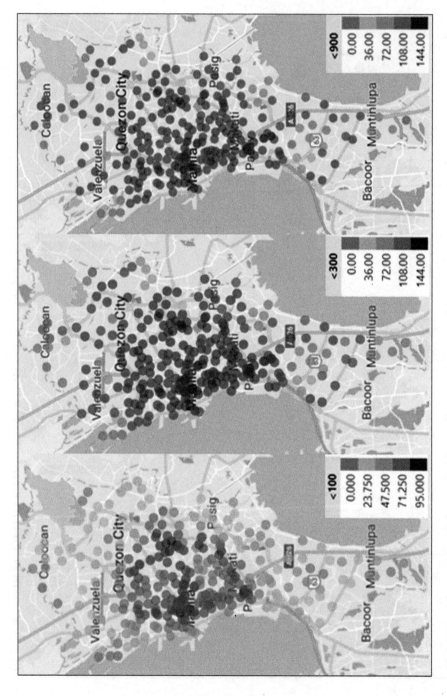

*Figure 10.3    Cumulative accessibility via public modes, increasing travel budget*

developing countries where data is scarce and resources are limited, such a methodology can be very useful. It was demonstrated using an illustrative case study for healthcare facilities in Metro Manila, Philippines. Furthermore, equity was assessed from both a spatial and modal perspective. From a spatial perspective, it was shown that inequity is only significant when the travel budget is low (i.e. 100 PhP). With a low budget, the inequity prohibits people from the peripheral areas to choose their preferred healthcare facility. From a modal perspective, there is severe inequity within private mode users when the assumed travel budget is low, while the inequality becomes insignificant beyond a moderate budget (i.e. 300 PhP). For public transport users, it is alarming to find out that a few peripheral zones have zero access to public transport even with a very high budget already (i.e. 900 PhP). These findings have led the authors to recommend increasing access to public transport in the peripheral areas and reducing the cost of accessing healthcare from the same.

In this vein, it is important to advocate for data-driven planning in developing countries, as accessibility or lack of is sometimes not obvious, and the population suffering from poor accessibility are usually those with less resources, and moreover, a weaker voice in politics and planning.

With regards to the calculated inequity score used in this study, interpretation is crucial since it only takes the difference between the minimum and maximum accessibility in the study area. A very large difference might look alarming, but it is also important to look at the value of the minimum accessibility. As shown in section 10.3.2, it is possible to have very large inequity, but when the least accessible area is already very accessible to begin with, the difference between least and most might not really matter anymore. The authors believe there is good potential for the equity measure based on the gap between least and most accessibility because of its inclusivity. A high accessibility score cannot be obtained until the last person or zone with poor accessibility is addressed. However, more improvement is still necessary on the simple formulation used in this study. Readers are encouraged to innovate and formulate better ways to express equity based on the same concept.

## ACKNOWLEDGEMENTS

The authors would like to acknowledge the Commission on Higher Education of the Philippines for their generous support in the conduct of this study, through the Grants-in-Aid Program and the Faculty Development Program. The authors also appreciate the valuable comments received from the NECTAR community, which helped improved this study.

## REFERENCES

Department of Health, Philippines. (2017). *List of Licensed/Accredited Health Facilities* [online]. Available at: https://hfsrb.doh.gov.ph/index.php/services/list-of-licensed-accredited-health-facilities. Last accessed 12 August 2017.

Department of Labor and Employment, Philippines. (2017). *Current Minimum Daily Wage Rates* [online]. Available at: www.nwpc.dole.gov.ph/pages/ncr/cmwr.html. Last accessed 22 December 2017.

Geurs, K.T. and van Wee, B. (2004). Accessibility evaluation of land-use and transport strategies: review and research directions. *Journal of Transport Geography*, 12(2), 127–140.

Guagliardo, M.F. (2004). Spatial accessibility of primary care: concepts, methods and challenges. *International Journal of Health Geographics*, 3(3), 1–13.

Hickman, R., Lopez, N., Cao, M., Lira, B.M. and Biona, J.B.M. (2018). "I drive outside of peak time to avoid traffic jams – public transport is not attractive here." Challenging Discourses on Travel to the University Campus in Manila. *Sustainability*, 10, 1462.

Japan International Cooperation Agency (JICA), Department of Transportation and Communications (DOTC). (2015). *Metro Manila Urban Transportation Integration Study Update and Enhancement Project (MUCEP). Technical Report: Transportation Demand Characteristics.*

Luo, R. and Shen, Y. (2009). The design and implementation of public bike information system based on Google Maps. In *Proceedings of 2009 International Conference on Environmental Science and Information Application Technology*, 156–159.

Neutens, T. (2015). Accessibility, equity and health care: review and research directions for transport geographers. *Journal of Transport Geography*, 43, 14–27.

Okafor, F.C. (1990). The spatial dimensions of accessibility to general hospitals in rural Nigeria. *Socio-Economic Planning Sciences*, 24(4), 295–306.

Páez, A., Moniruzzaman, M., Bourbonnais, P.L. and Morency, C. (2013). Developing a web-based accessibility calculator prototype for the Greater Montreal area. *Transportation Research Part A: Policy and Practice*, 58, 103–115.

Pereira, R.H.M., Schwanen, T. and Banister, D. (2017). Distributive justice and equity in transportation. *Transport Reviews*, 37(2), 170–191.

Santos, L., Coutinho-Rodrigues, J. and Antunes, C.H. (2011). A web spatial decision support system for vehicle routing using Google Maps. *Decision Support Systems*, 51, 1–9.

Sheppard, E., Leitner, H. and Maringanti, A. (2013). Provincializing global urbanism: a manifesto. *Urban Geography*, 34(7), 893–900.

Vasconcellos, E.A. (2013). *Urban Transport Environment and Equity: The Case for Developing Countries.* New York, Earthscan Publications.

Wang, F. (2012). Measurement, optimization, and impact of health care accessibility: a methodological review. *Annals of the Association of American Geographers*, 102(5), 1104–1112.

Wang, F. and Xu, Y. (2011). Estimating O-D travel time matrix by Google Maps API: implementation, advantages, and implications. *Annals of GIS*, 17(4), 199–209.

# 11. Working women and unequal mobilities in the urban periphery
## Eda Beyazit and Ceyda Sungur

## 1. INTRODUCTION

The urban periphery is often put as a counter argument to what constitutes the urban. Defined as the urban edge, urban fringe, urban ring or even the anti-city and non-city, 'the periphery is a historical and continually changing formation, not linked to any specific distances/measurements' (Foot, 2000, p.8). Istanbul has always been a destination for labour migration and forced dislocation, which shaped the urban dichotomy of core and periphery. Moreover, following the rise of urban development projects and decentralisation in Istanbul, the restructuring processes of the inner city caused a pervasive displacement of the working class from the core (Islam, 2005; Gündoğdu and Gough, 2009; Koçak, 2011). This economic, demographic, cultural and spatial restructuring formed diverse relations of centre and periphery. Depending on the household structure as well as economic level of families and preferences, parallel with the formation of a 'new gentry', the urban centre is no longer the best option for many. On the contrary, it is the periphery where the majority of the urban population increasingly live. While the core loses its residents leading to negative growth rates, peripheral areas grow exponentially in cities (Donoghue, 2014). Although it is by and large the urban poor living in the urban periphery due to its affordability, the periphery is also home to many who do not prefer urban lifestyles but more of the amenities the periphery has to offer, such as spacious houses, security, parks and recreational facilities. In this sense, it does not come as a surprise that new investments are being made more increasingly in the urban periphery by the private sector as well as governments, especially in emerging economies.[1] Moreover, new regulatory frameworks make this transition much easier. However, academic debates lack comprehensive analysis of what is really going on in urban peripheral areas (Basten, 2004; Dembski et al., 2017). Therefore, there is a necessity to move our focus to the urban periphery if we are to understand the future of cities (Foot, 2000).

By empirically exploring the wider definitions of the periphery in Istanbul, this chapter focuses on gendered mobilities in the urban periphery. It aims to explore the impact of the socio-spatial organisation of cities on gender, employment and mobility and discuss whether it is the gendered roles and/or living in the urban periphery which constitutes a constraint on women's daily mobilities. As the 'urban' becomes more 'peripheralised' due to continuously changing dynamics of residential mobility, this chapter asks whether gender gains a more substantial role in defining daily mobilities. It is informed by the findings of a study conducted with female domestic workers in Istanbul who experienced

---

[1]  For example in Istanbul the 3rd Bridge, 3rd airport, Canal Istanbul projects pronounced in the last 5 years aim to open new settlement areas in the periphery.

socio-spatial injustices due to lack of transport services where they live, which is often the urban periphery (Beyazit et al., 2016).

An increasing volume of the transport studies literature is devoted to gender and mobility especially in the last two decades. In fact, gender has been one of the most researched areas in transport research in understanding inequalities generated by transport systems and policies as well as other social, economic and demographic factors (e.g. Hanson and Johnston, 1985; Grieco et al., 1989; Hanson and Pratt, 1995; McLafferty and Preston, 1997; Law, 1999; Dobbs, 2007; Uteng and Cresswell, 2008; Uteng, 2009). Yet, since daily mobilities are continuously being reconstructed by the relations of power, interwoven with the relations of gender, class, ethnicity and labour, urban geography needs to adopt interdisciplinary and dynamic lenses that put working women in the centre of analysis.

Long and flexible working hours combined with work–home travel time between centre and periphery increases women's time cost of being in the labour market. Therefore, working becomes a major obstacle to fulfilling household responsibilities burdened on women in patriarchal societies (Özer, 2017; Ilkkaracan, 2010). Consequently, women's everyday mobilities remain as a medium of time and space adjustment to reconfigure their work and life balance in urban space. Investigating the relations of class, gender and everyday mobilities between home and work would help transect the socio-spatial inequalities constructed by the dialectics of centre and periphery. In that sense the geography of the ever-sprawling city of Istanbul, where life and work precarity force its women workers to be more mobile, becomes a fertile ground to explore the construction of the gendered and classed nature of everyday mobilities.

Focusing on women's oppression under the intertwined forces of capitalism and patriarchy as well as the invisibility and triviality of female labour, the study on mobility practices of female domestic workers revealed similarities with the existing literature on gender, mobility and inequalities (Beyazit et al., 2016). Yet, it also demonstrated how the narratives of female domestic workers were built not only on gendered power hierarchies, as Uteng and Cresswell (2008) pointed out, but also on class distinctions due to the nature of their work and the ways in which they travel to and from work. Therefore, it is seen that class persists to be an important determinant of gendered mobilities (Hanson and Pratt, 1995).

By building on the previous scholarly work and using household travel surveys conducted in 2012, this chapter aims to critically discuss the impacts of transport network in Istanbul on the 'peripheralization of the periphery' (Hall and Tewdwr-Jones, 2011) by contributing to the spatial entrapment of women.

## 2.   GENDERED MOBILITIES IN THE PERIPHERY

Unequal wages, a world-wide phenomenon nesting in the heart of gender equalities so as in transport inequalities (Rosenbloom, 2006), alongside patriarchal societal and household structures (Limtanakool et al., 2006; Adetunji, 2013) and men's dominance in transport (Venter et al., 2007; Naess, 2008; Salon and Gulyani, 2010; Duchène, 2011) confine women's daily mobilities within close proximity to their residential places (Hanson and Pratt, 1995; Naess, 2008; Salon and Gulyani, 2010) and even within their homes. Transport studies present rich and voluminous debates on gendered mobilities, drawing attention to relationships between residential–work location choice, travel mode choice and women's daily practices of commuting. Yet, to a great extent, these studies take time and/or distance to local amenities as main factors affecting gendered accessibility. However, distance (and/or travel time) is only one of the dimensions of what makes the periphery, and if taken solely presents a dull, shallow and simple definition of it. As Foot (2000) states 'the peripheral nature of the space is no longer linked in any way with a sense of spatial isolation or distance' (p. 10). Therefore, there is a need to deepen our knowledge on the urban–periphery divide by adopting an interdisciplinary perspective involving historical, anthropological, political, social and economic debates if we are to understand its relationship with gendered mobilities.

## 3. 'PLURAL PERIPHERIES' OF ISTANBUL

Defining the periphery of Istanbul is a highly complicated task. The complex, ever-so-changing macroform of the city with its polycentric employment structure (Alpkokin et al., 2008) and increasing residential density further from the downtown area, due to new developments, changing travel patterns between and within the two parts of the city, requires different parameters to be considered together.

From a historical perspective, the formation of the periphery in Istanbul begins following the Second World War. Tezer (2004) demonstrates that the built-up areas in Istanbul were confined within the historical centre, a few surrounding districts and settlements around the Bosphorus Strait by the early 1950s. As the sprawl accelerated with increasing population and decentralisation (Güvenç, 1993), the city grew towards its edges to include former squatter areas and villages within its borders. Terzi and Kaya (2011) discussed that low-density spatial development dominated the periphery of the city until 1995 with some neighbourhoods becoming denser and more compact from 1980s onwards (Terzi and Bolen, 2009). As Istanbul's spatial growth continuously absorbed its periphery (Aysu, 2002; Pérouse, 2011), it was no longer accurate to associate the periphery merely with squatter and illegal settlements (e.g. Erman and Eken, 2004). More 'modernist' projects followed in the 1990s (Aksoy and Robins, 1997) and in a more structured and planned form accompanied with the state's neoliberal agenda after 2000s (Aksoy, 2014). According to Keleş (2003) the centre and the periphery in Turkish cities have had both a spatial and a socio-cultural content directed by urban and national politics.

However, many scholars refrain from drawing clear lines pointing out the periphery of the city. This is partly due to the lack of comprehensive research regarding Istanbul's periphery (Pérouse, 2011; Logie and Morvan, 2014), although partial empirical work focusing on certain neighbourhoods or districts in Istanbul presents a thorough narration of peripheral areas in Istanbul (Erder, 1996; Işık and Pinarcioglu, 2001; Aslan, 2004; Türkün, 2014; Logie and Morvan, 2014). Despite lack of a holistic approach to Istanbul's periphery, scholars actually agree on the definition of the urban core as the space where global flows generate by all means (Tekeli, 2001; Keyder, 2014). Therefore, spatial development of the city throughout the history along with changes in residential and employment densities in relation to polycentricity have been taken as key criteria in understanding the core–periphery dichotomy as well as understanding the city in a more holistic manner.

As Keyder (ibid.) points out, urban flows can only be understood fully if only the urban core is evaluated with its hinterland, i.e. the periphery.

In order to define and map our units of analysis, we took inspiration from previous studies focusing on gendered patterns of labour in the city (Güvenç, 2009; Dedeoglu, 2008; 2014). While almost all sectors are male dominated in Istanbul, the manufacturing sector, located outside the historical core and in low income neighbourhoods, is mainly dominated by women workers (ibid.). Moreover, we reviewed the role of the transport network on the spatial growth of the city, which is likely to continue to sprawl towards North as well as East–West directions (Tezer, 2004; Ayazli et al., 2015). The road network in Istanbul is much denser in the south of the Trans-European Motorway (TEM) compared to other areas in the city. This is where also the majority of rail transit and bus rapid transit (BRT – Metrobus) investments have been made increasingly in the last decade and continuing as a part of a 6-year plan aiming at year 2023 with a motto: 'Metro everywhere'.

Existing literature on the geography of urban transformation in Istanbul presented another area to be investigated in order to define the urban periphery. Previous research points out the ways in which transformation processes take different forms in the city in relation to its changing socio-spatial and economic characteristics (Yalçıntan et al., 2014). As a result of the unequal development policies, urban sprawl continues uncontrollably towards Northern forests, wetlands and natural conservation sites by filling up the land in-between existing settlement areas and new development zones where the Third Bridge[2] and the Third Airport[3] have been planned to act as catalysts to this growth, along with previous regulations on the renewal of squatter areas, historical centres and earthquake-risk zones. It is mainly the low-income neighbourhoods where urban transformation projects are implemented while luxurious residential projects emerge in core areas and along the corridors by the highways and junctions of Istanbul (ibid.).

Drawing on the existing scholarly work that deepens our understanding of the core–periphery division in Istanbul, we have identified six zones with different characteristics which juxtapose with stratified class characteristics of the inhabitants and the historical development of the city (Figure 11.1). However, it should be noted that such stratification is solely done for the purposes of the analysis carried out in this chapter. Considering its polycentric structure, yet, also the perpetual existence of a powerful, large centre extending to three small peninsulas, these borders are less defined and often blurred in Istanbul, like in other cities with a similar historical, cultural and economic background.

The first zone is the historical urban core that all the aforementioned scholars have agreed upon; the second zone represents the historical sprawl of the first zone; the third zone is the transition or the peri-urban zone that carries limited characteristics of the core, such as historical and cultural amenities along the Bosphorus Strait and historical centres along the Marmara Sea; the fourth and the fifth zones are defined as the urban periphery where public transport infrastructure is insufficient. The former is composed of areas that are under threat of urban transformation, squatter settlements and low-income neighbourhoods, while the latter is composed of wealthy neighbourhoods with gated community settlements (partially based on Yalcintan et al., 2014 and authors' own

---

[2]  Opened in August, 2016.
[3]  Opened in October, 2018.

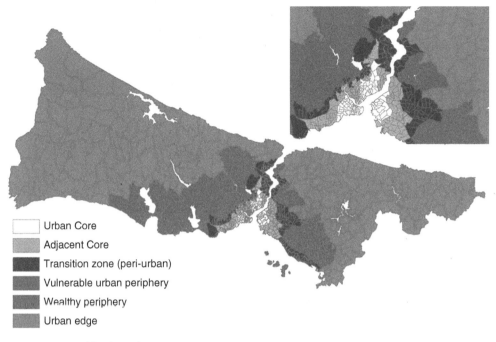

Urban Core

Adjacent Core

Transition zone (peri-urban)

Vulnerable urban periphery

Wealthy periphery

Urban edge

*Source:*   Prepared by the authors.

*Figure 11.1   Istanbul's peripheries*

evaluations). This approach, i.e. describing the periphery as vulnerable/poor versus gated/ wealthy is also proposed by Pérouse (2011). The sixth category includes areas that are further from the core of Istanbul, with rural characteristics and/or more connections with surrounding villages and cities than Istanbul. In this sense, our definition of the urban periphery is in line with Foot (2000), who urges the plurality of the term.

## 4.   ANALYSIS AND RESULTS

The initial analysis in this chapter involved a description of zones. Based on this definition, the second part takes a quantitative approach. Transport Household Surveys conducted in 2012 by the Istanbul Municipality are analysed to see whether gender comes across as a factor identifying the daily mobility practices of residents in urban peripheries. A random selection of a sample of 6,575 travel diaries was obtained from the Istanbul Metropolitan Municipality. After eliminating non-home-based trips and individuals below 15 years of age, we ended up with 4,429 trips completed by different individuals. Table 11.1 demonstrates the socio-economic characteristics of survey respondents based on their location of residence.

Table 11.1 confirms how the urban–periphery divide in Istanbul falls in line with the socio-economic stratification of the survey population. Employment comes across as a key component of living in the periphery, especially for women. In 2012, the female labour

*Table 11.1  Household surveys sample typology, 2012*

| | | Urban Core | | Adjacent Core | | Peri-urban | | Vulnerable Periphery | | Wealthy Periphery | | Urban Edge | |
|---|---|---|---|---|---|---|---|---|---|---|---|---|---|
| | | Count | Average | Count | Average | Count | Average | Count | Average | Count | Average | Count | Average |
| Sex | Female | 269 | 46 | 326 | 43 | 517 | 45 | 979 | 44 | 83 | 49 | 136 | 38 |
| | Male | 310 | 54 | 428 | 57 | 640 | 55 | 1261 | 56 | 86 | 51 | 219 | 62 |
| | Total | 579 | 100 | 754 | 100 | 1157 | 100 | 2240 | 100 | 169 | 100 | 355 | 100 |
| Employment | Employed women | 96 | 38 | 89 | 30 | 115 | 26 | 181 | 22 | 15 | 25 | 25 | 22 |
| | Unemployed women | 154 | 62 | 211 | 70 | 333 | 74 | 638 | 78 | 44 | 75 | 87 | 78 |
| | Total | 250 | 100 | 300 | 100 | 448 | 100 | 819 | 100 | 59 | 100 | 112 | 100 |
| | Employed men | 191 | 65 | 256 | 65 | 363 | 64 | 689 | 65 | 46 | 62 | 125 | 65 |
| | Unemployed men | 103 | 35 | 140 | 35 | 207 | 36 | 372 | 35 | 28 | 38 | 68 | 35 |
| | Total | 294 | 100 | 396 | 100 | 570 | 100 | 1061 | 100 | 74 | 100 | 193 | 100 |
| Employment skill levels | Women in skilled jobs | 62 | 67 | 53 | 60 | 64 | 56 | 72 | 41 | 4 | 27 | 11 | 44 |
| | Women in unskilled jobs | 31 | 33 | 36 | 40 | 50 | 44 | 105 | 59 | 11 | 73 | 14 | 56 |
| | Total | 93 | 100 | 89 | 100 | 114 | 100 | 177 | 100 | 15 | 100 | 25 | 100 |
| | Men in skilled jobs | 87 | 46 | 120 | 48 | 146 | 41 | 223 | 33 | 18 | 40 | 42 | 34 |
| | Men in unskilled jobs | 102 | 54 | 131 | 52 | 208 | 59 | 462 | 67 | 27 | 60 | 81 | 66 |
| | Total | 189 | 100 | 251 | 100 | 354 | 100 | 685 | 100 | 45 | 100 | 123 | 100 |
| Education | No schooling | 30 | 6 | 66 | 10 | 106 | 11 | 284 | 16 | 11 | 8 | 27 | 9 |
| | Mandatory education | 239 | 45 | 329 | 49 | 540 | 55 | 1085 | 60 | 82 | 63 | 188 | 63 |
| | High School | 131 | 25 | 161 | 24 | 219 | 22 | 276 | 15 | 22 | 17 | 57 | 19 |
| | University and above | 133 | 25 | 114 | 17 | 125 | 13 | 155 | 9 | 16 | 12 | 25 | 8 |
| | Total | 533 | 100 | 670 | 100 | 990 | 100 | 1800 | 100 | 131 | 100 | 297 | 100 |

| | 1 | | 2 | | 3 | | 4 | | 5 | | 6 | |
|---|---|---|---|---|---|---|---|---|---|---|---|---|
| | n | % | n | % | n | % | n | % | n | % | n | % |
| **Driving licence** | | | | | | | | | | | | |
| Women with DL | 97 | **43** | 91 | **36** | 109 | **30** | 122 | **19** | 18 | **38** | 20 | **24** |
| Women without DL | 129 | 57 | 162 | 64 | 258 | 70 | 507 | 81 | 30 | 63 | 64 | 76 |
| Total | 226 | 100 | 253 | 100 | 367 | 100 | 629 | 100 | 48 | 100 | 84 | 100 |
| Men with DL | 177 | 68 | 257 | 76 | 366 | 75 | 585 | 68 | 49 | 79 | 117 | 70 |
| Men without DL | 85 | 32 | 82 | 24 | 119 | 25 | 278 | 32 | 13 | 21 | 49 | 30 |
| Total | 262 | 100 | 339 | 100 | 485 | 100 | 863 | 100 | 62 | 100 | 166 | 100 |
| **Household composition** | | | | | | | | | | | | |
| Household size (mean) | 3.6 | | 3.8 | | 4.0 | | 4.3 | | 4.3 | | 4.1 | |
| **Income parameters** | | | | | | | | | | | | |
| Home owner | 296 | 56 | 395 | 59 | 597 | 60 | 1047 | 58 | 82 | 63 | 181 | 61 |
| Tenant or state residence | 235 | 44 | 276 | 41 | 395 | 40 | 745 | 42 | 48 | 37 | 116 | 39 |
| Total | 531 | 100 | 671 | 100 | 992 | 100 | 1792 | 100 | 130 | 100 | 297 | 100 |
| Rent (avg.paid) (2012 TL) | 635 | | 575 | | 577 | | 448 | | 487 | | 426 | |
| One or more cars | 404 | 70 | 446 | 59 | 717 | 62 | 1513 | 68 | 104 | 62 | 226 | 64 |
| No cars | 175 | 30 | 308 | 41 | 440 | 38 | 727 | 32 | 65 | 38 | 129 | 36 |
| Total | 579 | 100 | 754 | 100 | 1157 | 100 | 2240 | 100 | 169 | 100 | 355 | 100 |

participation rate in Turkey was calculated as 29.5 per cent, while for men it was 71 per cent (TUIK, 2013). In the urban core and adjacent core, the female labour participation rate is above the country average, while it is below this level in peri-urban areas, the vulnerable periphery, wealthy periphery and the urban edge. Although male labour participation is below the country average in all areas, ratios are almost the same throughout Istanbul. Another key point is the ratio of women and men in skilled and unskilled jobs. When employment skills are assessed in relation to the core–periphery divide, based on the jobs specified by survey respondents, it is seen that women in skilled jobs mostly reside in the core and adjacent core, while the ratio of women in skilled jobs drops as we move towards peripheral areas. This situation fluctuates for men; yet, the majority of men in unskilled jobs reside in the vulnerable periphery.

The residential location of skilled and unskilled population also corresponds with the education levels. The population in core areas demonstrates higher education levels compared to peripheral areas. Driving licence holders also present a gendered residential pattern. The proportion of females holding a driving licence drops as we move away from core areas while ratios fluctuate for their male counterparts. Based on the available data, other characteristics of the core–periphery division are household size and income parameters. According to these, household size gets larger away from the core, an indicator of small-size families residing in central areas. Also, house rents drop and homeownership increases towards the periphery. Moreover, car ownership is almost similar in the urban core and the vulnerable periphery without any information on the model/year of the cars owned. Almost steady ratios of car owners in all zones compared to decreasing ratios of women licence holders are evident as we move away from the core. This reflects patriarchal relationships in households where the man is the main user of the family car (Naess, 2008), especially in the periphery. Overall, gender differences are found to be greater as we move from the core to peripheral areas.

In order to respond to the questions posed in this chapter, the next sections involve a series of tests on selected transport and social parameters. The data set used is not as large as the original city-wide surveys and, therefore, it does not have a normal distribution which is a requirement for parametric tests (Healey, 1996). Thus, travel diaries have been analysed by using non-parametric tests: Mann-Whitney test for two-sample cases and Kruskal-Wallis test for cases with more than two samples. Both tests are based on a ranking of the median scores. Moreover, chi-square testing was used in order to understand the relationship between categorical variables such as transport mode. Chi-square testing does not provide information on whether the relationship is positive or negative, but it helps to demonstrate the strength of the relationship between variables. Therefore, it is to some extent explanatory.

At the aggregate level, men have statistically longer travel times compared to women in Istanbul (median$=30/20$; mean$=35/28$, $p<0.05$). They tend to travel longer distances (50 per cent); drive (23 per cent) and use public transport (32 per cent) more than women who tend to walk extensively (52 per cent). Such results indicate the geographical confinement of women in Istanbul, similar to other cities, a phenomenon widely discussed as a consequence of the 'traditional assignment of gender roles' (Noack, 2010, p.90). This chapter takes this argument further by investigating the impacts of the core–periphery divide on gendered mobilities, as accessibility and transport are found to be important determinants of participation to daily life, especially in rural areas (Belton-Chevallier et al., 2018). Previously, employment and education have been found to be the key criteria producing gendered travel patterns in Istanbul (Beyazit, 2013). Therefore, in our analysis we use employment, occupation and education levels as key socio-economic criteria, while travel time, mode choice and commuting distance are taken as mobility parameters.

## 4.1 Commuting Time

As seen in Table 11.2, average commuting time is slightly higher for men than women in all zones. Yet, differences are not statistically significant. However, results vary when average commuting time is analysed by occupation and education. Although no gender-bias has been found between workers in skilled and unskilled jobs in all zones, the fourth zone, which is the vulnerable periphery, reveals interesting results. In the vulnerable periphery, women workers in unskilled jobs spend less time travelling (avg. 26min, median 20min) than their male counterparts (avg. 35min, median 30min) ($p<0.05$). This result coincides with the sector-labour dependent location choice in Istanbul. According to Dedeoglu (2014) the ready-made clothing sector in Istanbul is strategically located in areas where under-educated, low-income women reside in large numbers. Women working in these small to large scale factories either walk if their workplaces are close to their homes, or take company services provided by these firms. Some even work from their homes where firms, sometimes their relatives, bring them clothing materials to work on (ibid.). A pool of women workers attracts certain sectors, in this case the manufacturing sector, to the surroundings of their residential areas which in turn produce concentrations of women working in unskilled, sex-segregated, low-wage occupations. In this sense, we see travel time as an important parameter demonstrating increased immobility levels for women in the periphery.

When commuting time for women and men working in different occupations are compared within the same gender groups, it is found that women workers in unskilled jobs spend significantly less time than women workers in skilled jobs for commuting in all zones, except in the wealthy periphery where the commute times do not have significant differences between men and women. For men, significant differences are found in only the adjacent core (nine minutes) and the vulnerable periphery (12min). In zones one to four, the difference in commuting time between women in skilled and unskilled jobs is 11 to 16 minutes, while in the urban edge the difference is 23 minutes on average, making workers in skilled jobs more mobile. Travel time is significantly lower for men and women living in the periphery and working in unskilled jobs. Yet, working in unskilled jobs is far more defining for women in all zones, as working in skilled jobs may reduce the risks of geographical confinement. Therefore, class (captured here in terms of working in skilled jobs and being highly educated) becomes a distinctive element regarding women's mobility. Previous research has shown that gaining new skills is likely to open up a larger job market for women (see for example, Dominguez and Watkins, 2003).

Regardless of zones, education is an important criterion defining the travel time. As education level increases travel time increases, therefore, individuals with higher-education profiles spend longer 'spatially-mobile time' and have increased likelihood of travelling further for work (Salon and Gulyani, 2010). Yet, when commuting time of women workers is compared according to their education levels, the only significance found is in the 'vulnerable periphery' where the travel time increases as a result of higher education levels,

Table 11.2  *Average travel time for employed population*

| | | Core | | Adjacent Core | | Transition Zone | | Vulnerable Periphery | | Wealthy Periphery | | Urban Edge | |
|---|---|---|---|---|---|---|---|---|---|---|---|---|---|
| | | Male | Female | Male | Female | Male | Female | Male | Female | Male | Female | Male | Female |
| Travel time (minutes) | | 44 | 42 | 40 | 38 | 37 | 40 | 37 | 33 | 35 | 30 | 39 | 39 |
| Occupation | Skilled | 46 | 47 | 45 | 44 | 40 | 45 | 43 | 42 | 33 | 27 | 38 | 52 |
| | Unskilled | 43 | 31 | 36 | 30 | 35 | 34 | 35 | 26 | 36 | 31 | 39 | 29 |
| Education | Primary | 44 | 38 | 35 | 31 | 37 | 36 | 35 | 26 | 27 | 29 | 41 | 30 |
| | High School | 40 | 42 | 47 | 40 | 34 | 45 | 43 | 35 | 54 | 60 | 34 | 34 |
| | University | 49 | 45 | 44 | 45 | 30 | 44 | 46 | 46 | 28 | 25 | 43 | 54 |

*Note:* 'o' statistically significant difference between different gender groups; '-' statistically significant difference among the same gender group i.e. working women with primary school education have lower commuting time on average than women with higher education whose commuting time is also lower than women with university education (26<35<46 avg. minutes, respectively, p<0.05). Similar to the results seen in the comparison between workers in skilled and unskilled jobs, education tends to be an important criterion for accessing a larger job market where certain skills are required. Actually, education is an important factor for accessing skilled jobs for women in Turkey. When primary school graduation is sufficient for men to find jobs, women would need more skills to be employed (Dayioglu and Kirdar, 2010). Moreover, in the 'vulnerable periphery', education seems to be an important determinant of travel time amongst employed men as well. Men who have completed primary education tend to spend longer time travelling compared to women with the same education levels (26<35, p<0.05). Therefore, the gender gap persists regardless of education levels (ibid.) However, since there is no significant difference in travel time between employed men and women of higher education levels, education is also explanatory to some extent.

## 4.2   Commuting Mode

Commuting mode is an important determinant of gendered mobilities. Women tend to use public transport more compared to men who are more likely to drive (e.g. Rosenbloom, 2006; Schaffer and Schulz, 2008; Prashker et al., 2008; Elias and Shiftan, 2014). Aggregate data on commute modes explains gendered modes of transport to some extent. In Istanbul, 27 per cent of employed men tend to travel by motorised private transport (private car, taxi[4] and motorbike) while only 16 per cent of women commute using similar modes. On the contrary, while 23 per cent of employed women commute using company services,[5] only 15 per cent of employed men tend to use these services. Ratios regarding the use of public transport modes and walking to work are similar for men and women. Thus, when the working population is analysed all together, travelling solo seems to have a masculine pattern, while collective transport by company cars is dominated by female workers. This can be explained partly due to the comfort and security of company cars as opposed to public transport when access to car is limited either due to male dominance and/or low-income levels (i.e. the wage gap).

Disaggregating the data by the core–periphery divide increases the variety in results (Table 11.3). In the core and the adjacent core, the choice of transport modes by employed men and women does not hold significant relationships (p>0.05). Yet, in the transition zone and the vulnerable periphery, significant relationships are found between gender and the choice of commuting mode. In the former, while 30 per cent of employed men tend to drive to work only 17 per cent of employed women have access to car. Employed women tend to use company shuttles more than men (26 per cent > 15 per cent) as well as informal transport (17 per cent > 11 per cent) while men tend to use public transport more. While the use of company shuttles can be explained due to the comfort and security

---

[4]   Only 28 out of 2183 respondents mentioned the use of taxis to work while there were only 7 motorbike users.

[5]   Minibuses provided by employers that pick up employees from predetermined locations or their residences.

Table 11.3  *Commuting modes of employed population*

| | | Core | | Adjacent Core | | Transition Zone | | Vulnerable Periphery | | Wealthy Periphery | | Urban Edge | |
|---|---|---|---|---|---|---|---|---|---|---|---|---|---|
| | | Male | Female | Male | Female | Male | Female | Male | Female | Male | Female | Male | Female |
| Transport mode (percentages) | walking | 23 | 23 | 26 | 22 | 23 | 24 | (29) | (38) | 13 | 20▲ | 18 | 24 |
| | motorised private transport | 23 | 20 | 28 | 16 | (30) | (17) | (23) | (11) | 43▲ | 40▲ | 36 | 24 |
| | company shuttle | 6 | 11 | 9 | 15 | (15) | (26) | (18) | (28) | 17 | 27 | 25 | 36 |
| | formal public transport | 42▲ | 41▲ | 27▲ | 34▲ | (20)▲ | (17)▲ | 15▼ | 11▶ | 13▶ | 7▶ | 10▶ | 8▶ |
| | informal public transport | 6 | 5 | 11 | 13 | 11 | 17 | 15 | 12 | 13 | 7 | 11 | 8 |
| Unskilled | walking | 26 | 39 | 33 | 31 | 23 | 34 | (34) | (51) | 11 | 18 | 18 | 36 |
| | motorised private transport | 24 | 13 | 26 | 17 | 31 | 8 | (21) | (1) | 33 | 36 | 38 | 14 |
| | company shuttle | 8 | 3 | 8 | 11 | 17 | 26 | (16) | (31) | 22 | 27 | 24 | 36 |
| | formal public transport | 36 | 42 | 24 | 25 | 18 | 12 | (12) | (5) | 15 | 9 | 13 | 7 |
| | informal public transport | 6 | 3 | 9 | 17 | 10 | 20 | (17) | (12) | 19 | 9 | 9 | 7 |
| Skilled | walking | 17 | 16 | 18 | 17 | 23 | 17 | 18 | 19 | 17 | 25 | 20 | 9 |
| | motorised private transport | 22 | 24 | 31 | 15 | 29 | 23 | 28 | 25 | 56 | 50 | 34 | 36 |
| | company shuttle | 5 | 15 | 10 | 17 | 12 | 27 | 21 | 24 | 11 | 25 | 27 | 36 |
| | formal public transport | 49 | 39 | 29 | 40 | 23 | 20 | 20 | 18 | 11 | 0 | 5 | 9 |
| | informal public transport | 7 | 6 | 12 | 11 | 12 | 13 | 13 | 14 | 6 | 0 | 15 | 9 |

158

| | | | | | | | | | | | | | |
|---|---|---|---|---|---|---|---|---|---|---|---|---|---|
| primary | walking | 25 | 53 | 36 | 44 | 22 | 36 | **33** | **54** | 19 | 22 | 23 | 33 |
| | motorised private transport | 25 | 6 | 24 | 8 | 28 | 7 | **17** | **4** | 27 | 22 | 29 | 11 |
| | company shuttle | 9 | 0 | 8 | 4 | 15 | 20 | **18** | **24** | 19 | 44 | 24 | 44 |
| | formal public transport | 38 | 35 | 21 | 28 | 21 | 11 | **14** | **5** | 15 | 0 | 13 | 0 |
| | informal public transport | 3 | 6 | 11 | 16 | 14 | 27 | 18 | _14_ | 19 | 11 | 10 | 11 |
| high school | walking | 31 | 22 | 14 | 12 | 28 | 19 | 19 | _28_ | 8 | 0 | 13 | 25 |
| | motorised private transport | 11 | 15 | 27 | 15 | 31 | 13 | 36 | _9_ | 58 | 0 | 35 | 13 |
| | company shuttle | 4 | 11 | 9 | 19 | 18 | 44 | 19 | 30 | 8 | 0 | 32 | 50 |
| | formal public transport | 38 | 48 | 41 | 38 | 17 | 13 | 15 | _12_ | 17 | 100 | 3 | 0 |
| | informal public transport | 16 | 4 | 9 | 15 | 6 | 13 | 12 | _21_ | 8 | 0 | 16 | 13 |
| university | walking | 10 | 12 | 12 | 15 | 18 | 12 | 12 | _17_ | 0 | 20 | 0 | 13 |
| | motorised private transport | 32 | 29 | 43 | 18 | 42 | 32 | 42 | _29_ | 86 | 80 | 77 | 50 |
| | company shuttle | 2 | 14 | 10 | 18 | 10 | 18 | 15 | _31_ | 14 | 0 | 8 | 13 |
| | formal public transport | 52 | 39 | 23 | 38 | 22 | 29 | 24 | _21_ | 0 | 0 | 8 | 25 |
| | informal public transport | 4 | 6 | 12 | 12 | 8 | 9 | 7 | _2_ | 0 | 0 | 8 | 0 |

*Notes:*
'o' statistically significant difference between different gender groups
'‗' statistically significant difference among the same gender group
▲ indicates significant differences between zones regardless of gender (pointing at accessibility of transport services)

they provide, the reasons for the use of informal transport by women are likely to be the flexibility of these services (also of company services), as women's travel patterns are likely to involve multiple chain trips (e.g. Turner and Grieco, 2000), and also the affordability of these services.

An expected finding is on the relationship between modes and zones. For both men and women, the use of formal public transport is significantly higher in the core and the adjacent core, compared to other zones, giving indication about the accessibility of public transport services in the centre of the city. Peripheral areas are often associated with poor and inadequate public transport (Turner and Fouracre, 1995; Sohail et al., 2003; Venter et al., 2007). Not surprisingly, the use of motorised private transport is higher in the wealthy periphery.

In the vulnerable periphery, employed women tend to walk to work (38 per cent) more than men (29 per cent) who drive to a larger extent (23 per cent > 11 per cent). When combined with the results on low commuting times of women in the same zone, this finding also supports the argument on the geographical confinement of women in the vulnerable periphery. Walking as the main mode of transport and shorter travel times are consequences of a limited job market for women living in the vulnerable periphery. Here, women also tend to use company shuttles (28 per cent) more compared to employed men who use public transport widely (30 per cent).

No significant relationship has been found between choice of transport modes based on residential location amongst men and women working in skilled and unskilled jobs, except in the vulnerable periphery where strong relationships are evident. In this sense, women workers in unskilled jobs tend to commute on foot in larger volumes compared to men (51 per cent > 34 per cent respectively) and use company shuttles to a greater extent, while working men in unskilled jobs tend to use public transport and private transport more. This finding deepens our understanding of the spatial entrapment thesis, as it is the women in unskilled jobs who work close to their residential units.

Similarly, when education levels are analysed, further differences are found especially in the vulnerable periphery. Employed men with primary education tend to walk less (33 per cent < 54 per cent), use company shuttles less (18 per cent < 24 per cent) than employed women with similar education levels living in the vulnerable periphery, while women tend to drive less and use public transport more, once again pointing at the role of gender and education in the vulnerable periphery. Moreover, when women living in the vulnerable periphery are compared based on their education levels, it is seen that as education levels increase the tendency to walk decreases and the use of car, company shuttles and public transport increases. This is also in line with the finding on women working in skilled jobs. Working in skilled jobs results in similar commuting patterns as having higher education levels. This highlights the role of class and social capital in accessing a more competitive job market.

### 4.3    Commuting Distance

Distance measure is not directly gathered in household surveys. For this purpose, we categorised the trips according to their origins and destinations. Trips are grouped in three categories, low, medium and long distance, based on whether the trip is done within the neighbourhood borders, within the district or outside the district respectively. According to this, gendered mobilities have been detected for employed men and women only in the vulnerable periphery (Table 11.4).

Table 11.4  *Commuting distance of employed population*

| Distance (percentage) | | | Core | | Adjacent Core | | Transition Zone | | Vulnerable Periphery | | Wealthy Periphery | | Urban Edge | |
|---|---|---|---|---|---|---|---|---|---|---|---|---|---|---|
| | | | Male | Female | Male | Female | Male | Female | Male | Female | Male | Female | Male | Female |
| skilled | low | | 11 | 13 | 16 | 15 | 17 | 17 | 21 | 22 | 17 | 20 | 28 | 20 |
| | medium | | 24 | 22 | 18 | 26 | 32 | 31 | 23 | 36 | 33 | 27 | 23 | 28 |
| | long | | 66 | 66 | 65 | 60 | 52 | 51 | 56 | 42 | 50 | 53 | 48 | 52 |
| | low | | 7 | 6 | 9 | 11 | 13 | 16 | 16 | 13 | 17 | 25 | 24 | 18 |
| | medium | | 18 | 21 | 20 | 23 | 27 | 25 | 19 | 29 | 22 | 0 | 26 | 0 |
| | long | | 75 | 73 | 71 | 66 | 60 | 59 | 65 | 58 | 61 | 75 | 50 | 82 |
| unskilled | low | | 14 | 26 | 23 | 19 | 19 | 20 | 23 | 29 | 19 | 18 | 30 | 21 |
| | medium | | 27 | 26 | 17 | 31 | 34 | 38 | 24 | 40 | 41 | 36 | 22 | 50 |
| | long | | 59 | 48 | 60 | 50 | 47 | 42 | 52 | 31 | 41 | 45 | 48 | 29 |
| primary | low | | 10 | 24 | 21 | 28 | 16 | 24 | 24 | 35 | 31 | 22 | 29 | 22 |
| | medium | | 25 | 35 | 20 | 32 | 34 | 36 | 24 | 36 | 35 | 33 | 27 | 67 |
| | long | | 65 | 41 | 59 | 40 | 50 | 40 | 53 | 29 | 35 | 44 | 44 | 11 |
| high school | low | | 14 | 19 | 11 | 4 | 22 | 13 | 15 | 7 | 0 | 0 | 28 | 13 |
| | medium | | 32 | 15 | 17 | 23 | 33 | 32 | 20 | 44 | 33 | 0 | 16 | 13 |
| | long | | 55 | 65 | 71 | 73 | 45 | 55 | 65 | 49 | 67 | 100 | 56 | 75 |
| university | low | | 8 | 4 | 10 | 12 | 9 | 12 | 10 | 15 | 0 | 20 | 15 | 25 |
| | medium | | 10 | 23 | 17 | 21 | 24 | 24 | 23 | 17 | 33 | 20 | 23 | 0 |
| | long | | 82 | 73 | 73 | 68 | 67 | 55 | 68 | 68 | 67 | 60 | 62 | 75 |

161

In the vulnerable periphery, employed men tend to commute longer distances than employed women, pointing to a more restricted job market for women. Yet, while there is no significant relationship in terms of distance between men and women working in skilled jobs according to their residential location, women workers in unskilled jobs tend to commute to closer locations than men. This finding highlights the impact of gendered roles affecting especially the women working in unskilled jobs in the vulnerable periphery.

In the vulnerable periphery while men and women university graduates show similar patterns in terms of the distance travelled to work place, differences have been found between primary school and high school graduates as employed men travel longer distances than employed women of similar education levels. In other areas such as the urban core, adjacent core, transition zone and the wealthy periphery, no significant difference has been found between travel patterns of employed men and women.

## 5.   CONCLUSIONS

This chapter adopted a centre–periphery lens in order to investigate the commuting patterns of working women in Istanbul. Through our analysis of travel patterns in previously identified centre and peripheral zones in Istanbul, we found out that gendered and class-based disparities not only do exist but also take different forms in the city.

Occupation, education and living in the 'vulnerable periphery' come across as definitive motives of travel time, mode choice and commuting distance. In this sense, women workers in unskilled jobs spend less time commuting than both working men in unskilled jobs and working women in skilled jobs, especially in the vulnerable periphery. They are also more likely to walk if they are living in these areas as opposed to their women counterparts living in more central areas of the city where public transport network is denser. Women workers in unskilled jobs also travel shorter distances for work.

Education is the second identifying factor combined with the centre–periphery division. According to our analysis as education levels increase, the ratio of walking as the primary mode decreases as access to private motorised transport and public transport increase as well as the use of company shuttles. This pattern is observed especially among women living in the vulnerable periphery.

Building on the existing literature on women's spatial entrapment, our analysis revealed that under-educated women workers in unskilled jobs who live in the vulnerable periphery are more likely to be subject to unequal mobilities compared to their working-class counterparts in either gender groups. They are highly exposed to inequalities regarding access to the job market, transport services and the use of urban space. Yet, in the central areas of the city such inequalities are negligible. Therefore, class and gender-based mobilities are more of a characteristic of the periphery – in our case, the 'vulnerable periphery'. We arrived at the conclusion that women with low education levels, working in unskilled jobs and residing in the vulnerable periphery are the most disadvantaged of all groups.

Aside from the findings from household transport surveys, one of our observations regarding the centre–periphery divide is that the similarities between the first, second and the third zones (core, adjacent-core and the transition zone) in terms of mobility patterns may point towards the expansion of the core. The adjacent core and the transition zone 'act' like the core areas of the city in terms of mobilities even though they have a different historical background and urban textures. In this sense, it can be suggested that the core of Istanbul is larger than it was initially thought, an argument worth exploring through an in-depth analysis of socio-spatial and spatio-economic processes in the city in future studies.

The data also has its limitations. Gender studies consider household structure as a crucial component of daily life within the urban space. However, this information is limited in the household travel surveys. For instance, the marital status (e.g. being a single mother) is one important variable we could not retrieve from the surveys. This is a consequence of gender-blind transport policy. Single mothers have different life struggles, which take place in different urban scales, and lack of access to the transport system might become more of a burden for them. Therefore, changing household structures need to be considered in travel surveys. Moreover, understanding women's networks, e.g. the type of social networks for finding jobs and/or for finding day care for children could help defining women's relationship with the urban and transport space. Further research could be designed to uncover this information, along with other dimensions that accompany mobility gaps in women's access to more opportunities. Qualitative research would fulfil this gap by providing an in-depth understanding of the combination of factors that lead to unequal mobilities and diminished levels of participation to urban life.

Another area for future studies is the investigation of not only horizontal but also vertical mobility inequalities in the city. Studies investigating gendered experiences of transition from squatter areas to apartments, due to urban transformation processes led by city authorities and central governments, highlight the importance of access to the street level for women. For instance, Erman (2014) points out that for women who used to live in gecekondu (squatter) settlements in Ankara, 'going out' no longer meant 'going outside the door' but 'going down the stairs' when they moved to state apartments. Thus, we believe that future studies should investigate the urban–periphery transition not only in the horizontal urban space but also in the vertical space in order to understand whether women from vulnerable communities may also become peripheralised due to the changes in the urban form. Moreover, in these new settlements, newly established class identity through new jobs (becoming members of working class via part-time or subcontracted jobs) and/or household responsibilities (becoming middle-class housewives) are likely to affect the daily travel patterns of women. As the labour participation rate is higher for women in Istanbul compared to the rest of the country (İlkkaracan, 2016), how will working class women respond to city's ever-shifting core–periphery divide through their daily gendered and classed negotiations of space and time?

Clearly, development of 'just' transport and urban policies is not the sole solution to women's problems interwoven with patriarchal relationships. Yet, it is an important dimension. If the poor are continuously pushed towards peripheral areas, inequality gaps only become larger. Expansion of affordable transport networks, increasing their spatial, temporal and economic accessibility would reduce the burdens of transport. Affordable housing in core and adjacent-core areas (Belton-Chevallier et al., 2018) along with affordable and accessible child-care facilities would increase the chances of women participating in work life. Last, but not least, government policies targeting equal division of household labour, increasing women's participation in politics and decision-making processes would bring women out of their homes, and 'just' transport and urban policies can pave the road ahead.

# REFERENCES

Adetunji, M. (2013) Gender Travel Behaviour and Women Mobility Constraints in Ilesa, Nigeria. *International Journal for Traffic and Transport Engineering*, 3(2), 220–229.
Aksoy, A. (2014) 'İstanbul'un Neoliberalizmle İmtihanı' in *Yeni İstanbul Çalışmaları Sınırlar, Mücadeleler, Açılımlar*. A. Bartu Candan and C. Özbay (eds) Istanbul: İletişim Yayınları, 27–46.
Aksoy, A. and Robins, K. (1997) Modernism and the Millennium. *City*, 2(8), 21–36.
Alpkokin, P., Cheung, C., Black, J. and Hayashi, Y. (2008) Dynamics of Clustered Employment Growth and its Impacts on Commuting Patterns in Rapidly Developing Cities. *Transportation Research Part A: Policy and Practice*, 42(3), 427–444.
Aslan, Ş. (2004) *1 Mayıs Mahallesi. 1980 Öncesi Toplumsal Mücadeleler ve Kent*. İstanbul: İletişim Yayınları.
Aysu, Ç. (2002) İstanbul Şehrinden Metropoliten İstanbul'a Mahallelerin Mekansal Dağılışı 1950–2001. *İstanbul Dergisi*, 40, 51–58.
Basten, L. (2004) Perceptions of Urban Space in the Periphery: Potsdam's Kirchsteigfeld. *Tijdschrift voor Economische en Sociale Geografie*, 95(1), 89–99.
Belton-Chevallier, L., Motte-Baumvol, B., Fol, S. and Jouffe, Y. (2018) Coping with the Costs of Car Dependency: A System of Expedients Used by Low-Income Households on the Outskirts of Dijon and Paris. *Transport Policy*, 65, 79–88.
Beyazit, E. (2013) Socio-spatial Inequalities and Transport: The Case of the Istanbul Metro. Unpublished PhD thesis, School of Geography and the Environment, University of Oxford.
Beyazit, E., Sungur, C. and Karabatak, İ. (2016) Social Inequalities in Urban Transport: Home–Work Journeys of Female Workers in Istanbul. Final Project Report, TUBITAK: Ankara.
Dedeoglu, S. (2008) *Women Workers in Turkey: Global Industrial Production in Turkey*. London: I.B. Tauris.
Dedeoglu, S. (2014) 'İstanbul'da Mekan, Cinsiyet ve Endüstriyet İstihdam' in *Yeni İstanbul Çalışmaları: Sınırlar, Mücadeleler, Açılımlar*. A.B. Candan and C. Özbay (eds) İstanbul: Metis Yayınları, 198–211.
Dembski, S., Schulze Bäing, A. and Sykes, O. (2017) What About the Urban Periphery? The Effects of the Urban Renaissance in the Mersey Belt. *Comparative Population Studies*, 42, 219–244.
Dobbs, L. (2007) Stuck in the Slow Lane: Reconceptualizing the Links between Gender, Transport and Employment. *Gender, Work and Organization*, 14(2), 85–108.
Domínguez, S. and Watkins, C. (2003) Creating Networks for Survival and Mobility: Social Capital Among African-American and Latin-American Low-Income Mothers. *Social Problems*, 50 (1), 111–135.
Donoghue, D. (2014) *Urban Transformations: Centres, Peripheries and Systems*. Surrey: Ashgate.
Duchène, C. (2011) *Gender and Transport*. Paris: *OECD Discussion Paper*, International Transport Forum, OECD (11).
Elias W. and Shiftan, Y. (2014) Gender Differences in Travel Behavior in The Arab World: Comparison of Case Studies from Jordan And Israel, 47–58. Women's Issues in Transportation (Wiit), Bridging the Gap, 5th International Conference, Paris.
Erder, S. (1996) *İstanbul'da Bir Kentkondu: Ümraniye*. İstanbul: İletişim Yayınları.
Erman, T. (2001) Rural Migrants and Patriarchy in Turkish Cities. *International Journal of Urban and Regional Research*, 25(1), 118–133.
Erman, T. (2014) 'Kentin kıyısında kadın olmak Gecekondudan TOKİ kentsel dönüşüm sitesine geçişte kadın deneyimleri' in *Kenarın Kitabı*. F.Ş. Cantek (ed.) İstanbul: İletişim Yayınları, 89–119.
Erman, T. and Eken, A. (2004) The 'Other of the Other' and 'Unregulated Territories' in the Urban Periphery: Gecekondu Violence in the 2000s With a Focus on the Esenler Case, Istanbul. *Cities*, 21(1), 57–68.
Foot, J. (2000) The Urban Periphery, Myth and Reality: Milan, 1950–1990. *City*, 4(1), 7–26.
Grieco, M., Pickup, L. and Whipp, R. (1989) *Gender, Transport and Employment*. Aldershot: Avebury.
Gündoğdu, İ. and Gough, J. (2009) 'Class Cleansing in Istanbul's World City Project' in *Whose Urban Renaissance: An International Comparison of Urban Regeneration Policies*. L. Porter and K. Shaw (eds) Abingdon: Routledge, 6–24.
Güvenç, M. (1993) Metropol Değil Azman Sanayi Kenti. *İstanbul Dergisi*, 5, 75–81.
Güvenc, M. (2009) 'Social Geography of Istanbul: An Overview' in *Mapping Istanbul*. P. Dervis and M. Oner (eds) Istanbul: Garanti Gallery.
Hall, P. and Tewdwr-Jones, M. (2011) *Urban and Regional Planning*. 5th ed., Abingdon: Routledge.
Hanson, S. (2010) Gender and Mobility: New Approaches for Informing Sustainability. *Gender, Place and Culture*, 17(1), 5–23.
Hanson, S. and Johnston, I. (1985) Gender Differences in Work Trip Length: Explanations and Implications. *Urban Geography*, 6, 193–219.
Hanson, S. and Pratt, G. (1995) *Gender, Work, and Space*. New York, NY: Routledge.
Healey, J. (1996) *Statistics: A Tool for Social Research*. California: Wadsworth Publishing Company.

İlkkaracan, İ. (2010) 'Uzlaştırma Politikalarının Yokluğunda Türkiye Emek Piyasalarında Toplumsal Cinsiyet Eşitsizlikleri' in *Emek Piyasasında Toplumsal Cinsiyet Eşitliğine Doğru İş ve Aile Yaşamını Uzlaştırma Politikaları*. İ. İlkkaracan (ed.) İstanbul: İTÜ Bilim, Mühendislik ve Teknolojide Kadın Araştırmaları ve Uygulamaları Merkezi, (s. 21–58).

İlkkaracan, İ. (2016) İstanbul İsgücü Piyasasının Toplumsal Cinsiyet Eşitsizliği Perspektifinden Analizi, International Labour Organization, ILO Office for Turkey. Ankara.

Işık, O. and Pınarcıoğlu, M. (2001) *Nöbetleşe Yoksulluk. Sultanbeyli*. İstanbul: İletişim Yayınları.

Islam, T. (2005) 'Outside the Core: Gentrification in Istanbul' in *Gentrification in a Global Context: The New Urban Colonialism*. R. Atkinson and G. Bridge (eds) New York and London: Routledge, 121–136.

Keleş, R. (2003) The Periphery in the Center: Some Political Features of Turkish Urbanization. *Ekistics* 70(420/421), 211–217.

Keyder, Ç. (2014) 'Sunuş' in *Yeni İstanbul Çalışmaları: Sınırlar, Mücadeleler, Açılımlar*. A.B. Candan and C. Özbay (eds), 127–132.

Koçak, H. (2011) İstanbul 'Emeksizleştirilirken'. *İstanbul Üniversitesi Siyasal Bilgiler Fakültesi Dergisi*, 44, 41–48.

Law, R. (1999) Beyond 'Women and Transport': Towards New Geographies of Gender and Daily Mobility. *Progress in Human Geography*, 23(4), 567–588.

Limtanakool, N., Dijst, M. and Schwanen, T. (2006) On the Participation in Medium- and Long-Distance Travel: A Decomposition Analysis for the UK and the Netherlands. *Tijdschrift Voor Economische en Sociale Geografie*, 97(4), 389–404.

Logie, S. and Morvan, Y. (2014) *Istanbul 2023*. Istanbul: İletişim Yayınları.

MacDonald, H. and Peters, A. (1993) Employment and Commuting by Rural Women in the Metropolitan Periphery, MidWest Transportation Centre, University of Iowa.

McLafferty, S. and Preston, V. (1997) Gender, Race and Determinants of Commuting: New York in 1990. *Urban Geography*, 18(3), 192–212.

Naess, P. (2008) 'Gender Differences in the Influences of Urban Structure on Daily Travel' in *Gendered Mobilities*. T. Uteng and T. Cresswell (eds) Aldershot: Ashgate.

Noack, E. (2010) Are Rural Women Mobility Deprived? A Case Study from Scotland. *Sociologia Ruralis*, 51(1), 79–97.

Özer, M. M. (2017) Ataerkil Kapitalist Çalışma Yaşamından Kadın Tanıklıkları. *Çalışma ve Toplum*, 54(3), 1397–1424.

Pérouse, J. F. (2011) 'Büyüyü Bozma Pahasına İstanbul Yaklaşımını Merkezden Çıkarmak' in *İstanbul'la Yüzleşme Denemeleri*. J. F. Pérouse (eds) İstanbul: İletişim Yayınları, 17–28.

Prashker, J., Shiftan, Y. and Hershkovitch-Sarusi, P. (2008) Residential Choice Location, Gender and the Commute Trip to Work. *Tel Aviv Journal of Transport Geography*, 16, 332–341.

Rosenbloom, S. (2006) Understanding Women's and Men's Travel Patterns: The Research Challenge. *Research on Women's Issues in Transportation*, 1, Conference overview and plenary papers. TRB Conference proceedings 35, 7–28.

Salon, D. and Gulyani, S. (2010) Mobility, Poverty, and Gender: Travel 'Choices' of Slum Residents in Nairobi, Kenya. *Transport Reviews*, 30(5), 641–657.

Schaffer, A. and Schulz, C. (2008) Women's and Men's Role in Passenger Transport. Employment and Mobility Patterns. *International Journal of Transport Economics*, 35(2), 231–250.

Sohail, M., Mitlin, D. and Maunder, D. (2003) Partnerships to Improve Access and Quality of Public Transport – Guidelines, Loughborough.

Tekeli, İ. (2001) Dünya Kenti Olma Süreci İçinde Akımlar Mekanını Yeniden Biçimlendiren İstanbul. *İstanbul Dergisi*, 37, 88–97.

Terzi, F. and Bolen, F. (2009) Urban Sprawl Measurement of Istanbul. *European Planning Studies*, 17(10), 1559–1570.

Terzi, F. and Kaya, S. (2011) Dynamic Spatial Analysis of Urban Sprawl Through Fractal Geometry: The Case of Istanbul. *Environment and Planning B: Planning and Design*, 38, 175–190.

Tezer, A. (2004) Modelling of Land Use – Transportation Interaction in Istanbul. *ITU A|Z*, 1(2), 12–25.

The Urban Task Force (2003) *Towards an Urban Renaissance*. Taylor & Francis.

Türkün, A. (2014) *Mülk, Mahal, İnsan: İstanbul'da Kentsel Dönüşüm*. İstanbul: Bilgi Üniversitesi Yayınları.

Turner, J. and Fouracre, P. (1995) Women and Transport in Developing Countries. *Transport Reviews*, 15(1), 77–96.

Turner, J. and Grieco, M. (2000) Gender and Time Poverty: The Neglected Social Policy Implications of Gendered Time, Transport and Travel. *Time & Society*, 9(1), 129–136.

TUIK (2013) Women in Statistics, www.tuik.gov.tr/PreHaberBultenleri.do?id=13458.

Uteng, T. (2009) Gender, Ethnicity and Constrained Mobility: Insights into the Resultant Social Exclusion. *Environment and Planning A*, 41, 1055–1071.

Uteng, T. and Cresswell, T. (2008) *Gendered Mobilities*. Aldershot: Ashgate.

166    *A companion to transport, space and equity*

Venter, C., Vokolkova V. and Michalek, J. (2007) Gender, Residential Location, and Household Travel: Empirical Findings from Low-income Urban Settlements in Durban, South Africa. *Transport Reviews*, 27(6), 653–677.

Yalçıntan, M.C., Çalışkan, Ç. O., Çılgın, K. and Dündar, U. (2014) 'İstanbul Dönüşüm Coğrafyası' in *Yeni İstanbul Çalışmaları: Sınırlar, Mücadeleler, Açılımlar.* A.B. Candan, C. Özbay (eds), 47–70.

# 12. Planning transport to meet the needs of children and young people

*Janet Stanley, John Stanley and Brendan Gleeson*

## 1. INTRODUCTION

The demand for transport is generally a derived demand. For personal travel, it is usually travel to meet personal needs, which might be working, attending school, shopping, visiting friends and so on. Somewhat curiously, however, transport analysts typically focus on the trip itself as the unit of interest in deciding on which policy or project initiatives to pursue. Hence commonly the focus is on problems such as traffic congestion and solutions defined in terms of trip level outcomes (travel time savings and lower fuel costs) that are usually viewed as the largest benefit from major new urban road projects. The vital question of who is undertaking the travel, the quality of the journey experience and what activities can be accessed, is quietly overlooked in favour of more abstract calculus.

While this issue is relevant to many groups of people, this chapter particularly explores the issue in relation to children. Perhaps the most specific differentiation of children and young people in transport policy and planning relates to the common practice of providing young people with discounted public transport fares up to a certain age (subject to conditions) and to the provision of a separate school bus services. A comprehensive school bus service operates, for example, in rural/regional areas of Australia as well as in many other countries. However, there are commonly regulations about who can and cannot travel, defined by distance of living location from the school, as well as age, and type of educational service the person wishes to attend, resulting in many children and youth deemed not eligible to travel on the bus. In this case, distance is a poor measure of social difference and need for transport by children and young people.

This chapter looks at children and young people as significant users of transport. It examines how, traditionally, transport evaluations are judged on the actual trip, rather than how transport meets the needs of the travelling public. It reviews how equity is understood in the literature according to the major theorists and points out the unequal distribution of the benefits of mobility or accessibility opportunities. The benefits and costs are examined for children and youth. This is followed by discussion about the place of the '20-minute city' as a means of improving transport for children and universally. Finally, there is brief recognition of the importance of involving children in transport decisions.

## 2. THE SIGNIFICANCE OF CHILDREN AND YOUNG PEOPLE

Children and young people deserve attention in transport planning for many reasons: sheer numbers are one important reason. We illustrate this with reference to our home

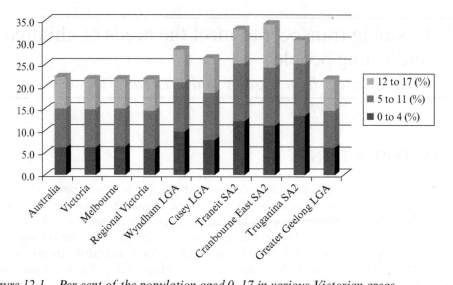

*Figure 12.1    Per cent of the population aged 0–17 in various Victorian areas*

city, Melbourne, with all data being taken from the Australian Bureau of Statistics (ABS 2017). Melbourne's population in 2015 was 4.5 million, of whom 21.7 per cent were aged 0–17. The Regional Victoria share was marginally higher at 21.8 per cent, with the national share slightly higher again at 22.3 per cent. Thus, over one in five people are children/youth in these areas, meaning that, in total, they number more than total daily public transport users. Public transport receives considerable focus in transport planning: children do not.

Figure 12.1 shows the proportions aged 0–4, 5–11 and 12–17 for Australia, Victoria, Melbourne, Regional Victoria and for a number of local government areas (LGAs), and some smaller geographies. The latter, in particular, includes three of Australia's 10 fastest growing areas at SA2 level[1] (average population of SA2s is ~10,000), in absolute numbers: Truganina, Cranbourne East and Tarneit, which are located within the Casey (Cranbourne East) or Wyndham LGAs (Truganina and Tarneit). It is noteworthy that, in the three fast-growing SA2s, the proportion of children and youth sums to around one in three of the local population, with high concentrations in all age groupings shown and the highest proportions aged 0–4. The aggregate proportions of children and youth in the fast growing areas is thus very high, about half as high again as the state and metropolitan Melbourne proportions. Numerical significance indicates that children and young people in these fast growing areas deserve particular priority in transport planning. However, given the locations of the areas referred to above, that is on the fringe of Metropolitan Melbourne, the transport options of the higher proportion of children in these areas are much poorer than the smaller proportion of children located in inner Melbourne areas. Thus the children and youth experience a double-hit of disadvantage.

---

[1]    Statistical area level 2 (SA2) – there are 2,310 SA2 regions covering the whole of Australia.

## 3.   COMMON METHODS OF TRANSPORT PROJECT EVALUATION

Welfare economics suggests that the level of focus on the trip itself is appropriate when there are competitive markets and no external benefits or costs associated with trips. However, urban travel, in particular, is replete with external costs and some external benefits, which mean a focus on the trip only can often provide misleading outcomes. Thus, if people choose to use travel time-savings to travel further, many economists argue that this is just taking their benefits in another way. Fair enough if there is no such thing as changing land use, such as increased urban sprawl. Housing and transport initiatives that foster urban sprawl, for example, are likely to add significant external costs of congestion, greenhouse gas emissions, greater obesity levels, a higher road toll, and so on, highlighting the need for integrated land use transport thinking.

The transport planning and policy process should, but rarely does, include an early-stage focus on *needs identification*. A failure to take this approach tends to severely constrain imagination about what the real issue or opportunity is and what range of options there might be to provide better outcomes. This needs identification should result in the pursuit of particular valued societal outcomes, identified through integrated land use transport planning processes that include extensive community engagement. These *valued societal outcomes* typically comprise some variant of improved productivity, reduced social exclusion, a lower environmental footprint, better health, connecting people and ensuring a safe community. Integrated land use transport planning should also extend further into related policy areas such as affordable housing and key services. There is also little estimation given of progress towards these policy goals, an issue that needs to be monitored and included in transport modelling.

Jurisdictions that are best at planning their transport systems, like London, Freiburg and Vancouver, understand these complexities and usually start from a position of seeking to identify what kind of city they want. They then tease out how transport can help them achieve that city, rather than jumping to narrowly conceived conclusions about more/bigger roads as the solution. This is inherently a people centred approach that avoids taking the shortcut to abstract thinking about mobility needs as metrics.

After need identification, the transport planning process has a focus on option/solution identification, then *appraisal or evaluation*,[2] to reveal options that best meet the intended outcome goals. Evaluation commonly involves the application of cost–benefit analysis (CBA), a tool that frequently exercises a powerful influence on the way jurisdictions think about the planning process. CBA is an analytical approach that seeks to identify preferred courses of action for society from among competing alternatives, based on identifying and measuring all the respective benefits and costs of these alternatives, as far as possible in money terms. It is about needs evaluation rather than needs identification.

CBA is very widely used to guide decision-making in transport (see, for example, Stopher and Stanley 2014), so needs little elaboration here. We note, however, that CBA is usually blind to the *distributional or equity consequences* of the matters under assessment.

---

[2]   UK practice is to distinguish between appraisal, which is ex ante, and evaluation, which is ex post. Both terms are used interchangeably in the current chapter.

It is usually assumed that if the benefits are larger than the costs (as measured), and if the gainers from a particular initiative *could* compensate the losers (Hicks 1939; Kaldor 1939), then the proposal is worthwhile. However, this approach favours wealthy people who are likely to be more mobile, and usually there is no compensation offered in transport anyway (Hickman and Dean 2017). This approach makes no distinction between members of the society in terms of their degree of deservingness or their needs and, we contend, its use has tended to divert attention away from an up-front focus on the needs that *particular groups* of people might have, when policy and other initiatives are developed. Predominance is usually given to travel to work, which in many city contexts is a steadily declining proportion of overall transport need. Such an approach is to reward investment where a high benefit can be demonstrated, although the benefits of social inclusion, although available, are not utilised (Stanley et al. 2011a).

Equity weighting approaches have sometimes been used to move away from the assumption that a dollar of benefit is of equal worth to all, irrespective of personal circumstances (see, for example, Nash, Pearce and Stanley 1975; HM Treasury 2012). These approaches incorporate weights that reflect the relative value to be placed on benefits/costs accruing to particular categories of people (ultimately a matter of value judgement). Application of this approach requires identification of *who* benefits and who incurs costs (defining the particular categories of people for whom distributional consequences are of concern), measuring the extent of their respective benefits/costs and then specifying the relative worth (equity weights) of benefits/costs to each of the categories of people who are of interest. Stanley and Stanley (2016) discuss this process in more detail. This approach is much more likely to encourage need identification that is sensitive to differences between various categories of people than the conventional Hicks-Kaldor approach to CBA.

Pearce et al. (2006) point out that there is considerable debate about choosing the 'correct' set of weights. It is important to note, however, that the failure to specify particular weights is not a value free approach to policy/evaluation. It is simply an approach that uses the (usually implied) value judgement that benefits/costs to all groups/people should be weighted equally, irrespective of their personal circumstances (e.g. income, physical capacities, age, etc.).

Income is the most common dimension on which equity or distributional weights are applied in transport policy/planning evaluation. The UK Treasury Green Book (HM Treasury 2012) sets out a methodology for deriving possible weights, the application of which implies that a dollar of benefit to a household in the top household income quintile is worth only about one fifth as much as a dollar of benefit to a household in the bottom quintile. Here, social difference, in all of its complexity, is measured in money units.

Notwithstanding the focus in some countries (particularly the UK) over the last decade or so on deriving equity weights, Geurs, Boon and van Wee (2012, p. 84) comment that: 'Both OEI [the Dutch transport evaluation guidelines] and WebTAG [the UK guidelines] provide little guidance on the evaluation of the distribution of impacts amongst population groups'. While income is the usual basis for equity weighting, if adopted, Geurs et al. (2012) quite correctly suggest that such differentiation might also be on a basis of social differences (e.g. gender), economic differences (income, wealth) and/or spatial differences (geography), to which they might have equally added (for example) age differences (e.g. children, older persons), physical and intellectual capacities and mental health.

As noted, the process of deciding that distribution matters in evaluation, and the associated search for ways of incorporating distributional weights within the evaluation framework, requires the analyst and decision-maker to focus on the who as well as on the how much of policy and evaluation. We believe that adopting an evaluation approach that is more attuned to distribution is likely to lead to better targeted policies and programs and outcomes more aligned with high-level societal values.

## 4. RAWLS AND SEN'S CONTRIBUTIONS TO EQUITY AND NEED IDENTIFICATION

The theories of distributive justice proposed by Rawls (1971) and Sen (2009) provide a values basis for focussing on children as a particular group in need identification and initiative evaluation. Rawls used the concept of a 'veil of ignorance' to ask what social choice rules a society might adopt. Under this veil a member of a society does not know what particular position they will occupy in that society. Rawls suggests that, under the veil, society is likely to agree to first safeguard their basic political and personal liberties and to then judge social and economic institutions according to how well they promote the primary social goods of those in the worst off social group (the greatest benefit of the least advantaged). This is Rawls' difference principle, founded on what he sees as rational self-interested thought. A policy interpretation is that society should maximise the welfare of the least well off (the maximin rule).

If the Rawls approach is to be applied to transport, van Wee (2012) points out that it might involve seeking to identify which particular travel purposes might be considered as primary social goods. He emphasises the role of accessibility in this regard, as an indicator of need. Accessibility planning approaches often stress the importance of access to employment education, health services, shops and the like. Other research, however, has shown the importance of trip making to connect with people to build social capital, as well as a 'sufficient' income, as the means to enhance social inclusion and promote wellbeing (Stanley et al. 2011a, 2011b). A lesson from this research is that, rather than nominate what a transport planner believes the person should be accessing, as is often done, if good transport options are offered, the person is free to improve their engagement and inclusion in a way that is important to them, enabling them to meet their self-determined needs. The needs of children commonly vary from the needs of adults and it is vitally important to cater for these, especially in the formative states of human development.

Psychology has given consideration to the nature of generalised human needs. Maslow (1954) defined these needs in a hierarchy, the most fundamental being physiological (food, water, shelter, sleep) and safety needs. The next level of general needs are interactional, identified by Maslow as inter-personal, later theorists viewing this as critical for the building blocks of healthy child development (Shonkoff and Phillips 2000). Contemporary research is also showing the importance of interaction with the natural environment, with building evidence of the importance on health and wellbeing, as well as physical and mental health restorative functions (Rook 2013; Ward Thompson, Aspinall and Roe 2014). Again, interaction with nature and unstructured play has been found to be particularly important for young children in terms of cognitive and motor skills development, and for older children in terms of creativity, independence and spontaneity, leading to confidence, self-esteem and self-actualisation (Christian et al. 2015; Lang and Deitz 1990).

The other key requirement for applying the Rawls approach is identifying those who are most disadvantaged. Research in regional and rural Australian areas suggests that children and youth are generally the most disadvantaged cohort, from a transport perspective (Currie et al. 2005; Stanley and Banks 2012; Stanley et al. 2017). This is particularly so for children living on farms or in small urban centres which lack a regular bus service.

Sen (2009) took a different approach and argued that welfare should be assessed in terms of a person's capabilities. How the person then used those capabilities was a matter for the individual. Capabilities are a basis for freedom to choose what a person wants to do and be, within their personal features and situation. Nussbaum (2001), building on Sen's work, set out 10 capabilities that she thought were relevant cross-culturally as a basis for wellbeing and freedom. These can be summarised as (Nussbaum 2005, p. 41):

- normal length of human life
- physical health
- bodily integrity (freedom from violence, sexual satisfaction and reproduction choice)
- being able to use senses to imagine, think and reason – thus also having access to an adequate education, freedom of speech and religion
- being able to express emotions – attachment, being able to experience full emotional development
- practical reason – being able to form a conception of good and engage in planning of one's life
- affiliation – being able to live with others and having the social bases of self-respect and treated as a dignified human being
- concern for other species
- control over one's environment – participation in political choices and material capacities such as property rights, employment

The ability to be mobile can be seen as an intermediate capability to the achievement of many of the outcomes listed above, many of which are especially important for the healthy formation of children. In a sense this capabilities approach encompasses meeting human needs but includes the idea that people have differing means to meet these needs.

An example of the capabilities and/or needs approach in action is the implementation of social safety net public transport service levels, where service standards are designed to enable:

- most people (not just those with some disability) to access
- most of the things they might wish to do
- most of the time

'All' might be better than 'most' but, within an economic paradigm, would raise questions of feasibility. This approach does not presume to specify which particular activities people might choose to access, leaving them the freedom to choose between those choices that are available. This process of choice itself has value. Recent work by two of the present authors (Stanley et al. 2018) has shown that those who are at most risk of social exclusion are more likely to believe that they are not able to control their life circumstances, as compared with those who are included in society. There is a risk, therefore that those experiencing exclusion will feel disempowered and further disengage from society. Providing the possibilities of choices to achieve goals would improve their beliefs about their personal capabilities. Freedom of choice itself has considerable value. However, up-take of choice usually implies improvement in more than one experience of disadvantage. For example, a person needs to also obtain employment to fulfil the need to travel to the job and needs the confidence to apply for the job in the first place.

## 5.   IDENTIFYING NEED IN TERMS OF TRANSPORT FOR CHILDREN AND YOUTH

*Need identification* is an early stage in a transport policy cycle. In the transport policy context, this need will usually be some particular transport or transport-related situation that is having a perceived adverse impact on achievement of high level societal goals or a beneficial opportunity that is being foregone but which might possibly be realised, if certain steps are taken. Those high level societal goals are wider than meeting personal needs, and include societal social goals (a well-functioning and healthy society, responsive to future challenges and extreme events), environmental, economic, governance and cultural goals. The need might relate, for example, to reducing greenhouse gas emissions from international aviation, lowering a high national road toll, reducing traffic congestion in a city, lowering urban air pollution concentrations along a busy road or providing a more equal distribution of the benefits of transport accessibility between different groups in the community, including to children and youth.

It is important at this stage to note a language disconnection between transport policy and social policy on the concept of *need*. Transport analysts from engineering and economic backgrounds tend to use measures of disadvantage as indicators of underlying *need*. Measuring disadvantage is only one part of the equation, as this does not tell us whether or not people's needs are being met, despite the disadvantage (Stanley and Read 2012). A person may be viewed as transport disadvantaged because they do not own a car and there is no available public transport. However, it may be that a neighbour has a car and is very happy to drive the person without a car anywhere they may wish to go. Perhaps this arrangement is meeting the social capital needs of the neighbour, so the arrangement suits both parties. In consequence, there remains a gap in understanding how policies designed to promote social inclusion (reduce disadvantage) will actually benefit those for whom the policies are designed. In transport, the informal system is frequently overlooked. Recent research on links between mobility, social inclusion and wellbeing should assist in teasing out these complexities (Stanley et al. 2011a, 2011b).

In terms of equity, an unequal distribution or incidence of the benefits of mobility or accessibility opportunities and/or of the costs from the provision and/or operation of transport systems/services (e.g. noise, air pollution) are common potential sources of transport *need* with an equity face. The equity face requires attention to the question of 'accessibility for whom'? In the current context this equals children and young people.

## 6.   THE IMPORTANCE OF TRANSPORT FOR CHILDREN AND YOUNG PEOPLE

Certain conditions are important in order to achieve good child development outcomes (Gleeson, 2010). Societal expenditure to achieve these conditions for children gives a higher rate of return on investment than using the same level of resources for adults, indeed the return is higher the younger the child (Heckman 2008) (Figure 12.2). Delayed early development leads to either poorer outcomes in terms of health and/or employment for adults, or more costly later interventions to change this trajectory. The sooner a child receives access to healthcare, intellectual and social stimulation and is supported by loving, attentive parents, the more likely that child will grow up to be happy, healthy and productive (The Smith Family 2010). Investment in transport is especially important for those children experiencing some form of disadvantage, to enable them to receive needed societal supports.

For children in the very early years, transport is needed to provide connections for parents in relation to health care and to build social capital and connections with the community to build a supportive environment for the family and meet the child's material, physical, affective and psychological needs (Prilleltensky and Nelson 2000). As the child grows, access to pre-school education has been found to be critical for education success, school retention and future employment. As noted above, this has been found to be especially problematical for some children with poor transport options who live in rural/regional areas of Australia. The Australian average sits at 11.1 per cent of children having two or more developmental delays in five critical areas, on reaching school age,

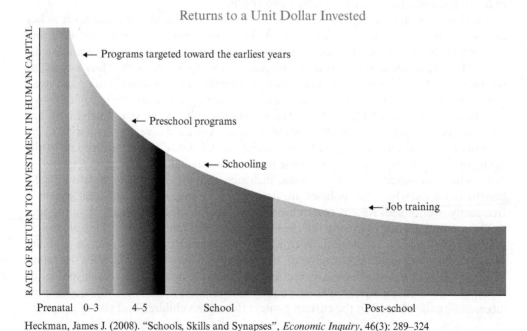

Heckman, James J. (2008). "Schools, Skills and Synapses", *Economic Inquiry*, 46(3): 289–324

*Figure 12.2   Rate of return on investment in childhood*

with pockets reaching much higher levels (Australian Government 2016). For example, the town of Peterborough in South Australia, has close to one-quarter of children due to enter school (24.8 per cent) with significant developmental delays. Parents are not permitted to accompany their pre-school children on the school bus and pre-school places on the bus are only available on some occasions. In other areas, Maternal and Child Health Nurses estimate about one in four children aged 0–5 have transport difficulties (Stanley and Stanley 2016). However, poor accessibility is rarely connected with Australia's poor level of average education attainment in international comparisons (Perry and Lublenski 2017). NIEIR (2016) estimates that the cost to society per person over a life-time is calculated to be approximately $1.4 million, due to a failure to move a person from disadvantaged to advantaged. Thus, the life-time costs of a lack of early opportunity are substantial and mobility is one important element therein.

As the child grows, so does the importance of growth of interactional needs with peers and the environment, and room to explore and play including in natural settings. 'Children are active participants in their own development, reflecting the intrinsic human drive to explore and master one's environment' (Shonkoff and Phillips 2000, p. 4). Part of this is self-directed activities, growth in confidence and gaining independent learning in life skills (Zigler, Singer and Bishop-Josef 2004). The ability to be mobile is a critical component in the achievement of these developmental stages. An international study auspiced by the UK Policy Studies Institute (Shaw et al. 2015) found that the independent mobility of children is declining, resulting in significant adverse consequences for the children. Australia ranked poorly on independent mobility when compared to other countries. The absence of public transport, particularly on the urban fringe, is a handicap for many older children and youth. This was found to be so in the LaTrobe Valley, Victoria (Stanley et al. 2018). While youth used active transport (bikes, skate boards, walking) to engage with peers and build bonding social capital, it was the absence of public transport that impeded bridging social capital, that is connections with education, employment and broader societal structures, that led to reduced opportunities, difficulties obtaining employment and risks poor levels of functioning and wellbeing.

## 7.   TRANSPORT MAY HAVE A NEGATIVE IMPACT ON CHILDREN

The argument presented above centres around a requirement to consider the needs of children in the provision of transport in a quest for a more equitable society, and to avoid possible personal and societal costs, which may manifest later in life. However, it is also argued that some aspects of the predominant form of transport risks a negative impact on children. This particularly refers to the dominance of cars and other vehicles that create the shape of urban spaces, reducing opportunities for outdoor play and informal neighbourhood interactions. Child safety concerns commonly limit independent travel and recreational activities for younger children, often necessitating a car-based escort for children. This is strongly evidenced in the large increase in children being driven to and from school in the major urban centres in Australia (Gleeson and Sipe 2006). Such concerns may restrict active mobility for children and informal street play.

Many children are confined to inside play and engage in considerable screen time, losing opportunities for play in open and green spaces. There is accumulating scientific evidence that children are 'getting fatter, sicker and sadder', reflected in rising obesity and health problems such as asthma and diabetes (Gleeson 2006). Research evidence is growing about the link between green spaces and young children's cognitive and motor skills development, in addition to psychological strengths such as growth in self-reliance and self-esteem (McFarland and Laird 2017). A study of 4,562 children aged seven to ten years of age in 36 primary schools in Barcelona, Spain, showed a beneficial association between exposure to green space and cognitive development, which was partly mediated by reduction in exposure to air pollution (Dadvand et al. 2015).

## 8.    IMPROVING TRANSPORT EQUITY FOR CHILDREN

The above discussion suggests that the interests of children have been neglected in transport policy and planning, an issue that needs to be corrected. Responding at an adequate level to children's needs is also likely to improve outcomes for many other people, those at risk of experiencing inequality and others who would like to see less car domination for their own health and wellbeing.

Planning urban structure around the principle of a 20-minute city, where most services and places can be achieved within a 20-minute public or active transport trip, would reduce inequality (Stanley, Stanley and Davis 2015). This entails the provision of good transport options and services, such as frequent bus headways (at least 20 minutes) with a wide coverage and separated good quality bike and walkways. It also involves a local provision of the most commonly used services, reducing the need to travel longer distances. Such developments are supported by urban densities of around 80 persons plus jobs per hectare, as recently provided for in designated greenfield areas in Toronto (OMMA 2017). This would need a substantial increase in density for most Australian cities, as they have very low densities when compared with UK and European cities particularly. For example, population density (excluding large parks, industrial areas and airports) is an average of 26 persons per hectare in Melbourne, compared with 80 in London (Loader 2017). Of course transition to density must be managed carefully, avoiding the bleak high rise forms that worsen not improve the wellbeing of children by entirely neglecting their need for creative and free space.

Within a 20-minute city model, local parks and centres for children should be available. Blocking off roads, turning them into open/green space and traffic calming in other streets to offer more safe outdoor play areas for children, such is being increasingly undertaken in European cities, such as Freiberg im Breisgau, Germany, which provides opportunities to better meet child development needs. Access to public transport for older children should be a short five to 10-minute walk or safe cycle ride. A 20-minute neighbourhood is likely to offer a greater sense of place, safety and community responsibility for children, as the use of public and active transport offers more opportunities for localised interactions and social capital development (Stanley, Stanley and Hansen 2017). Such needs would also be met by cultural and social change that supports physical activity and the fostering of independence in young people, such that they are allowed and encouraged to travel and play outdoors, especially in the last mile trip to school and shops (Shliselberg and Givoni 2016).

## 9.   PROCESS EQUITY

A society might place value not only on particular outcomes from policy initiatives that are to be pursued but also on how decisions are taken (procedural goals). For example, a common public policy value position is that people have a right to input on public policy decisions that are likely to affect their wellbeing. This often takes the form of community engagement around particular major initiatives. Children are generally left out of this engagement and need to be included as part of the process of reducing inequality, along with the voices of racial and other excluded groups (Whitzman 2013). Alternatively, the participation of children and youth can sometimes be at the level of tokenism and adult controlled (Hart 1992). This necessitates offering a context where children feel they have equal power with adults and their views are valued and taken forward with the view of adult participants (Mathews 2003).

## 10.   CONCLUSIONS

This chapter argues that transport project evaluation should take greater account of the broader goals of society and whether the transport project takes the social, as well as economic and environmental outcomes, into account. This should encompass an exploration of the costs and benefits of who the traveller is, and if the project will meet their needs. The transport needs of children, as well as specific other groups of people, should be particularly catered for, in place of the frequent assumption that travellers are work commuters who want to get from home to work and back in the shortest time. The premise of this chapter is that planning should focus on human need measured variously in its manifold diversity not the abstract calculus of mainstream transport and urban metrics. The chapter focuses particularly on children, as an investment in child development is for the future benefit of all of society, and expenditure while the child is developing will prevent far larger investments in the future needed to repair developmental omissions.

What specifically is to be done for children to improve their urban wellbeing? The Policy Studies Institute (Shaw et al. 2015) makes several recommendations from their research. These include putting the needs of children at the heart of spatial planning, as places that work for children work for others as well, and reducing the dominance of road traffic. The 20-minute city provides a valuable integrating framework within which to locate this thinking. The importance of such changes go beyond what the Institute has defined as the 'rights of children' to encompass the role of transport planning in the healthy development of children within society. A society that neglects the needs of children is not concerned with the future (Gleeson and Sipe 2006). If planning is about anything, it is about the future, and thus its inheritors, today's children.

It would be of great value to have the opportunity to undertake action research and longitudinal measurement on a project that implements many of the ideas of a neighbourhood for children, along the lines of a 20-minute neighbourhood. Such a case example would assist understanding of the extent of urban and transport modification needed, the threshold points where change could happen, the interaction between the components of transport and urban structure, and the full benefits/costs and the process of transition. Of course, it would be important to include the voices of children and young people, seeking their priorities and views, and their opinion of the success, or otherwise, of such a project.

# REFERENCES

Australian Bureau of Statistics (ABS) (2017) *2016 Census of Population and Housing: Community Profile*, Cat. 2001.0 viewed 30 October 2017 www.abs.gov.au/websitedbs/D3310114.nsf/Home/2016%20Census%20 Community%20Profiles.

Australian Government (2016) *Australian Early Development Census*, www.aedc.gov.au/data/data-explorer.

Christian, H., Zubrick, S., Foster, S., Giles-Corti, B., Bull, F., Wood, L., Knuiman, M., Brinkman, S., Houghto, S. and Boruff, B. (2015) The influence of the neighbourhood physical environment on early child health and development: a review and call for research. *Health and Place*, 33, 25–36.

Currie, G., Gammie, F., Waingold, C., Paterson, D. and Vandersar, D. (2005) *Improving Access to Transport for Young People in Rural and Regional Australia: A Report to the National Youth Affairs Research Scheme*. Australian Government, Canberra.

Dadvand, P., Nieuwenhuijsena, M., Esnaolaa, M., Fornsa, J., Basagaña, X., Alvarez-Pedrerola, M., Rivasa, L., López-Vicentea, M., De Castro Pascuala, M., Suf, J., Jerrettg, M., Querole, X. and Sunyera, J. (2015) Green spaces and cognitive development in primary schoolchildren. *PNAS*, 112(26), 7937–7942.

Geurs, K., Boon, W. and van Wee, B. (2012) Social impacts of transport: literature review and the state of the practice of transport appraisal in the Netherlands and the United Kingdom. *Transport Reviews*, 29(1), 69–90.

Gleeson, B. (2006) Australia's toxic cities: modernity's paradox? In, Gleeson, B. and Sipe N. (eds), *Creating Child Friendly Cities: Reinstating Kids in the City*. London, New York: Routledge, pp. 33–48.

Gleeson, B. (2010) *Lifeboat Cities*. Sydney: UNSW Press.

Gleeson, B. and Sipe, N. (2006) Reinstating kids in the city. In, Gleeson, B. and Sipe, N. (eds), *Creating Child Friendly Cities: Reinstating Kids in the City*. London, New York: Routledge, pp. 1–10.

Hart, R. (1992) *Children's Participation from Tokenism to Citizenship*. Florence, Italy: UNICEF.

Heckman, J. (2008) Schools, skills and synapses. *Economic Inquiry*, 46(3), 289–324.

Hickman, R. and Dean, M. (2017) Incomplete cost – incomplete benefit analysis in transport appraisal. *Transport Reviews*, online https://doi.org/10.1080/01441647.2017.1407377.

Hicks, J. R. (1939) The foundations of welfare economics. *Economic Journal*, 49, 696–712.

HM Treasury (2012) *The Green Book: Appraisal and Evaluation in Central Government, Annex 5 – Distributional Impacts*. London: TSO.

Kaldor, N. (1939) Welfare comparisons of economics and interpersonal comparisons of utility. *Economic Journal*, 49, 549–555.

Lang, M. and Deitz, S. (1990) Creating environments that facilitate independence: The hidden dependency trap. *Children's Environments Quarterly*, 7(3), 2–6.

Loader, C. (2017) *Charting Transport*, https://chartingtransport.com/2015/12/06/how-do-australian-and-european-cities-compare-for-population-and-area/.

McFarland, L. and Laird, S. (2017) Parents' and early childhood educators' attitudes and practices in relation to children's outdoor risky play. *Early Childhood Education Journal*, 1–10. DOI 10.1007/s10643-017-0856-8

Maslow, A. (1954) *Motivation and Personality*, 3rd ed. New York: Harper and Row Publishers.

Mathews, H. (2003) Children and regeneration: setting an agenda for community participation and integration. *Children and Society*, 17, 264–276.

Nash, C., Pearce, D. and Stanley, J. (1975) An evaluation of cost-benefit analysis criteria. *Scottish Journal of Political Economy*, 22(2), 121–134.

NIEIR (National Institute of Economic and Industry Research) (2016) *Regional Statistical Profile – Mornington Peninsula, 2011 to 2015*, April, unpublished report, author.

Nussbaum, M. (2001) *Upheavals of Thought: The Intelligence of Emotions*. Cambridge: Cambridge University Press.

Nussbaum, M. (2005) Wellbeing, contracts and capabilities. In, Manderson, L. (ed.) *Rethinking Wellbeing*. South Australia: Griffin Press.

OMMA (Ontario Ministry of Municipality Affairs) (2017) *Growth Plan for the Greater Golden Horseshoe*, author, Ontario, http://placestogrow.ca/index.php?option=com_content&task=view&id=430&Itemid=14.

Pearce, D., Atkinson, C. and Mourato, S. (2006) *Cost Benefit Analysis and the Environment: Recent Developments*. Paris: OECD.

Perry, L. and Lublenski, C. (2017) Australian schools: engines of inequality. *The Conversation*, March 13, https://theconversation.com/australian-schools-engines-of-inequality-23979.

Prilleltensky, I. and Nelson, G. (2000) Promoting child and family well-ness: priorities for psychological and social interventions. *Journal of Community and Applied Social Psychology*, 10, 85–105.

Rawls, J. (1971) *A Theory of Justice*. Cambridge, MA: Harvard University Press.

Rook, G. (2013) Regulation of the immune system by biodiversity from the natural environment: an ecosystem service essential to health. *Proceedings of the National Academy of Science*, 110(46), 18360–18367.

Sen, A. (2009) *The Idea of Justice*. London: Penguin Books.

Shaw, B. Bicket, M., Elliott, B., Fagan-Watson, B. and Mocca, E. (2015) *Children's Independent Mobility: An International Comparison and Recommendations for Action*. University of Westminster, London: Policy Studies Institute.

Shliselberg, R. and Givoni, M. (2016) Cultural differences in children's one-mile mobility. *Built Environment*, 42(4), 554–572.

Shonkoff, J. and Phillips, D. (2000) Executive summary, in Institute of Medicine (ed.) *From Neurons to Neighborhoods: The Science of Early Childhood Development*. Washington, DC: The National Academies Press, pp. 1–15.

Stanley, J. and Banks, M. (2012) *Transport Needs Analysis for Getting There and Back: Report for Transport Connections: Shires of Moyne and Corangamite*, June.

Stanley, J. and Read, P. (2012) Documented Community Needs in the City of Boroondara, Monash Sustainability Institute, Monash University, June.

Stanley, J. and Stanley J. (2016) *Improving mobility opportunities in Regional South Australia: Case Studies from the Riverland, Mount Gambier and Port Pirie*, unpublished report, Bus Industry Confederation.

Stanley, J. and Stanley, J. Balbontin, C. and Hensher, D. (2018) Social exclusion: The role of mobility and bridging social capital in regional Australia. *Transportation Research A*, https://doi.org/10.1016/j.tra2018.05.015.

Stanley, J., Hensher, D., Stanley, J., Currie, G. and Greene, W. (2011a) Social exclusion and the value of mobility. *Journal of Transport Economics and Policy*, 45(2), 197–222.

Stanley, J. K., Hensher D., Stanley, J. and Vella-Brodrick, D. (2011b) Mobility, social exclusion and well-being: exploring the links. *Transportation Research A*, 45, 789–801.

Stanley, J., Stanley, J. and Davis, S. (2015) *Connecting Neighbourhoods: The 20-minute city, Bus and Coach Industry Policy Paper 4*. Bus Industry Confederation, Australia, ACT.

Stanley, J., Stanley J. and Hansen, R. (2017) *How Great Cities Happen: Integrating People, Land Use and Transport*. Cheltenham, UK and Northampton, MA, USA: Edward Elgar.

Stopher, P. and Stanley, J. (2014) *Introduction to Transport Policy: A Public Policy View*. Cheltenham, UK and Northampton, MA, USA: Edward Elgar.

The Smith Family (2010) *The Mental Health and Wellbeing of Children and Young People in Western Australia*, November, Author.

Van Wee, B. (2012) How suitable is cost benefit analysis for the ex ante evaluation of transport projects and policies? A discussion from the perspective of ethics. *Transport Policy*, 12(1), 1–7.

Ward Thompson, C., Aspinall, P. and Roe, J. (2014) Access to green space in disadvantaged urban communities: evidence of salutogenic effects based on biomarker and self-report measures of wellbeing. *Social and Behavioural Sciences*, 153, 10–22.

Whitzman, C. (2013) Harnessing the energy of free-range children, transforming urban transport, in, Lowe, N. (ed.) *The Ethics, Politics and Practices of Sustainable Mobility*. London: Routledge, pp. 186–201.

Zigler, E., Singer, D. and Bishop-Josef, S. (2004) *Children's Play: The Roots of Reading, ZERO TO THREE*. Washington, DC: National Center for Infants, Toddlers and Families.

# 13. Social assessment of transport projects in Global South cities using community perceptions of needs
*Karen Lucas, Nihan Akyelken and Janet Stanley*

## 1. INTRODUCTION

Investment in large transport infrastructure projects has traditionally been seen as an important economic driver for developing countries. Billions of dollars are spent annually on building major new transport projects all around the world with this end in mind (International Transport Forum, 2015). These investments have been shown to act as a catalyst for local, national, regional and even international economic growth, but their contribution to social development and poverty reduction is questionable. However, the critics of such investments point to the unequal social distribution of their economic and environmental benefits and burdens, as well as their long term negative quality of life impacts (see Dimitriou, 2011, for a full discussion of these issues). This is because the benefits of these strategic projects often accrue to the wealthiest populations in Global South cities, and often leave in their wake highly negative, localised social and environmental problems for the poorest populations (see e.g. Mahapa and Mashiri, 2001; Van de Walle, 2002; Bryceson et al., 2008).

Many of the funded road infrastructure projects that are currently being brought forward are mainly aimed at addressing traffic congestion, and/or to provide strategic links between cities. Meanwhile the shift to motorised vehicles directly conflicts with the indigenous mobility practices of the low-income population in developing cities, the majority of whom still rely on walking to access their daily activity needs (Dimitriou and Gakenheimer, 2011). Also, the growing demand for road-based infrastructures to meet the mobility needs of the motorised minority is usually at the cost of non-motorised and transit options, with the consequence of decreased accessibility for low-income populations (Banister, 2005).

In tandem, there are also very wide inequalities in mobility, accessibility and associated activity participation within Global South cities, including by income, gender, age, disability and other social factors. Also, very little funding is available to apply the conventional quantitatively focused transport analysis approach used within best practice transport appraisal in the Global North (for example the WebTAG approach to the appraisal of social and distributional impacts of major road schemes in the United Kingdom[1]). In most cases, social and distributional assessments are standalone exercises conducted after the standard economic cost benefit analysis (CBA) has been completed (Vanclay, 2002).

---

[1]   For more about this see WebTAG Units 4.1 (December 2017) Social Impact Assessment https://assets.publishing.service.gov.uk/government/uploads/system/uploads/attachment_data/file/670358/tag-4.1-social-impact-appraisal-dec17.pdf and Unit 4.2 (December 2015) https://www.gov.uk/government/publications/webtag-tag-unit-a4-2-distributional-impact-appraisal-december-2015.

We posit that, particularly in the Global South, it is necessary to develop systematic understandings of the contextual evidence of the local welfare conditions of communities 'before and after' projects are introduced, in order to make evident the social development contribution of different project options (i.e. in the form of real world case studies).

The main purpose of this chapter, therefore, is to help to raise scholarly and policy awareness of the crucial role that transport plays in worsening or enhancing the livelihood outcomes of low-income populations in Global South cities through the lens of the Social Development Goals (SDGs), which are seen as having increasing importance to the social development aspirations of Global South cities because of their links with external funding aid (Sperling and Gordon, 2009). It is within this context, that we propose an assessment framework, which is grounded in local community perspectives of 'mobilty and accessibility' needs, as they relate to the maintenance of people's livelihoods (Lucas and Porter, 2016) to assess the role of new transport projects in developing cities.

The approach we identify specifically focuses on the social development outcomes (sometimes referred to as 'pro-poor' projects within the policy literature) of project investments, rather than solely on their mobility outcomes. Ellis's (2000, p.10) definition of livelihoods is adopted:

> The assets. . . the activities, and the access to these. . . that together determine the living gained by the individual or household.

Until now, social development policy has tended to pay little attention to the problems that are associated with growing inequalities in transport within Global South cities, such as the health effects of life-threatening levels of exposure to traffic-related pollutions (UN Habitat, 2014), lack of adequate physical activity, increased deaths and casualties from road traffic accidents (WHO, 2015), as summarised in a recent World Health Organization report (Schweizer et al., 2014). Neither does it appear to recognise the severe and increasing threat to livelihoods of the inaccessibility of low-income populations to markets, employment, goods and services (Bryceson et al., 2003; Salon and Guylani, 2010). There is now much greater appreciation of these social concerns amongst the funders of transport infrastructure projects such as the Multinational Development Banks (MDBs). This can be evidenced by a proliferation of recent policy guidance on the social appraisal of transport projects (e.g. Cooke et al., 2005; Department for International Development, 2004; Thynell, 2009; World Bank 2006; 2013).

## 2.   LITERATURE REVIEW

Studies of the social consequences of transport investment decisions began in the 1990s and primarily focused on Global North urban and rural area (see, for example, Gannon and Liu, 1997). The more contemporary literature demonstrates a continued interest in the issue of transport equity (e.g. Beyazit, 2011; Martens, 2006) in contexts where transport poverty is a problem for an underserved *minority* of the population. In contrast, transport poverty in the Global South is a problem for the *majority* of people whether they live in urban environments, or at the centre or edge of cities, or in rural area. The phenomenon persists whether there is more or less of a supply of transport services in these locations, and despite considerable investments in new transport infrastructures by many Global South cities in recent years.

The general lack of access to goods and services as a consequence of this transport poverty has become critical to the delivery of SDGs for many Global South cities and their rural hinterlands. However, many of the transport policies and projects of Low and Middle Income Countries (LIMCs) and some cities appear to be in direct contravention of the SDG targets for transport, potentially worsening rather than improving the poverty plight and quality of life outcomes of local populations in the areas where they are delivered (e.g. SDG 11). This is because there has been a past tendency amongst politicians and other decision makers to favour investment in large road-building programmes to meet the increased demand for motorised transport (Bryceson et al., 2003). Their decisions are based on the widely questioned (see, for example, Stiglitz et al., 1999) neo-liberal ideology that economic growth will automatically benefit the poor through a 'trickle-down effect'.

Perversely, many commentators (as do we) now criticise the policy rational that major transport infrastructure investment can act as a 'quasi' social development tool in this way. For example, Mahapa and Mishiri (2001) note the preoccupation of transport policymakers with higher technology fixes and efficiency savings rather than the travel needs of local 'beneficiary' communities, which they claim could have resulted in different, less expensive and more context-specific and gender-sensitive solutions. However, the funding has always been minimal for local community-based transport projects to directly benefit poor and other disenfranchised groups in Global South cities.

Recently, these negative trends have been compounded by the global economic downturn and slow recovery from the 2008 global economic crisis, which has led to a reduction in the levels of finance that are available to support projects in developing countries (United Nations, 2015a, 2015b). Dimitriou and Gakenheimer (2011) suggest that it is likely that new less expensive and alternative solutions will be needed for the delivery of mass transit in rapidly urbanising cities, together with new financial models combining private and individual investments in transport infrastructure projects. Stanley (2010) and Lucas et al. (2016a), among others, argue that transport policymakers and urban planners urgently need to find new ways to evaluate the new transport infrastructures which are being proposed for Global South cities, in order to integrate the social and environmental impacts and value of transport projects as an integral part of their upstream and downstream appraisal.

Indeed, many academic and policy literatures now suggest that radically new transport policies and programmes are needed to reduce the highly unequitable transport landscapes of developing cities in the Global South. A study in the Mardin region of southeast Turkey (Akyelken, 2013) revealed that political instability combined with a lack of investment by government in social infrastructure, low educational levels and a dominant patriarchal mind-set has meant that women have largely not benefited from the significant investments that have gone into new transport infrastructure projects in the region over the last ten years. It is partly in recognition of this need for future transport investments to deliver pro-poor policy outcomes, that major investors in new transport infrastructure projects are beginning to make efforts to assess their social and distributional impacts, some of which have materialised as toolkits, as exemplified by the Asian Development Bank (Cook et al., 2005) and World Bank (World Bank, 2006). However, the approach we are proposing here goes beyond these current social assessment protocols by offering a set of social criteria and indicators for the assessment of transport projects from the perspectives of local communities, based upon the evidence of several case studies with 300 participants from different community groups in South Africa and Brazil (see Lucas, 2011; Maia et al., 2016 for full details of these studies).

## 3.   METHODOLOGY

Several previous studies have previously recommended indicator frameworks and methodologies to assess the social outcomes of transport projects (e.g. in Uganda, Zimbabwe and Zambia, see Bryceson, et al. (2003) and Davis (2000)). These studies have shown that many of the 'unintended' negative social outcomes of current transport decisions in the Global South are due to a systematic failure to include *the perspectives of affected communities* within the project decision process.

Our suggested framework is based on the evidence of these community perspectives, and rather than deciding the appropriatness of investments externally, should be used to provide *the starting point for a process of dialogue* and evidence gathering between the various decision-makers of new transport projects on the social contribution and equity of different project options. The main rationale behind this decision tool is that in order to understand the social contribution of transport projects it is necessary to first gather the evidence of what is important to *the livelihoods the local people who may be affected* by the proposed intervention. Thus, the selected evaluation criteria should, as far as possible, be based upon a revealed evidence-base of *what matters to local people* and this should seek to include consideration of the *needs and perspectives of all members of the communities that will be affected by the project*, and not just those of project investors, politicians, policymakers and powerful local elites.

This section of the chapter sets out the different stages of our social assessment methodology. Table 13.1 presents the overview of the three key stages of our framework specification and Table 13.2 identifies the specific indicators and their suggested social disaggregation. The next sections explain how each indicator was devised based upon the research evidence.

*Table 13.1    Three pillars of social development on transport*

| Social progress | Social distribution | Social justice |
| --- | --- | --- |
| <ul><li>Livelihoods:<ul><li>o Access to formal and informal transport</li><li>o Access to key social services</li><li>o Wider impacts</li></ul></li><li>Health and safety</li><li>Planning and integration</li></ul> | <ul><li>Distribution of costs and benefits</li><li>Segregation of population groups</li><li>Identifying thresholds</li></ul> | <ul><li>Redistribution of benefits and costs</li><li>Equality of direct and indirect opportunities and outcomes</li><li>Potential for policy accountability</li></ul> |

*Source:*   Based on Lucas et al. (2007).

*Table 13.2  Social justice transport appraisal framework*

| Area of progress | Indicator of progress | Disaggregation criteria E.g. Gini index can be used to compare different identified groups with average population or local study area(s) with the whole city | | | | |
| --- | --- | --- | --- | --- | --- | --- |
| | | *Income distribution* | *Gender* | *Age* | *Disability* | *Ethnicity* |
| 1 SDG 1 and 11: Poverty reduction and mobility<br>a) Access to local facilities<br>b) Access to transport services (formal and informal)<br>c) Affordability (transport) | a) Increase % of residents living within 15 min 'safe walk' to key local facilities (e.g. schools, clinics, local shops, police station, welfare centres, etc.)<br>b) Increase % of population within 15 min safe walk to regular public transit services (bus stop, bus station, rail stations)<br>c) Reduce total household expenditure on travel to below 10% of income (zero for low income households) | Poorest 30% in study area vs. the rest | Total % of women affected % of girls affected By age 5–11, 11–18 and 18–25 years | *% of children affected:* % older people affected By age bands | % of disabled people affected By mobility impaired, other physical impairments and mental disabilities | Classify any key ethnic minorities in study area: % of key ethnic minorities affected |
| 2 SDG 1, 3 and 4: Improving access to jobs, markets, education, healthcare and public sector services | Increase availability of low cost housing within 30 min public transit journey time of key employment centres<br>Increase % of urban population within 30 min public transit journey times to key economic and life opportunities (e.g. gainful employment, markets, tertiary education, hospitals) | | | | | |
| 3 SDG 3 and 13: Improving the health and safety of the transport environment | a) Reduce number of child and adult pedestrian casualties<br>b) Reduce incidence of crime on and waiting for public transit<br>c) Reduce levels of population exposure to traffic related noise and air pollution (especially children and older people) | | | | | |
| 4 SDG 16: Strengthening transport governance | a) Increase levels of community participation in local decision-making processes for local transit service provision<br>b) Introduce mechanisms for recourse to legal justice where populations experience negative transport externalities (e.g. participation in citizen's panels) | | | | | |

*Source:*  Adapted from Lucas et al. 2007, p. 32: Table 1.

## 3.1   Providing the Evidence Base

To develop the indicator framework, the chapter draws upon the evidence of the authors' qualitative grassroots research in development contexts with low-income and disadvantaged population groups to identify what matters for the people who are living in poverty in terms of their transport, mobility and accessibility needs. We synthesise this evidence base in Section 4 of the chapter.

### 3.1.1   Case study I: Tshwane, South Africa

The South African case studies were conducted in the Tshwane Metropolitan Municipality and in particular the Sunnyside district of the City of Tshwane (Pretoria) and two periurban districts, Mamelodi and Soshanguve, which are located within relatively close travel distances to the city. Seven focus groups were conducted with low-income local residents across these three communities; two were in Sunnyside with non-paid carers and disabled people, three were in Mamelodi with unemployed adults, female single parents, and low-income workers (earning less than 1,000 rand per month) and two in Soshanguve with child heads of households (under 18 years) and students in full-time tertiary education.

### 3.1.2   Case study II: Recife, Brazil

The Brazilian case study involved the residents of two low-income settlements in the metropolitan region of Recife. A series of four focus groups were conducted by local facilitators with a total of 73 local residents participating across the two communities, 41 from Coque and 32 from Santa Terezinha. The Coque settlement is located less than a mile from the main centre of the City of Recife and is well served by local facilities and services. Alto Santa Terezinha is a more peripheral urban hillside community, located about ten kilometres to the north of the city but is still considered to be part of the main urban conurbation of Recife. Separate focus groups were held with housewives, employed women, unemployed men and secondary students (females in Coque and males in Santa Terezinha).

### 3.1.3   New proposed transport projects

At the time of both the Brazilian and South African studies, the local metropolitan authorities of Recife and Pretoria were in negotiation with local politicians and national government to facilitate significant investment in the public transport infrastructure in both cities in the form of new bus rapid transit (BRT) or light rail transit (LRT) systems. A key research question for both studies was how far the new planned transit systems were likely to meet the mobility and accessibility needs of low-income and socially disadvantaged groups living within these cities. The decision makers we interviewed as part of the study did not have any clear understanding of how to make a judgment call on this question when considering the various options available to them. In many ways, this promoted our initial development of a social assessment framework.

The overall validity of the framework was tested in October 2015 with 25 project officers and project consultants from the Asian Development Bank (ADB) during a training course on Designing Socially Inclusive Transport Projects. The feedback from the course suggested that participants found it to be a useful high-level tool for initial scrutiny of the likely SDIs of transport projects. They recommended that it would be most useful once the indicators could be quantitatively measured, which was recognised as difficult due to the lack of freely available and appropriate quantitative datasets.

### 3.2   Setting the High-level Objectives

The first stage in any evaluation process is to establish a clear set of high-level project objectives, in this case in terms of their contribution to social development. Precisely what constitutes social development in any given situation is open to interpretation and may largely depend upon the moral codes of a given society (Martens, 2006). For the purposes of this chapter, we base our interpretation on Brundtland's (1987) definition of sustainable development (Table 13.1):

1.   To achieve social progress in terms of poverty alleviation, improve health and wellbeing, reduce illiteracy and improve educational attainment.
2.   To provide an equal distribution of benefits and responsibilities (or at least equality of opportunity) both within and between nations.
3.   To ensure social justice is delivered in terms of the protection of vulnerable social groups and between nations.

Brundtland's intention (as for our own research) is that these social goals will be promoted *alongside, and integrated with*, a broader set of criteria for economic stability and environmental protection, so as to achieve a more balanced approach to social development that is also within the capacity of the Earth's environment and to the benefit of current and future generations.

### 3.3   Identify Indicators of Social Progress – Case Study Research

Having established these three broad objectives for social development, we next identify a set of metrics or indicators with which to measure 'what counts' (in this case for transport), as well as helping to determine the weights (or importance) that should be given to each indicator (see Table 13.2 above). The important questions to explore are: a) what are the main benefits and dis-benefits of transport that might have an impact on social progress in terms of the transport delivery; b) which social groups should be the target to increase equity; and c) how should the benefits and burdens of the transport system be distributed to be considered to be fair?

## 4.   DISCUSSION OF THE CASE STUDY EVIDENCE FOR FRAMEWORK SPECIFICATION

In this section, we discuss the evidence to support the indicator framework in Table 13.2 based on the 11 South African and eight Brazilian focus groups that were conducted with low income residents in the two case studies.

## 4.1   Establishing Indicators of Social Progress

Each of the indicators is discussed serparately as it is presented in Table 13.2, but we recognise that many of the issues overlap and are often cumulative in their affects on social progress. It was clear from the case study evidenc that where people live interacts with the availability and quality of the local facilities in these areas, which then has knock-on consequences for their mobility practices, activity outcomes and ultimately social inclusion. For some indicators, the evidence was more comprehensive than in others, and further research would be necessary to fully establish the concerns of local communities in some instances where the data is sparser.

**Indicator 1: poverty and mobility**
This first indicator comprises three sub-indicators of: a) access to local facilities, b) access to transport services, and c) transport affordability.

*Indicator 1a: access to local facilities*   In all of the case studies, the participants overwhelmingly accessed most of their daily activities on foot. Having to pay for transport to access jobs and services significantly increased their impoverishment. As such, their greatest concerns related to the quality and accessibility of local facilities (e.g. stores, clinics, schools, welfare centres) within their neighbourhoods. Travel was often necessary, however, due to the poor quality of these local services, particularly in the case of primary care clinics, which were found to be understaffed and lacking in basic medical provisions in both Brazil and South Africa.

However, being more mobile per se will not necessarily lead the residents of these communities to improve their levels of activity participation (e.g. in employment or education or health care), and so both mobility and the wider accessibility benefits of improved local services need to be monitored as indicators of social progress. This suggests that the extent to which a proposed new project increases the potential for non-served populations to access their daily activities should be a primary consideration in the investment decision process. Once it is established that more transport is what is needed (rather than better local services or walking facilities), then all new projects should be universally accessible (in terms of their availability, cost and usability, including the aged and those with a disability) and integrated with land use and the wider transport network (e.g. through feeder routes, community vans, etc.).

*Indicator 1b: access to transport services*   Public transport access was a key area of concern in both the Brazilian case studies, but for quite different reasons. Although, Coque is very close to the city centre, the absence of community transport and motorbike taxis within the settlement causes particular problems for bringing home shopping from the local market and connecting with formal public transport services outside the area. There was also a lot of concern about getting to the hospital in an emergency, particularly at night because the ambulance and taxi drivers will not drive into the area due to a fear of crime.

Previous studies have observed (e.g. Cheety and Phayane, 2012) the availability of transport services also needs to be checked in terms of the frequency of service and operating times, as many formal transit services may only operate during the morning and evening peaks and not during the middle of the day or at night when they may be more socially necessary than employment-related. For these reasons, securing a community van service was seen as a major local political achievement for the Santa Teresinha community.

*Indicator 1c: transport affordability*   This issue of transport affordability is a key for many low income residents who tend to live in peripheral areas of the city in slum or informal settlements. Salon and Gulyani (2010) also identified that access to affordable transit services was a key issue for urban slum dwellers in their Nairobi case study for similar reasons of income poverty combined with the relatively high cost of fares for the use of these services, which are largely unregulated in most African cities.

For example, in the South African case studies, most participants raised this issue. They needed to use informal shared-taxi services (kombis) at least once or twice a month to buy food and they were particularly reliant on them for getting to hospital in the case of a medical emergency. The cost of the fare for these services was seen as very high (approximately 25 rand for a single trip), given that all of the people who participated in the study were on incomes of less than 1,000 rand a month (approx. $80).

By contrast, affordability was not a major concern for most people living in the inner city Coque area of Brazil because all their activities were deemed to be quite local and so they mostly walked everywhere and very rarely used public transit services. People in Santa Terezinha were more reliant on public transit services due to the peripheral location of the area. Their community van is free to connect with the regular public transport at the bottom of the hill. Nevertheless, travelling into the city centre was described as '*beyond the reach of city workers*', especially for trips involving the whole family (R$20).

However, even these vans cannot penetrate the higher areas of the alto settlement, and so people are almost solely reliant on privately operated and totally unregulated motorbike taxis. The fare is R$1 (R$1 = approx. $0.45) for local trips, and hence both were seen as affordable options. These are seen as a cheap and easy way to connect people who cannot walk down the hillside to the shops and local services at the bottom of the settlement. Nevertheless, they are also a highly risky form of transport and are also seen as a nuisance factor by other residents because they compete with pedestrian space on the narrow roads that serve the community lower down the hill.

**Indicator 2: strategic accessibility and housing supply**
As indicated within our evaluation framework (see Table 13.2), there are two main elements that fall under this theme: a) the level of formal housing supply that is available within close proximity to the supply of public transport to employment; and b) increasing the connectivity of public transport to strategic destinations within the city, such as hospitals, colleges and specialist centres. All too often current transport evaluation in development contexts fails to recognise these inherent policy interactions in the planning of new transport infrastructures, thus often worsening the plight of low-income populations (UN Habitat, 2016). The assessment approach helps to raise the important issue of these policy interactions between housing and land use planning.

*Indicator 2a: housing supply*   Many transport projects involve enforced housing displacements and/or gentrification of the housing stock in the areas around these new developments. This leads to increased social segregation and reduced social progress for affected populations as they get pushed further into peripheral and marginalised areas. There can also be severance effects, due to an absence or loss of adequate pedestrian facilities associated with these projects. So that while the project itself may respect the principles of universal access, it may not be adequately integrated with the surrounding walking environment leading to reduced local accessibility.

For example, many of the houses in Santa Terezinha are in a precarious position on the hillside and some have already collapsed. In Coque, the issue is that the settlement is situated on land that is increasingly encroached upon by major transport infrastructure (road and rail). There is also no opportunity to develop further housing in either of these areas due to physical land use constraints. Possible relocation was not up for discussion with either of the communities. The position was that residents have fought hard to gain permission to get their settlements formally registered by the state and they do not want to move away from them. *'We are here to stay whatever happens around us'* is a local campaign slogan for the hillside communities.

*Indicator 2b: strategic accessibility*   Another issue is the poor connectivity of public transport systems with employment and other important destinations within the city. This is particularly prevalent in countries where there are lax or non-existent planning polices for land use development and so facilities such as hospitals, colleges and other important activities are located without any reference to the availability of the public transport supply to reach them.

In a number of the South African case studies, people referred to 'working for the transport'. Understandably, they were averse to this idea, preferring instead to try to eke out a living from the informal sale of goods and services. Beyond this constraint, most people said that they would take any kind of work as long as they could get to it. In practice most of the focus group participants were not working on a regular basis and so their job search activities took them to different parts of the city. Many of them in the Mamelodi groups would use the train for this purpose, although this was described as slow and unsafe, and probably not a viable option on a regular basis. Most people looked to the city centre as the main employment location, although there were some limited opportunities for employment in the periphery.

In both the Brazilian groups, strategic access to hospitals also was raised as a serious problem, especially at night. This was largely because the ambulances would not enter into the neighbourhood for fear of criminal damage and driver safety, and so people described long and unsafe walks to get to hospital even when they were in the throes of childbirth. Other strategic facilities that were also mentioned as problematic were schools and educational colleges. Getting to welfare services was a big issue for people in the disabled group because this required travelling to the other side of the city centre and they often could not use kombi taxis to get there because of their wheelchairs.

**Indicator 3: healthy and safe environments**
There are three main considerations that fall under this theme heading: a) high incidences of pedestrian casualties and road deaths, b) crime and fear of crime whilst travelling and c) high levels of exposure to traffic-relayed pollutants.

*Indicator 3a: pedestrian casualties and road deaths*   Reducing pedestrian accidents, especially amongst the child population, is a key performance health indicator for transport internationally (UN Habitat, 2014). Whereas these accidents rates are now relatively low in cities in the developed world, they are on the rapid increase in Global South cities, especially for pedestrians. However, much of the attention within the transport policies of Global South countries focuses on reducing traffic collisons, and often pedestrian casualties and deaths are either not recorded or are not disaggregated by income, age and gender. It is overwhelmingly the poorest and women and children who experience the worst outcomes in this respect because they walk more and so are more exposed to traffic.

It was most notable from the case study evidence that the issue of pedestrian safety is greatly overlooked by local residents living alongside busy roads. This is most likely because people are so used to travelling in these dangerous conditions that they accept these conditions as normal. For example, in the Coque group, it was surprising that despite a highly congested major road passing right through the area and a total absence of any pedestrian crossing or footpaths, the issue of road casualties was absent from the discussions. Similarly, in South Africa, people were more likely to talk about the heat associated with punitive walking distances than fear of traffic-related casualties or deaths. This is not to undermine the importance of exploring the issue of pedestrian safety within the design of transport projects, but may partly explain why it is currently so often overlooked by the planners and designers of these large infrastructure projects.

*Indicators 3b: personal safety*    Personal safety whilst travelling is also an important indicator of the social sustainability of the transport system. Porter (2011) reports that when researching in a development context it is important to distinguish between male perceptions of a safe journey and the actual safety needs of female travellers. Safety issues have also been identified as particularly important for young people's daily mobility, especially for young girls. It has also been observed that boys have more freedoms than girls due to less danger of rape and impregnation. Transport safety issues are, therefore, interconnected with broader safety issues as well as local cultural perceptions in terms of age and gender.

In particular, the perception of Coque as an area of high crime was seen as a major barrier to incoming transport service providers due to this stigma. Additionally, the issue of night-time crime was raised in Santa Terezinha and there was also some mention of pedestrian danger from motorbike taxis in some of the groups. In the South African groups, the issue was more about personal safety whilst travelling especially for women, where the main concern for women and young girls was fear of rape whilst walking and also by taxi drivers when using the kombi taxis. The dangerous drunk driving behaviours of taxi drivers was also raised as a big problem for personal safety.

*Indicator 3c: exposure to air and noise pollution*    The World Health Organization (2009) estimates that 531,000 premature deaths occur annually in developing Asian countries due to air pollution, much of which is road transport related. The transport networks of many Global South cities are already at breaking point, with chronically high levels of congestion, traffic-related accidents, noise and air pollution. Research has also demonstrated that low-income sectors of the population are disproportionately affected by the negative health impacts of road-based transport, such as poor air quality, noise, community severance and traffic fatalities (Kent and Simon, 2007).

Despite this global evidence, air quality and traffic noise were not recognised as an issue by particpants in any of the focus groups. This was not because there is not a problem, as traffic congestion and levels of pollution are high, but because people seem to be unaware of this as a problem for their health and wellbeing. This could be explained as due to the numerous other threats to human health that local residents experience on a daily basis or to a lack of information about the problem or for other reasons which were not explored in the groups. Clearly, this is an important gap in the evidence of our research and should be explored in more depth in future research.

### Indicator 4: transport justice

Several authors have noted the need to dramatically improve transport governance structures within developing countries if any progress is to be made on transport justice aspects of transport (e.g. see Dimitriou and Gakenheimer, 2011). However, the specific issue of transport justice did not emerge as an important issue within the context of our case study research, but this is not to say that it should be ignored. As such, we identify two indictors for transport justice within our assessment framework:

*Indictor 4a: community participation in decision-making processes*   In the Brazilian case studies, a local government scheme to allow local communities to determine their own local spend on transport with small devolved budgets was seen by participants as one way to ensure that the needs of local populations were being met. Local participants were enthusiastic about the potential for this fund to improve local walking facilities and, in the case of Coque, to secure a community van for trips to the local market. In South Africa, there was no such evidence of any devolved responsibilities for local transport or bottom-up initiatives, although there was mention in the focus groups that this was beginning to happen to a certain extent in Johannesburg and Cape Town. Devolving decisions and at least some budgets to communities is a key aspect of the social justice agenda and can lead to much more targeted spending to meet local needs. One important concern that is regularly raised by policymakers in this respect, however, is the levels of corruption which are evident within the local gangs and power-bases in many of these communities, which is an issue that cannot be overlooked.

*Indicator 4b: recourse to legal justice*   It was evident that most of the people that partici-pated in the case studies did not expect to be consulted at all about any aspect of their lives. The idea that they personally could have any influence over the type of transport provision that was provided in their local areas or the city at large did not occur to them. Most people had experienced instances where the complaints that they had made were ignored by officials and in many instances people said they would not know who to go to with their transport problems.

### 4.2   Measuring the Social and Spatial Distributions of Impacts

Once the evidence base to support indicators have been identified in this way (i.e through meaningful enagagement with local affected communities in the areas where new transport projects and policy interventions are planned), the next step in the assessment process is to establish appropriate disaggregation metrics to gauge the impacts of projects (positive and negative) on *different sectors* of the local population. The proposed disaggregations are indicated in the five columns under 'disaggregation criteria' in Table 13.2.

One useful way to establish equity of outcome between different population sectors is through the use of the Gini coefficient, which to can be used compare one group with another, e.g. women with men, or one place with another, e.g. the study area with the city as a whole. The full explanation of this approach is not discussed within this chapter due to space constraints, but can be found in Lucas et al. 2016b.

The social policy literatures are helpful to understand which population groups are of most interest for the purposes of disaggregation, as they clearly and consistently identify key population groups that should be targeted and protected by development policy. The most commonly identified vulnerable population sectors noted for attention are:

- The *urban poor* (who are defined as individuals living on less than $1.5 per day). They mostly rely on walking and other non-motorised modes and so it is also important to disaggregate by the percentage of the population with access to the different modes of transport before and after the introduction of a new project (Lucas et al., 2016a).
- *Women* have been identified as one of the most disadvantaged groups in reaping the benefits of transport in a developing country context, while they still face challenges given the widely accepted gender roles in daily life (Porter, 2011; Porter et al., 2012).
- McMillan (2010) identifies that, despite the fact that *children and youth* are a growing proportion of the population in many urban areas around the world (children and young people under 24 represent 47 per cent of the total population in developing countries and 29 per cent of the population in developed countries), in terms of urban transport they are an overlooked and vulnerable segment of the population.
- The mobility and accessibility needs of *older people and those with a disability* (who will represent nearly third of the world's population by 2050) are also often insufficiently considered by transport providers (UN Habitiat, 2014).

Less often identified and reported are the additional vulnerabilities of *people with disabilities* and *minority ethnicity communities*, but the specific needs of both populations sectors have huge implications for how transport systems are developed and delivered in cities worldwide.

## 5.   CONCLUDING REMARKS

The assessment framework and qualitative case study evidence which underpins it presented in this chapter is illustrative, and we recognise that robust quantitative data and analysis is needed to test the validity and viability of our approach in a live project setting. To collect all the data that is needed for this would require a significant new research effort, which is beyond the scope of our current enquiry. Nevertheless, we have taken the first steps to demonstrate that a community-scale, mobility and livelihoods approach to transport project assessment can provide useful insights on the contribution of transport projects to social progress and country-specific SDGs.

Our approach significantly diverges from the currently recommended 'best practice' approaches to the social appraisal of transport projects in the Global North where transport planning has been developed over the last 70 years as primarily quantitative exercises. This privileges the use of often complex econometric or modelling approaches in the selection of projects and prioritisation of policy strategies, which are not likely to be replicated in the Global South, as there are usually not the levels of funding available for transport analysis to be carried out in this complex manner. There are also increasing concerns that these quantitative approaches do not adequately reflect the complexities of human behaviours and that new qualitatively-based approaches need to be developed to help cities invest in more people-centred and socially inclusive transport systems worldwide.

Further qualitative and quantitative research is necessary to support this approach, not only in terms of targeted data collection efforts, but also to establish appropriate threshold levels to set the minimum levels of transport provision necessary for social progress in each given context. A considerable challenge in this respect is the almost total absence or non-availability of appropriate quantitative datasets with which to assess the diffferent social and distributional parameters we have identified. One recommendation from our research, therefore, is the need for the funders of all future transport projects to collect, archive and release appropriate data for the social and distributional assessment of new transport projects in the Global South, and ideally to make them publically available for analysis for non-commercial research purposes.

As we have demonstrated, applying community perspectives in the social assessment of new transport projects allows decision makers to not only identify the benefits and burdens that accrue from them, but to also consider the *a priori* conditions of the different communities that they affect, and so to assess whether or not they are 'fit for purpose' where social development is the key delivery aim. If targeted towards the specific delivery of SDGs, it is important to *first* identify the unmet mobility and accessibility needs of low-income, vulnerable and disadvantaged populations and to assess whether the proposed project will meet their social needs *in some significant way,* e.g. it will reduce poverty by providing better access to skills-appropriate employment locations, or it will reduce health inequalities by improving air quality.

Ultimately, however, these decisions are often out of the hands of project evaluators and funders because the upfront decision concerning their introduction has already been decided politically before the financial appraisal process begins. In these instances, a comprehensive social assessment can, at the very least, be used to enhance the project design, so as to maximise its overall contribution to social development, and to help to mitigate any of its negative social consequences for local communities.

# REFERENCES

Akyelken, N. (2013) Development and gendered mobilities: narratives from the women of Mardin, Turkey. *Mobilities*, 8, 424–439.

Banister, D. (2005) *Unsustainable Transport: City Transport in the New Century*. London: Routledge.

Banister, D. and Berechman, J. (2001) Transport investment and the promotion of economic growth. *Journal of Transport Geography*, 9, 209–218.

Beyazit, E. (2011) Evaluating social justice in transport: lessons to be learned from the capability approach. *Transport Reviews*, 31(1), 117–134.

Bruntland and World Commission on Environment and Development (1987) *Our Common Future* (Vol. 383). Oxford: Oxford University Press.

Bryceson, D., Bradbury, A. and Bradbury, T. (2008) Roads to poverty reduction? Exploring rural roads' impact on mobility in Africa and Asia. *Development Policy Review*, 26, 459–482.

Bryceson, D., Mbara, T. and Maunder, D. (2003) Livelihoods, daily mobility and poverty in sub-Saharan Africa. *Transport Reviews*, 23, 177–196.

Cook, C., Duncan, T., Jitsuchhon, S., Sharma, A. and Guobao, W. (2005) *Assessing the Impact of Transport and Energy Infrastructure on Poverty Reduction*. Manila: Asian Development Bank.

Department for International Development (UK) (2004) *Inclusion Of Social Benefits In Transport Planning – Review Of Developing Country Experience* www.transportlinks.org/transport_links/filearea/documentsto re/322_Literature%20Survey%203.doc.

Dimitriou, H. (2011) Transport and city development: understanding the fundamentals. In, Dimitriou, H. and Gakenheimer, R. (eds). *Urban Transport in the Developing World: A Handbook of Policy and Practice*. Cheltenham: Edward Elgar.

Dimitriou, H. and Gakenheimer, R. (eds) (2011) *Urban Transport in the Developing World: A Handbook of Policy and Practice*. Cheltenham: Edward Elgar.

Ellis, F. (2000) *Rural Livelihoods and Diversity in Developing Countries*. Oxford: Oxford University Press.

Gakenheimer, R. and Dimitriou, H. (2011). Introduction. In, Dimitriou, H. and Gakenheimer, R. (eds). *Urban Transport in the Developing World: A Handbook of Policy and Practice*. Cheltenham: Edward Elgar.

Gannon C. and Liu, Z. (1997) TWU30, Transport Division Poverty and Transport, Discussion Paper September, Washington, DC: World Bank.

Goldman, T. and Gorham, R. (2006) Sustainable urban transport: four innovative directions. *Technology in Society*, 28, 261–273.

International Transport Forum (2015) *Transport infrastructure Spending and maintenance figures*, OECD http://stats.oecd.org/Index.aspx?DataSetCode=ITF_INV-MTN_DATA.

Kent, L. and Simon, M. (2007) *Safeguarding or Disregarding? Community Experiences with the Asian Development Bank's Safeguard Policies*. Australia: Oxfam.

Lucas, K. (2011) Making the connections between transport disadvantage and the social exclusion of low income populations in the Tshwane Region of South Africa. *Journal of Transport Geography*, 19, 1320–1334.

Lucas, K. and Porter, G. (2016) Mobilities and livelihoods in urban development contexts: introduction. *Journal of Transport Geography*, 55, 129–131.

Lucas, K., Brooks, M., Marsden G. and Kimble, M. (2007) Assessment of capabilities for examining long-term social sustainability of transport and land use strategies. *Transportation Research Record*, 30–37, doi: 10.3141/2013-05.

Lucas, K., Mattioli, G., Verlinghieri, E., and Guzman, A. (2016a) Transport poverty and its adverse social consequences. *Proceedings of the Institution of Civil Engineers: Transport*, 169, 353–365.

Lucas, K., van Wee, B. and Maat, K. (2016b) A method to evaluate equitable accessibility: combining ethical theories and accessibility-based approaches. *Transportation*, 43, 473–490.

Mahapa, S. and Mashiri, M. (2001) Social exclusion and rural transport: Gender aspects of a road improvement project in Tshitwe, Northern province. *Development Southern Africa*, 18, 365–376.

McMillan, T. (2010) Children and Youth and Sustainable Urban Mobility. Thematic study prepared for Sustainable Urban Mobility: *Global Report on Human Settlements 2013*.

Maia, M., Lucas, K., Marinho, G., Santos, E. and de Lima, J. (2016) Access to the Brazilian city – from the perspectives of low-income residents in Recife. *Journal of Transport Geography*, 55, 132–141.

Martens, K. (2006) Broad transport planning on principles of social justice. *Berkeley Planning Journal*, 19, 1–17.

Porter, G. (2011) 'I think a woman who travels a lot is befriending other men and that's why she travels': mobility constraints and their implications for rural women and girls in sub-Saharan Africa. *Gender, Place and Culture: A Journal of Feminist Geography*, 18, 65–81.

Porter, G., Hampshire, K., Abane, A,. Robson, E., Munthali, A., Mashiri, M., Tanle, A., Maponya, A. and Dube, S. (2012) Perspectives on young people's daily mobility, transport and service access in Sub-Saharan Africa. In, Grieco, M. and Urry, J. (eds). *Mobilities: New Perspectives on Transport and Society*. Ashgate, 65–90.

Salon, D. and Gulyani, S. (2010) Mobility, poverty and gender: travel 'choices' of slum residents in Nairobi, Kenya. *Transport Reviews*, 30, 641–657.

Schweizer, C., Racioppi, F. and Nemer, L. (2014) *Developing national action plans on transport, health and environment*. World Health Organization, Regional Office for Europe.

Sperling, D. and Gordon, D. (2009) *Two Billion Cars: Driving Towards Sustainability*. Oxford: Oxford University Press.

Stanley, J. (2010). The social value of transport. *Proceedings of World Transport Conference*, 12–19 July, Lisbon, Portugal.

Stanley, J., Hensher, D., Currie, G., Greene, W. and Vella-Brodrick, D. (2011) Social exclusion and the value of mobility. *Journal of Transport Economics and Policy*, 45, 197–222.

Stiglitz, J., Sen, A. and Fitoussi, J. (2009) Report by the Commission on the Measurement of Economic Performance and Social Progress. Commission on the Measurement of Economic Performance and Social Progress. Available online at: www.stiglitz-sen-fitoussi.fr/documents/rapport_anglais.pdf. [Accessed 25 February 2010].

Thynell, M. (2009) *Social Impact Assessment of Public Transport in Cities: An approach for people involved in the planning, design, and implementation of public transports systems: final consultant's report.* Asian Development Bank and Clean Air Initiative for Asian Cities, http://cleanairinitiative.org/portal/system/files/SIA_Report_FINAL_Nov09_0.pdf.

United Nations (2015a) *World Economic Situation and Prospects 2015*, Chapter 1 Global Economic Outlook, UN, New York.

United Nations (2015b) As Developing Countries Strive to Enhance Economic Performance, Developed Partners Should Honour or Surpass Aid Pledges, Addis Conference Hears, 14 July, www.un.org/press/en/2015/dev3187.doc.htm.

UN Habitat (2014) *Planning and Design for Sustainable Development: Global Report on Human Settlement 2013*, https://unhabitat.org/planning-and-design-for-sustainable-urban-mobility-global-report-on-human-settlements-2013/.

UN Habitat (2016) Housing and slum upgrading, http://unhabitat.org/urban-themes/housing-slum-upgrading/.

Van de Walle, D. (2002) Choosing rural road investments to help reduce poverty. *World Development*, 30, 575–589.

Vanclay, F. (2002) Conceptualising social impacts. *Environmental Impact Assessment Review*, 22, 183–211.

World Bank (2006) *Social Analysis in Transport Project: Guidelines for Incorporating Social Dimensions into Bank-Supported Projects.* Washington, DC: The World Bank.

World Bank (2013) South Africa Economic Update: Focus on Financial Inclusion. *World Bank Group Africa Region Poverty Reduction and Economic Management Issue 4*, www.worldbank.org/content/dam/Worldbank/document/Africa/South%20Africa/Report/south-africa-economic-update-2013.05.pdf.

World Health Organization (WHO) (2015) *Traffic Accident Injuries, May*, www.who.int/mediacentre/factsheets/fs358/en/.

# PART IV

# EMERGING APPROACHES TO SOCIO-SPATIAL EQUITY ANALYSIS

# 14. Reasonable travel time – the traveller's perspective

*David Banister, Yannick Cornet, Moshe Givoni and Glenn Lyons*

## 1. INTRODUCTION

Travel time is central to our understanding of transport, and to analysis and decision making in the transport sector. Currently, transport planning is based on the rationale that all travel is 'wasteful' (Hamilton, 1989) and therefore travel time savings are beneficial to the individual traveller and to society as a whole. It means that travel time ought to be minimised. It is complemented by the argument that greater choice between activities at alternative destination options is beneficial. Hence, a better transport system is one that provides a wider range of destinations that can be reached in the time available to any individual. The inevitable consequence of this thinking is to promote speed as the primary objective of transport systems with a view to 'saving time' (Banister, 2011). This leads to longer travel distances, has distributional outcomes (greater inequality), and results in greater use of resources, as higher speed increases energy consumption and carbon emissions.

This chapter discusses the notion of reasonable travel time as a wider objective for transport planning and investment. Reasonable travel time (RTT) addresses the way we value and perceive the consumption of time while travelling, and it recognises the role that travel time use has in our lives alongside the more traditional purpose of transport systems seeking to get us from A to B as quickly as possible. The argument is illustrated with reference to High-Speed Rail (HSR), where both high speed (minimisation of time) and high quality service (opportunities to use time effectively) are combined. We argue that these two essential qualities can be traded against one another when investment funding is limited. The debate around travel time is first outlined, and we then detail the elements of RTT arguing that such an approach might help reassess priorities and lead to a more equitable transport system.

## 2. CONSIDERATIONS OF TRAVEL TIME

### 2.1 Commodification of Travel Time

Transport provides the means to overcome distance in order to take part in activities at other locations, and it has traditionally been seen as a means to an end. Transport is derived from the demand to be somewhere to reach and realise valuable opportunities – hence the term 'derived demand' (e.g. Geurs and van Wee, 2004). Travel time is considered a disutility, where the disbenefit or cost is represented by having to invest time to travel in order to realise destination's benefits. If the transport system can help minimise this disutility then more time is available for economically productive activities. Such logic has provided the underpinning for economic appraisal of transport schemes internationally (Watts and Urry, 2008; Small, 2012). It has provided the motivation to monetise the benefits of saved travel time that result from investments in transport in order to justify the investment costs, where even tiny reductions in travel time can, when aggregated, generate substantial benefits.[1]

Amongst economists concerned with examination of valuation of travel time savings (VTTS) in transport as part of economic appraisal, there is an acknowledgement that not all travel time is wasted. Indeed, there is an important distinction between valuing travel time and valuing travel time savings.[2] Fowkes (2001) suggests that provided not all travel time is productive, then any time that is saved by speeding up a journey will relate to the unproductive part of journey time. This is argued to support a long-held appraisal assumption (for travel during the course of work) that saved time is released from being unproductive within the journey to being put to productive use in activities involving paid work outside the journey (Watts and Urry, 2008; Small, 2012). Conceptually, Hensher (1977) outlined how productive use of travel time might influence VTTS (later codified by Fowkes et al., 1986) and recent work by the UK Department for Transport has revisited the valuation of travel time savings using a willingness-to-pay approach that sought to incorporate consideration of travel time use when assessing travellers' willingness to trade travel time savings for money (Department for Transport, 2015).

Milakis et al. (2015) translate the understanding that not all travel time is 'wasteful' to argue that for each journey there is an 'acceptable travel time' and an 'ideal travel time' for the traveller. Acceptable travel time represents the travel time that corresponds to peak overall utility when combining the utility to be derived from the activity at the destination and disutility of travelling itself. Ideal travel time is the point at which the marginal utility of additional travel time diminishes (but can still be positive). Reasonable Travel Time aligns with Milakis et al.'s acceptable travel time, but it moves away from the notion of utility as the measurement unit of time towards a much broader concept of time (see Section 3).

The commodification of time and the concept of (dis)utility both have merits, but they remain controversial (Næss, 2006), as they do not provide a complete picture in terms of making sense of travel time. They should not be the dominant guiding principles in transport planning, as this overly simplifies the planning and investment considerations. The existing paradigm's apparently enduring 'need for speed' is not simply a product of the approaches used in transport analysis – it points to the modernist 'mindset' underpinning the utilitarian view of commoditised time (Wardman and Lyons, 2016).

---

[1]   Although some countries apply a discount to 'small time savings' as a way to reduce the bias towards seemingly large cumulative benefits that may not be relevant from a user's perspective (Mackie et al., 2014).

[2]   While the former could (and we later in this chapter argue should) be a (more) important aspect of transport investment, the latter has nevertheless been a dominant consideration in the process of justifying investment.

## 2.2 Door-to-Door Travel Time

The transport system is commonly planned as a set of separately operated networks, with each catering for one or more specific modes of transport. Many of the limitations of the current system are associated with the lack of an integrated transport system (Givoni and Banister, 2010). But for the passenger there is only one transport system, made up of different modes and transfers between them. Thus, the travel time and speed should relate to the total journey time from door-to-door. Alternatives to the car usually involve a combination of modes and thus expose users to the issues associated with changing between modes during a door-to-door journey. While HSR, for example, provides fast travel and relatively short travel time station to station (given the distance covered), the journey to and from the HSR station is often considerably slower resulting in a long door-to-door travel time and a poor overall experience. This is even more apparent with air travel. Most travel surveys only consider the main part of the journey, often the 'trunk' section that covers the main mode and time (or distance), but not the time taken to access the main mode and the time and means needed to reach the final destination (the 'egress' journey). Each door-to-door journey, with the exception of walking, consists of several segments in which the experience will vary substantially and this is affected by factors such as intermodal connectivity.

Many journeys involve 'transfer' time, during which speed and distance covered are close to zero (waiting time is often the main element of the transfer), and this needs to be considered. The implications for door-to-door travel time are important, as it means that it is not only the total travel time that matters, but how this time is divided between different segments of the journey and between different modes of transport. It is already current practice in transport planning to allocate a different value of time for in-vehicle travel time and out-of-vehicle travel time, and further to break down the latter into several categories (wait and walk being the main ones). Empirical evidence shows that the disutility of out-of-vehicle travel time is considerably larger than in-vehicle time (Wardman, 2001). In other words, not all minutes are equal, and our attention has been focused on the 'wrong' minutes.

In planning terms, the concern should be over the efficient operation of the transport system as a whole and how the various elements complement each other. One means by which this can be measured is the interconnectivity ratio, calculated as the access and egress time as a proportion of total trip time (Krygsman et al., 2004). In a multimodal journey, this interconnectivity ratio would need to include transfer and wait time, as well as access and egress travel times. Givoni and Rietveld (2007) and Brons et al. (2009) have concluded that in order to increase its number of passengers, Dutch Railways ought to invest in the stations and in the access and egress journeys to/from them rather than investing in the actual rail journey.

## 2.3 Experienced Time

A broader social science perspective on travel time has examined and promoted its value and meaning in terms of the range of activities that can be undertaken whilst travelling. For example, travel time can be spent on a range of technology-enabled activities (Holley et al., 2008; Lyons et al., 2013; see also Kenyon and Lyons, 2007, for an extensive list of activities). This implies a level of benefit to the traveller from travel time (Mokhtarian and Salomon, 2001). Time spent travelling can become useful in and for itself, which some authors have called the 'joy of travel' (Milakis et al., 2015) or the 'gift of travel time' (Jain and Lyons, 2008). In its more extreme form, 'travel' can be the only journey purpose – travel for its own sake (Mokhtarian and Salomon, 2001), or 'travel with meaning' – which underpins the nascent slow travel movement (Lumsdon and McGrath, 2011). This experienced time affects the value of time in a more normative sense, and by implication could affect travel behaviour.

The value of experienced time depends on a range of external factors that provide the option for time to become useful, and there will be situations where there simply is no opportunity for using travel time purposefully.[3] Lyons et al. (2013), referring to Stradling (2006), offer a simple typology of three different forms of effort that may impinge on how travel time is experienced: physical effort, cognitive effort, and affective effort. Physical effort is the effort asked of and imposed on the body in undertaking travel. Cognitive effort is the mental focus that is needed to execute the journey successfully. Affective effort is the emotional influence of undertaking the journey. Lyons et al. (2013) infer that 'less effort devoted to travel itself yields more potential opportunity for the fruitful spending of travel time' (p. 563). It should be noted that such efforts do not always have a negative connotation – for instance physical effort can provide a positive stimulus for a sense of emotional wellbeing, which in turn heightens the (perceived) fruitfulness of time use, for example while cycling.

Travel experience determines the extent to which travel time is seen as a cost or a benefit to the individual and it depends very much on the extent to which the travel environment provides a setting to use travel time for 'something', other than for travelling. There are many ways to improve aspects of the travel experience and to improve the conditions to use time. These include: reducing transport connections and 'smoothing' them by integrating the transport networks (Banister and Givoni, 2013); improving comfort (e.g. through reduced crowding and available seating, or through vehicle design and operation to minimise travel sickness); reducing unwanted distractions; improving the perceived security or pleasantness of travel; improving the familiarity with the transport system; improving the ability to plan the journey effectively; and improving overall reliability. The goal should be to avoid letting travel time turn into lost time. We define lost time as 'time that individuals cannot choose to allocate to an activity they need or wish to participate in (apart from travel itself) due to physical, cognitive or affective efforts imposed by the transport system'. In this respect, the transport system should be planned with the intention to allow travellers to reclaim the lost time that has been invested in travelling, and to turn this into useful time.

## 2.4   Destination Time and Multiple Activities

Travel time and travel experience are situated in a wider context of the combined time invested both in getting to and participating in activities, and how this combined time is distributed

---

[3]   Purposeful should not only imply 'economically productive' but rather any use of time, over and above the act of travelling itself, that is felt to be useful to the individual concerned.

(spatially and temporally). A journey is not necessarily only from point A to point B, and for a single purpose. A traveller may justify a trip by planning to undertake a number of activities at or near to the primary destination (Lyons, 2013). Alternatively, a traveller may plan activities at different locations along an overall route to an end destination. Schwanen and Dijst (2002) explored the notion of a travel–time ratio (see also Dijst and Vidakovic, 2000; Susilo and Dijst, 2010 and Hunink, 2013). This travel–time ratio is obtained by dividing the travel time by the sum of the travel time and activity duration, and it provides one means to measure the relationship between the time spent travelling and the time spent at the destination, or in the various activities undertaken whilst away from the home.

There are interdependencies between the destination activity and travel time. If the journey is undertaken then it generally means the utility to be derived at the destination is larger than the disutility from travel, as illustrated by Milakis et al. (2015). Alternatively, to compensate for the efforts involved in reaching a destination, other activities might also be added, to increase the utility to be derived at the destination. This means that the journey characteristics (time, comfort and cost) could influence the (number of) destination and activity choices, and not only the other way round. The purposes and means of traveling are closely related and interdependent.

## 3.   DEFINING REASONABLE TRAVEL TIME (RTT)

These dimensions of travel time (Section 2) provide the context for defining the notion of Reasonable Travel Time (RTT). There is clearly an imperative to being able to travel with some degree of speed, unless all our needs for accessing people, goods, services and opportunities can be met quite literally on our doorsteps. It is also apparent that travel involves much more than time minimisation, as it provides, at least in part, an opportunity to carry out different activities during travel. When considering travel time from the passenger's perspective, RTT provides a much richer and complex set of relationships that go beyond the simplification given by 'clock time'. RTT is defined as the door-to-door journey time that is acceptable to the individual traveller for reaching a particular destination, and its associated activities, given the conditions provided to turn 'lost time' into 'useful time' while travelling.

RTT provides a normative conceptualisation of travel time which is designed to highlight what is really important to the traveller and what determines travel choices and behaviours. Reducing travel time typically improves RTT, but RTT can also be improved through other factors that are relevant to travellers. These include the total door-to-door travel time, the ability to carry out multiple activities at destinations, and importantly the means to improve the travel experience. In each case, the RTT may be increased as the total journey time is increased (through all parts of the journey being considered), as the destination activities become more attractive (through multiple activities), as the positive experience is enhanced (through greater comfort and convenience), and as lost time is recaptured (through making use of travel time while travelling). This richer interpretation of travel time would suggest that there might be a benchmark RTT (say 30 minutes for the journey to work in a medium-sized city of about 500,000), but this could be increased or reduced according to the other dimensions highlighted here and through the different priorities allocated by travellers (Table 14.1).

*Table 14.1   The dimensions of RTT and the equity impacts*

| Equity dimensions | Dimensions of reasonable travel time | | |
| --- | --- | --- | --- |
| | Door-to-door travel time | Travel experience | Destination characteristics |
| Reliability | Uncertainty relates to all segments of a journey | Variable crowding levels, seating availability | Availability of people and activities |
| Mobile technology – user side (ICT) | Increases possibility for useful travel time | Reduces efforts in planning and undertaking travel | Possibility for 'virtual' mobility |
| Technologies – supply side (ITS) | Enables multi-modal seamless connections | Allows real-time monitoring and management of transport system | Potential to create flexibility in time and proximity or closeness of activities |
| Traveller characteristics | Perceptions affect understanding of useful time | Attitude and abilities shape travel experience | Needs define purpose and choice of destinations |

These priorities cover the different needs of travellers, and relate explicitly to equity through their particular requirements (service reliability), their competences (access to technology), and abilities (individual characteristics). Each segment of door-to-door travel time can face uncertainty (departure time, waiting time, in-vehicle time, arrival time, transfer time, ticketing time), and these may affect the total journey time, or necessitate extra buffering, or result in delays. Reliability influences the perception of time, as improved reliability reduces the effort and therefore the effective journey time. In turn, unreliable travel times can increase anxiety and discomfort, and therefore impact on the experience of travel by imposing extra cognitive, physical and/or emotional efforts upon the traveller. Finally, characteristics of the destination(s) can be subject to uncertainties (associated with or compounding travel time reliability), such as opening hours, the duration of a meeting, or the availability of people or activities at the destination.

Secondly, technology in general, and information and communications technology (ICT) in particular, has a direct effect on RTT and experiential time especially (Lyons et al., 2016; Wardman and Lyons, 2016). ICT can also be relevant for planning, paying and tracking a seamless, door-to-door multimodal journey, as well as potentially discovering new activities en-route or at destination. In other words, ICT impacts on all components of RTT including addressing some underlying issues relating to travel reliability, whether it is through the use of mobile devices (on the user side) or the provision of intelligent transport systems (ITS) delivering real-time information to travellers (on the supply side). Different users have different levels of knowledge and access to technologies, and these together with affordability, have clear equity implications.

Thirdly, there are important factors that relate to an individual's ability to travel. Travel is often viewed as something that we can all engage with, but in reality there is a huge diversity between individuals. Each person needs to define their travel purpose, and this will influence the overall experience together with their attitudes, abilities and perceptions towards speed, reliability, travel time, access and egress requirements, previous experiences and any other particular requirements (e.g. cost constraints and disability). RTT varies substantially across the population according to their individual constraints, their location, their budgets and their preferences.

Not all transport modes offer the same opportunity for useful travel time. Car drivers can use their travel time productively by making phone calls, or as valuable time-out, or 'me-time' for transitioning between work and home (Jain and Lyons, 2008; Wardman and Lyons, 2016). Empirical evidence shows productive time is particularly prevalent on train journeys, where a greater range of activities can be undertaken. A modal hierarchy seems to be apparent in relation to economically productive travel time use with rail at the top, followed by air, bus, and finally car (Lyons and Urry, 2005; Wardman and Lyons, 2016). This does not stem from the unique characteristics of a particular mode, but from its current design, and the potential to combine speed with a positive experience. The case of HSR is used to illustrate the RTT perspective, where station to station travel combines both high speed and a positive experience, but door-to-door travel provides substantially poorer speeds and experiences.

## 4. EXAMINING HIGH-SPEED RAIL FROM A RTT PERSPECTIVE

Many studies have analysed the contraction of space from reduced travel times for high-speed rail (HSR), examining weighted average travel time and contours in China (Cao et al., 2013), territorial cohesion in Spain and Portugal (Ortega et al., 2015, 2012), wider economic impacts in sub-regions of France and the UK (Chen and Hall, 2012), the importance of system connectivity and interchanges (Hickman et al., 2015), and time-space effects of existing (Chen and Hall, 2011) and future (Martínez Sánchez-Mateos and Givoni, 2012) high-speed lines in the UK. The standard definition of HSR relates only to speed (see Givoni, 2006), with much less attention being given to aspects of the experience of travelling by HSR.

From a traveller perspective, crowding, comfort and other quality features play an important role in making rail attractive (Wardman and Whelan, 2011; Blainey et al., 2012) and HSR even more so. It is these aspects of the travel, not the speed (vehicle speed or city centre to city centre travel time) that make HSR a preferred choice by passengers over the aircraft (on routes up to about 1000 km). Greater comfort and better quality of services have been shown to attract business travellers away from flying (Hall, 2009; Givoni and Dobruszkes, 2013). For example, some travellers may feel physically constrained by the limited seating space in planes or cars. Others experience motion-sickness in road transport, therefore physically limiting the possibility of using travel time. Cognitively, the HSR traveller is freed from any obliged tasks – like driving – the main advantage over the car, and from lengthy check-in and security processes, and from restrictions on some activities (mainly during take-off and landing) – the main advantage over the plane, creating the possibility of turning lost time into useful time. In other words, HSR typically offers a higher ratio of main mode travel time to door-to-door travel time – its main advantage over the much faster plane (Givoni and Banister, 2013). This may help explain why Eurostar (HSR) has captured more than 74 per cent of the market share between London and Paris, and 68 per cent for the London to Brussels route.[4]

The qualities of HSR need to be examined as part of the full door-to-door journey. HSR infrastructure is prone to the 'excitement engineers and technologists get in pushing the envelope for what is possible in "longest-tallest-fastest" types of projects' (Flyvbjerg, 2014). HS2 in the UK is designed for a state-of-the-art maximum speed of 400 km/h (250mph). However, achieving higher speeds imposes a limit on the number of stations along the way as each additional stop increases the journey time by 10 to 15 minutes (Givoni and Banister, 2012). From a multi-modal door-to-door perspective, using HS2 will require long access and transfer times for many travellers, eroding its potential travel time savings once the door-to-door journey is considered. Analysis has shown that many cities along the proposed HS2 line will, as a result of developing the HSR, experience longer door-to-door travel times by rail to London (Martínez Sánchez-Mateos and Givoni, 2012). Based on their analysis of the Amsterdam area, Givoni and Rietveld (2014) conclude that 'it may be worthwhile to let high-speed trains stop in more than one station in large cities', which will slow them down, but will ease access to stations and overall reduce travel time door-to-door.

Although most attention has been given to the 'high speed' part of the journey, from the passenger's perspective it is the average speed from door-to-door that is most important (Brons et al., 2009; Givoni and Banister, 2012). Similarly, the travel experience relates to the whole journey and it is the 'non high speed' sections that create a poor experience. In a study of intermodal hubs in China, Hickman et al. (2015) observed that poor experience was prevalent, largely due to problems including 'Wi-Fi availability, waiting and seating, the availability of door-to-door ticketing, crowdedness, access to the hub, time of travel through and waiting in the hub' (p. 175).

From an equity perspective, there are additional issues relating to technology and the traveller (Table 14.1) that are also important. On the French TGV, 40 per cent of all journeys are made by the top 20 per cent of income groups, and for the UK the corresponding figure is 63 per cent, and there is also a strong spatial focus on Paris and London respectively. Paris residents use the TGV nearly four times more than the national average (Banister, 2018, pp. 128 and 143). The rich living in Paris (and London) make much more use of HSR, and they also have the competence to use technology to ensure a more positive experience by maximising useful time while travelling. HSR seems to be viewed as a separate transport network, rather than as part of the overall rail or transport system. This means that some elements of RTT are not included (Table 14.1) and that there are strong spatial and social equity consequences, as passengers are concentrated spatially in the capital cities and socially in the top income groups.

## 5.   CONCLUSIONS AND IMPLICATIONS FOR EQUITY

The notion of 'time is money' dominates thinking on transport through the commodification of time and monetisation of travel time savings (Banister, 2008, 2011). While the idea

---

[4]   www.telegraph.co.uk/travel/rail-journeys/Eurostars-20th-anniversary-what-now-for-the-rail-operator/.

that time is money may be true for some travellers, this does not mean that travel time invested in reaching a destination is entirely lost time. Travel time can be reclaimed and turned into useful time, some of which may well be termed 'productive' in economic and social terms. The broader concept of RTT recognises both the complexity of travel time and the diversity of travellers. A passenger should be considered to be 'better off' not only when the door-to-door travel time is shortened, but when there are more and better opportunities to use travel time for 'something useful' and when there are more potential activities relevant to the traveller in close proximity at destinations. This situation is further complicated by the requirements, competences and abilities of the passengers themselves.

All aspects of RTT should be improved, and this means prioritising more than just travel time and speed. It can be argued that as a general rule, improving the journey experience would be an easier and cheaper means to achieve this, as compared with reducing the door-to-door travel time. As discussed earlier, increasing travel comfort (by improving seating availability), reducing travel anxiety (improving the reliability or the ability to plan a trip effectively) or simply improving the pleasantness of the travel environment could contribute substantially towards improving the travel experience. Lyons et al. (2016) note that improving travel experience is also in the hands of the traveller themselves, in terms of how travellers equip themselves physically and mentally for engaging in the travel activity.

Speeding up the journey is still important. However, in terms of return on investment in doing so, we suggest that greater priority should be given to speeding up those parts of a journey that are least amenable to turning lost time into useful time for the traveller. Meanwhile for parts of a journey that best lend themselves to opportunities for useful time use, the alternative to speeding them up may instead be to take steps to enhance the time use experience. Such an approach must still appreciate the huge variety in the travelling public, and be sensitive to any individual's requirements, and not assume that we all have the same values, limitations and objectives when we travel. Social and spatial differences mean that it is difficult to respond to all these requirements when providing transport services, but it is essential when thinking about equity that this diversity of needs are recognised and acted upon.

Secondly, in terms of equity, it is also important to consider the slower modes of transport within the same framework, as the bus and active modes are those that are most commonly used by the poor (Banister, 2018). Their journeys tend to be shorter, with a poor quality experience and less opportunity to make use of travel time. But there may also be less potential for turning lost travel time into useful travel time.

Travel time is sometimes conceptualised as a 'wicked' problem (Wardman and Lyons, 2016), as it consists of complex interdependencies, with no obvious single 'right' or 'best' solution. The concept of RTT developed here can be seen as a shift from functionalist science towards a paradigm of 'complexity' and systems science (Leleur, 2008), and acknowledge deep uncertainty where new challenges to our conventional processes are being introduced (Lyons and Davidson, 2016). Innovative transport technologies are now focused more on the travel experience rather than speed, for example by taking away the 'driving' function from the car through automation.

Our treatment of travel time cannot remain unchanged and we must move on by adopting new concepts such as reasonable travel time. This chapter has attempted to provide a broader framework within which to understand travel behaviour, and this includes an appreciation of the richness of time in terms of its quality and how it is used. We all have the same amount of time, and it is important that we accept the diversity of uses when discussing what is reasonable, and how much should be allocated to the travel activity. That diversity should also be extended to our understanding of how the travel experience can be made more pleasurable for all of us.

## ACKNOWLEDGEMENTS

This chapter was partly funded by the Strategic Research Council of Denmark (Innovationsfonden).

## REFERENCES

Banister, D. (2008) 'The sustainable mobility paradigm', *Transport Policy*, 15(2), 73–80, doi: 10.1016/j.tranpol.2007.10.005.

Banister, D. (2011) 'The trilogy of distance, speed and time', *Journal of Transport Geography*, 19(4), 950–959, doi: 10.1016/j.jtrangeo.2010.12.004.

Banister, D. (2018) *Inequality in Transport*, Marcham: Alexandrine Press, p.250.

Banister, D. and Givoni, M. (2013) 'High-speed rail in the EU27: trends, time, accessibility and principles', *Built Environment*, 39(3), 324–338.

Blainey, S., Hickford, A. and Preston, J. (2012) 'Barriers to passenger rail use: a review of the evidence', *Transport Reviews*, (February 2015), 675–696, doi: 10.1080/01441647.2012.743489.

Brons, M., Givoni, M. and Rietveld, P. (2009) 'Access to railway stations and its potential in increasing rail use', *Transportation Research Part A*, 43(2), 136–149, doi: 10.1016/j.tra.2008.08.002.

Cao, J., Liu, X. C., Wang, Y. and Li, Q. (2013) 'Accessibility impacts of China's high-speed rail network', *Journal of Transport Geography*, 28, 12–21, doi: 10.1016/j.jtrangeo.2012.10.008.

Chen, C. L. and Hall, P. (2011) 'The impacts of high-speed trains on British economic geography: a study of the UK's InterCity 125/225 and its effects', *Journal of Transport Geography*, 19(4), 689–704, doi: 10.1016/j.jtrangeo.2010.08.010.

Chen, C. L. and Hall, P. (2012) 'The wider spatial-economic impacts of high-speed trains: a comparative case study of Manchester and Lille sub-regions', *Journal of Transport Geography*, 24, 89–110, doi: 10.1016/j.jtrangeo.2011.09.002.

Department for Transport (2015) *Provision of market research for value of travel time savings and reliability – Phase 2 Report*. London. Available at: https://www.gov.uk/government/publications/values-of-travel-time-savings-and-reliability-final-reports.

Dijst, M. and Vidakovic, V. (2000) 'Travel time ratio: the key factor of spatial reach', *Transportation*, (1979), 179–199.

Flyvbjerg, B. (2014) 'What you should know about megaprojects and why: an overview', *Project Management Journal*, 45(2), 6–19, doi: 10.1002/pmj.

Fowkes, A. S. (2001) *Principles of Valuing Business Travel Time Savings, Working Paper 562*. University of Leeds, Institute for Transport Studies. Available at: http://eprints.whiterose.ac.uk/2064/1/ITS39_WP562_uploadable.pdf.

Fowkes, A. S., Marks, P. and Nash, C. A. (1986) *The value of business travel time savings, Working Paper 214*. University of Leeds, Institute for Transport Studies.

Geurs, K. T. and van Wee, B. (2004) 'Accessibility evaluation of land-use and transport strategies: review and research directions', *Journal of Transport Geography*, 12(2), 127–140, doi: 10.1016/j.jtrangeo.2003.10.005.

Givoni, M. (2006) 'Development and impact of the modern high speed train: a review', *Transport Reviews*, 26(5), 593–611, doi: 10.1080/01441640600589319.

Givoni, M. and Banister, D. (2010) *Integrated Transport: From Policy to Practice*. Routledge. Available at: https://www.routledge.com/Integrated-Transport-From-Policy-to-Practice/Givoni-Banister/p/book/9780415548939.

Givoni, M. and Banister, D. (2012) 'Speed: the less important element of the high-speed train', *Journal of Transport Geography*, 22, 306–307, doi: 10.1016/j.jtrangeo.2012.01.024.

Givoni, M. and Dobruszkes, F. (2013) 'A review of ex-post evidence for mode substitution and induced demand following the introduction of high-speed rail', *Transport Reviews*, 33(6), 720–742, doi: 10.1080/01441647.2013. 853707.

Givoni, M. and Rietveld, P. (2007) 'The access journey to the railway station and its role in passengers' satisfaction with rail travel', *Transport Policy*, 14(5), 357–365, doi: 10.1016/j.tranpol.2007.04.004.

Givoni, M. and Rietveld, P. (2014) 'Do cities deserve more railway stations? The choice of a departure railway station in a multiple-station region', *Journal of Transport Geography*, 36, 89–97, doi: 10.1016/j. jtrangeo.2014.03.004.

Hall, P. (2009) 'Magic carpets and seamless webs: opportunities and constraints for high-speed trains in Europe', *Built Environment*, 35(1), 59–69, doi: 10.2148/benv.35.1.59.

Hamilton, B. W. (1989) 'Wasteful commuting again', *Journal of Political Economy*, 97(6), 1497–1504.

Hensher, D. A. (1977) *Value of Business Travel Time*. Oxford: Pergamon Press.

Hickman, R., Chen, C.-L., Chow, A. and Saxena, S. (2015) 'Improving interchanges in China: the experiential phenomenon', *Journal of Transport Geography*, 42, 175–186, doi: 10.1016/j.jtrangeo.2014.12.004.

Holley, D., Jain, J. and Lyons, G. (2008) 'Understanding business travel time use and its place in the working day', *Time and Society*, 17(1), 27–46, doi: 10.1177/0961463X07086308.

Hunink, D. (2013) *Travel–time ratios for commuters in the Netherlands between 2005, Unpublished paper*. University of Utrecht, Department of Geography. Available at: http://dennishunink.nl/wp-content/uploads/2013/07/ Travel-time-ratios-for-commuters-in-the-Netherlands-between-2005-and-2009-Dennis-Hunink.pdf?bd19aa.

Jain, J. and Lyons, G. (2008) 'The gift of travel time', *Journal of Transport Geography*, 16(2), 81–89, doi: 10.1016/j.jtrangeo.2007.05.001.

Kenyon, S. and Lyons, G. (2007) 'Introducing multitasking to the study of travel and ICT: examining its extent and assessing its potential importance', *Transportation Research Part A: Policy and Practice*, 41(2), 161–175, doi: 10.1016/j.tra.2006.02.004.

Krygsman, S., Dijst, M. and Arentze, T. (2004) 'Multimodal public transport: an analysis of travel time elements and the interconnectivity ratio', *Transport Policy*, 11(3), 265–275, doi: 10.1016/j.tranpol.2003.12.001.

Leleur, S. (2008) 'Systems science and complexity: some proposals for future development', *Systems Research and Behavioral Science*, (25), 67–79, doi: 10.1002/sres.860.

Lumsdon, L. M. and McGrath, P. (2011) 'Developing a conceptual framework for slow travel: a grounded theory approach', *Journal of Sustainable Tourism*, 19, 265–279, doi: 10.1080/09669582.2010.519438.

Lyons, G. (2013) 'Business travel: the social practices surrounding meetings', *Research in Transportation Business and Management*, 9, 50–57, doi: 10.1016/j.rtbm.2013.03.001.

Lyons, G. and Davidson, C. (2016) 'Guidance for transport planning and policymaking in the face of an uncertain future', *Transportation Research Part A*, 88, 104–116, doi: 10.1016/j.tra.2016.03.012.

Lyons, G. and Urry, J. (2005) 'Travel time use in the information age', *Transportation Research Part A: Policy and Practice*, 39(2–3), 257–276, doi: 10.1016/j.tra.2004.09.004.

Lyons, G., Jain, J., Susilo, Y. and Atkins, S. (2013) 'Comparing rail passengers' travel time use in Great Britain between 2004 and 2010', *Mobilities*, 8(4), 560–579, doi: 10.1080/17450101.2012.743221.

Lyons, G., Jain, J. and Weir, L. (2016) 'Changing times: a decade of empirical insight into the experience of rail passengers in Great Britain', *Journal of Transport Geography*, 57, 94–104, doi: 10.1016/j.jtrangeo.2016.10.003.

Mackie, P., Worsley, T. and Eliasson, J. (2014) 'Transport appraisal revisited', *Research in Transportation Economics*, 47, 3–18, doi: 10.1016/j.retrec.2014.09.013.

Martínez Sánchez-Mateos, H. S. and Givoni, M. (2012) 'The accessibility impact of a new High-Speed Rail line in the UK – a preliminary analysis of winners and losers', *Journal of Transport Geography*, 25, 105–114, doi: 10.1016/j.jtrangeo.2011.09.004.

Milakis, D., Cervero, R., van Wee, B. and Maat, K. (2015) 'Do people consider an acceptable travel time? Evidence from Berkeley, CA', *Journal of Transport Geography*, 44, 76–86, doi: 10.1016/j.jtrangeo.2015. 03.008.

Mokhtarian, P. L. and Salomon, I. (2001) 'How derived is the demand for travel? Some conceptual and measurement considerations', *Transportation Research Part A: Policy and Practice*, 35(8), 695–719, doi: 10.1016/ S0965-8564(00)00013-6.

Næss, P. (2006) 'Cost–benefit analysis of transportation investment: neither critical nor realistic', *Journal of Critical Realism*, 5(1), 32–60.

Ortega, E., López, E. and Monzón, A. (2012) 'Territorial cohesion impacts of high-speed rail at different planning levels', *Journal of Transport Geography*, 24, 130–141, doi: 10.1016/j.jtrangeo.2011.10.008.

Ortega, E., Martín, B., Gonzalez, E. and Moreno, E. (2015) 'A contribution for the evaluation of the territorial impact of transport infrastructures in the early stages of the EIA: application to the Huelva (Spain)-Faro (Portugal) rail link', *Journal of Environmental Planning and Management*, 59(2), 302–319, doi: 10.1080/09640568.2015.1009628.

Schwanen, T. and Dijst, M. (2002) 'Travel–time ratios for visits to the workplace: the relationship between commuting time and work duration', *Transportation Research Part A: Policy and Practice*, 36(7), 573–592, doi: 10.1016/S0965-8564(01)00023-4.

Small, K. A. (2012) 'Valuation of travel time', *Economics of Transportation*, 1(1–2), 2–14, doi: 10.1016/j.ecotra.2012.09.002.

Stradling, S. G. (2006) *The Psychology of Travel. Review commissioned for the Foresight 'Intelligent Infrastructure Systems' project, Office of Science and Technology, Department for Trade and Industry*. London. Available at: http://researchrepository.napier.ac.uk/2590/.

Susilo, Y. O. and Dijst, M. (2010) 'Behavioural decisions of travel–time ratios for work, maintenance and leisure activities in the Netherlands', *Transportation Planning and Technology*, 33(1), 19–34, doi: 10.1080/03081060903429280.

Wardman, M. (2001) 'A review of British evidence on time and service quality valuations', *Transportation Research Part E: Logistics and Transportation Review*, 37(2–3), 107–128, doi: 10.1016/S1366-5545(00)00012-0.

Wardman, M. and Lyons, G. (2016) 'The digital revolution and worthwhile use of travel time: implications for appraisal and forecasting', *Transportation*, 43(3), 507–530, doi: 10.1007/s11116-015-9587-0.

Wardman, M. and Whelan, G. (2011) 'Twenty years of rail crowding valuation studies: evidence and lessons from British experience', *Transport Reviews*, 31(3), 379–398, doi: 10.1080/01441647.2010.519127.

Watts, L. and Urry, J. (2008) 'Moving methods, travelling times', *Environment and Planning D: Society and Space*, 26(5), 860–874, doi: 10.1068/d6707.

# 15. Using different approaches to evaluate individual social equity in transport

*Mengqiu Cao, Yongping Zhang, Yuerong Zhang, Shengxiao Li and Robin Hickman*

## 1. INTRODUCTION

There is growing inequality in the distribution of opportunities and activities, particularly with regard to income and wealth,[1] not only in the so-called developing countries (Ravallion, 2014), but throughout the world (Alvaredo et al., 2018). The World Inequality Report shows that the richest 10 per cent of people received approximately 61 per cent, 55 per cent, 55 per cent, 47 per cent, 46 per cent, 41 per cent and 37 per cent of national income in the Middle East, India, Brazil, USA, Russia, China and Europe, respectively, in 2016 (ibid.). These are fairly damning statistics globally from the perspective of social equity. In addition, Dorling (2015) argues that the top one per cent of people generally exacerbate this inequality, because they have an excessive amount of money and benefit disproportionately from this extreme wealth, whereas there is less potential for the remaining 99 per cent of people to enhance their financial status. Hence, the rich become richer, and the poor become poorer (OECD, 2015). Inequalities not only exist in the field of economics in relation to income and wealth, but also in other areas, such as the transport sector, where access to and use of different transport modes varies markedly across population groups, and provides the means to access activities necessary in life (Martens, 2017; Banister, 2018; Litman, 2018).

In the transport context, it has been found that the rich tend to make longer distance journeys, often by rail and air, and travel more frequently. This means that wealthier cohorts generally have higher levels of mobility than their less well-off counterparts, which may in turn contribute to rising transport inequality (Banister, 2018). In addition, it has also been argued that inequality in transport has extended beyond the traditional measures of travel undertaken by different people, such as travel time, travel distance, travel mode and travel cost. Instead, it now covers a wide range of effects relating to social exclusion, freedom, well-being and the ability to access opportunities and resources (Lucas, 2004, 2012; Delbosc and Currie, 2011a, 2011b; Hickman et al., 2017; Banister, 2018; Cao and Hickman, 2019a, 2019b). In order to address the aforementioned issues, an important question to resolve is what type of methods can be used to measure inequalities in transport most effectively. Some econometric measures of income inequality have already been adapted and used to a limited extent in the transport sector, such as the Gini coefficient (Delbosc and Currie, 2011c; Lucas et al., 2016; Guzman et al., 2017), which is more widely used in development studies. However, it can be argued that if people have very similar

---

[1] The difference between income and wealth is explained by Banister (2018, p. 19).

levels of accessibility to local transport services (e.g. using the Underground), the Gini coefficient may not be the most suitable method to use, and perhaps alternative approaches could prove useful. The Capabilities Approach (CA) (Sen, 1985, 1999, 2009) has attracted increasing interest in transport, but with some difficulties noted in application (Hickman et al., 2017, Cao and Hickman, 2019a, 2019b). Beyond these approaches, it is useful to consider whether other methods can also be used to measure social equity in the transport context. To our knowledge, there are very few empirical studies[2] that have attempted to examine different inequality measures and their use in assessing individual social inequity in transport (Banister, 2018). Furthermore, only a few empirical studies have applied the CA in the transport context to examine the differences between real opportunities and actual travel and participation in activities (Hickman et al., 2017). Finally, existing literature has not provided sufficient empirical studies on immigrants' travel behaviour (Blumenberg and Smart, 2010; Lovejoy and Handy, 2011), especially in developing countries (Li and Zhao, 2018). Thus, this chapter aims to fill the aforementioned research gaps using the relatively migrant-rich lower-income neighbourhood of Tuqiao, in Beijing, as a case study. As well as the CA, the following six inequality indices, namely the Gini coefficient, the Atkinson index, the Palma ratio, the Pietra ratio, the Schutz coefficient and the Theil index, are also applied and compared, in order to identify the differences between them with respect to measuring transport-related social inequity in the case of Tuqiao.

The chapter is organised as follows: Section 2 introduces the case study, research framework and data; Section 3 discusses the different methods used to measure social inequity; and Section 4 gives the modelling results and provides a commentary. Finally, Section 5 summarises the findings, highlights the key contributions and discusses the policy implications.

## 2.    CASE STUDY, RESEARCH FRAMEWORK AND DATA

East Beijing, and the Tongzhou District in particular (formerly located in a peripheral or suburban area covering 906 km$^2$, with approximately 747,000 permanent residents), was promoted to the deputy administrative centre of Beijing in July 2015, according to the "Outline of Coordinated Development for the Beijing-Tianjin-Hebei Region" (MLR, 2015). The aim was to relocate non-essential functions within Beijing while exploring a new model of optimised integrated development in a region with a dense population, as well as maintaining a good balance between jobs and housing. In Beijing, most jobs and public facilities are concentrated within the Fourth Ring Road, rather than in suburban areas like Tongzhou, which was formerly referred to as a "dormitory satellite town". This changed focus has led to social inequalities, including in terms of the commuting burden, due to a mismatch between jobs and housing (Zhang et al., 2018), as well as causing smog-related air pollutants and carbon dioxide emissions generated by on-road vehicles (Cao et al., 2017). Tuqiao, located within the Tongzhou District, adjacent to the East Sixth Ring Road, was selected as the case study in order to illustrate features of a mixed-transitional, relatively migrant-rich lower-income neighbourhood. This contrasts

---

[2]    E.g. see Banister (2018, Chapter 4, Travel Patterns in Great Britain, pp. 103–110).

to a relatively high-income neighbourhood, Guomao, in the Central Business District, which is considered in related research (Cao, 2019; Cao and Hickman, 2019b). Tuqiao subway station was opened in December 2003 and is located on the Batong Line, which is also a Line 1 extension (Figure 15.1).

Figure 15.2 gives the theoretical framework for the analysis using the CA. Nussbaum's central human capabilities (Nussbaum, 2000, 2003, 2011) are modified and applied in the transport context (Cao and Hickman, 2019a, 2019b; Cao, 2019). The key concepts used from the CA are capabilities (an individual's real opportunities for travel and participation in activities) and functionings (the activities which they are currently performing). Capabilities are the most difficult to apply in transport, and we interpret this in this chapter as perceived ideal accessibility. This is then compared to functionings, which are the realised activities (see further discussion in Hickman et al. 2017; Cao and Hickman 2019a, 2019b; Cao, 2019). This distinction is very useful in transport planning, as often there are barriers to using accessibility through a particular public transport service, including cost of travel, education and skills, aspiration, etc. Examining the differences between real opportunities and realised activities can help us understand why particular population groups do not use public transport services despite living near to them. The following type of survey question is therefore used relative to different activities, such as access to employment, education and leisure.

There are two main interpretations of transport-related social inequity in this context (Figure 15.2). Firstly, there are statistically significant differences between capabilities (i.e. the difference between a and a') and functionings (i.e. the difference between b and b') respectively, across the various socio-demographic characteristics of individuals. Secondly, the distribution of the difference between capabilities and functionings is regarded as a form of travel inequity (i.e. the difference between a minus b, and a' minus b') – if individuals have differences between their perceived ideal accessibility and realised mobility, then this represents a form of travel inequity.

The data used in this study was collected in 2016 with face-to-face interviews in Tuqiao, with 622 valid responses (Cao, 2019). We employed a simple random sampling approach (Fink, 2003) to select and interview participants who were walking either near the station or in the communities within the station catchment area. Additionally, we also used a systematic sampling approach to select households (Fink, 2003; Pfeffermann and Rao, 2009) and carry out interviews in the communities within the station catchment area. All the respondents lived in Tuqiao, within a 1km radius of the station catchment area, and therefore had easy access to the Batong Line through Tuqiao subway station. Descriptions of the data variables are provided in Table 15.1.

## 3.  METHOD

Different approaches to measuring transport-related social inequity were tested, including the CA and statistical F-test to explore differences across population groups, and an additional six approaches, namely the Gini coefficient, the Atkinson index, the Palma ratio, the Pietra ratio, the Schutz coefficient and the Theil index. The same case study and dataset were used with the different approaches and more detailed explanations of the methods and formulae are provided below.

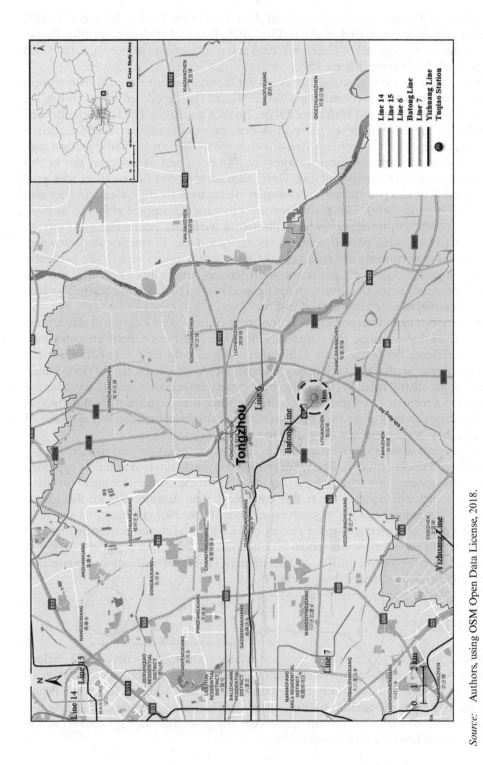

*Source:* Authors, using OSM Open Data License, 2018.

*Figure 15.1  Case study of Tuqiao, showing Tuqiao subway and surrounding neighbourhood, East Beijing*

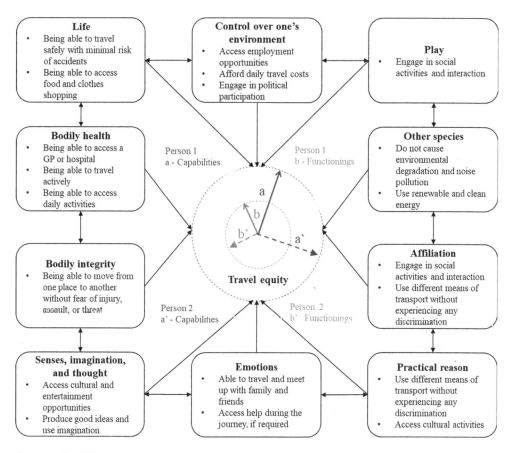

*Source:   Cao, 2019.*

*Figure 15.2   Research framework of capabilities and functionings*

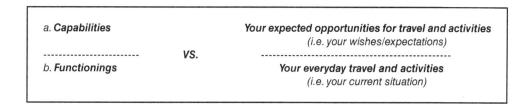

## 3.1   Capabilities Approach and F-test

The Capabilities Approach and F-test (Blackorby et al., 1981; Foster and Shneyerov, 1996) is adapted from a study by Lorgelly et al. (2008), who used a similar approach to test their findings regarding inequalities in individual capabilities in order to understand the patterns and causes of enduring poor health among various groups of people in Glasgow. In the transport context, it is assumed that differences in capabilities, func-

*Table 15.1   Descriptions of data variables*

| Categories | Variable names | Description (measure and value) |
| --- | --- | --- |
| *Socio-demographics* | | |
| Gen | Gender | 1(female); 0(male) |
| Age | Age | 1(18–24); 2(25–34); 3(35–44); 4(45–54); 5(55–64); 6(65 or over) |
| Huk | Hukou status | 1(Beijing hukou holders); 0(otherwise) |
| Inp | Incumbent population | 1(moved to the area before the Tuqiao Underground station was opened); 0(otherwise) |
| Pmi | Personal monthly income | Monthly personal gross income in Chinese Yuan (¥): 1(<1,000); 2(1,000–2,000); 3(2,001–6,000); 4(6,001–10,000); 5(10,001–20,000); 6(20,001–30,000); 7(>30,000) |
| Cao | Car ownership | 1(yes); 0(otherwise) |
| *Capabilities and functionings* | | |
| Life | | |
| LItrs | C&F_travel safety (accidents) | Index of functionings/capabilities |
| LIshp | C&F_access grocery/clothes shopping | Index of functionings/capabilities |
| Bodily health | | |
| BHhos | C&F_access hospitals | Index of functionings/capabilities |
| BHact | C&F_active travel | Index of functionings/capabilities |
| Bodily Integrity | | |
| BItrs | C&F_travel safety (violent assault) | Index of functionings/capabilities |
| Senses, imagination, and thought | | |
| SItre | C&F_access training and education | Index of functionings/capabilities |
| SIcri | C&F_creativity and imagination | Index of functionings/capabilities |
| SIree | C&F_ exercise freedom of religious/ worship/practise | N/A |
| Emotions | | |
| EMtrv | C&F_travel and visit family/friends | Index of functionings/capabilities |
| Practical reason | | |
| PRcua | C&F_access cultural activities | Index of functionings/capabilities |
| Affiliation | | |
| AFreh | C&F_respect and get help | Index of functionings/capabilities |
| Other species | | |
| OSend | C&F_against environmental degradation | Index of functionings/capabilities |
| Play | | |
| PLler | C&F_leisure and recreation | Index of functionings/capabilities |
| Control Over One's environment | | |
| COwoo | C&F_seek work opportunities | Index of functionings/capabilities |
| COtra | C&F_travel affordability | Index of functionings/capabilities |
| COpop | C&F_political participation | N/A |

*Notes:*
1.   C&F = Capabilities and functionings.
2.   "Not applicable" responses in the survey research are treated as missing values in statistical terms. Therefore, the sample size used in the analysis is 622.

tionings and the distance between these are all forms of social inequity, hence we are interested in the value of the variability in the numerator of the F-statistic (see Equation 1). A higher F value gives an indication of greater transport-related social inequity across population groups.

$$F = \frac{\sum_{i=1}^{\mu} n_i (\overline{Y}_i - \overline{Y})^2 / (\mu - 1)}{\sum_{i=1}^{\mu} \sum_{j=1}^{n_i} n_i (Y_{ij} - \overline{Y}_i)^2 / v} \tag{1}$$

Where:
- $F$: F value
- $\overline{Y}_i$: the sample mean in the $i^{th}$ group
- $n_i$: the number of observations in the $i^{th}$ group
- $\overline{Y}$: the overall mean of the sample size
- $\mu$: the number of groups
- $Y_{ij}$: the $j^{th}$ observation in the $i^{th}$ out of $\mu$ groups
- $n$: the overall sample size
- $v$: degrees of freedom under the null hypothesis (i.e. $n - \mu$)

## 3.2   Gini Coefficient (and Lorenz Curve)

The Gini index is a well-established approach, developed by the Italian statistician, sociologist and demographer Corrado Gini in 1912. It has conventionally been used to measure income inequality (Gini, 1912) (see Equation 2). This approach has already been applied as a statistical measure of inequality evaluation in the field of transport (see Delbosc and Currie, 2011c; van Wee and Geurs, 2011; Bhouri et al., 2016; Lucas et al., 2016; Guzman et al., 2017). In this context, a high Gini ratio (concave curve, see Figure 15.3 – Lorenz curve) indicates that people experienced high levels of overall transport-related social inequity. It has previously been applied in terms of functionings (i.e. realised mobility) rather than capabilities, and is useful for examining differences between neighbourhoods.

$$G = 1 - \sum_{m=1}^{n} (X_m - X_{m-1})(Y_m + Y_{m-1}) \tag{2}$$

Where:
- $G$: Gini coefficient ($G \in [0, 1]$)
- $X_m$: the cumulative proportion of the population variable, for $m = 0, \ldots, n$, with $X_0 = 0$, $X_n = 1$
- $Y_m$: the cumulative proportion of the functionings variable, for $m = 0, \ldots, n$, with $Y_0 = 0$, $Y_n = 1$

## 3.3   Atkinson Index

The Atkinson index was developed by the British economist Anthony Barnes Atkinson, who used it to measure income inequality (Atkinson, 1970) (see Equation 3). In our case, a high Atkinson parameter implies high levels of transport-related social equity across the respondents. This measurement is particularly helpful to determine which end of the overall functionings scores contributed most to the observed transport-related social inequity.

$$A = 1 - \left[\frac{1}{n}\sum_{m=1}^{n}\left[\frac{x_m^{1-e}}{\bar{u}}\right]\right]^{\frac{1}{1-e}}$$

(3)

Where:
– *A*: Atkinson parameter (A ∈ [0, 1])
– *e*: inequality aversion parameter
– *ū*: the average overall functionings
– *m*: the m[th] observation
– *n*: the overall sample size

## 3.4   Palma Ratio

The Palma ratio is also a measure of income inequality which is based on the work of Jose Gabriel Palma (Palma, 2011; Palma and Stiglitz, 2016). He argued that middle class incomes account for approximately half of gross national income, and are more stable, while the other half is unequally split between the richest (10 per cent) and the poorest (40 per cent), although their proportions vary considerably across countries. This approach has been applied in an empirical study to measure the inequality of the distribution of transport accessibility (Guzman and Oviedo, 2018). In our case, the Palma ratio is useful for measuring the differences between the top 10 per cent of individuals who experienced the lowest levels of transport-related social inequity and the bottom 40 per cent of people who suffered the most severe transport-related social inequity issues. The larger the Palma ratio, the higher the levels of transport-related social inequity. If *Pi* is the top *i* per cent of the population's share of overall functionings scores, then the formula for calculating the Palma ratio is as follows (Equation 4):

$$P = \frac{P_{i=10}}{P_{i=100} - P_{i=60}}$$

(4)

Where:
– *P*: Palma ratio
– *i*: the top i percentage of the overall functionings

## 3.5   Pietra Ratio

The Pietra ratio is an additional indicator for the Lorenz curve, as a measure of inequality for resource distribution across the population, which is particularly used in relation to health and income measurements. In this context, the Pietra ratio indicates that the proportion of overall functionings scores should have been transferred from those experiencing the least transport-related social inequity to those who suffered higher levels of transport-related social inequity in order to achieve a state of perfect equality. The Pietra ratio is shown below in Equation (5).

$$P' = \frac{1}{2} \sum_{m=1}^{n} \left| \frac{X_m}{X'} - \frac{Y_m}{Y'} \right| \qquad (5)$$

Where:
- $P'$: Pietra ratio
- $n$: the number of quantiles
- $X_m$: the overall functionings in the $m^{th}$ quantile
- $X'$: the sum of overall functionings for all quantiles
- $Y_m$: the size of the $m^{th}$ person (i.e. the number of persons)
- $Y'$: the sum of all persons

### 3.6 Schutz Coefficient

The Schutz coefficient is also used as a measure of income inequality (Schutz, 1951) (Equation 6). In this context, it compares the overall functionings level of each person with the average overall functionings of the population, and then sums the absolute values of the differences between them, and views it as a proportion of the total functionings.

$$S = \sum_{m=1}^{n} |X - Y_m| Xn \qquad (6)$$

Where:
- $S$: Schutz coefficient
- $n$: the overall sample size
- $X$: the average overall functionings of the population
- $Y_m$: the $m^{th}$ individual overall functionings

### 3.7 Theil Index

The Theil index is another measure of economic inequality developed by a Dutch econometrician Henri Theil (Theil, 1967, 1972), which uses entropy measures based on statistical information theory (Equation 7). This index is also used to measure inequality in relation to multi-group segregation (Reardon and Firebaugh, 2002). In this study, it provides a way to measure the discrepancy between the structure of the overall functionings across groups and the overall functionings across the same groups. In other words, a higher Theil value implies greater transport-related social inequity across groups.

$$T = \frac{1}{n} \sum_{m=1}^{n} \left( \frac{u_m}{\bar{u}} \times ln \frac{u_m}{\bar{u}} \right) \qquad (7)$$

Where:
- $T$: Theil value ($T \in [0, 1]$)
- $n$: the overall sample size
- $m$: the $m^{th}$ individual
- $u_m$: the overall functionings of individual m
- $\bar{u}$: the average overall functionings

## 4.   MODELLING RESULTS AND COMMENTARY

### 4.1   Descriptive Statistics

A brief descriptive analysis of the responses is provided in Table 15.2. These samples show that there were fewer male respondents (40 per cent) than females (60 per cent). Most respondents were non-agricultural hukou[3] residents living in a transitional neighbourhood. This may be due to the rapid urbanisation process that has occurred in China since the 1990s (Liu et al., 2010) as well as emerging neoliberal urbanism (He and Wu, 2009). Furthermore, 33 per cent of residents living in the neighbourhood were migrants. There was a fairly normal age distribution. The majority of respondents (65 per cent) were aged between 25 and 44. In addition, more than 72 per cent of respondents' personal incomes were less than the average income of ¥7,706 per month. Moreover, 43 per cent of respondents did not own cars. Finally, it should be noted that our samples are most likely to be representative of relatively migrant-rich lower-income cohorts living in areas close to the station, with good accessibility to local transport services, and are not representative of all people residing in Beijing.

### 4.2   Capabilities Approach (CA) F Test Results

The analysis examines whether capabilities and functionings show statistically significant differences across socio–demographic groups. It can be argued that conventional accessibility analysis overlooks the real opportunities (capabilities) and realised activities (functionings) elements of the CA as it examines a theoretical access to transport services, employment and other activities. All survey respondents live in the Tuqiao underground station catchment area with good accessibility to the local transport service, but there are substantial differences in their actual travel behaviours according to socio-economic characteristics and individual abilities. Six social equity groupings are taken into consideration: gender, age, hukou, incumbent population, personal income and car ownership. Significant findings with regard to differences in transport-related social inequity are marked with asterisks (*) in Table 15.3.

   With regards to gender, four of the capabilities categories (i.e. travel safety – accidents and violent assault, active travel, and respect and get help) have statistically significant differences (Column 2, Table 15.3). The results show that males are more likely than females to be able to get help if they need it, whilst travelling across Beijing. Moreover, men again have higher levels of overall capabilities than women in terms of travel safety (accidents and violent assault) and active travel across Beijing. The findings imply a gendered inequality, meaning that females are more likely to experience transport-related safety issues, which is also in line with the existing literature illustrating how gender shapes mobility differently (Uteng and Cresswell, 2008; Uteng, 2009; Adeel et al., 2016),

---

[3]   Hukou refers to the household registration scheme used in China and is used to identify a person as resident in an area. Benefits such as education, health care and retirement pensions are particularly related to an urban local hukou, and migrants do not qualify for these, hence there is much inequity in the system.

*Table 15.2   Descriptive statistics*

| Individual characteristics | | Survey sample (2016) | |
|---|---|---|---|
| | | Count | Percentage |
| Gender | Male | 248 | 39.9 |
| | Female | 374 | 60.1 |
| Hukou | Non-agricultural residence | 540 | 86.8 |
| | Agricultural residence | 82 | 13.2 |
| | Beijing urban hukou holders | 400 | 64.3 |
| | Beijing agricultural hukou holders | 16 | 2.6 |
| | Non-Beijing urban hukou holders | 140 | 22.5 |
| | Non-Beijing agricultural hukou holders | 66 | 10.6 |
| Age | 18–24 | 108 | 17.3 |
| | 25–34 | 230 | 37.0 |
| | 35–44 | 172 | 27.6 |
| | 45–54 | 62 | 10.0 |
| | 55–64 | 44 | 7.1 |
| | 65 or more | 6 | 1.0 |
| Personal income | <1,000 | 76 | 12.2 |
| (RMB / month) | 1,000–2,000 | 36 | 5.8 |
| | 2,001–6,000 | 336 | 54.0 |
| | 6,001–10,000 | 126 | 20.3 |
| | 10,001–20,000 | 42 | 6.8 |
| | 20,001–30,000 | 4 | 0.6 |
| | >30,000 | 2 | 0.3 |
| Car ownership | Yes | 356 | 57.2 |
| | No | 266 | 42.8 |

and that women's freedom of mobility to engage in daily life activities is more likely to be constrained (Shin, 2011; Turdalieva and Edling, 2017).

In terms of age, it was found that most categories display highly statistically significant differences. More specifically, in a relatively low-income neighbourhood, the results show that middle-aged people (35–54) have much higher scores for both capabilities and functionings than people who are over 55, and this is particularly noticeable for respondents aged over 65, in relation to activities such as "accessing grocery and clothes shopping", "being able to travel safely (accidents and violent assault)", "accessing training and education", "creativity and imagination", "seeking work opportunities" and "travel affordability". The results imply that with advancing age, people seem to be more vulnerable when travelling and are struggling to adapt to rapid social change and unfavourable environmental and technological conditions (Mollenkopf et al., 1997), despite having good accessibility to local transport services. Some may also be experiencing a deterioration in physical function which could make travelling more problematic for them. However, people over 65 had the highest capabilities scores in relation to "accessing cultural activities" while respondents aged between 18 and 34 scored comparatively lower in this respect. A possible explanation for this may be that the younger generation are gradually losing interesting in going to concerts, live events and exhibitions, or at least

Table 15.3  Summary test statistics (F tests) for differences in individual transport-related social equity in Tuqiao, Beijing

| Capabilities and functionings | Gender | Age | Hukou | Incumbent population | Personal income | Car ownership |
|---|---|---|---|---|---|---|
| **Life** | | | | | | |
| C_travel safety (accidents) | 4.404* | 3.369** | 0.261 | 0.441 | 4.401*** | 0.712 |
| F_travel safety (accidents) | 0.097 | 3.929** | 0.635 | 1.381 | 6.739*** | 2.532 |
| C_access grocery/clothes shopping | 0.227 | 6.693*** | 0.264 | 16.763*** | 5.222*** | 0.110 |
| F_access grocery/clothes shopping | 0.081 | 3.045** | 4.116* | 5.997* | 1.463 | 1.713 |
| **Bodily health** | | | | | | |
| C_access hospitals | 1.068 | 6.765*** | 1.692 | 22.658*** | 6.471*** | 1.675 |
| F_access hospitals | 0.262 | 1.554 | 3.024 | 5.089* | 4.441*** | 0.023 |
| C_active travel | 3.660* | 0.705 | 0.678 | 2.020 | 2.719* | 2.820 |
| F_active travel | 3.158 | 3.025** | 0.336 | 1.156 | 5.375*** | 1.114 |
| **Bodily integrity** | | | | | | |
| C_travel safety (violent assault) | 15.346*** | 4.342*** | 0.147 | 4.972* | 2.883** | 1.667 |
| F_travel safety (violent assault) | 0.829 | 4.200*** | 0.115 | 2.359 | 3.801*** | 2.820 |
| **Senses, imagination, and thought** | | | | | | |
| C_access training and education | 1.367 | 3.957** | 1.835 | 2.253 | 3.638*** | 0.082 |
| F_access training and education | 0.385 | 8.095*** | 4.694* | 0.054 | 2.425* | 8.922** |
| C_creativity and imagination | 0.702 | 6.373*** | 2.088 | 3.875* | 11.458*** | 2.677 |
| F_creativity and imagination | 0.072 | 4.013*** | 0.001 | 1.917 | 13.364*** | 1.005 |
| C_religious exercise | N/A | | | | | |
| F_religious exercise | N/A | | | | | |
| **Emotions** | | | | | | |
| C_travel and visit family/friends | 0.186 | 6.223*** | 0.000 | 18.680*** | 5.491*** | 0.359 |
| F_travel and visit family/friends | 1.496 | 1.772 | 5.103* | 7.498** | 3.265** | 3.078 |
| **Practical reason** | | | | | | |
| C_access cultural activities | 2.949 | 5.026*** | 0.014 | 12.925*** | 7.993*** | 0.591 |
| F_access cultural activities | 3.391 | 1.801 | 3.334 | 12.097*** | 2.655* | 1.149 |
| **Affiliation** | | | | | | |
| C_respect and get help | 3.926* | 0.832 | 1.029 | 1.303 | 2.242* | 0.190 |
| F_respect and get help | 0.737 | 1.964 | 0.033 | 0.285 | 3.541** | 0.010 |

**Other species**

| | | | | | |
|---|---|---|---|---|---|
| C_against environmental degradation | 2.686 | 0.997 | 0.340 | 0.592 | 0.896 | 0.167 |
| F_against environmental degradation | 0.509 | 2.201 | 4.672* | 4.051* | 5.200*** | 0.073 |
| **Play** | | | | | | |
| C_leisure and recreation | 2.681 | 3.392** | 0.201 | 0.910 | 3.809*** | 3.289 |
| F_leisure and recreation | 2.800 | 0.597 | 3.416 | 5.607* | 1.219 | 1.713 |
| **Control over one's environment** | | | | | | |
| C_seek work opportunities | 2.428 | 6.523*** | 0.078 | 1.829 | 5.375*** | 0.036 |
| F_seek work opportunities | 1.856 | 5.521*** | 0.008 | 0.952 | 1.556 | 9.327** |
| C_travel affordability | 3.152 | 2.717* | 1.158*** | 16.821*** | 8.171*** | 8.424** |
| F_travel affordability | 3.336 | 2.964* | 3.565* | 5.483* | 9.137*** | 0.144 |
| C_political participation | N/A | | | | | |
| F_political participation | N/A | | | | | |

(n = 622)

*Notes:*

1. *$p < 0.05$, **$p < 0.01$, ***$p < 0.001$.
2. Key results are highlighted with a dotted outline box and discussed in the text.
3. More detailed statistical analysis and further interpretation of the findings can be found in Cao (2019).

have less time to do this. More in-depth interviews are required to explore the reasons for these findings.

The Chinese registration system known as hukou has a significant influence on transport and related inequity, as has been shown in the case of Beijing (Zhao and Howden-Chapman, 2010; Zhao and Li, 2016; Cao and Hickman, 2019b). It particularly affects commuting behaviour and access to jobs and housing, with migrants likely to be excluded from jobs, healthcare and educational resources. For Tuqiao, a relatively migrant-rich area, our results are in line with much of the previous literature, and reveal that migrants without a Beijing hukou experience transport-related social inequity and remain disadvantaged, i.e., they have much lower functionings-related scores compared to local Beijing residents with an urban hukou. In addition, immigrants' (migrants in the context of Beijing) friendships tend to be largely within their own ethnic group, which could have the effect of constraining their accumulation of social capital and preventing them from exploring wider social networks (Schwanen et al., 2015). Migrants are also excluded from urban educational resources (Li and Zhao, 2018), and hence their children may find it difficult to gain entry to grammar schools due to not having Beijing hukou. The differences between migrants and local Beijing hukou holders will not be eliminated until further effective hukou reform policy is implemented in China. However, surprisingly, our findings appear to suggest that migrants did not face significant barriers to accessing jobs. This can be attributed, in the context of Tuqiao, to there being many lower-skilled migrants who are likely to have a casual working contract with their employers and be informally employed (Zhang et al., 2018), doing jobs such as delivering parcels (e.g. YTO Express, ZTO Express, SF Express, etc.) or food (e.g. Meituan, ele.me, etc.) due to the growth of e-commerce. This may allow them to eventually increase their job opportunities without being too restricted by their lack of hukou status, but of course the skill and pay levels will remain low.

In terms of the differences between incumbent residents and newcomers, it was found that although the travel equity gaps between the two groups are similar, the incumbent population appeared to have higher capabilities and functionings scores than newcomers. This may be because most newcomers in Tuqiao are relatively low-income migrants, perhaps doing temporary low-skilled jobs, and do not have Beijing hukou. Thus, they may gain fewer benefits and lack access to opportunities and resources compared to incumbent residents.

Income has always been taken into account as a key indicator when measuring accessibility and transport-related social inequity especially between better- and worse-off groups (de Vasconcellos, 2005; Guzman and Oviedo, 2018), as lower-income groups and the most socially disadvantaged within society are more likely to experience transport disadvantage than their higher-income counterparts (Lucas, 2004, 2012). Not surprisingly, almost all categories of capabilities and functionings have statistically significant differences based on respondents' personal monthly incomes. For instance, higher-income groups (personal income > ¥30,000) had capabilities and functionings scores which were over 33 per cent higher than relatively low-income respondents (personal income between ¥1,000 and ¥6,000) in terms of travel affordability. This implies that the lower-income population may have to spend a much higher share of their income on transport or perhaps travel less due to the unaffordability of travel costs (Stokes and Lucas, 2011; Titheridge et al., 2014; Stokes, 2015). This may eventually cause people with lower incomes to have lower overall mobility levels and to miss out on opportunities to access key life activities, in contrast to higher-income cohorts. However, it should be noted that, in relation to "active travel", lower-income groups appeared to have much higher capabilities and functionings scores than higher-income cohorts. This finding can be attributed to lower-income groups travelling less and finding jobs in nearby areas. Thus, they may be able to walk or cycle which would incur lower travel costs than travelling by Underground or driving private vehicles. Higher-income groups are more likely to drive private vehicles.

Finally, with regards to car ownership, although the results show that only three indicators have statistically significant differences, people who drive private vehicles are more likely to be able to access training, seek a wider array of job opportunities and afford the cost of travelling, across Beijing. This may imply that having access to a car could make additional opportunities available to people, particularly in terms of job accessibility; thus, there is still transport-related social inequity between car owners and non-car owners, especially in a relatively low-income neighbourhood.

## 4.3  Wider Inequality Indices Results

In this research, we believe that effect sizes can be used to describe to what extent each of the different approaches can reflect transport equity issues. For example, in terms of functionings (i.e. realised mobility), effect sizes can be used rather than specifying a range of threshold values for each of the indices. There is some debate about whether it is still appropriate to use similar threshold values drawn from the economics domain to measure and represent inequalities in the transport context, such as using a benchmark value of 0.4 for the Gini coefficient (OECD, 2014, 2015). This is because there have been significant differences in the past few years between economic inequality and transport-related inequality and it is unlikely that thresholds will transfer well across topics and contexts (Banister, 2018).

A summary of results obtained using different evaluation approaches to measure individual transport-related social inequity in Tuqiao is provided in Table 15.4, showing two main aspects: (1) Effect sizes: how sensitive the approach is (see Hagenauer and Helbich, 2017) when it is used to examine transport equity issues; (2) Interpretation: how easily the results can be interpreted and understood in the transport domain.

The results reveal the different findings that can be used with the various approaches. The CA has the largest effect size, while the modelling results can be easily and clearly interpreted. The Palma ratio is useful for measuring the extreme differences between the top 10 per cent of individuals who experienced the lowest levels of transport-related social inequity and the bottom 40 per cent of people who suffered the most severe transport-related social inequity issues; it is also able to overcome the sensitivity to change in the middle of the functionings distribution (compared to the Gini coefficient (Figure 15.3) or Schutz coefficient, for example).

More specifically, for the CA in this context, the effect size indicates that there is a large difference in F value scores, which means that most residents living in Tuqiao are more likely to experience high levels of transport-related social inequity in terms of functionings. The Gini coefficient produces a low effect size, with a score of 0.078. The Lorenz curve (Figure 15.3) implies that Y per cent of aggregated functionings' scores for X per cent of residents in Tuqiao experienced severe transport-related social inequity issues.

*Table 15.4   Summary of results using different evaluation tools to assess individual transport-related social inequity in Tuqiao, Beijing*

| Measurement approach | Ratio / Parameter | Effect size[a] | Interpretation[b] |
| --- | --- | --- | --- |
| Capabilities approach | F values (see Table 3) | 3 | 3 |
| Gini coefficient | 0.078 | 1 | 2 |
| Atkinson index | 0.007 | 1 | 1 |
| Palma ratio | 0.352 | 2 | 3 |
| Pietra ratio | 0.055 | 1 | 1~2 |
| Schutz coefficient | 0.155 | 1 | 1 |
| Theil index | 0.014 | 1 | 1 |

(n = 622)
*Notes:*
a.   Effect sizes: 1 – a small effect; 2 – a medium effect; 3 – a large effect.
b.   Interpretation: 1 – not easy; 2 – neutral; 3 – easy.

Furthermore, the Atkinson parameter, the Pietra ratio, the Schutz coefficient and the Theil index all indicate a relatively small effect size, meaning that most respondents do not appear to experience high levels of transport-related social inequity, at least in this case. Finally, the Palma ratio is 0.352, indicating a medium effect. This means that the top 10 per cent of individuals who experienced the lowest levels of transport-related social inequity have approximately 0.4 times higher overall functionings scores than the bottom 40 per cent of people who suffered the most severe transport-related social inequity.

## 5.   CONCLUSIONS

This chapter has not only used an emerging and innovative approach, the CA, but has also used six other measures of inequality to examine transport-related social inequity, at the individual level, for residents living in the subway station catchment area of Tuqiao, Beijing. It has also examined how different inequality tools can be used in assessing transport-related equity issues.

There are different approaches available, including the CA, the Gini coefficient, the Atkinson index, the Palma ratio, the Pietra ratio, the Schutz coefficient and the Theil index, which can be applied in different circumstances. Based on our findings, it is suggested that the CA is useful in assessing transport-related inequalities where there are significant barriers to the take up of accessibility, for example where there are high levels of disadvantaged groups, and where disaggregated analysis can be undertaken. The Palma ratio appears to have a larger effect when measuring transport-related social inequity than the Gini coefficient (Guzman and Oviedo, 2018) and the other inequality tools in this case. Furthermore, based on our findings, it is argued that many of the income inequality approaches adapted from econometrics may be useful for measuring transport-related social inequity. This can help compare differences between regions, cities or countries (Delbosc and Currie, 2011c; Lucas et al., 2016), or within the same area but at different

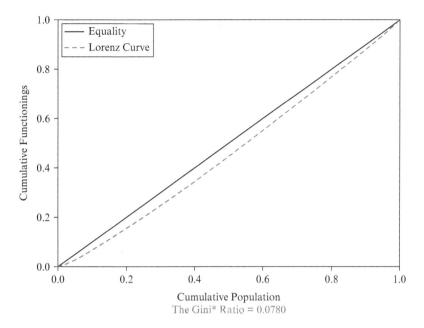

*Figure 15.3    Lorenz curve for transport-related social inequity (functionings) in Tuqiao*

points in time (Guzman and Oviedo, 2018), and also across individuals who have different levels of socio- or spatial-inequity related to transport accessibility (Guzman et al., 2017; Jang et al., 2017).

The analysis makes several key contributions to the existing literature and methodology. First, this study provides new evidence on the potential limitations of investigating the effects of a relatively migrant-rich (i.e. without Beijing local hukou) lower-income neighbourhood, emphasising that hukou still plays a significant role as a barrier to transport equity (Zhao and Howden-Chapman, 2010). Second, gendered transport inequality is clearly evident (Uteng, 2009; Adeel et al., 2016), not only in a relatively wealthy neighbourhood (Cao and Hickman, 2019b), but also in a lower-income area. Not surprisingly, higher-income cohorts had both higher levels of capabilities and functionings scores compared to their less well-off counterparts, meaning that lower-income groups are still more likely to be socially disadvantaged (Lucas, 2004, 2012). Moreover, owning a car appeared to have little effect on the residents living in a wealthy neighbourhood (Cao and Hickman, 2019b), but it was significant for people residing in a lower-income area, as non-car owners experienced constraints in terms of the job and educational opportunities and resources available to them, which may in turn prevent them from realising their human capital potential. Finally, in terms of the methodological contribution, six different income inequality measures were adapted and applied in the transport context, which enabled us to compare each approach and comment on their effectiveness.

In terms of policy implications relating to the transport equity domain, we suggest that politicians and transport planners should take their context-specific situations into account and then carefully select an appropriate measurement approach in order to evaluate the impacts of transport-related social equity. Each gives a subtly different answer to a similar question. In addition, based on our analysis (e.g. comparisons between Gini coefficient and Palma ratio), it would seem that political intervention should focus on the bottom 40 per cent of people who are most severely affected by transport-related social inequity, through long-term social investment, rather than simply subsidising transport fares or giving discounts for travel. In particular, efforts should be made to help migrants who primarily live and work in Beijing in order to facilitate accessibility to a wide range of key life activities, and offer them more opportunities and resources to address the inequality issues that they face. In a general sense, the CA can be seen as a useful approach to evaluate transport-related social inequity, and therefore it can be added to the existing inequality measurement approaches for use in the transport context. As ever, the choice of assessment approach greatly effects the assessment and conclusions made – and, ultimately, the progress that can be made in reducing inequalities.

## ACKNOWLEDGMENTS

This research is partly funded by the National Natural Science Foundation of China (Project No. 51808392). The authors would like to extend their appreciation to Dr Andy Ho (LSE) for his mathematics contributions and Dr Daniel Oviedo (UCL) for sharing his opinions on the discussion of the Palma ratio. Thanks also to the reviewers for their useful feedback on the initial manuscript.

## REFERENCES

Adeel, M., Yeh, A. and Zhang, F. (2016) Transportation disadvantage and activity participation in the cities of Rawalpindi and Islamabad, Pakistan. *Transport Policy*, 47, 1–12.
Alvaredo, F., Chancel, L., Piketty, T., Saez, E. and Zucman, G. (2018) World Inequality Report 2018. Available at: https://wir2018.wid.world/files/download/wir2018-full-report-english.pdf (accessed 1 August 2018).
Atkinson, A. (1970) On the measurement of inequality. *Journal of Economic Theory*, 2, 244–263.
Banister, D. (2018) *Inequality in Transport*. Oxon: Alexandrine Press.
Bhouri, N., Aron, M. and Scemama, G. (2016) Gini index for evaluating bus reliability performances for operators and riders. *Transportation Research Board*, January, Washington, USA.
Blackorby, C., Donaldson, D. and Auersperg, M. (1981) A new procedure for the measurement of inequality within and among population subgroups. *Canadian Journal of Economics*, 4, 665–685.
Blumenberg, E. and Smart, M. (2010) Getting by with a little help from my friends and family: immigrants and carpooling. *Transportation*, 37(3), 429–446.
Cao, M. (2019) *Exploring the relation between transport and social equity: Empirical evidence from London and Beijing*. Unpublished PhD thesis, London, UCL.
Cao, M. and Hickman, R. (2019a) Urban transport and social inequities in neighbourhoods near Underground stations in Greater London. *Transportation Planning and Technology*, 42(5), 419–441.
Cao, M. and Hickman, R. (2019b) Transport, social equity and capabilities in East Beijing. In, Chen, C-L., Pan, H., Shen Q. and Wang, J. (eds), *Handbook on Transport and Urban Transformation in China*. Cheltenham: Edward Elgar.
Cao, M., Chen, C-L. and Hickman, R. (2017) Transport emissions in Beijing: a scenario planning approach. *Proceedings of the Institution of Civil Engineers – Transport*, 170(2), 65–75.
De Vasconcellos, E. (2005) Transport metabolism, social diversity and equity: the case of São Paulo, Brazil. *Journal of Transport Geography*, 13(4), 329–339.
Delbosc, A. and Currie, G. (2011a) Exploring the relative influences of transport disadvantage and social exclusion on well-being. *Transport Policy*, 18(4), 555–562.
Delbosc, A. and Currie, G. (2011b) The spatial context of transport disadvantage, social exclusion and well-being. *Journal of Transport Geography*, 19(6), 1130–1137.

Delbosc, A. and Currie, G. (2011c) Using Lorenz curves to assess public transport equity. *Journal of Transport Geography*, 19(6), 1252–1259.

Dorling, D. (2015) *Inequality and the One Percent*. London: Verso.

Fink, A. (2003) *How to Sample in Surveys*. London: Sage Publications.

Foster, J. and Shneyerov, A. (1996) *Path Independent Inequality Measures*. Vanderbilt University: Department of Economics.

Gini, C. (1912) *Variability and Mutability, Contribution to the Study of Statistical Distributions and Relations*. Studi Economico-Giuricici della R. Universita de Cagliari.

Guzman, L. and Oviedo, D. (2018) Accessibility, affordability and equity: assessing "pro-poor" public transport subsidies in Bogotá. *Transport Policy*, 68, 37–51.

Guzman, L., Oviedo, D. and Rivera, C. (2017) Assessing equity in transport accessibility to work and study: the Bogotá region. *Journal of Transport Geography*, 58, 236–246.

Hagenauer, J. and Helbich, M. (2017) A comparative study of machine learning classifiers for modeling travel mode choice. *Expert Systems with Applications*, 78, 273–282.

He, S. and Wu, F. (2009) China's emerging neoliberal urbanism: perspectives from urban redevelopment. *Antipode*, 41(2), 282–304.

Hickman, R., Cao, M., Mella Lira, B., Fillone, A. and Biona, J.B. (2017) Understanding capabilities, functionings and travel in high and low income neighbourhoods in Manila. *Social Inclusion*, 5(4), 161–174.

Jang, S., An, Y., Yi, C. and Lee, S. (2017) Assessing the spatial equity of Seoul's public transportation using the Gini coefficient based on its accessibility. *International Journal of Urban Sciences*, 21(1), 91–107.

Li, S. and Zhao, P. (2018) Restrained mobility in a high-accessible and migrant-rich area in downtown Beijing. *European Transport Research Review*, 10(4), 1–17.

Litman, T. (2018) Evaluating transportation equity: guidance for incorporating distributional impacts in transportation planning. Available at: www.vtpi.org/equity.pdf (accessed 25 July 2018).

Liu, Y., He, S., Wu, F. and Webster, C. (2010) Urban villages under China's rapid urbanization: unregulated assets and transitional neighbourhoods. *Habitat International*, 34(2), 135–144.

Lorgelly, P., Lorimer, K., Fenwick, E. and Briggs, A. (2008) *The Capability Approach: Developing an Instrument for Evaluating Public Health Interventions*. University of Glasgow: Public Health and Health Policy.

Lovejoy, K. and Handy, S. (2011) Social networks as a source of private vehicle transportation: the practice of getting rides and borrowing vehicles among Mexican immigrants in California. *Transportation Research Part A*, 45(4), 248–257.

Lucas, K. (2004) *Running on Empty: Transport, Social Exclusion and Environmental Justice*. Bristol: The Policy Press.

Lucas, K. (2012) Transport and social exclusion: Where are we now? *Transport Policy*, 20, 105–113.

Lucas, K., van Wee, B. and Maat, K. (2016) A method to evaluate equitable accessibility: combining ethical theories and accessibility-based approaches. *Transportation*, 43(3), 473–490.

Martens, K. (2017) *Transport Justice: Designing Fair Transportation Systems*. New York: Routledge.

Mollenkopf, H., Marcellini, F., Ruoppila, I., Flaschenträger, P., Gagliardi, C. and Spazzafumo, L. (1997) Outdoor mobility and social relationships of elderly people. *Archives of Gerontology and Geriatrics*, 24(3), 295–310.

Nussbaum, M. (2000) *Women and Human Development: The Capabilities Approach*. Cambridge: Cambridge University Press.

Nussbaum, M. (2003) Capabilities as fundamental entitlements: Sen and social justice. *Feminist Economics*, 9(2–3), 33–59.

Nussbaum, M. (2011) *Creating Capabilities: The Human Development Approach*. Cambridge: Belknap.

OECD (2014) *How was Life? Global Wellbeing since 1820* (in collaboration with OECD Development Centre and the CLIO-INFRA Project). Paris: OECD.

OECD (2015) *In it Together: Why Less Inequality Benefits All*. Paris: OECD.

Palma, J. (2011) Homogeneous middles vs. heterogeneous tails, and the end of the "Inverted-U": it's all about the share of the rich. *Development and Change*, 42(1), 87–153.

Palma, J. and Stiglitz, J. (2016) Do nations just get the inequality they deserve? The "Palma ratio" re-examined. In, Basu, K. and Stiglitz, J. (eds) *Inequality and Growth: Patterns and Policy*. Volume II: Regions and Regularities. London: Palgrave Macmillan.

Pfeffermann, D. and Rao, C. (2009) *Handbook of Statistics. 29A – Sample Surveys: Design, Methods and Applications*. Oxford: North Holland.

Ravallion, M. (2014) Income inequality in the developing world. *Science*, 344, 851–855.

Reardon, S. and Firebaugh, G. (2002) Measures of multigroup segregation. *Sociological Methodology*, 32(1), 33–67.

Schutz, R. (1951) On the measurement of income inequality. *The American Economic Review*, 41(1), 107–122.

Schwanen, T., Lucas, K., Akyelken, N., Solsona, D., Carrasco. J. and Neutens, T. (2015) Rethinking the links between social exclusion and transport disadvantage through the lens of social capital. *Transportation Research Part A*, 74, 123–135.

Sen, A. (1985) *Commodities and Capabilities.* Oxford: Elsevier Science Publishers.

Sen, A. (1999) *Development as Freedom.* Oxford: Oxford University Press.

Sen, A. (2009) *The Idea of Justice.* London: Allen Lane.

Shin, H. (2011) Spatial capability for understanding gendered mobility for Korean Christian immigrant women in Los Angeles. *Urban Studies*, 48(11), 2355–2373.

Stokes, G. (2015) Incomes, accessibility and transport poverty. In, Hickman, R., Givoni, M., Bonilla, D. and Banister, D. (eds) *Handbook on Transport and Development.* Cheltenham: Edward Elgar.

Stokes, G. and Lucas, K. (2011) *National Travel Survey Analysis.* Working Paper, Oxford, University of Oxford.

Theil, H. (1967) *Economics and Information Theory.* Chicago: Rand McNally and Company.

Theil, H. (1972) *Statistical Decomposition Analysis.* Amsterdam: North-Holland Publishing Company.

The Ministry of Land and Resources (MLR) (2015) *Outline of Coordinated Development for the Beijing-Tianjin-Hebei Region.* Beijing: MLR (in Chinese).

Titheridge, H., Christie, N., Mackett, R., Oviedo, D. and Ye, R. (2014) Transport and poverty: a review of the evidence. Available at: www.ucl.ac.uk/transport-institute/pdfs/transport-poverty (accessed 3 November 2015).

Turdalieva, C. and Edling, C. (2017) Women's mobility and "transport-related social exclusion" in Bishkek. *Mobilities*, Online, 1–16.

Uteng, T. (2009) Gender, ethnicity, and constrained mobility: insights into the resultant social exclusion. *Environment and Planning A*, 41, 1055–1071.

Uteng, T. and Cresswell, T. (2008) *Gendered Mobilities.* Aldershot: Ashgate.

van Wee, B. and Geurs, K. (2011) Discussing equity and social exclusion in accessibility evaluations. *European Journal of Transport and Infrastructure Research*, 11(4), 350–367.

Zhang, M., He, S. and Zhao, P. (2018) Revisiting inequalities in the commuting burden: institutional constraints and job-housing relationships in Beijing. *Journal of Transport Geography*, 71, 58–71.

Zhao, P. and Howden-Chapman, P. (2010) Social inequalities in mobility: the impact of the Hukou system on migrants' job accessibility and commuting costs in Beijing. *International Development Planning Review*, 32(3–4), 363–384.

Zhao, P. and Li, S. (2016) Restraining transport inequality in growing cities: can spatial planning play a role? *International Journal of Sustainable Transportation*, 10(10), 947–959.

# 16. Why the Capability Approach can offer an alternative to transport project assessment
*Beatriz Mella Lira*

## 1. INTRODUCTION

Nowadays, there is a worldwide problem regarding growing social inequality and there are significant gaps that must be addressed to achieve better levels of equity and social justice in cities. Stiglitz (2012) reminds us of the financial crisis in 2007–2008, the problems of unemployment, house repossessions, homelessness, student debt, and the difficulties of the market economy in contributing to greater income equality over the last three decades:

> We are paying a high price for our large and growing inequality, and because our inequality is likely to continue to grow – unless we do something – the price we pay is likely to grow too. Those in the middle, and especially those at the bottom, will pay the highest price, but our country as a whole – our society, our democracy – will also pay a very high price. (Stiglitz, 2012, p. 104)

However, economic welfare and differences in income are just some of the dimensions that must be addressed in order to change the injustice precepts, and should be interpreted in relation to the contexts, circumstances and the underlying opportunities (Atkinson, 2015). Prosperity, measured in terms of GDP outcomes and other economic indices, has not been enough to capture wide-ranging social issues, despite being the most used metric of "progress" in industrialised and many emerging countries. Sen (1999) has argued that we should instead examine the freedoms that people enjoy, and this led to the development and use of the wide-ranging Millennium Development Goals by actors such as the World Bank. Wider equity measurement parameters have been suggested to consider issues of social welfare, such as health and well-being (Jackson, 2009), considering shifting the attention "from material standards and economic growth to ways of improving the psychological and social well-being of whole societies" (Wilkinson and Pickett, 2010, p. 4).

There has been an increasing focus on social equity issues in transport planning, particularly the linkages between transport and social exclusion, over the last 20 years. This has had a pronounced focus, considering the distribution of impacts over space and time, with the aim of achieving better-distributed attributes across the population. Consequently, better standards of accessibility to goods and services have been promoted, as well as the efficient distribution of human capital, as mediated through transport systems, in order to enhance access to job and other opportunities for disadvantaged population cohorts. A diverse literature has developed examining the potential reduction of social exclusion through transport interventions (Church et al., 2000; Lucas, 2001, 2006, 2012). The many barriers experienced by some groups with transport disadvantages have been considered (Hine and Mitchell, 2001, 2003) and the relevance of users' perceptions to facilitate the understanding of their social inclusion (Rajé, 2007). The spatial component has been conceptualised as an important transport-related element to social exclusion (Preston and

Rajé, 2007) and the concept of well-being has been examined to promote clearer linkages to public policy (Stanley et al., 2011; Delbosc and Currie, 2011; Schwanen et al., 2015). In this regard, accessibility has been widely discussed as a key element for addressing the inclusion of certain groups of society (Geurs and van Wee, 2004; Handy and Niemeier, 1997). Particularly in the UK, and in other countries in Europe, North America and Australia, accessibility planning has been applied in practice, with various distance, time and utility-based measurements used to assess the accessibility of population cohorts to different activities. Physical and social mobility, in the form of motility (Kaufmann et al., 2004), has been also considered and framed in terms of the role that transport has for increasing access to opportunities and activities.

Alongside, the discussion concerning how social issues can be better addressed in project appraisal and evaluation is increasingly important. While cost–benefit analysis (CBA) has been widely used in the assessment of transport projects, it has also been strongly criticised (Ackerman and Heinzerling, 2004; Næss, 2006, 2016; Hickman and Dean, 2017), for issues such as quantification, discounting, and distribution, and giving more importance to economic factors rather than social, environmental or even educational, cultural and institutional conditions. In the UK, there has been some use of multiple appraisal criteria in WebTAG (Web-based Transport Appraisal Guidance), but the coverage of social impacts is weak – there is still too much focus on the economic efficiency of projects in ante (before the fact) appraisal and post (after the fact) evaluation.

Some authors (including Robeyns, 2005; Beyazit, 2011; Hananel and Berechman, 2016) have argued for use of different evaluation tools in transport projects, with a better assessment of social justice issues. There is some potential in using the Capability Approach (CA) (Sen, 1985, 2009; Nussbaum and Sen, 1993; Nussbaum, 2000, 2011); however, the approach is only beginning to be considered in the transport field.

The chapter elaborates three arguments that allow the connection of the CA to the analysis of normative conflicts within transport project assessment. A comprehensive literature review of existing sources on the CA and the potential use in transport planning is used for the analysis. Therefore, the aim of the chapter is examining the application of CA in promoting better transport projects, focused on the resolution or reduction of social conflicts. It considers relevant concepts such as freedom and opportunities, for the most vulnerable groups, especially under the lens of social equity. First, CA is discussed in view of the wider literature on social equity. Second, a framework is developed for using CA in transport, based on needs, capabilities and functionings. Finally, the application of this framework is discussed, including the use of qualitative methodologies in decision-making. In conclusion, the chapter argues that CA might be seen as a complementary evaluation method for assessing the social impacts of transport projects, based on the analysis of users' expectations and attitudes towards transport and daily activities which they are able to perform.

## 2.   DEFINING CA IN TRANSPORT

### 2.1   Building Upon Concepts of Social Equity

CA was originally developed by Sen (1985, 2009) as a response to the lack of understanding on the social dimensions of equity, related not just to material resources but also to the opportunities that people have. In CA, the main focus is on what individuals are able to do, taking us beyond the role of institutions and the identification of ideal social arrangements. The framework is focused on two dimensions of substantive equity (Hickman et al., 2017):

- Capabilities: represent the "alternative combinations of doings and beings [functionings] that are feasible [for a person] to achieve" (Sen, 1999, p. 75). Capabilities are located in the field of the person's freedoms and opportunities of the things she can do or be. The definition of capabilities strongly relies on the understanding and attainment of functionings.
- Functionings: defined by Sen as the "various things a person may value doing and being" (Sen, 1999, p. 75), which includes the actions that individuals are able to perform and achieve. In transport, this could be interpreted as the person's experienced levels of accessibility, and the actual travel and participation in activities.

CA can be useful within transport as it moves beyond concepts of social inclusion or use of accessibility planning. The CA elaborates an understanding of substantive equity, considering: "not only the various things we succeed in doing, but also in the freedoms that we actually have to choose between different kinds of lives." (Sen, 2009, p. 18). The "different kinds of lives" also represents a challenge when elaborating on the psychological and societal dimensions that shape individual's freedoms. Some aspects to consider include: ability, income, education, aspiration, political and cultural context and societal norms. Hence, the understanding of capabilities takes us beyond the conventional framing of social impact assessment in understanding the shaping of individual capabilities, and also in the understanding of the actual achievement. The CA progresses beyond conventional accessibility planning, focused on the theoretical accessibility to particular activities, by considering the obstacles that might stop people from using the accessibility provided. Accessibility planning was a major step forward conceptually from the more conventional mobility planning, yet is limited in assuming that there is a "free choice" in using the accessibility provided. Issues such as income, education, aspiration, etc. limit the free choice. Hence there is a link back to Harvey (1973), who is insistent on the importance of structural factors to urban development and, by implication, transport.

In the literature, there are additional overlaps with more recent research in transport planning, such as the importance of individual attitudes (Anable, 2005) and societal influences (Urry, 2007; Shove, 2012) relative to travel, which suggests there are psychological and societal dimensions to travel. However, the CA focuses the attention on the achievement of opportunities, that can be seen as predecessors of quality of life for individuals (Anand, Hunter, and Smith, 2005). What people achieve "plays a crucial role in determining the relation between capability and well-being" (2005, p. 12). Therefore, the CA has potential in bringing together different approaches in the emerging transport field and applying them in terms of social equity. The freedom to choose our opportunities, within certain constraints, also brings with it responsibilities, to the extent that each activity is a selected action (Sen, 2009) – where there is some relation back to the Socratic notion of virtue.

Outside the transport field, Robeyns (2005) also reflects on some of the important characteristics of CA as a normative, interdisciplinary and multidimensional concept.

Robeyns suggests that the key to CA is in understanding the differences between the means and the ends of well-being and development (Robeyns, 2005, p. 95). In transport, this relationship between means and ends can be a useful distinction. For example, accessibility is a means rather than end. No one aspires "to be accessible", but having accessibility allows achieving and reaching activities and resources. The "end" is the actual functioning – the realisation of substantive equity. In this conceptualisation, accessibility (and transport provision) might be seen as a means to achieve social equity or justice, modified by particular individual's capabilities.

This difference and interdependence between capabilities and functionings is then of special interest. In particular, defining (or measuring) the gap between them might determine the existent level of equity between individuals (or social segments), alongside the actual levels of capabilities and functionings. This information can help understand what these groups expect to perform and what they are actually able to do, with transport as one element in the means to reach the required outcomes.

Despite the positive contribution that CA generates from the individual's perspective, Sen (2009, p. 295) remind us about the limitations of this approach:

> [. . .] Capability is only one aspect of freedom, related to substantive opportunities, and it cannot pay adequate attention to fairness and equity involved in procedures that have relevance to the idea of justice. [. . .] The central issue here concerns the multiple dimensions in which equality matters, which is not reducible to equality in one space only, be that economic advantage, resources, utilities, achieved quality of life capabilities. (Sen, 2009, p. 295)

## 2.2    Personal Freedoms and Choices

The freedom to choose is a relevant aspect considered by Sen related to how people are able to manage their own lives. In this regard, the capability to perform different activities is valuable in itself, as well as people having to decide how to use the freedom they possess. Poor transport networks or services often limit the choice of modes, impacting on the access to employment and other activities:

> The freedom to choose our lives can make a significant contribution to our wellbeing, but going beyond the perspective of wellbeing, the freedom itself may be seen as important. The freedoms and capabilities we enjoy can also be valuable to us, and it is ultimately for us to decide how to use the freedom we have. (Sen, 2009, pp. 18–19)

The individual freedom to choose implies at the same time the consideration of the subjectivity for each individual. In this regard, Sen highlights the importance of the use of objective reasoning in the field of feelings in order to think about issues of justice and injustice (Sen, 2009, p. 41). This is partially because it would be argued, from the analysis of subjective elements from users' feelings and preferences, that some elections are not necessarily related to rationality but emanate from the efficiency of systems.

Personal elections and freedoms are relevant aspects considered by Sen (1985) in order to inform how people are able to manage their own lives. The capacities of reasoning and choosing – inherent to human beings – are tested and even constrained under institutional frameworks ruled by inflexible norms. The same occurs when contexts are not prepared to receive transformations and changes made by individuals. When this relates to transport, the individual's scope of action could be constrained when transportation systems do not meet individuals' needs and requirements, making it difficult for users to respond to the system that is available. On the contrary, the provision of a wide range of transport alternatives, in terms of modes and trips flexibility, allows people to have more opportunities and freedoms to perform their activities and to meet their needs.

The significance given to personal elections has shaped an important criticism of CA, regarding its individualistic focus which places individual requirements over collective demands. Personal needs have the potential, of course, to be directly encouraged to be consistent with societal requirements. Sen (1985) takes this into account, criticising the principles of justice from Rawls (1971), giving more weight to equal individual liberties rather than the distribution of communitarian resources. Even though the Rawlsean approach was mainly focused on primary goods rather than income, this is the reason that sustains Rawlsean theory, prioritising liberty over social justice assessment. On the contrary, the CA brings more attention to the opportunities that individuals might have from the ownership of those goods, adapting and adjusting those resources into characteristics of good living.

The dichotomy between personal choice and collective demands has importance in the applicability of CA in transport. How could a collective transport system of goods, services and people, be planned under these principles? Can individual needs be aggregated into a communitarian context? How much focus should we give to the user perspective? In transport, perhaps the difference is not so stark – that individual and collective advantages are close to the idea of the common good.

## 2.3 Recognising the Importance of Opportunities

There is a strong association between poverty and transport and this has been well researched (Beyazit, 2011; Lucas, 2001, 2004; Church et al., 2000; Preston and Rajé, 2007; among others). However, socio-economic factors are just one of the valuable aspects regarding the opportunities that can be attained by people. A lack of income may even lead to a different range of activities that could be a match with well-being – indeed there is evidence that the focus on GDP growth has not led to increases in well-being and that the gains from higher wealth on individual happiness tail off at a relatively low threshold (Layard, 2005; Wilkinson and Pickett, 2010).

One of the fundamental points made by Sen (1985) concerns the inadequacy of the utilitarian approach to capture the different and heterogeneous aspects of development. Utilitarianism does not take into account the adaptive preferences of users. Nussbaum (2011), developing Sen's work, considers people's conditions as a strong factor in the attainment of development goals. Nussbaum often works directly with gender, considering the deficiencies not only in the utilitarian approach but also in CA.

Regarding opportunities and resources, these may be cut down by different factors related (or not) to individuals, and capabilities are: "no more than a perspective in terms of which the advantages and disadvantages of a person can be reasonably assessed" (Sen, 1985, p. 296). Sen defines the real poverty as the lack of opportunities, which can be a result of capability deprivation. In this sense, disadvantaged groups, such as the elderly, ethnic, racial or sexual minorities could have even more difficulties than low-income groups. In the transport field, these specialist needs should be taken into account in terms of configuring plans where less advantaged people can stretch and achieve their capabilities as well as people without these restrictions.

## 3.    APPLYING THE CA IN TRANSPORT

### 3.1    Quantification of Capabilities

Nussbaum (2011), when considering fundamental entitlements, suggests that there is a minimum level of capability that must be accomplished as a response to the ambiguity in the quantification of capabilities. The problem of the ambiguity of the concepts used in Sen's work is evident when attempting to operationalise the theory in an applied field such as transport. Functioning seems fairly straightforward in terms of being represented by actual travel, but capability can be interpreted in transport in various ways. It could be the aspiration of individuals to access particular activities, which are then moderated by various constraints to produce the actual functioning. Each person's capability is moderated by physical and attitudinal attributes and by the political and cultural context and societal norms. It could also be represented by the highest capabilities experienced in a sample group, with other respondents compared relative to these levels of freedom. This chapter takes the former approach, but the difficulty still remains in determining the level of theoretical capability for each individual.

In Nussbaum's work there is a link made between the goals of development and individual needs as presented above. Hence the capability could be a target level. From the perspective of equality, the problem of needs coverage – either from the individual's perspective or the systemic societal perspective – relies not only on the lack of resources but also on the abilities that individuals possess to take advantage of resources. The analysis of constraints that might affect individuals' abilities could be analysed through multi-level perspectives, such as developed by Geels (2011, 2012) and others (Whitmarsh, 2012; Nykvista and Whitmarsh, 2008). These respond mainly to socio-technical regimes grounded in norms that have oriented the activities of social groups. Informative, educational and communicational skills also play an important role in the attainment of social abilities as well as physical skills that might be constraints especially in terms of transportation abilities.

The work of Alkire (2005) in this regard is interesting for discussing the question of the applicability and operationalization of the capability approach. She suggests "even if we acknowledge the considerable value of the 'more general' framework, the pragmatic and insistent questions about how to use the approach in different contexts are still well worth asking for a number of reasons" (p. 116). This is particularly important for the developing of the research, as it experiments with the possibility of applying CA in a Latin American city.

Defining the more operational part of the CA – which leads more easily to the application of it on the field of transport planning – requires us to revisit the main objectives: the expansion of the freedoms of deprived people, for them to enjoy "valuable beings and doings", which brings both justice and poverty reduction. This comes along with the fundamental access to the necessary resources and people's possibility to make their own choices (Alkire 2005, p. 117).

The openness in terms of interpretations and lack of indicators from the CA produce certain levels of uncertainty for measuring and using this approach in an empirical context. The opportunities and capabilities potentially executable are more difficult to measure in terms of impacts in order to be translated into public policy.

### 3.2   Measuring Capabilities and Functionings in Transport

One of the main problems of CA is to find an approach to measurement and hence application. In this regard, the levels and differentiation between capabilities and functioning are of special interest, as this might determine the level of equity relative to what individuals expect to perform and what they are actually able to do – and also between individuals. The problem of measuring transport equity might be tackled from this angle – the levels and difference between capability and functioning can be viewed as "transport equity", with higher levels and a reduced gap being more equitable. Physical accessibility would be at a higher level than capability, modified into the capability by various factors that affect the "free choice" of accessibility, such as physical ability, income, education, aspiration, political and cultural context and societal norms.

In the context of Manila, the Philippines, we carried out a survey-based approach study for the measurement of capabilities and functionings (Hickman et al., 2017). The purpose of the study aimed to understand the social equity implications of different access to transport, in different low- and high-income neighbourhoods in Manila. The surveys included questions on individual and household characteristics, and questions referring to a range of central human capabilities related to the users' perceptions on transport and urban planning issues in Manila. The questions were defined based on the assessment of certain aspects related to travel and the built environment (functionings) and the desired levels of those aspects for measuring capabilities.

The impact and measurement of functionings can also be explored more in depth. We developed an approach for measuring functionings in health-related factors affecting transport users in their daily commutes, distinguishing between functionings and "weighted functionings". Weighted functionings consider the levels of assessment and the value people assign to the factors assessed. This allows understanding the gap between people's current states and their aspirations, which lead towards their capabilities. This consideration has revealed significant differences between segments, especially in disadvantaged groups such as public transport users, women and low-income segments.

The variation between capabilities and functionings between individuals, neighbourhoods and other jurisdictions, and the gap between capabilities and functionings are all of interest – hence there is much potential for fruitful analysis. Kronlid (2008) explores the relationship between capabilities and mobility, suggesting that this relationship strengthens the significance towards the individual's wellbeing. This definition of mobility is based essentially in the same theoretical structure to CA, but associating physical movement to opportunities. He argues that mobility should be in the list of capabilities, as being mobile could be considered as an opportunity, placing the practical reasons for its incorporation in the work of Alkire and Black (1997).

Martens (2016) replaces mobility with accessibility, and we would support this as the stronger position to take. The concepts presented are interesting as they locate mobility as an intrinsic element of peoples' well-being. Although Kronlid (2008) suggests a relationship between social and spatial mobility, none of the authors have presented, so far, a solution to the complexity of measurement of capabilities in transport. This consequently leads us to consider to what extent the concepts presented may help to articulate a transport planning approach based on the parameters of CA.

Previous research on the use of capabilities (Hickman et al., 2017; Mella Lira, 2019) has articulated the design of the qualitative tool based on the list of central human capabilities developed by Nussbaum (2003). The list was modified for considering the transport and urban planning context. Nussbaum's list is a comparative quality of life measurement and as a proposal for measuring capabilities. She considers the list of 10 capabilities as central requirements of a life with dignity in different spheres of life, where intrinsic to these capabilities is the idea of the "minimum account of social justice":

1. Life
2. Bodily health
3. Bodily integrity / comfort and built environment
4. Senses, imagination and thought
5. Emotions
6. Practical reason / planning one's life
7. Affiliation: respecting, valuing, appreciating people / social interaction / discrimination
8. Species / nature
9. Play / recreational activities
10. Control over environment / able to influence decisions in the local area

The translation of concepts from the Central Human Capabilities into transport would be an important conceptual step forward in assessing the social impacts of transport infrastructure. Considering the 46 CA categories, or similar, would be beneficial in that wider, inherent aspects of transport affecting individuals would be revealed relative to the conventional social impact assessments carried out in transport. This would increase our level of understanding, relative to approaches such as WebTAG, including categories such as impacts on feelings and emotions. These types of impacts are likely to be important to various modes, including walking and cycling, and to the travel experience and the wellbeing of travellers. As argued earlier in this chapter, the increase in wellbeing has its ultimate goal as the attainment of happiness.

## 4. CONCLUSIONS: APPLICABILITY AND POLICY-MAKING

This chapter began by questioning why the CA can offer an alternative for transport project assessment. Three arguments are proposed concerning the changes in the way current transport project assessment works, under the analysis of normative and ethical considerations, building on social equity's concepts; looking upon personal freedoms and choices; and recognising the attainment of individual's opportunities.

1. CA allows understanding, measuring and using concepts such as capabilities and functions, enabling to measure the differences between individuals and societal cohorts. The lower the levels and higher the gap between the current and expected achievement of opportunities, the farther we are from achieving equity.
2. CA reflects on the importance of individual decisions, attributing value to the preferences and freedoms that people require. A public transport network, for example, must be flexible enough to allow room for the exercise of these freedoms. The mode

choice, as well as the scope of the needs and activities that people perform, are some examples of this.

3. CA goes beyond the commonly placed associations between deprivation and lack of economic resources. The CA allows measuring the development of a person, group or community, through the opportunities that people can achieve.

However, there is difficulty in applying CA in transport planning, largely in terms of quantifying the capability dimension. The functioning element is relatively straightforward, representing actual travel – and is the part that transport planners usually measure in analysis. However, the reason for choosing CA as a complementary instrument is based on the idea that the evaluation of social justice in transport should include an assessment of potential physical (and perhaps social) mobility as well as actual mobility. The main problem is in data collection, and this chapter presents the possibility of using a survey and/or in-depth interview based on CA criteria, to be incorporated in the process of a widened participatory approach to project development and impact assessment. The process is, however, more than a revised set of criteria covering social issues – it also requires some judgement, quantification and discussion on capabilities and functionings, and on the gap between.

The CA can be used as an inclusive tool, using a bottom-up approach from the users' perspective, and as a mechanism for evaluating required and real access to opportunities and activities through the use of transport, as far as there can be an effective measurement of functionings and capabilities. To achieve this, it is necessary to openly ask people about their current requirements and achievements relative to travel. The scoring of criteria, weighting and impact scoring allows the user to reflect on their travel behaviours, including the opportunities and constraints impacting on these processes.

Transport should be understood, then, as a facilitator in the development of fairer societies. If transport is the means that supports some social transformations, then equity and social justice should be seen as critical goals in transport planning and need much strengthened definition and debate.

If capabilities can be measured effectively, then CA might be used in the planning and appraisal of transport, indeed in wider public policy interventions. This provides us with a much stronger accomplishment-based understanding of social justice. If inequity is rising in many contexts, then we would expect that transport inequity is too, yet there is little evidence to help us conclude on this topic. Accessibility planning, whilst a major progression from mobility planning, has not been used to the extent it might have been – and is underestimating the problem. CA offers us a way forward to consider social equity in transport more effectively, focusing the analysis on the freedoms we might like to choose in our lives.

# REFERENCES

Ackerman, F. and Heinzerling, L. (2004). *Priceless: On Knowing the Price of Everything and the Value of Nothing*. New York, New Press.

Alkire, S. (2005). *Valuing Freedoms: Sen's Capability Approach and Poverty Reduction*. Oxford, Oxford University Press.

Anable, J. (2005). 'Complacent car addicts' or 'aspiring environmentalists'? Identifying travel behaviour segments using attitude theory. *Transport Policy*, 12, 65–78.

Anand, P., Hunter, G. and Smith, R. (2005). Capabilities and well-being: evidence-based on the Sen–Nussbaum approach to welfare. *Social Indicators Research*, 74(1), 9–55.
Atkinson, A. (2015). *Inequality: What Can Be Done?* Cambridge, Harvard University Press.
Beyazit, E. (2011). Evaluating social justice in transport: lessons to be learned from the capability approach. *Transport Reviews*, 31(1), 117–134.
Church, A., Frost, M. and Sullivan, K. (2000). Transport and social exclusion in London: exploring current and potential indicators. *Transport Policy*, 7, 195–205.
Delbosc, A. and Currie, G. (2011). Using Lorenz curves to assess public transport equity. *Journal of Transport Geography*, 19(6), 1252–1259.
Geels, F. (2011). The multi-level perspective on sustainability transitions: responses to seven criticisms. *Environmental Innovation and Societal Transitions*, 1(1), 24–40.
Geels, F. (2012). A socio-technical analysis of low-carbon transitions: introducing the multi-level perspective into transport studies. *Journal of Transport Geography*, 24, 471–482.
Geurs, K. and van Wee, B. (2004). Accessibility evaluation of land-use and transport strategies: review and research directions. *Journal of Transport Geography*, 12, 127–140.
Hananel, R. and Berechman, J. (2016). Justice and transportation decision-making: the Capabilities Approach. *Transport Policy*, 49, 78–85.
Handy, S. and Niemeier, D. (1997). Measuring accessibility: an exploration of issues and alternatives. *Environment and Planning A*, 29, 1175–1194.
Harvey, D. (1973). *Social Justice and the City*. Georgia, University of Georgia Press.
Hickman, R. and Dean, M. (2017). Incomplete cost–incomplete benefit analysis in transport appraisal. *Transport Reviews*, online, DOI: 10.1080/01441647.2017.1407377.
Hickman, R., Cao, M., Mella Lira, B., Fillone, A. and Bienvenido Biona, J. (2017). Understanding capabilities, functionings and travel in high and low income neighbourhoods in Manila. *Social Inclusion*, 5(4), 161–174.
Hine, J. and Mitchell, F. (2001). Better for everyone? Travel experiences and transport exclusion. *Urban Studies*, 38(2), 319–332.
Hine, J. and Mitchell, F. (2003). *Transport Disadvantage and Social Exclusion: Exclusionary Mechanisms in Transport in Urban Scotland*. Aldershot, Ashgate.
Jackson, T. (2009). *Prosperity Without growth: Economics for a Finite Planet*. Abingdon, Routledge.
Kaufmann, V., Bergman, M. and Joye, D. (2004). Motility: mobility as capital. *International Journal of Urban and Regional Research*, 28(4), 745–756.
Kronlid, D. (2008). Mobility as capability. In, Uten, Tanu Priya and Cresswell, Tim (eds), *Gendered Mobilities*, 1st edn. Abingdon, Routledge.
Layard, P.R.G. (2005). *Happiness: Lessons from a New Science*. London, Allen Lane.
Lucas, K. (2001). *Transport, the Environment and Social Exclusion*. York, York Publishing Services.
Lucas, K. (2004). *Running on Empty: Transport, Social Exclusion and Environmental Justice*. Bristol, The Policy Press.
Lucas, K. (2006). Providing transport for social inclusion within a framework for environmental justice in the UK. *Transportation Research A*, 801–809.
Lucas, K. (2012). Transport and social exclusion: where are we now? *Transport Policy*, 20, 105–113.
Martens, K. (2016). *Transport Justice: Designing Fair Transportation Systems*. New York, Routledge.
Mella Lira, B. (2019). *Transport planning towards urban and social equity in Santiago de Chile*. Unpublished PhD, Bartlett School of Planning, UCL.
Næss, P. (2006). Cost benefit analyses of transportation investments: neither critical nor realistic. *Journal of Critical Realism*, 5, 32–60.
Næss, P. (2016). Inaccurate and biased: cost–benefit analyses of transport infrastructure projects. In, Næss, P., Price, L. and Despain, H. (eds) *Crisis System: A Critical Realist and Environmental Critique of Economics and the Economy*. Abingdon, Routledge.
Nussbaum, M. (2000). Women's capabilities and social justice. *Journal of Human Development*, 1(2), 219–247.
Nussbaum, M. (2003). Capabilities as fundamental entitlements: Sen and social justice. *Feminist Economics*, 9, 33–59.
Nussbaum, M. and Sen, A. (eds) (1993). *The Quality of Life*. Oxford, Oxford University Press.
Nykvista, B. and Whitmarsh, L. (2008). A multi-level analysis of sustainable mobility transitions: niche development in the UK and Sweden. *Technological Forecasting and Social Change*, 75(9), 1373–1387.
Preston, J. and Rajé, F. (2007). Accessibility, mobility and transport-related social exclusion. *Journal of Transport Geography*, 15(3), 151–160.
Rajé, F. (2007). Using Q methodology to develop more perceptive insights on transport and social inclusion. *Transport Policy*, 14, 467–477.
Rawls, J. (1971). *A Theory of Justice*. Cambridge, MA, Harvard University Press.
Robeyns, I. (2005). The capability approach: a theoretical survey. *Journal of Human Development and Capabilities*, 6(1), 93–114.

Schwanen, T., Lucas, K., Akyelken, N., Cisternas, D., Carrasco, J., and Neutens, T. (2015). Rethinking the links between social exclusion and transport disadvantage through the lens of social capital. *Transportation Research Part A*, 74, 123–135.

Sen, A. (1981). *Poverty and Famines: An Essay on Entitlement and Deprivation*. Oxford, Clarendon Press.

Sen, A. (1985). *Commodities and Capabilities*. Amsterdam; New York, North-Holland; New York, Elsevier Science Pub. Co.

Sen, A. (1999). *Development as Freedom*. Oxford, Oxford University Press.

Sen, A. (2009). *The Idea of Justice*. London, Penguin.

Shove, E. (2012). Putting practice into policy: reconfiguring questions of consumption and climate change. *Contemporary Social Science*, 9, 1–15.

Stanley, J., Hensher, D., Stanley, J. and Vella-Brodrick, D. (2011). Mobility, social exclusion and well-being: exploring the links. *Transportation Research, Part A: Policy and Practice*, 45(8), 789–801.

Steg, L. (2005). Car use: lust and must. Instrumental, symbolic and affective motives for car use. *Transportation Research, Part A*, 39, 147–162.

Stiglitz, J. (2012). *The Price of Inequality*. New York, Penguin.

Urry, J. (2007). *Mobilities*. Cambridge, Polity.

Whitmarsh, L. (2009). Participation of experts and non-experts in a sustainability assessment of mobility. *Environmental Policy and Governance*, 19, 232–250.

Whitmarsh, L. (2012). How useful is the multi-level perspective for transport and sustainability research? *Journal of Transport Geography*, 24, 483–487.

Wilkinson, R. and Pickett, K. (2010). *The Spirit Level*. London, Penguin Books.

# 17. Assessing utility, feasibility and equity with competence-based multi criteria analysis
*Geert te Boveldt, Imre Keseru and Cathy Macharis*

## 1. INTRODUCTION

There are several rationales behind the growing trend of participation in transport planning. Authorities might be genuinely concerned about the needs and desires of stakeholders, but also about identifying and overcoming potential resistance during the planning and delivery of projects (Arnstein, 1969; Glass, 1979; Ward, 2001; Bickerstaff et al., 2002). In spatial planning, participation has become so ubiquitous that, since the 1990s, it is said to have taken a 'communicative turn' (Healey, 1992; Innes and Booher, 1999).

Nonetheless, in project appraisal, participation plays a remarkably small role, even though this is one of the key phases in the planning process. The goal of appraisal is to inform decision makers on the advantages and disadvantages of potential project candidates (Mackie et al., 2014). Economic, social and environmental effects are estimated and valued, using appraisal methods such as Cost-Benefit-Analysis (CBA)[1] or Multi-Criteria Analysis (MCA).[2]

Appraisal is typically performed from a single-actor perspective, estimating the aggregate effects of projects on society. This approach, however, does not take into account the difference between effects on different groups within society or living in different places. Though methods have been developed for taking distributional effects into account from a single-actor viewpoint (Thomopoulos, Grant-Muller and Tight, 2009; Lucas et al., 2016), this chapter makes the case for 'opening up' the evaluation-decision making process for stakeholders. It also discusses the use of stakeholder inclusion for both ethical and pragmatic considerations, that is, in cases where stakeholder support is required for a successful implementation of the decision that is being evaluated. In addition, building on Multi Actor Multi Criteria Analysis (MAMCA) (Macharis, 2005; Macharis et al., 2012), the chapter proposes a framework for applying MCA for questions that require input or support from multiple stakeholders with divergent interests and different levels of salience: Competence-based Multi Criteria Analysis (COMCA).

The chapter starts with a short account of methods to evaluate impacts of transport on society. Then, the use of multi-actor multi-level appraisal for ethical motives is discussed. The next section deals with the use of multi-actor multi-level appraisal for pragmatic

---

[1]   When wider societal effects are taken into account, the method is also referred to as Social Cost-Benefit Analysis (SCBA). Following the majority of literature, this chapter uses CBA.

[2]   Depending on the source, also referred to as Multi(ple) Criteria Decision Analysis/Aid(ing) (MCDA), Multi(ple) Criteria Decision Evaluation (MCDE), Mutli(ple) Criteria Decision Making (MCDM), Multi(ple) Attribute Decision Analysis (MADA) or Multi(ple) Attribute Decision Making (MADM).

reasons, especially in multi-actor issues, such as cross-border projects. The following section focuses on MCA and the various existing methods for involving stakeholders in MCA. Then, the framework of COMCA is introduced and demonstrated using the complex political-geographical situation in Brussels, Belgium.

## 2.   EVALUATING WELFARE AND SUSTAINABILITY

In transport planning, the process of making major decisions is typically supported by ex-ante evaluation or appraisal methods. In the most common appraisal methods, CBA and (most techniques of) MCA, transport planning is treated as an optimisation problem. The methods help identifying decision options with an optimal ration between negative effects (costs) and positive effects (benefits).

Appraisal of public projects often not only deals with financial implications for the project's commissioner, but also with the project's (non-financial) impacts on the overall welfare of society, or the welfare of society in the long run (sustainability). In CBA, all impacts are quantified through translation into economic benefits for the whole of society. MCA, on the other hand, is explicitly designed to evaluate decisions with several incommensurable criteria, which may include whatever criterion the decision maker deems important (Munda, 2004).

CBA is the most widely used appraisal method for transport (Grant-Muller et al., 2001; Haezendonck, 2007; Annema et al., 2015). At the same time, it is strongly criticised for numerous reasons (Beukers et al., 2012; van Wee, 2012; Jones et al., 2014; Annema, 2015; Hickman and Dean, 2017; Kębłowski and Bassens, 2017), the most important of which, for the purpose of this chapter, is its inadequacy to deal with distribution effects (Thomopoulos, Grant-Muller and Tight, 2009; Beyazit, 2011; Lucas et al., 2016).

In many countries, the choice and quantification rate of the effects to measure in CBA are set by national guidelines (Geurs, Boon and Van Wee, 2009). In doing so, these guidelines explicitly define what is 'good' and 'bad' for society. In MCA, on the contrary, both the selection and the quantification of the importance of the effects depend on the standards of the person or institution that evaluates them. This subjectivity is often regarded as a main drawback of MCA (Eijgenraam et al., 2000; Gamper and Turcanu, 2007; van Wee and Tavasszy, 2008; Bakker, Koopmans and Nijkamp, 2010; Beria, Maltese and Mariotti, 2012).

## 3.   MULTI-ACTOR APPRAISAL FOR EQUITY CONCERNS

### 3.1   Costs and Benefits Depend on Perspective

Whether a person benefits from a specific transport project depends on many factors and individual characteristics, such as place of residence, work and other activities, physical and cognitive capabilities, income, gender, cultural preferences, and so on. For example, a new transport link is desirable for those in need of better accessibility in the places that it connects, but undesirable for neighbouring residents who only experience the noise and pollution it generates. Even when a project does not produce immediate nuisance, some groups will be relatively disadvantaged by the fact that public funds are spent on projects from which they do not benefit. Also, the different aspects of sustainability (environmental vs. social vs. economic) are often conflicting (Boussauw and Vanoutrive, 2017).

The distribution of costs and benefits of transport projects are unevenly distributed over society, space and time (Beyazit, 2011; Pereira et al., 2017; van Wee, 2012). Transport projects are hardly ever pareto-efficient (Van Wee and Molin, 2012), which implies that they virtually always (re)produce winners and losers (Verhoef et al., 1997; Rietveld, 2003).

CBA, however, only uses aggregate values, in which costs and benefits are calculated for society as a whole. This approach assumes Kaldor-Hicks efficiency; the possibility of compensation of negative effects on one group by the positive effects on another group (Boadway, 1974), or in other words, the benefits for the winners pay the costs for the losers. Logically, when aggregates are used, the impacts on specific groups within society (e.g. elderly or lower-income groups), are not taken into account. Whether a project benefits society or not depends on the perspective. Of course, it depends on the project's performance on welfare indicators, but also on the choice of which indicators are used, as well as the place and period for which the performance is measured.

### 3.2  Ethics are Political

Critiques on current practices of appraisal (for an overview, see Kębłowski and Bassens, 2017) concern the fact that authorities frame many transport problems and their solutions as merely 'technical', requiring a 'neutral' evaluation by 'experts', in order to make 'rational' decisions. This criticism particularly targets the underlying utilitarian philosophy, which prescribes maximising the total sum of net benefits for all people. Especially the methods of willingness-to-pay or willingness-to-accept as means to derive weights for the relative importance of non-monetary effects are criticised, as this approach generates provisions in transport for those who can afford the demand, who are not necessarily those with the highest needs (Thomopoulos et al., 2009; Beyazit, 2011; van Wee, 2012).

Following utilitarian ethics, an ethically 'just' decision means choosing the alternative with the highest performance on welfare. Yet, as discussed above, an alternative's performance on welfare depends on the scope of evaluation (area, period, population), and as a consequence, so does the answer as to whether a decision is good or bad. Whether the expansion of an airport, for example, is a good decision, largely depends on whether the perspective of evaluation is national (better connections vs. costs), local (jobs vs. noise), global (climate change), or foreign (competition with own airport).

Decisions in transport planning necessarily involve trade-offs between the interests of different groups of people at different places at different spatial and temporal scales. Assessing a decision with a single indicator of welfare implies the choice to only be concerned about a specific population in a specific area and can therefore be considered subjective.

Utilitarianism, however, is only one philosophy according to which ethics could be formulated. Several scholars (Thomopoulos et al., 2009; Beyazit, 2011; Lucas et al., 2016; Martens, 2017) explore alternative ethical frameworks for transport planning, such as egalitarianism (Rawls, 1971) or Sen's Capability Approach (Sen, 2006), striving for a 'just' distribution of benefits, taking into account the desires of the most needy.

Projects that are equally optimal for everyone do not exist. A project striving to maximise the total cost-benefit ratio for all people of society, i.e. maximising 'happiness' according to the utilitarian principle, inevitably requires sacrifices of certain groups, some of which might be deemed unacceptable. For example, when aspiring to a 'sustainable' society that requires minimal use of unrenewable resources (the long-term social optimum), to what extent is it acceptable to restrict travel for individuals? On the other hand, when the egalitarian (Rawls, 1971) principle of ethics is applied (i.e. that no person should suffer for increasing the wellbeing of others), very few transport projects could actually be realised (van Wee, 2012).

In short, decisions that claim to maximise welfare imply trade-offs on several levels: (1) between the different components of welfare; (2) between the interests or needs of different subgroups that together make up society; (3) between the interest of people in different places and different spatial scales; and (4) between the different ethical principles for a fair or just distribution of welfare over society.

## 3.3   The Benefits of Stakeholder Inclusion in Appraisal

Several methods have been proposed for evaluating the distribution of effects (Thomopoulos et al., 2009; Lucas et al., 2016). These methods, however, still use a single-actor viewpoint. This section puts forward several reasons for including perspectives from multiple actors in evaluation.

First, the attitude of a stakeholder vis-à-vis a certain decision is not only a function of a rationally estimated impact on his or her life, not even when the estimation is specified for the person's socio-spatial situation. Rather, the person's rational preferences are shaped within the boundaries of the person's cognition, values (Audi, 2007) and habitus (Bourdieu, 1972). Inclusion of individual stakeholder views helps to take these individual preferences into account. Also, stakeholder inclusion prevents the process from any possible criticisms of paternalism (van Wee, 2012). Instead of authorities assuming what is 'good' for them, stakeholders themselves are allowed to express their preferences. This also fits to Sen's notion of capabilities, meaning that the value of (basic) goods is not absolute, but depends on how they make different people capable in fulfilling their personal needs. Lastly, stakeholder-based evaluation can provide solutions in cases where information is ambiguous or contested (De Bruijn and Leijten, 2008; Martens and van Weelden, 2014).

Finding a definite, absolute indicator for the welfare impacts of decisions is problematic, which, of course, does not mean that all decisions are equally good or bad. Multi-actor evaluation allows to show the impacts on and preferences of different groups of people at different places and scales, thereby informing the decision makers on the impacts of potential decisions, providing transparency in whose interests they take into account and the choices they make between the interests of different groups of people. By doing so, a certain complexity is maintained, which, as Stirling (2010) argues, is necessary to hold politicians accountable for the choices they make.

## 3.4   Classification of Stakeholders

Through multi-actor evaluation, multiple individual preferences can be revealed. If the goal is to guide decision-making, a comprehensive interpretation of these multiple preferences is needed. This is difficult in projects with high numbers of stakeholders. Also, stakeholders often have different degrees of salience, which means that an aggregation of individual preferences into a group preference would not be a solution. For example, when a tramline is constructed, authorities might be interested in the preferences of citizens who will use the service, but might have special concern about the interests of shopkeepers or residents along the tram line who are likely to experience nuisance. The question is then, how can the interests of those groups be represented? In other words: how to deal with different degrees of salience?

A first option is to invite committees or associations that represent the interests of specific groups as stakeholders in the process. This, however, poses problems when stakeholders (citizen or shopkeepers) have opposing views within their own group. Moreover, such interest groups might simply not exist. In such cases, the process might be organised such that all stakeholders give individual input, which is then aggregated for each group that is given special consideration. A second option is to classify the stakeholders in groups according to their interest regarding the project in question. Doing so provides insight in the overall desirability for specific interest groups, while stakeholders can retain their individual objectives and priorities.

## 4.   MULTI-ACTOR APPRAISAL FROM A PRAGMATIC PERSPECTIVE

Motives behind stakeholder inclusion might not only be ethical but also practical. As for other citizen participation initiatives, a reason can be to identify and accommodate potential resistance to decisions. In some situations, however, there is a need for genuine multi-actor decisions, such as in policy contexts without one overarching or omnipotent decision maker. Examples are transport projects that cross administrative borders, such as international transport corridors or metropolitan transport areas.

Inter-governmental decision making is complicated for two main reasons. Firstly, different governments might have different priorities or (political) values. Secondly, if governments act as rational agents, they will aim to maximise the cost-benefit ratio in favour of their own territory or constituency. Due to the uneven spatial distribution of costs and benefits of infrastructure, the ideal decision version of a project would look different for each of the governments involved, even if they are on the same ideological line. Each government opts for the project alternative that maximises benefits against minimal costs and nuisances on their respective territory only. This is problematic in issues that exceed administrative boundaries and therefore require joint solutions by multiple governments. As stated earlier, each transport project inevitably creates winners and losers. So, multi-institutional decision problems, where each institution, rationally acting in its own interest, has a de facto veto power, typically leads to two situations. Either no decision is made at all, because no possible decision alternative improves the situation of all actors (i.e. the status-quo is pareto-optimal), or the agreed-upon decision is a compromise far from the social optimum. This situation is coined the *joint decision trap* by Scharpf (1988). Governments have no incentives to act beyond the confines of their own territory or constituency, since there is no mechanism that internalises the externalities of their decisions (Hooghe and Marks, 2003). For this type of problem, actor-based appraisal is useful to map local interests, global interests and help finding an equilibrium between utilitarian and egalitarian ideal situations, i.e. defining the degree of local nuisance that is acceptable to compensate global interests.

## 4.1 Multi-Level Governance

Some inter-institutional decision problems do not only require horizontal arrangements between governments of the same institutional level, but also vertical arrangements between different levels. This is the case in many international organisations, such as the EU, but also in federal states like Belgium.

A higher institutional level and larger spatial scale typically entail a greater possibility for larger projects. More positive externalities can be internalised, which allows for a greater mobilisation of funds and a greater capacity to compensate local nuisance. All transport projects require a certain territorial solidarity. So, all transport projects also need their decisions to be taken at a scale that is large enough to internalise sufficient benefits to compensate the local costs. Indeed, if every municipality were sovereign, finding a site for large-scale infrastructure, such as an airport or a waste facility plant, would be very difficult. In projects that need support or collaboration from governments from different institutional levels, multi-level evaluation can help to map global interests (e.g. the need for supra-local infrastructure), local interests (the benefits or nuisance to a specific place) and help finding equilibria between those interests.

## 4.2 Stakeholder Inclusion in Multi-Criteria Analysis

In contrast to CBA, MCA is not one standardised method, but rather a family of widely varying evaluation techniques, with different underlying philosophies. Some of the most well-known methods are MAUT/MAVT (Multi Attribute Utility/Value Theory) (von Neumann and Morgenstern, 1947), AHP (Analytic Hierarchy Process) (Saaty, 1980), PROMETHEE (Preference Ranking Organization METHod for Enrichment of Evaluations) (Brans and Vincke, 1985) and ELECTRE (ELimination Et Choix Traduisant la REalité) (Roy, 1968; Roy, et al., 1986). The sequential steps typically include: (1) problem statement; (2) identification of decision alternatives; (3) definition of criteria; (4) assessment of the performances of the alternatives on the criteria; (5) weighting of the criteria; (6) an overall preference ranking of the alternatives.

Stakeholder inclusion can help MCA to overcome one of its greatest weaknesses. MCA is often criticised for its arbitrariness: the choice of criteria, the rating of the performances of the alternatives on the criteria and the weight of those criteria are completely subjective. It is unlikely that a single evaluator manages to adequately represent society as a whole. Yet, by involving stakeholders, relevant parts of society can be represented. Moreover, rather than using socio-spatial aggregates, the choice of socio-economic groups and areas to be represented is made explicit.

Numerous frameworks have been developed for including stakeholders in MCA, including group applications of AHP and ANP (Analytic Network Process) (Saaty and Peniwati, 2008; Thomopoulos et al., 2009), Multi Criteria Mapping (Stirling and Mayer, 1999), Social Multi Criteria Evaluation (Munda, 2004), MAMCA (Multi Actor Multi Criteria Analysis) (Macharis, 2005; Macharis et al., 2012), TEBA (Transportation Elimination-By-Aspects) (Khraibani et al., 2016) and Policy-led Multi Criteria Analysis

(Ward et al., 2016). For the selection of stakeholders, most authors refer to existing stakeholder theories, such as proposed by Savage et al. (1991) or Whitehead et al. (1989).

In most participatory MCA methods (Banville et al., 1998; Bana e Costa, 2001; Munda, 2004; Saaty and Peniwati, 2008) stakeholders use a common set of criteria, resulting in a single preference ranking of alternatives representing the common interest and priorities of the group. However, reaching consensus on the criteria set might prove difficult in groups with markedly divergent interests and perspectives on the problem. Moreover, when stakeholders have different functions or responsibilities, a group preference ranking without stakeholder differentiation provides little information on the feasibility of the alternatives. Indeed, in large-scale infrastructure projects and associated decision problems, stakeholders typically have distinctive functions or levels of responsibility. If the aim of the evaluation is to assess the socio-political feasibility of alternatives, these different roles must be reckoned with.

Various techniques exist for according weights to stakeholders in MCA (Ramanathan and Ganesh, 1994; Saaty and Peniwati, 2008), but due to practical problems, such as coalition forming or the difficulty of quantifying salience, they are not well suited to political-institutional contexts (Bogetoft, 1992; Van Den Honert, 2001).

Another group of methods, including MAMCA (Macharis, 2005), Multi Criteria Mapping (MCM) (Stirling and Mayer, 1999), or participatory MCA (Hickman and Dean, 2017) bypasses both problems. Here, each actor defines its individual criteria set, leading to individual preference rankings. There is no group ranking; individual rankings are juxtaposed with the aim to facilitate comparison. In doing so, the problem of stakeholder hierarchy is circumvented, but the question of which option is preferred is left open for discussion between the actors.

### 4.3   Competence-Based Multi Criteria Analysis

COMCA is a framework for applying MAMCA in a multi-level context, i.e. in decision problems where multiple actors have different roles, tasks or levels of responsibility. This implies that actors have different levels of salience, but in COMCA, this is not expressed by according values to actors. Instead, the evaluator classifies the actors in groups according to the role they play in the problem that is at stake, i.e. their competence. In addition to MAMCA, the impacts of project alternatives are not only assessed for each actor individually, but also for each group of actors with a specific role or interest in the implementation of the decision.

As argued earlier in this chapter, rationales for including stakeholders in the evaluation process can be ethical or pragmatic. COMCA can be applied to integrate these ethical or pragmatic considerations in evaluation and therefore also in decision making. For the ethical aspect, the social utility of alternatives (the total net utility for multiple stakeholders combined), but also equity (the distribution of positive and negative effects among certain groups of stakeholders) can be assessed. From a pragmatic point of view, COMCA can be applied to assess the social feasibility of alternatives, i.e. the desirability of alternatives for each group of actors whose support is needed for the implementation of the alternatives.

Competence therefore does not only refer to legal competences (authority), but also to technical, intellectual or financial resources; in short, any resource or role the initiator

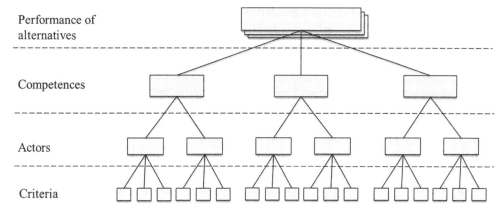

*Source:*   Author.

*Figure 17.1   The structure of COMCA*

of the evaluation deems relevant. Classifying stakeholders by competence allows for the verification of the availability of the required resources (permissions, money, technical skills, support among the relevant social groups) for the implementation of the decisions. One must bear in mind, however, that it is very difficult to assess the exact power of an actor to realise or obstruct a project, as power is often exerted through channels other than its official competences. The goal here, however, is not to provide a definitive assessment, but rather an exploratory indication, providing transparency on whose interests are taken into consideration.

The structure of COMCA is given in Figure 17.1 and includes the following steps: (1) problem statement and identification of decision alternatives; (2) identification of required competences; (3) identification of actors; (4) definition of criteria by actors; (5) assessment of the performances of the alternatives on each criterion; (6) weighting of the criteria by each actor; (7) preference ranking for each actor; (8) preference ranking for each competence domain; (9) overall analysis. The steps do not have to follow this order. Often, evaluation is carried out on the initiative of a problem owner, typically a public actor, seeking solutions for a problem. For a bottom-up or 'co-creative' approach, competences and actors can be selected earlier in the process, so problems and alternatives are identified or constructed by the actors, using their competences.

## 4.4   Assessing Utility, Feasibility and Equity in the Brussels North-South Railway Corridor Project

COMCA was applied in a project commissioned by the Belgian Federal Authority for Mobility and Transport, with the goal to study alternatives for the Brussels North-South railway corridor, a heavily saturated tunnel that forms the main bottleneck of the Belgian railway network (Abu Jeriban et al., 2015). The goal of the analysis is not to appoint the best solution, but to show the use of COMCA in decision making according to different ethical principles in problems that require cooperation of multiple actors in multiple societal domains or institutional levels (Boveldt, Van Raemdonck and Macharis, 2018).

In the project, eight alternatives were identified. Then, competences and corresponding actors were determined: the Belgian federal government, the governments of the three Belgian regions (Brussels, Flanders and Wallonia), the national railway company, regional transport operators, the railway infrastructure manager, citizens' organisations, travellers and employers' associations. The alternatives were assessed on criteria that were selected by each of the actors. It is important to note that the criteria, wherever needed, were specified to the situation of the actor in question. For example, for the criterion 'environmental impact', different assessments were made for Brussels, Flanders and Wallonia, as the alternatives have different impacts in each of the regions.

Based on data from earlier studies, experts rated the performances of the alternatives on a nine-point scale from negative to positive, as compared to the *do-nothing* alternative. Weights for the criteria were given by each of the actors to each of the criteria that were relevant to them, using a point-allocation method. The Simple Multiplicative Attribute Rating Technique (SMART) (Von Winterfeldt and Edwards, 1986) was chosen as aggregation method, as, for its transparency, it is preferable over more mathematically sophisticated methods (Stirling and Mayer, 1999).

As argued in Section 3 of this chapter, one of the main criticisms on appraisal methods (both MCA and CBA) concerns the fact that alternatives are only assessed on their net utility, allowing for the sometimes inappropriate compensation of negative effects by positive effects. For this reason, in this study, it was chosen not to calculate net benefits, but keep positive and negative impacts disaggregated. This was possible as the performances of the alternatives were compared to the do-nothing alternative.

Figure 17.2 shows the strength of the total positive and negative impacts of the alternatives for all actors, with impacts aggregated by competence domain. This classification was made to assess social feasibility: alternatives should enjoy sufficient support within each of the competence domains in order not to be blocked. Support of some actors, such as the railway company, the infrastructure manager and the federal government was considered so crucial that they were classified as a competence domain on their own. Technically, regional governments, especially the Brussels government, would be able to block the project. Here it was chosen, however, to aggregate their impacts in order to obtain a view on project-area wide, common utility instead of local, individual, utility.

A first look on the chart indicates that the alternative 'South-East tunnel' has the highest net benefits. If all competence domains were considered equal, this alternative would be the 'just' choice from a utilitarian perspective. However, we also see that for the competence domains 'citizens' organisations' and 'regional governments' this alternative has more negative than positive impacts. If the decision maker chooses to implement the 'South-East tunnel' alternative the concerns of the regional governments in this competence domain must be addressed.

In order to gain more insight into the variation in preferences within key competence domains (Figure 17.3), the distribution of impact on each of the regional governments is shown. It shows that the 'South-East tunnel' is especially problematic for Wallonia. If territorial equity is used as a guiding principle, the decision maker might consider choosing an alternative with a lower overall utility, but with a better distribution of negative impacts among the regions, such as 'Upgrade Eastern ring railway'. Another option would be to compensate or mitigate the negative effects of the 'South-East tunnel'.

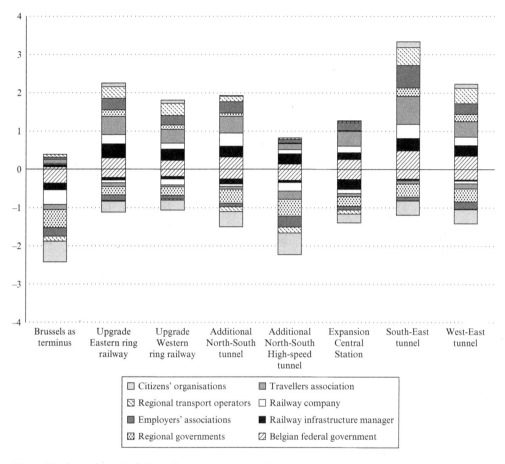

*Note:* Maximum impact of alternative per competence domain = 1

*Source:* Abu Jeriban et al. (2015), figure by author.

*Figure 17.2 Strength of total positive and negative impacts of alternatives for competence domains*

Figure 17.4 shows the positive and negative impacts of the alternative 'South-East tunnel' for each of the regional governments on the evaluation criteria they have chosen. This chart shows that the regional governments have mostly used different criteria (criteria with negligible impacts are not shown). While the impact on climate change seems to concern all three regional actors, we see that negative impacts for Wallonia are mostly due to the low performance of the alternative on financial feasibility, a criterion that was deemed especially important by the Walloon government. If the 'South-East tunnel' alternative were implemented, taking into account territorial equity among the regions, this would be a primary aspect to address.

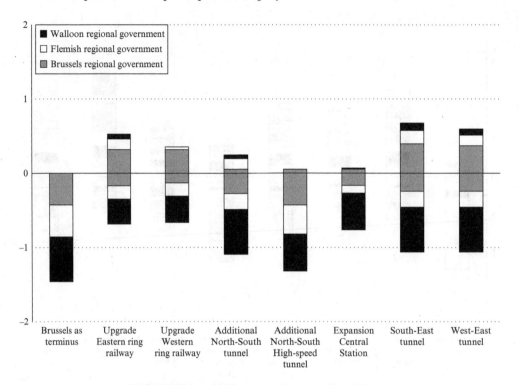

*Note:*   Maximum impact of alternative per actor = 1

*Source:*   Abu Jeriban et al. (2015), figure by author.

*Figure 17.3    Strength of total positive and negative impact of alternatives for regional governments*

## 5.   CONCLUSION

The performance of a transport project in terms of contribution to societal welfare depends on how society is delineated in space and time, and according to which ethical principles society's needs are defined. The ratio between advantages and disadvantages depends on place, scale, income, lifestyle, habits, values, etc. Attempts to summarise a project's performance on societal welfare or sustainability in a single indicator therefore necessarily imply political or moral values and so do the decisions based on the indicator.

The purpose of COMCA, as presented in this chapter, is not normative or prescriptive (Bell, Raiffa and Tverski, 1988), but heuristic and descriptive. The participatory evaluation method presented does not provide guidelines for choosing the 'right' criteria or stakeholders for making ethical or sustainable decisions. It does, however, provide a framework for decision makers, helping them to make their own vision on ethics or sustainability explicit and evaluate decisions accordingly.

It aims to help decision makers find equilibria between the importance of different factors and different actors, different places and different spatial or temporal scales. Also,

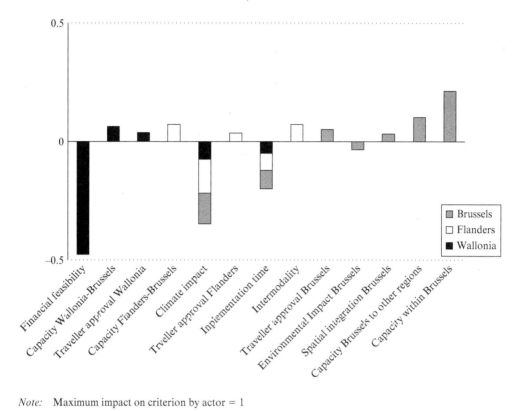

*Note:* Maximum impact on criterion by actor = 1

*Figure 17.4 Impacts of the alternative 'South-East tunnel' for regional governments by criterion*

it shows the consequences of the application of different ethical principles and helps in defining the extent to which local or individual interests can be sacrificed in favour of the greater good.

In many decision problems, such as transport projects in the metropolitan area of Brussels, decisions cannot be taken by one actor alone, but require the support of multiple actors at multiple levels. In such a context, multi-actor evaluation can be also useful to assess the feasibility of decision options, taking into account the support among the actors without whom the decisions cannot be implemented.

Even in situations where participatory appraisal does not influence the final decision in a direct way, it can function as a public evaluation tool, revealing impacts of the public decisions, thereby increasing the accountability of decision makers. It helps to make clear the distinction between the technical aspects of a decision and the political aspects and thereby supports the public debate on those decisions.

Further research could focus on providing guidelines for standardising (participatory) MCA in order to improve inter-project comparability, which is now a key strength of CBA. The bewildering amount of different methods, as well as their complexity can be a significant obstacle (Lahdelma and Hokkanen, 2000; Gamper and Turcanu, 2007).

Research is also needed to enhance the practical aspect of participatory evaluation, for example in how to reach citizens and ensure representativeness using on-line technology. Also, it would be interesting not to use evaluation only at one moment in the planning process, but find ways to use it in a more dynamic way as a framework for structuring decision making during the course of an open planning process, adaptive to changing information, goals, actors and alternatives.

# REFERENCES

Abu Jeriban, S. et al. (2015) *Rail 4 Brussels. Etude en vue de l'amélioration de la traversée et de la desserte fer-roviaire de Région Bruxelles-Capitale dans un contexte multimodale.* Available at: https://mobilit.belgium.be/sites/default/files/r4b_rapport_final_fr_deel2.pdf (accessed: 2 December 2017).

Annema, J., Mouter, N. and Razaei, J. (2015) 'Cost-benefit analysis (CBA), or multi-criteria decision-making (MCDM) or both: Politicians' perspective in transport policy appraisal', *Transportation Research Procedia*, 10, 788–797, doi: 10.1016/j.trpro.2015.09.032.

Arnstein, S. (1969) 'A ladder of citizen participation', *Journal of the American Institute of Planners*, 35(4), 216–224.

Audi, R. (2007) *Moral Value and Human Diversity.* Oxford: Oxford University Press.

Bakker, P., Koopmans, C. and Nijkamp, P. (2010) 'Appraisal of integrated transport policies', in Givoni, M. and Banister, D. (eds) *Integrated Transport From Policy to Practice.* Abingdon: Routledge, pp. 117–136.

Bana e Costa, C. (2001) 'The use of multi-criteria decision analysis to support the search for less conflicting policy options in a multi-actor context: case study', *Journal of Multi-Criteria Decision Analysis*, 125, 111–125, doi: 10.1002/mcda.292.

Banville, C. et al. (1998) 'A stakeholder approach to MCDA', *Systems Research and Behavioral Science*, 15, 15–32.

Bell, D., Raiffa, H. and Tverski, A. (1988) *Decision Making: Descriptive, Normative and Prescriptive Interactions.* Cambridge: Cambridge University Press.

Beria, P., Maltese, I. and Mariotti, I. (2012) 'Multicriteria versus cost benefit analysis: a comparative perspective in the assessment of sustainable mobility', *European Transport Research Review*, 4(3), 137–152, doi: 10.1007/s12544-012-0074-9.

Beukers, E., Bertolini, L. and Brömmelstroet, M. Te (2012) 'Why cost benefit analysis is perceived as a problematic tool for assessment of transport plans: a process perspective', *Transportation Research Part A*, 46, 68–78. Available at: https://ac.els-cdn.com/S0965856411001376/1-s2.0-S0965856411001376-main.pdf?_tid=0907c134-da9a-11e7-bd0c-00000aab0f01&acdnat=1512574257_ca802159dae48f1682eb27716c162697 (accessed: 6 December 2017).

Beyazit, E. (2011) 'Evaluating social justice in transport: lessons to be learned from the capability approach', *Transport Reviews*, 31(1), 117–134, doi: 10.1080/01441647.2010.504900.

Bickerstaff, K., Tolley, R. and Walker, G. (2002) 'Transport planning and participation: the rhetoric and reali-ties of public involvement', *Journal of Transport Geography*, 10, 61–73. Available at: https://ac.els-cdn.com/S0966692301000278/1-s2.0-S0966692301000278-main.pdf?_tid=1019beca-d764-11e7-8e14-00000aacb35f&acdnat=1512221223_288b2d326f86a67790be2f95d8056ad0 (accessed: 2 December 2017).

Boadway, R. (1974) 'The welfare foundations of cost-benefit analysis', *The Economic Journal*, 84(336), 926–939. Available at: www.jstor.org/stable/pdf/2230574.pdf (accessed: 7 December 2017).

Bogetoft, P. (1992) 'A note on conflict resolution and truthtelling', *European Journal of Operational Research*, 60(1), 109–116, doi: 10.1016/0377-2217(92)90338-A.

Bourdieu, P. (1972) *Outline of a Theory of Practice.* Cambridge: Cambridge University Press.

Boussauw, K. and Vanoutrive, T. (2017) 'Transport policy in Belgium: translating sustainability discourses into unsustainable outcomes', *Transport Policy*, 53, 11–19, doi: 10.1016/j.tranpol.2016.08.009.

Boveldt, G. te, Van Raemdonck, K. and Macharis, C. (2018) 'A new railway tunnel under Brussels? Assessing political feasibility and desirability with competence-based multi-criteria analysis', *Transport Policy*, 66, doi: 10.1016/j.tranpol.2018.03.002.

Brans, J. and Vincke, P. (1985) 'A preference ranking organisation method: (the PROMETHEE Method for Multiple Criteria Decision-Making)', *Management Science*, 31(6), 647–656.

De Bruijn, H. and Leijten, M. (2008) 'Mega-projects and contested information', in Priemus, H., Flyvbjerg, B., and van Wee, B. (eds) *Decision-Making on Mega-Projects.* Cheltenham: Edward Elgar, pp. 84–101, doi: 10.4337/9781848440173.

Eijgenraam, C. et al. (2000) *Evaluation of Infrastructural Projects; Guide for Cost–Benefit Analysis, Sections I and II.* Rotterdam: The Hague.

Gamper, C. and Turcanu, C. (2007) 'On the governmental use of multi-criteria analysis', *Ecological Economics*, 62, 298–307, doi: 10.1016/j.ecolecon.2007.01.010.

Geurs, K., Boon, W. and Van Wee, B. (2009) 'Social impacts of transport: literature review and the state of the practice of transport appraisal in the Netherlands and the United Kingdom', *Transport Reviews*, 29(1), 69–90, doi: 10.1080/01441640802130490.

Glass, J. (1979) 'Citizen participation in planning: the relationship between objectives and techniques', *Journal of the American Planning Association*, 45(2), 180–189, doi: 10.1080/01944367908976956.

Grant-Muller, S. et al. (2001) 'Economic appraisal of European transport projects: the state-of-the-art revisited', *Transport Reviews*, 21(2), 237–261, doi: 10.1080/01441640151098097.

Haezendonck, E. (2007) *Transport Project Evaluation, Extending the Social Cost–Benefit Approach*. Cheltenham: Edward Elgar.

Healey, P. (1992) 'Planning through debate: the communicative turn in planning theory', *Town Planning Review*, 63(2), 143, doi: 10.3828/tpr.63.2.422x602303814821.

Hickman, R. and Dean, M. (2017) 'Incomplete cost–incomplete benefit analysis in transport appraisal', *Transport Reviews*, 1–21, doi: 10.1080/01441647.2017.1407377.

Hooghe, L. and Marks, G. (2003) 'Unravelling the central state, but how? Types of multi-level governance', *Reihe Politikwissenschaft*, 97(2), 233–243.

Innes, J. and Booher, D. (1999) 'Consensus building and complex adaptive systems', *Journal of the American Planning Association*, 65(4), 412–423, doi: 10.1080/01944369908976071.

Jones, H., Moura, F. and Domingos, T. (2014) 'Transport infrastructure project evaluation using cost–benefit analysis', *Procedia – Social and Behavioral Sciences*, 111, 400–409, doi: 10.1016/J.SBSPRO.2014.01.073.

Kębłowski, W. and Bassens, D. (2017) '"All transport problems are essentially mathematical": the uneven resonance of academic transport and mobility knowledge in Brussels', *Urban Geography*, 3638, 1–25, doi: 10.1080/02723638.2017.1336320.

Khraibani, R. et al. (2016) 'A new evaluation and decision making framework investigating the elimination-by-aspects model in the context of transportation projects' investment choices', *Transport Policy*, 48, 67–81, doi: 10.1016/j.tranpol.2016.02.005.

Lahdelma, R. and Hokkanen, J. (2000) 'Using multicriteria methods in environmental planning and management', *Environmental Management*, 26(6), 595–605, doi: 10.1007/s002670010118.

Lucas, K. et al. (2016) 'A method to evaluate equitable accessibility: combining ethical theories and accessibility-based approaches', *Transportation*, 43, 473–490, doi: 10.1007/s11116-015-9585-2.

Macharis, C. (2005) 'The importance of stakeholder analysis in freight transport', *European transport / Trasporti Europei*, 25–26, 114–126.

Macharis, C., Turcksin, L. and Lebeau, K. (2012) 'Multi actor multi criteria analysis (MAMCA) as a tool to support sustainable decisions: state of use', *Decision Support Systems*, 54(1), 610–620, doi: 10.1016/j.dss.2012.08.008.

Mackie, P., Worsley, T. and Eliasson, J. (2014) 'Transport appraisal revisited', *Research in Transportation Economics*, 47, 3–18, doi: 10.1016/J.RETREC.2014.09.013.

Martens, K. (2017) *Transport Justice. Designing Fair Transportation Systems*. New York: Routledge.

Martens, K. and van Weelden, P. (2014) 'Decision-making on transport infrastructure and contested information: a critical analysis of three approaches', *European Planning Studies*, 22(3), 648–666, doi: 10.1080/09654313.2013.783665.

Munda, G. (2004) 'Social multi-criteria evaluation: methodological foundations and operational consequences', *European Journal of Operational Research*, 158(3), 662–677, doi: 10.1016/S0377-2217(03)00369-2.

Pereira, R., Schwanen, T. and Banister, D. (2017) 'Distributive justice and equity in transportation', *Transport Reviews*, 37(2), 170–191, doi: 10.1080/01441647.2016.1257660.

Ramanathan, R. and Ganesh, L. (1994) 'Group preference aggregation methods employed in AHP: an evaluation and an intrinsic process for deriving members' weightages', *European Journal of Operational Research*, 79, 249–265.

Rawls, J. (1971) *A Theory of Justice*. Cambridge, MA: Harvard University Press.

Rietveld, P. (2003) 'Winners and losers in transport policy: on efficiency, equity, and compensation', in Hensher, D. and Button, K. (eds) *Handbook of Transport and the Environment (Handbooks in Transport, Volume 4)*. Emerald Group Publishing Ltd, pp. 585–601.

Rietveld, P., Rouwendal, J. and Vlist, A. van der (2007) 'Equity issues in the evaluation of transport policies and transport infrastructure projects', in Geenhuizen, M. van, Reggiani, A., and Rietveld, P. (eds) *Policy Analysis of Transport Networks*. Aldershot: Ashgate, pp. 19–36.

Roy, B. (1968) 'Classement et choix en présence de points de vue multiples', *Revue française d'automatique, d'informatique et de recherche opérationnelle*, 2(6), 57–75.

Roy, B., Présent, M. and Silhol, D. (1986) 'A programming method for determining which Paris metro stations should be renovated', *European Journal of Operational Research*, 24, 318–334.

Saaty, T. (1980) *The Analytic Hierarchy Process: Planning, Priority Setting, Resources Allocation*. New York: McGraw Hill.

Saaty, T. and Peniwati, K. (2008) *Group Decision Making. Drawing out and Reconciling Differences*. Pittsburgh: RWS Publications.

Savage, G. et al. (1991) 'Strategies for assessing and managing organizational stakeholders', *The Academy of Management Executive*, 5, 61–75.

Scharpf, F. (1988) 'The joint-decision trap: lessons from German federalism and European integration', *Public administration*, 66(3), 239–278.

Sen, A. (2006) 'What do we want from a theory of justice?', *The Journal of Philosophy*, 103(5), 215–238.

Stirling, A. (2010) 'Keep it complex', *Nature*, 468, 1030–1031.

Stirling, A. and Mayer, S. (1999) *Rethinking Risk. A pilot multicriteria mapping of a genetically modified crop in agricultural systems in the UK*. Available at: http://users.sussex.ac.uk/~prfh0/Rethinking Risk.pdf (accessed: 2 December 2017).

Thomopoulos, N., Grant-Muller, S. and Tight, M. (2009) 'Incorporating equity considerations in transport infrastructure evaluation: current practice and a proposed methodology', *Evaluation and Program Planning*, 32(4), 351–359, doi: 10.1016/J.EVALPROGPLAN.2009.06.013.

Van den Honert, R. (2001) 'Decisional power in group decision making: a note on the allocation of group members, weights in the multiplicative AHP and SMART', *Group Decision and Negotiation*, 10, 275–286, doi: 10.1023/A:1011201501379.

van Wee, B. (2012) 'How suitable is CBA for the ex-ante evaluation of transport projects and policies? A discussion from the perspective of ethics', *Transport Policy*, 19(1), 1–7, doi: 10.1016/J.TRANPOL.2011.07.001.

van Wee, B. and Molin, E. (2012) 'Transport and ethics: dilemmas for CBA researchers. An interview-based study from the Netherlands', *Transport Policy*, 24, 30–36, doi: 10.1016/j.tranpol.2012.06.021.

van Wee, B. and Tavasszy, L. (2008) 'Ex-ante evaluation of mega-projects: methodological issues and cost–benefit analysis', in Priemus, H., Flyvbjerg, B., and van Wee, B. (eds) *Decision-Making on Mega-Projects*. Cheltenham: Edward Elgar, pp. 40–66.

Verhoef, E. et al. (1997) *Benefits and costs of transport classification, methodologies and policies*. Rotterdam. Available at: https://www.econstor.eu/bitstream/10419/85521/1/97084.pdf (accessed: 25 November 2017).

von Neumann, J. and Morgenstern, O. (1947) *Theory of Games and Economic Behavior*. Princeton: Princeton University Press.

Von Winterfeldt, D. and Edwards, W. (1986) *Decision Analysis and Behavioral Research*. Cambridge: Cambridge University Press.

Ward, D. (2001) 'Stakeholder involvement in transport planning: participation and power', *Impact Assessment and Project Appraisal*, 19(2), 119–130, doi: 10.3152/147154601781767131.

Ward, E., Dimitriou, H. and Dean, M. (2016) 'The application of policy-led multi-criteria analysis to mega transport infrastructure project appraisal', *Research in Transportation Economics*, doi: http://dx.doi.org/10.1016/j.retrec.2016.08.003.

Whitehead, C. et al. (1989) 'Stakeholder supportiveness and strategic vulnerability: implications for competitive strategy in the HMO industry', *Health Care Management Review*, 14(3).

# 18. Understanding the potential for behavioural economics to inform more effective planning and delivery of cycling projects
*Matt Higgins*

## 1. INTRODUCTION

The reprioritisation of road space for cycling has become a politically mainstream policy objective in the UK (GLA, 2013), yet schemes that inconvenience motor traffic can provoke strong emotional responses that divide communities and lead to social protest (Hill, 2015). So-called bikelash has been experienced in many western countries and can be seen as a pervasive threat to the successful implementation of cycling projects (GLA, 2016; Walker, 2015). At the same time, there are crises in public health, air pollution and congestion; all of which have been attributed to car-dependence and to all of which cycling is proposed as part of the solution (Banister, 2008; GLA, 2013). This research was therefore inspired by an urgent need for policy-makers and scheme promoters to better understand public opposition to road space reallocation for cycling, or else fail to effectively tackle some of the most urgent transport planning problems of our time.

This chapter proposes that bikelash is a sign that planning processes are flawed. In particular, it challenges rational choice theory, which underpins the traditional approach to behaviour change initiatives and communications that are often used to support delivery of cycling schemes. Instead, this author looks to the field of behavioural economics – which provides evidence that human beings often do not make rational choices – to consider whether doing so can offer insights that have the potential to mitigate opposition. In fact, behavioural economics is already starting to become a foundation for policy-making in the UK (Metcalfe and Dolan, 2012) in many domains, yet there is very little evidence of its application in transport planning.

The research focused on a case study of the controversial Walthamstow Village Mini-Holland scheme to explore contemporary planning processes and investigate lessons for practitioners. The most critical themes and issues contributing to public opposition were drawn out through content analysis of interviews and secondary data. These were then linked to the most prominent human biases identified in the MINDSPACE framework (Dolan et al., 2010) in order to provide behavioural insights. The findings offer strong links between opposition to the scheme and behavioural economics principles, which have been translated into a number of recommendations for practitioners.

## 2. CONTEXT AND THEORY

The literature points to motorisation being at the core of a physical inactivity epidemic, not least because concerns for personal safety discourage walking and cycling (Jacobsen et al., 2009; Koohsari et al., 2012; Olabarria et al., 2014). The implications are far-reaching and include premature mortality, climate change (Jacobsen et al., 2016), poor air quality (TfL, 2014a) and reduced social cohesion (Appleyard and Lintell, 1972). With motorisation damaging the environment and limiting social and physical opportunities within communities, there must be continued and fervent re-appraisal of the dominance and prioritisation of cars in our cities.

With regards to cycling, Tapp et al. (2016) found that most British adults think that it is a good thing for society, yet 49 per cent would not support measures that penalise car use. They state that a significant number of the population hold deep-seated pro-car values, which Steg (2004) believes originate somewhat from prolonged exposure to potent affective and symbolic advertising. Consequently, we see that in practice, proposed reprioritisation of road space away from cars leads to hostile opposition (GLA, 2016). As such, we are left with an interesting conflict between what is good for society and individual freedom when it comes to driving. This conflict is what planners and practitioners must manage, using a range of push and pull factors to restrict car use and encourage active travel (Banister, 2008). A balanced approach often includes infrastructure, behaviour change initiatives and communications.

Communications are crucial for public engagement. Poor communications lead to poor engagement, and poor engagement is likely to lead to low trust in the authority putting forward proposals (COI, 2009), which can divide communities (Botes and Rensburg, 2000) and lead to active opposition (Davies, 2001). A compounding factor is a general perception of "them" and "us" amongst the public towards planning authorities, which is found to contribute towards scepticism, alienation and frustration (Davies, 2001). Consequently, planners and practitioners should be particularly careful when communicating their projects, not least because doing so stimulates powerful individual psychological and economic motivations (Avineri, 2012; Cairns et al., 2008). It is therefore easy to appreciate why this part of project delivery so-often provokes opposition.

In common planning practice, standard communications are said to be built on rational choice theory (Avineri, 2012). The problem with this approach is that it assumes that individuals make decisions based on a rational evaluation of the information provided (Dolan et al., 2012). However, observed behaviour has consistently found evidence to the contrary, instead identifying the "systematic errors and biases of human decision-making" (Sliwowski and Olejniczak, 2015, p.61). The field of behavioural economics focuses on these errors and biases and asserts that we are instead strongly influenced by unconscious factors (Dolan et al., 2010), especially images, symbols and their context. In this regard, the same information presented in different ways, known as framing, can lead to significant variances in behaviour (Avineri, 2012). Therefore, continuing to blindly follow rational choice theory comes with the risk of inadvertently framing information in a way that triggers negative biases, whilst ignoring the opportunity to use behavioural economics to an advantage.

MINDSPACE was developed by the UK's Institute for Government. It brings together the strongest principles from behavioural economics and presents them in a framework for practitioners (Metcalfe and Dolan, 2012). This author found that planners are often responsible for the framing of information, yet behavioural economics is rarely considered. Bickman knew in 1987 that those "armed with the knowledge of human behaviour, should be especially well suited for developing theoretically sound and effective models of interventions" (p.14), and it is therefore surprising to find that common planning practice has been slow on the uptake. This chapter proposes that behavioural economics offers this knowledge and that using a framework such as MINDSPACE can improve planning and communications. In turn, this research uses a case study to provide evidence that traditional communication methods can lead to scheme opposition, before suggesting where consideration of behavioural economics might provide mitigation.

## 3.   RESEARCH FRAMEWORK AND CASE STUDY

The research formed a retrospective case study evaluation. The aim was to discover important issues and themes that resulted in opposition, before identifying correlations with behavioural insights. A replicable methodology was not found in the literature and so a three-stage analytical framework was created (Figure 18.1).

### 3.1   Case Study

The London Borough of Waltham Forest faces typical challenges associated with a car-dependant culture and growing population (Waltham Forest, 2015b). The Mini-Holland programme – funded by the Mayor of London (GLA, 2013) – provided an opportunity for the borough to reduce short car trips, increase walking and cycling, improve public spaces and stimulate economic regeneration (Waltham Forest, 2013). To do so, planners decided to divide the borough into area-wide neighbourhood schemes and develop an extensive cycle network (Figure 18.2).

Walthamstow Village was one of the area-wide schemes. As part of the approach, physical features were installed on street at specific points across the neighbourhood to limit access to walking and cycling only. The purpose of these modal filters was to "return the streets to local people by removing through traffic, providing safer, quieter and more pleasant streets which make walking and cycling the obvious ways to get around" (ibid, p.28). The scheme was innovative (TfL, 2014b), received majority support from the public,

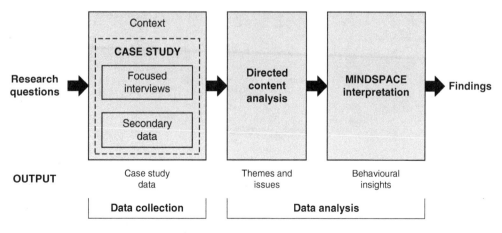

*Figure 18.1   Analytical framework*

*Source:* Walthamstow Village Residents' Association, 2015.

*Figure 18.2   Map of the Walthamstow Village scheme*

and was nominated for and won a number of awards (Davis, 2015; LCC, 2015; Waltham Forest, 2015a). However, it also proved to be highly controversial (Hill, 2015), with local groups emerging to both support and oppose the scheme. Protests marred the extensive public engagement process and a legal challenge was taken to the High Court, before being dismissed. Although the scheme was successfully implemented, the controversy continued to threaten delivery. As "the nature of people and systems becomes more transparent during their struggles" (Stake, 2005, p.16), this case study provided an important learning opportunity, considering that this type of opposition jeopardises project delivery across the UK and beyond.

## 3.2 Research Methods

Data collection came from a mixture of focused interviews and secondary data. Interviews were conducted across a representative breadth of views and a corroborative style of questioning was used to highlight gaps in knowledge, attitudes and understanding (Yin, 2003). Secondary data included council reports, communication materials and comments from social media and other online sources. Directed content analysis was conducted across data sources to "validate or extend conceptually a theoretical framework or theory" (Hsieh and Shannon, 2005, p.1279). In this case, the underlying theory was that planners and the planning process might influence the opposition faced during the initial stages of scheme engagement and delivery. Analysis discovered opposition themes and issues in the primary and secondary data, which were then brought together for triangulation. The strength of this approach is that it "enhances data quality based on the principles of idea convergence and the confirmation of findings" (Baxter and Jack, 2008, p.556).

The MINDSPACE framework was then used to uncover influences on behaviour (Metcalfe and Dolan, 2012). Such influences are vital for policy-makers to understand, as they "help explain and predict actual human responses to regulations and public programmes" (ibid, p.86). In this analysis, the interpretation formed a scheme evaluation, which in practice would be used to reshape the continued programme (Dolan et al., 2010), but that the retrospective nature of this research did not allow. Insights were gained by discovering links between the data and MINDSPACE principles, which could be interpreted as causational influences on outcomes. For this final step, each of the following MINDSPACE elements – defined in Dolan et al. (2010, p.8) – were studied in turn.

| | |
|---|---|
| MESSENGER: | We are heavily influenced by who communicates information |
| INCENTIVES: | Our responses to incentives are shaped by predictable mental shortcuts, such as strongly avoiding losses |
| NORMS: | We are strongly influenced by what others do |
| DEFAULT: | We "go with the flow" of pre-set options |
| SALIENCE: | Our attention is drawn to what is novel and seems relevant to us |
| PRIMING: | Our acts are often influenced by sub-conscious cues |
| AFFECT: | Our emotional associations can powerfully shape our actions |
| COMMITMENTS: | We seek to be consistent with our promises, and reciprocate acts |
| EGO: | We act in ways that make us feel better about ourselves |

## 4.   STUDYING OPPOSITION

Interviews were carried out with local residents, planners, campaigners and politicians. Common opposition issues were grouped together and distilled into distinct themes. Three themes in particular stood out as the most commonly raised and passionately debated by interviewees. As such, these are discussed below.

### 4.1   Views Were Influenced by General Negativity Towards the Council and a Lack of Trust

Distrust and ill feeling towards the council from local residents was a strong emergent theme:

> I've worked with pretty much half the local authorities in London doing this job at one stage or other, and pretty much every single one suffers from that lack of confidence in the council and accusations. (Respondent 1 2016, interview)

> I think there's quite a lot of animosity towards our council generally. (Respondent 7 2016, interview)

Perhaps this might have been expected, given that planners operate within a context of low levels of trust in authority (Sliwowski and Olejniczak, 2015). Regardless, this caused several ill-effects and difficulties for scheme delivery. First of all, the council and those supporting the council lost the ability to influence those in opposition:

> [A scheme supporter discussing those in opposition] Whatever people put out now, people say it's a lie, the anti-people say it's a lie. (Respondent 8 2016, interview)

Not only was influence lost, but conspiracy theories took hold as to whether consultation materials were received (Respondent 8, 2016, interview), manipulation of monitoring results (Respondent 7, 2016, interview), transparency of the consultation process (Respondent 10, 2016, interview) and council doctrine (Respondent 9, 2016, interview). According to the literature, this type of reaction is founded in both distrust and feelings of powerlessness (Jolley and Douglas, 2014), which also leads to polarisation of opinion (Botes and Rensburg, 2000). Overall, this suggests that distrust and feelings of powerlessness were pervasive in influencing opposition to the scheme, which was often grounded in perceptions of the council.

### 4.2   Strong Reactions to the Scheme Were in Abundance and Had a Variety of Origins

Opposition to the scheme was often very strong. This opposition could be traced directly to powerful, negative emotions inflamed by various incidents across consultation and delivery. Such incidents left some people feeling unable to influence outcomes, with the belief they had been deliberately excluded from the consultation process:

> People were very, very angry; very angry. They felt like the scheme was being done to them. (Respondent 3 2016, interview)

> I think it's they feel like their choice has been taken away. And what a lot of people at first didn't like is that they didn't receive any of those postcards [consultation materials]. They weren't

aware of what was happening and by the time that they were asked it was too late. (Respondent 6 2016, interview)

As previously noted, whether or not people received notification of the scheme was hotly debated and contributed to loss of trust in the process, whilst inspiring conspiracy theories. In tandem with the debate around public notification, the delivery mechanism itself – a two-week trial of the modal filter scheme – surfaced as the pivotal provocative incident:

> The trial went in and it was furore. Officers had eggs thrown at them, people were marching the streets. (Respondent 4 2016, interview)

Planners were aware that the trial would have an impact. However, they were under pressure to deliver at short notice and had little time to prepare residents in advance. Officers posted notifications through resident letterboxes and considered the trial itself to be a tool for engagement and demonstration of concept (Respondent 2, 2016, interview). Unfortunately, in this case the approach generated some very strong reactions, which led to anger that "never went away" (Respondent 3, 2016, interview). Therefore, it must be concluded that the delivery method aroused strong negative emotions that ultimately led to opposition.

### 4.3 Understanding of the Role of Consultation Was Confused and Contradictory

Understanding of the consultation process and its purpose was one of the most crucial issues, predicating many common arguments found in opposition. The following quotations illustrate confusion amongst decision-makers and local residents alike. Eventually this became problematic, with fierce debate centred on the question of majority support (Respondent 9, 2016, interview) and accusations of a rigged process:

> The expectation that you've got to have 51 per cent of people of a scheme is quite frankly bonkers. (Respondent 1 2016, interview)
> When we do consultations in Waltham Forest, if it's 51 per cent in favour then we go with the scheme. (Respondent 3 2016, interview)
> Consultation isn't market research . . . we're not going out to people and saying 'what shall we do?' because by the time we consult, we've already decided what we want to do. (Respondent 11 2016, interview)
> What they do is, they make their mind up already . . . it's false consultation and it's a common thing with councils. (Respondent 10 2016, interview)

The consultation was done through standard and legal practices (Bailii, 2015; COI, 2009) and many argued that the council went above and beyond what is normally expected. However, Arnstein (2007) would define this standard type of consultation as tokenism because citizens have some, but limited, power to change scheme outcomes. Though many participants did manage have a tangible influence on outcomes, it was clear that those that did not felt let down by the process: "I'm really sorry that I just blithely assumed everything was going to be fine" (Respondent 9, 2016, interview). As well as a lack of influence, many also opposed the scheme to say that a representative majority was not won (ibid; Respondent 10, 2016, interview). Interestingly, at no point during the interview process and nowhere in the secondary materials did planners of the scheme state that decisions would be made through majority support, yet there was an assumption amongst most that this was the due process.

In summary, it appeared that a greater share of power was expected by many residents, which Arnstein (2007) would label partnership or citizen power. Expectations were not matched by the type of consultation experienced, which resulted in opposition. Alternatively, this might be a case of those not in agreement with the result instead picking fault with the process, which is said to be a common outcome (Respondent 11, 2016, interview). When all is considered, the main issue seemed to rest on general confusion and contradictory ideas about the role of consultation.

### 4.4    Secondary Data and Triangulation

Consultation documents and communications, reports, meeting minutes, approvals and pertinent comments and images found online were included in secondary data analysis (examples are presented and discussed in Sections 5.2 and 5.3). Rather than finding new emerging issues, the secondary data converged around ten key themes that supported the interview data. Figure 18.3 illustrates the numerous relationships found between the interview themes and secondary data. To provide an example, interviews identified contradictory views around the role of consultation. This could then be linked to mixed messaging found in the consultation materials and information presented in ways that did not clearly set out the role of consultation, which led to opposition and the process being legally challenged. Together, interview and secondary data combined to offer triangulation across sources by providing strong links between themes.

The triangulation of sources substantiated claims made in interviews and offered evidence that opposition had in part been influenced by scheme planning and delivery methods, rather than the scheme itself. A primary example is that many residents had difficulty understanding information provided in the secondary materials and even felt that contentious details were deliberately obscured:

> [The consultation document] . . . was a six-page A4 document full of diagrams and symbols, and 'do you want more potted plants?' and 'would you like your bridges nice colours? Oh by the way, we're going to block some of your roads off.' But you only saw that if you actually looked at the splodges on the map and looked them up on the key. And a lot of the people that I'd spoken to hadn't done that. 'What is this? I don't understand, I'll look it up later' and they never did. (Respondent 9 2016, interview)

Individual assertions aside, the potential for misunderstanding could be found mostly in inconsistency, lack of clarity, and failure to set accurate expectations. The next step was to investigate whether these findings correlated with the strong human biases outlined in the behavioural economics literature.

## 5.    BEHAVIOURAL INSIGHTS

Interviews with the Mini-Holland planners established that behavioural economics was not considered, which was unremarkable considering that rational choice theory is the

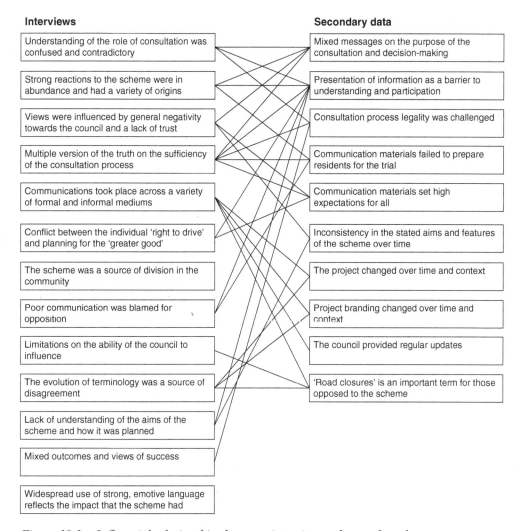

**Interviews**

| |
|---|
| Understanding of the role of consultation was confused and contradictory |
| Strong reactions to the scheme were in abundance and had a variety of origins |
| Views were influenced by general negativity towards the council and a lack of trust |
| Multiple version of the truth on the sufficiency of the consultation process |
| Communications took place across a variety of formal and informal mediums |
| Conflict between the individual 'right to drive' and planning for the 'greater good' |
| The scheme was a source of division in the community |
| Poor communication was blamed for opposition |
| Limitations on the ability of the council to influence |
| The evolution of terminology was a source of disagreement |
| Lack of understanding of the aims of the scheme and how it was planned |
| Mixed outcomes and views of success |
| Widespread use of strong, emotive language reflects the impact that the scheme had |

**Secondary data**

| |
|---|
| Mixed messages on the purpose of the consultation and decision-making |
| Presentation of information as a barrier to understanding and participation |
| Consultation process legality was challenged |
| Communication materials failed to prepare residents for the trial |
| Communication materials set high expectations for all |
| Inconsistency in the stated aims and features of the scheme over time |
| The project changed over time and context |
| Project branding changed over time and context |
| The council provided regular updates |
| 'Road closures' is an important term for those opposed to the scheme |

*Figure 18.3   Influential relationships between interview and secondary data*

traditional approach. The raison d'être of this research was to evaluate the potential impact that doing so would have had on outcomes and what the implications might be for planning. As previously discussed, in order to carry out such evaluation, each MINDSPACE element was considered in turn. Encouragingly, connections were found between the research data and each element, though some revealed themselves as much stronger than others. The three most compelling examples will now be discussed.

## 5.1 Messenger

*Messenger* is concerned with who is providing information, rather than the information itself. Many examples where the reception of information was strongly influenced by the messenger were found in the evidence, especially if it came from an opposing point of view.

... you give them a factual piece of information that has research and expert opinion behind it and you're told that you're pedalling lies. (Respondent 8 2016, interview)

In a similar vein to previous discussion, this became important as it meant that scheme supporters lost the ability to have influence within the debate. It also appears to lend support to Bickman's theory that information that is contradictory to one's beliefs does not have influence on already polarised opinion (1987). Moreover, it can be seen that *Messenger* was a key influence during engagement, which was all the more powerful within a context of low levels of trust and animosity towards the council. Dolan et al. (2010) suggest that mitigation might be achieved by involving third parties, which the council did attempt to some degree (Respondent 4, 2016, interview). However, the data did not provide a clear indication as to whether this was effective and it was not singled out as an important part of the communication strategy.

## 5.2   Incentives

Behavioural economics tells us that as humans, our responses to *Incentives* are shaped by a variety of mental shortcuts. For example, we place disproportionate high value on the short term (Dolan et al., 2010). While the longer terms benefits of the scheme were placed at the heart of its promotion, the findings show that it was in fact the initial trial had the biggest impact on attitudes and behaviour. An important factor was that people's expectations were not accurately set:

... people [were] coming across these closures and started flipping out at the council. (Respondent 2 2016, interview)

It was bigger than people were expecting. (Respondent 1 2016, interview)

In hindsight, this knowledge might have focused planners more on preparing residents for the short term impacts, lessening the levels of shock, antagonism and opposition that the delivery method brought about. Similarly, another example from *Insights* is that we are heavily averse to losses (Dolan et al., 2010). For motorists, the term *road closure* appeared to be interpreted as a loss. This may explain why the term was appropriated by opponents (Respondent 5, 2016, interview); featuring heavily in online campaigning (Figure 18.4).

*Source:*   Walthamstow Village Against Road Closure, 2014.

*Figure 18.4    "Road closed" featuring heavily on the opposition campaign Facebook profile*

The MINDSPACE literature advises practitioners to be wary of framing information in terms of losses, or else to frame losses in a way that can generate positive outcomes (Dolan et al., 2010). Consideration of loss-aversion may have steered planners away from the term *road closure*, which appeared to influence negative individual attitudes and was later used as a potent rallying tool for opponents.

## 5.3   Salience

The MINDSPACE element *Salience* offered the most pervasive link between behavioural economics and scheme opposition. Salience states that we are drawn to what is novel and seems relevant to us. It includes a number of different aspects, such as that our memory is governed by the most intense "peak" moments and that we have a limited attention span, which influences how we interpret information (Dolan et al., 2010). In this case, there are two particularly interesting examples to present.

Firstly, the first piece of information that we see on a given topic sets an *anchor*, which strongly influences how subsequent information is perceived (Dolan et al., 2010). It was discovered in the interview process that some residents reacted strongly when their initial understanding of the scheme changed.

> I'm the first one who spoke up against it . . . 'look guys, when I went to a meeting at TfL this is what I saw. *However, this is what's going to happen*'. Then the fury came out of people. (Emphasis added.) (Respondent 10 2016, interview)

In this example, the problem seemed to stem from the fact that changes made to early plans were not subsequently explained by the council. This oversight appears to have had remarkable implications, as people that read the early planning documents – and set anchors based on this information – ended up becoming founders of petitions (Respondent 10, 2016, interview) and influential mobilisers of opposition (Respondent 9, 2016, interview).

Secondly, content analysis across data sources identified issues with confusion, misunderstanding and inconsistency. When considering the role of consultation and decision-making, a telling link to Salience can be found in the consultation results document (Figure 18.5).

This consultation document placed significant emphasis on the amount of support received for proposals, given as percentages. The pie chart is colourful and stands out; it is very salient. Considering that the decision-making process was not determined by majority view (Respondent 1, 2016, interview), it could be argued that this presentation is misleading, and thus a source of the contradictory understanding of consultation that was found. Indeed, this is another example where consideration of behavioural economics might have led to a different approach that could have avoided triggering opposition through acknowledgement of our human biases.

## 5.4   Other MINDSPACE Elements

As discussed, links were also found between the data and the other MINDSPACE elements: *Norms, Default, Priming, Affect, Commitments* and *Ego*. However, the nature of

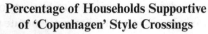

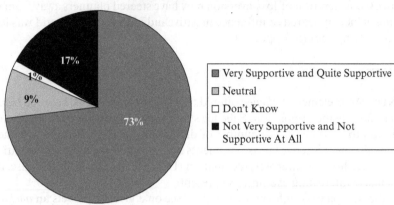

*Source:*    Waltham Forest, 2015c.

*Figure 18.5    Example presentation of consultation results*

the research topic leant itself most strongly to *Messenger, Incentives* and *Salience*. This is because the root of the experienced conflict centred around the relationship between the council and the public, the high impact of the scheme and the contradictory interpretation of communication materials. While there was evidence that behaviour was influenced by social norms and shaped by emotional responses, for example, *Norms* and *Affect* were not found to have been as impactful as the other highlighted links. It is natural to expect that different MINDSPACE elements will emerge more strongly than others – or not at all – when applying the framework in practice (Dolan et al., 2010).

## 6.    CONCLUSION

The research was driven by a desire to better understand public opposition to transport planning schemes that reprioritise road space away from cars for walking and cycling. This author sought to explore influences on public opposition and determine whether planning practitioners might unwittingly be contributing to it by following a typical approach; one that does not give conscious consideration to behavioural economics. In this case it appeared that planners and the planning process played a significant role in triggering the opposition faced, even though the scheme itself was delivered successfully to the accolade of multiple awards. This was founded in a context of general negativity towards the council and a lack of trust, but inflamed by a trial of the scheme that caused strong reactions and enduring negativity, as well as a lack of clarity about the role of consultation and decision-making.

Numerous links were found between the opposition faced and the behavioural economics literature, which were assessed through the MINDSPACE framework. Notably, the MINDSPACE element *Messenger* offered an explanation as to why the council lost the ability to influence the debate once opposition was formed; *Incentives* revealed that the strong negative reactions elicited by the trial might be founded in short term bias and loss-aversion; and the importance of anchoring within *Salience* explained the anger caused by changing plans. Lessons learnt from this particular case study suggest that the following strategies may lead to a more behaviourally-informed approach for schemes of this nature.

Bear in mind that due to anchoring, the first information shared is the most influential. It is subsequently difficult to change attitudes and perceptions after this point, especially if the information is being presented by those with an opposing view. Therefore, consider the framing of information at the beginning of a project and explain any changes made over time.

Consider and address the short term impacts, ensuring that expectations are accurately set. While transport planning schemes are often sold against their longer term benefits, which may take years to come to fruition, it is the short term impacts that influence behaviour most strongly. As such, recognising and addressing the immediate changes and setting expectations accordingly will lead to a more informed and effective approach.

Bear in mind that people have limited attention spans and therefore the most salient information will be the most influential. This means that the most important information for the reader should be the most prominent – whether through its placement or presentation – with the assumption that the reader is unlikely to read all of the information thoroughly. It also means that the content should be relevant to the reader and that care must be taken to present information clearly.

Avoid framing losses, or else consider positively framing losses, rather than gains. As people feel the pain of losses much more than they do the pleasure of gains, it is important not to present plans in a way that will be interpreted as a loss, which is likely to provoke strong negative reactions. Alternatively, loss aversion can be used to the benefit of the scheme. Instead of listing benefits, which is common practice in transport planning, it might be more impactful to list the losses associated with not going ahead with the scheme.

Consider using third party messengers that might be better placed to achieve positive outcomes. For example, if a business owner does not trust the local council, they may be less receptive to a local scheme being promoted by them. In this instance, it is likely to be more effective to ask a business that has been through similar changes to convey the message, rather than the council. Similarly, a cycling organisation may not be a trusted messenger for an anti-cycling audience.

Ensure that the role of consultation and the decision-making process is clearly explained. Leaving ambiguity in this domain opens the door to contention between supporters and opponents, a breakdown in trust between stakeholders and subsequent charges of conspiracy. The due process first needs to be agreed between scheme promoters and then communicated effectively at the start of the consultation period.

The findings and lessons learnt presented have important implications for future planning and delivery, contributing to an area of literature in which Avineri (2012) laments "a limited body of evidence" (p.519). Based on this research, it is recommended that behavioural economics – through the MINDSPACE framework or similar – is introduced into the planning process to ensure the principles contained within it are considered from the start of planning through to public engagement and delivery. In turn, this chapter opens the door to a number of different avenues for further research.

First, the recommendations set out in this chapter should be tested in practice. As a retrospective and evaluative study, it was beyond the scope of this research to do so. The most effective method would be to conduct field experiments, which "have the potential to shed some significant light on the underlying causes of changes in behaviour" (Dolan et al., 2010, p.56). Not only would this allow these particular lessons learnt to be applied and evaluated as part of real projects, it may be used to help to answer the question of whether this type of approach can compete with other strong emotional, social and cultural influences, such as pro-car values embedded through exposure to advertising (Steg, 2004) and other influences all around us (Thaler and Sunstein, 2008).

Second, further research might identify other potential areas of transport planning and project delivery to apply the lessons of behavioural economics to. It does not necessarily need to be thought of as a tool to study opposition or understand reactions to walking and cycling projects; there are potentially many other domains that could benefit from the application of this field of knowledge. Policy-makers in other sectors have already established behavioural economics as a fundamental tool (Metcalfe and Dolan, 2012) and Thaler and Sunstein (2008) provide a wealth of examples where the principles of behavioural economics have been effectively introduced across a range of disciplines, including environmental policy, health care and road safety.

Third, due to the surrounding controversy caused by the delivery method of the trial in this case, the level of public acceptability in reprioritising road space away from the private car for walking and cycling at a neighbourhood-wide scale could not be measured reliably. Rather, opposition that centred around distrust of the council and the consultation process distracted somewhat from the detail of the proposals. Within a context where bikelash is commonly experienced, it appeared that these larger issues also masked any opposition to cycling itself, which was not found in the data. Further research might answer the question of whether local residents and businesses are more anti-cycling or anti-car-restriction, which would be a valuable insight for policy-makers and practitioners.

Finally, it should be noted that there are ethical considerations and criticisms to take in to account in the application of behavioural economics. Thaler and Sunstein (2008) identify that potential abuses of power and exploitation are some of the most prevalent arguments against the use of behavioural economics. In the case of this research, some may argue that if the council had used MINDSPACE to frame information in a way that had reduced opposition, it would represent a form of manipulation. However, in the presentation of information "it is not possible to avoid influencing people" (ibid, p.247). The scheme promoter has to present information somehow, and even if that is in a behaviourally-informed way, the recipient maintains the freedom to make their own decisions. The literature identifies the most important factors being transparency and accountability. Policy-makers and practitioners should to be willing to defend the use of behavioural economics either to customers in the private sector, or voters in the public sector, and the right checks and balances need to be in place to reduce fraud and other abuses. With those in place, the benefits appear to significantly outweigh potential problems. Behavioural economics can have large impacts at low cost (Dolan et al., 2010) and generally speaking, knowledge of human behaviour can lead to more effective interventions (Bickman, 1987). There may certainly be greater efficiencies and exciting developments in store for the field of transport planning if it opens itself to the potential of behavioural economics.

**List of respondents**

Respondent 1      Planner, London Borough of Waltham Forest
Respondent 2      Planner, Transport for London (TfL)
Respondent 3      Councillor, London Borough of Waltham Forest
Respondent 4      Local resident and cycle campaigner, London Cycling Campaign
Respondent 5      Local resident and cycle campaigner, Waltham Forest Cycling Campaign
Respondent 6      Local resident and council officer, London Borough of Southwark
Respondent 7      Local resident, scheme support
Respondent 8      Local resident, scheme support
Respondent 9      Local resident and business owner, scheme opposition
Respondent 10    Local resident, scheme opposition
Respondent 11    Senior consultation practitioner, Transport for London (TfL)

# REFERENCES

Appleyard, D. and Lintell, M. (1972) The environmental quality of city streets: the residents' viewpoint, *Journal of the American Institute of Planners*, 38 (2), 84–101.

Arnstein, S. (2007) A ladder of citizen participation, *Journal of the American Institute of Planners*, 35 (4), 216–224.

Avineri, E. (2012) On the use and potential of behavioural economics from the perspective of transport and climate change, *Journal of Transport Geography*, 24, 512–521.

Bailii (2015) Williams v London Borough of Waltham Forest, accessed 25 August 2016 at: www.bailii.org/ew/cases/EWHC/Admin/2015/3907.html.

Banister, D. (2008) The sustainable mobility paradigm, *Transport Policy*, 15 (2), 73–80.

Baxter, P. and Jack, S. (2008) Qualitative case study methodology: study design and implementation for novice researchers, *The Qualitative Report*, 13 (4), 544–559.

Bickman, L. (1987) The functions of program theory, *New Directions for Program Evaluation*, 33, 5–18.

Botes, L. and Rensburg, D. Van (2000) Community participation in development: nine plagues and twelve commandments, *Community Development Journal*, 35 (1), 41–58.

Cairns, S., Sloman, L., Newson, C., Anable, J., Kirkbride, A. and Goodwin, P. (2008) Smarter choices: assessing the potential to achieve traffic reduction using soft measures, *Transport Reviews*, 28 (5), 593–618.

COI (2009) *Effective public engagement: a guide for policy-makers and communications professionals*, London: Cabinet Office, accessed 25 May 2016 at www.coi.gov.uk/documents/guidance/effective-public-engagement.pdf.

Davies, A. (2001) Hidden or hiding? Public perceptions of participation in the planning system, *The Town Planning Review*, 72 (2), 193–216.

Davis, B. (2015) Waltham Forest Council's mini Holland scheme up for another cycling award, accessed 28 August 2016 at www.guardian-series.co.uk/news/wfnews/13609949.Controversial_mini_Holland_scheme_up_for_a nother_cycling_award/.

Dolan, P., Hallsworth, M., Halpern, D., King, D., Metcalfe, R. and Vlaev, I. (2010) *MINDSPACE: Influencing Behaviour Through Public Policy*, London: Cabinet Office.

Dolan, P., Hallsworth, M., Halpern, D., King, D., Metcalfe, R. and Vlaev, I. (2012) Influencing behaviour: the mindspace way, *Journal of Economic Psychology*, 33, 264–277.

GLA (2013) *The Mayor's Vision for Cycling: an Olympic Legacy for all Londoners*, accessed 25 July 2016 at http://content.tfl.gov.uk/gla-mayors-cycle-vision-2013.pdf.

GLA (2016) *Human Streets: The Mayor's Vision for Cycling, Three Years On*, accessed 25 July 2016 at www.london.gov.uk/sites/default/files/human_streets_0.pdf.

Hill, D. (2015) Waltham Forest "Mini-Holland" row: politics, protests and house prices, accessed 28 August 2016 at www.theguardian.com/uk-news/davehillblog/2015/nov/07/waltham-forest-mini-holland-row-politics-protests-a nd-house-prices.

Hsieh, H. and Shannon, S. (2005) Three approaches to qualitative content analysis, *Qualitative Health Research*, 15 (9), 1277–1288.

Jacobsen, P., Racioppi, F. and Rutter, H. (2009) Who owns the roads? How motorised traffic discourages walking and bicycling, *Injury Prevention*, 15 (6), 369–373.

Jacobsen, P., Ragland, D. and Komanoff, C. (2016) Safety in numbers for walkers and bicyclists: exploring the mechanisms, *Injury Prevention*, 21 (4), 217–220.

Jolley, D. and Douglas, K. (2014) The social consequences of conspiracism: exposure to conspiracy theories decreases intension to engage in politics and the reduce one's carbon footprint, *British Journal of Psychology*, 105, 35–56.

Koohsari, M., Karakiewicz, J. and Kaczynski, A. (2012) Public open space and walking: the role of proximity, perceptual qualities of the surrounding built environment, and street configuration, *Environment and Behaviour*, 45 (6), 706–736.

LCC (2015) *London Cycling Campaign 2015: winners announced*, accessed 28 August 2016 at http://lcc.org.uk/pages/winners.

Metcalfe, R. and Dolan, P. (2012) Behavioural economics and its implications for transport, *Journal of Transport Geography*, 24, 503–511.

Olabarria, M., Perez, K., Santamarina-Rubio, E., Novoa, A. and Racioppi, F. (2014) Effect of neighbourhood motorization rates on walking levels, *European Journal of Public Health*, 25 (4), 740–747.

Sliowski, P. and Olejniczak, K. (2015) Towards behaviourally informed public interventions, *Management and Business Administration, Central Europe*, 23 (2), 61–91.

Stake, R. (2005) *The Art of Case Study Research*, London: Sage.

Steg, L. (2004) Car use: lust and must. Instrumental, symbolic and affective motives for car use, *Transportation Research Part A*, 39, 147–162.

Tapp, A., David, A., Nancarrow, C. and Jones, S. (2016) Great Britain adults' opinions of cycling: implications for policy, *Transportation Research Part A*, 89, 14–28.

TfL (2014a) *Improving the Health of Londoners*, accessed 25 July 2016 at http://content.tfl.gov.uk/improving-the-health-of-londoners-transport-action-plan.pdf.

TfL (2014b) *London Cycling Design Standards*, accessed 28 August 2016 at https://tfl.gov.uk/corporate/publications-and-reports/streets-toolkit#on-this-page-1.

Thaler, R. and Sunstein, C. (2008) *Nudge: Improving Decisions About Health, Wealth and Happiness*, London: Penguin.

Walker, P. (2015) Sabotage and hatred: what have people got against cyclists?, accessed 19 June 2016 at www.theguardian.com/lifeandstyle/2015/jul/01/sabotage-and-hatred-what-have-people-got-against-cyclists.

Waltham Forest (2013) *Mini-Holland*, London: Waltham Forest Council.

Waltham Forest (2015a) *Mini-Holland programme wins 2015 London cycling award*, accessed 28 August 2016 at www.enjoywalthamforest.co.uk/mini-holland-programme-wins-2015-london-cycling-award/.

Waltham Forest (2015b) *Waltham Forest Mini Holland*, accessed 28 August 2016 at http://studylib.net/doc/13826622/waltham-forest-mini-holland.

Waltham Forest (2015c) *Walthamstow Village*, accessed 28 August 2016 at www.enjoywalthamforest.co.uk/work-in-your-area/walthamstow-village/.

Walthamstow Village Against Road Closure (2014) Walthamstow Village Against Road Closure, Facebook Referencing Group, accessed 28 August 2016 at www.facebook.com/novillageclosures/.

Walthamstow Village Residents' Association (2015) Walthamstow Village area wide improvements, accessed 28 August 2016 at www.walthamstowvillage.net/wp-content/uploads/2015/02/Appendix-A-Map-of-Proposals.jpg.

Yin, R. (2003) *Case Study Research: Design and Methods*, London: Sage Publications.

# 19. Operationalising motility for transport policy
*Rebecca Shliselberg and Moshe Givoni*

## 1. INTRODUCTION

Motility, or mobility capital, is defined as the capacity to engage in travel and it is intended to reflect the relationship between spatial mobility and social mobility (Kaufmann, Bergman and Joye, 2004). Similar to other forms of individual capital, such as cultural or social capital, it is a set of personal resources used to accomplish life's tasks and has implications for class structures. Motility captures the stored value of mobility experiences (Shliselberg and Givoni, 2017), and like cultural capital it has different forms, including as embodied forms that relate to identity formation and personal growth (Hopkins, 2010; Kaufmann, 2011). Motility expresses the full set of personal resources necessary for mobility and can be described as comprised of three elements: personal access portfolios that often relate to life choices or constraints, for example owning a bicycle or living close to public transport; formal and informal skills needed to conduct travel, such as journey planning and along the way navigation; and cognitive appropriation that renders a particular travel choice relevant personally and subject to socio-cultural contexts (Flamm and Kaufmann, 2006). Motility as a capital resource is intended to capture the capacity for mobility to expand the realm of the possible. Certainly it has a role in enabling travel choices. However, the essence of capital resources is value through exchange with other forms, such that motility can be transformed into economic, cultural or social capital. For example, getting a better job because one has the capacity for travel either as a more valuable employee or because of the certain *savoir faire* that comes through in a job interview (Levy, 2014). Motility adds another perspective in relating transport policy to wellbeing.

Wellbeing can be defined through hedonic measures, such as subjective wellbeing or life satisfaction, to reflect positive life feelings and absence of negative experiences. This is a more common focus of transport policy, best captured by engagement in destination activities enabled by reducing travel costs (Abou-Zeid and Ben-Akiva, 2012). Travel can also be an activity in its own right, with potential positive experiences, as evidenced by excess travel, either entire trips or taking the long way around, indicating that travel can contribute to subjective wellbeing (Ory and Mokhtarian, 2005; Collantes and Mokhtarian, 2007).

An alternative definition is based on eudaimonia, personal wellbeing that promotes individual self-realisation and flourishing. Accessibility measures that gauge the range of activities from which an individual can choose (van Wee, 2016). This references the freedom of choice in destination activities that can contribute to self-realisation and flourishing. In this context, equity assessments can promote distributional equity in access opportunities (Martens, 2012). This captures the instrumental role of travel, focusing entirely on the value of the potential destination activities.

Motility completes the picture by emphasising travel as a valuable activity, addressing the intrinsic value of travel experiences in the way it can contribute to building up capabilities and promoting autonomy. Motility can help identify barriers to travel, especially in cases when travel opportunities appear readily available but are under subscribed. For example, new complex mass transit services that replaced direct bus services sometimes resulted in decreased travel activities that can be attributed to a lack of skills or other factors that made the adjustment difficult (Witter, 2012).

In addition to the immediate impact on mobility behaviour, the value of a capital resource has further implications. These capabilities can contribute to individual flourishing and being true to oneself not only through additional capacity for travel, but by promoting social or cultural capital as well (Shliselberg and Givoni, 2017). This intrinsic value is, as a capital resource, comparable with social capital and cultural capital, enriching personal life choices (Schwanen et al., 2015). The literature to date offers no clear means of operationalisation in policy design. Operationalisation requires a common understanding of what motility is and the value to society in promoting motility. These two points are necessary to establish motility as a policy objective. The next step is to understand how motility exhibits itself among different population groups and how it is generated so that policy can then be designed and implemented to address this need.

The challenge of operationalising motility is manifold. First, it can be elusive to understand and it is subjective. The study of accessibility often relies on network measures, combining spatial-temporal measures, bringing together travel time, hours of operation, type of activities (Geurs and van Wee, 2004; van Wee, 2016). Socio-economic variables can be insufficient for incorporating social-cultural factors or individual skills. For example, is it acceptable for women to ride a bicycle or does an individual have the skills to navigate a complex multi-modal public transport system? Understanding these constraints is key to understanding the role of motility. Secondly, it is very difficult to assess potentials, especially since inaction does not represent an absence of capacities. Furthermore, certain observable behaviours can belie limitations. For example, in the case of refugees who forcibly engage in long distance movement, but do not necessarily gain equally in motility when compared to similar journeys that might be taken for study abroad. Finally, in order to apply motility in policy and planning we need to have at minimum an ordinal scale. What is more motility, what can induce greater motility and if possible can we assess how much more motility is worth in increased wellbeing? And how much is it worth investing in it?

A methodology to take steps towards meeting these challenges is described in this chapter with two aims in mind:

- Establish a policy value for increased motility by relating it to increased social capital, cultural capital and/or to an individual's capacity for self-determination.
- To identify the variables that are indicative of a motility scale, so that there is some ordinal indication for high or low motility levels.

Motility as a policy objective for transport planning adds a mechanism beyond accessibility measures for addressing the social sustainability of transport. For this reason, motility is addressed in studies on social inclusion (Witter, 2012; Schwanen et al., 2015). While long distance travel to foreign locales is often thought of as freedom and expansive, the slow-paced movements in a mobile community can be the most meaningful (Kaufmann, 2011, 59). Motility provides a tool that can capture value in support of policies to promote short distance trips, slow travel modes, and group travel, by emphasising the personal growth, the relatedness, and the autonomy that can be generated through experiences that occur along the way, during travel.

The next section describes the use of motility in theoretical and empirical work to date. The value of the focus groups and the interviews is described in section 3. The structure of the cognitive assessment survey, which drew both from previous studies documented in the literature and from the focus groups in this research, is described in section 4. The last section discusses next steps in the research and the potential contribution of this research to incorporating motility in policy and planning.

## 2. ASSESSING MOTILITY

The theoretical discourse on motility establishes the role of travel experiences in promoting wellbeing in the context of individual flourishing and self-determination, coined as personal or eudaimonic wellbeing (De Vos et al., 2013; Reardon and Abdallah, 2013; Schwanen and Wang, 2014). Given the difficulties in assessing individual capacities or capabilities in general (Sen, 2007) makes this particular linkage of intrinsic value of travel difficult to target as a policy objective (Martens, 2012). However, the discourse on social exclusion has embraced this concept, using motility to bring into play those elements that go beyond economic means in limiting mobility and reciprocally tracing the impacts of the capacity for mobility that extend beyond travel behaviour in promoting social inclusion (Schwanen et al., 2015). Similarly, studies on the benefits of mobility for children or elderly raise developmental, cognitive and social benefits of journeying, sometimes with and sometimes without explicitly referring to motility (Hopkins, 2010; Jones et al., 2012; Nordbakke, 2013). Motility holds value for those with more obvious mobility opportunities, such as student exchange that adds cultural capital, business travellers that value the social network and added cultural capital and in opening up new work–home arrangements with clear implications for economic opportunities (Kesselring, 2006; Green et al., 2014; Gustafson, 2014).

Motility cannot be measured through observable network performance measures and nor can it be captured through observed travel behaviour. The use of motility as an explanatory variable in demand modelling was not successful (De Witte et al., 2013). Based on the qualitative research described in the following section, most people think of their immediate choices in the context of efficiency (travel time, costs) and it is a process to uncover the strategic choices that set in place their personal choice set, or access a portfolio in which these choices are framed. Motility requires understanding rationales of constraints and enablers of different capabilities that go beyond socio-economic variables.

Qualitative studies that address rationales are the more common means for studying motility and look beyond the context of the decision related to a particular travel choice, most often the target of travel behaviour analysis. For example, car ownership among young adults, leading to cruising, was central in identity formation, adding cultural capital and promoting self-determination and autonomy (Collin-lange, 2014). The role of on-the-way experiences are emphasised in the narratives on business travellers (Gustafson, 2014). The value of mobility capital in exchange for economic opportunities are discussed in the context of new remote work arrangements (Kesselring, 2006). The individual narratives demonstrate the decision process in personalising motility capital, how travel experiences contribute and the value added through the prism of additional cultural and social capital.

Individual capital is accrued through inheritance, through parental investment in children and through individual choices (Becker, 1962; Jaeger, 2009). The role of family and individual past experiences are key in defining skills and cognitive appropriation for different travel contexts, requiring a longitudinal element or personal mobility biographies. Families are key to this dynamic in transferring mobility capital between generations, but also in the process of maturation and moving away and staying connected (Kaufmann and Widmer, 2006). There is increasing awareness that childhood experiences are shaped by family but also can shape adult travel patterns later in life (Shliselberg and Givoni, 2016). To address this perspective, where possible longitudinal studies are best, but more accessible means are personal histories (Vincent-Geslin and Ravalet, 2015; Viry and Vincent-Geslin, 2015).

Two studies stand out as combining qualitative and quantitative elements, as well as longitudinal impacts in empirical research on motility. A study of a new transit system in Santiago de Chile looks to the changes in travel habits as a function of motility. Certain populations with limited motility had reduced travel with the opening of the new system, having failed to adjust to the change (Witter, 2010, 2012). Another study looks to long distance travel for work in Europe, with a particular focus on middle class workers such as teachers and professional drivers. This study highlights the informal skills and personal predispositions or cognitive appropriation framed by a willingness to engage in particular travel activities. This study used personal histories, incorporating questions such as housing relocation in childhood. These skills and attitudes contribute to an ability to successfully engage in high mobility for work, making long distance commuting, job relocation or frequent business-related travel a viable option (Kaufmann et al., 2015; Vincent-Geslin and Ravalet, 2015). In both cases the qualitative analysis helped identify the issues at hand, while the quantitative survey contributed to understanding the extent of the phenomena across a larger sample. Furthermore, post survey interviews were conducted to provide additional insight on findings that came across through the survey. This approach has been adopted to study women's motility in Israel.

There is ample justification for wellbeing to become a stronger driver for public policy, but insufficient methods and tools are at the core of policy making. In particular, policy making relies on operational objectives that focus on measurable results, with a preference for quantifiable, objective measures. Ex-ante and ex-post assessments are important procedures to ensure that public resources are applied effectively. Empirical research is needed to move from an understanding of motility to a prescriptive tool for applying motility in policy making. The research on motility remains descriptive, however it points to potential directions that could be useful for assessment of individual motility levels. Further empirical research is necessary to define measures that can be used in a motility scale and to establish the link between the inputs of mobility experiences to the outcomes of motility stocks. This is essential for motility to take on a role in transport policy and thereby to strengthen the avenues through which transport policy contributes to greater wellbeing.

## 3.  EXPLORATORY QUALITATIVE ANALYSIS

In developing the research process, it was clear that the first step needed was to establish the validity of motility by identifying its expressions through empirical research. The standing of motility as a capital resource also needed to be confirmed based on two elements: durability, including an inherited component and the lasting impact of personal experiences, and an exchange value with other forms of capital. Step one was to identify a population segment, in order to reduce cultural or geographical factors that would support a focus on intra-group differences in motility. The objective was to see how different mobility experiences created different motility stocks, and to see if this difference in motility could be a factor in other dimensions, such as social capital and self-determination. Gender is an important differentiation relevant to understanding cultural and social contexts in general and differences in expectations and experiences related to mobility (Kronlid, 2008; Viry, Vincent-Geslin and Kaufmann, 2015). Furthermore, in Israel there are dramatic differences in cultural context along ethnic-religious lines. To try and isolate the effects of mobility experiences in particular, the study targeted a relatively homogeneous group in order to mitigate the impact of geographical or cultural differences that would affect motility as well. The study was conducted among Jewish women between the ages of 25 and 65, who at the time of the study lived and worked in metropolitan Tel Aviv.

A semi-structured approach was used. Twenty-six women participated in a series of two in-depth interviews and four focus groups. Recruitment was done through social media, two informal social groups (e.g. a book club) and also through municipal social services agency. The sample of women was diverse in educational levels, of which nine had only a high school education, 19 of the women were employed full time and eight women had no access to a car. The discussion was guided through five topics, beginning with a description of current travel habits, after which the women were asked to describe a notable event that happened along the way that left a lasting impression. The next point for discussion was on the role of mobility in strategic life choices, such as housing location. The women were also asked to describe travelling to an unfamiliar destination, including the skills and willingness. Finally, the women were asked if they could draw a connection between mobility and self-fulfilment.

The narratives clearly expressed the role of personal histories, with important roles for both inheritance and on-the-way experiences in establishing motility. For example, Dana (professional singer, aged 45–54) describes how she built her personal access portfolio around owning a car. Dana noted her decision to purchase a car soon after getting a driver's licence and her proud purchase of a red Thunderbird when a foreign student in Los Angeles. These two decisions are attributed in her narrative about her father who was a professional driver and she referenced his shared passion with her brother for red Thunderbirds when she was a child. The role of personal experiences is exemplified by Shira (aged 35–44), who works at the Tel Aviv Municipality. Shira never drove long distances or out-of-town travel, until circumstances forced her to drive to a remote location in Israel's Negev region. This travel experience opened a new set of capabilities for Shira. This illustrates well how (travel) experience can be transformed into capital. Before that specific experience the resources needed for a long drive were not in hand, while after the experience they became available.

Personal narratives of on-the-way experiences also helped to understand part of the exchange value of motility. These narratives were confined to the way in which engaging in travel helped to promote both network and bonding social capital and cultural capital in the form of skills. The participants described making new acquaintances on the bus or train, as a form of network social capital. Bonding capital was part of getting to know your community, promoting acceptance for community diversity or finding a helping hand when travelling with children on a bus. Experiences that helped improve "tech savviness" included navigation applications and learning to use sophisticated fare systems. Travel both relies on and promotes other skills related to concepts of environmental mastery defined as handling life's unexpected events. This includes navigating the physical environment using navigation skills such as finding short cuts and shifting travel plans along the way.

A majority of the experiences described were about local, everyday travel experiences, for example local bus travel, which came across as influential for identity formation and capital stocks, with fewer references to leisure travel as having long lasting impact. The role of relocating was very dominant in setting a backdrop to current capabilities. High mobility experiences could be divided between those that do support and those that do not always support increased motility. Women who immigrated to Israel under difficult circumstances in the 1970s from the then Soviet Union, experienced difficult journeys but also were cut off from the country of origin, depleting social and cultural capital stocks. These women expressed very limited capacity for mobility in their lives. Conversely, women who studied abroad or immigrated under much easier conditions and maintained contact with their first homes (return visits or communications), clearly had enhanced motility.

What is illustrated through this analysis is the existence of motility as a benefit of travel experiences and that motility as a capital resource can influence life choices beyond travel. While the women do not necessarily consciously choose to promote their motility when choosing a particular journey option, it does influence strategic choices and even general preferences. What is also important to note, is that some of the benefits, such as social bonding and community diversity, may be unintended benefits, in effect positive externalities of travel behaviour. These findings both corroborate and build on the existing theoretical and empirical literature.

Thus, the qualitative analysis asserted that mobility capital, or motility, is not only a theoretical construct, but an empirical reality. This is a critical finding that can alert transport policy makers to account for motility in their policy making considerations. But how can a suitable policy be devised and then evaluated? In other words, in order for motility to be operationalised for policy purposes there is a need to have some measure of motility, preferably with some objective indicators. Working with narratives is a challenge in many policy contexts and is insufficient to influence most current policy mechanisms. The challenge is can motility be measured and how to measure it?

## 4.   COGNITIVE ASSESSMENT SURVEY

At this juncture, the need for a survey is two-fold. The first objective is to try and distil a motility scale or measure that could be derived from a series of questions on personal mobility history and attitudinal questions. The second objective is to try to ascertain the extent to which additional motility related to additional social/cultural capital and to eudaimonic wellbeing as defined in social psychology. The survey drew on findings from other qualitative studies, the limited cases of motility surveys, other relevant survey tools and the findings from the qualitative analysis conducted in this study. These different sources helped to form a list of questions that could help assess motility levels and identify contributory sources. The final product was a survey using cognitive assessment. The survey is intended to support the development of a motility index, by identifying which variables best indicate an individual's capacity for mobility. This motility index will then be used to seek potential linkages with the measures of social and cultural capital as well as the relationship between motility measures and a measure of self-determination.

The qualitative research was able to bring forward understandings and rationales based on personal narratives. The idea of a cognitive assessment survey is to structure these rationales and understandings in a questionnaire that can reach a wider audience. The drawbacks of a survey are the lack of depth of understanding, the directness may overstate certain themes and certainly the respondents can only rank or value what they are asked. There is no room for wider perspectives or rationales. While narratives are personal and even common themes across a few narratives can indicate a pattern, the limited sample is insufficient for defining a social pattern. The broader sample is necessary to understand if the pattern is common to all or to some, are there different forms and to understand under what conditions does motility take on another particular form. A survey format enables wide exposure across a large sample. This method can identify what in the narratives was particular or incidental and what is a pattern. It is a shift from exploratory narratives to assessing a social phenomenon. Generalisation and population segmentation is crucial for public policies, where targeted policies address a group. Furthermore, the quantitative analysis should provide at minimum a useful ordinal scale for motility and help to understand the relationship between more motility with more wellbeing. It may also contribute towards understanding which experiences or independent variables have a greater impact on motility. These elements are key to being able to develop interventions that can be effective in promoting motility.

The generalisation however needs to be done in steps. Gender, cultural heritage, and age cohort could be expected to result in different motility expressions and constraints. Building up empirical evidence on motility is probably best accomplished as one builds a quilt, formed through research on different populations that together form a whole picture. The focus groups were built to engender a conducive environment for self-expression and to some extent self-investigation. The groups were homogeneous, many of the women knew each other and were used to interacting together. This reduced the risk of ridicule or other inhibiting dynamics. The next step was to generalise from the small sample to representative of the group as a whole. It would be very difficult to extrapolate from the focus groups to a very heterogeneous population. Therefore the survey was built specifically for the same demographic sector as used in the focus groups.

The survey was built around seven units. Two sections provided general background related to socio-economic variables such as age and employment status and formative mobility experiences, such as relocation or where the women did their army service. The next three sections addressed motility based on the three components of personal access,

*Table 19.1    Survey structure*

| Unit | Description / Key questions |
| --- | --- |
| Socio-economic | Age, employment status, household structure, education |
| Mobility history | Formative experiences such as relocation and emigration, travel abroad, location of two-year army service |
| Personal access | Residential location and resulting access to services/destinations, car availability, bicycle/motorcycle, transport mode preferences |
| Skills | Use of navigation apps, languages spoken, journey planning, time usage, ease of interaction with others along the way |
| Cognitive assessment | Travel with children, relocate, travel for work, travel alone at night, travel alone long distances, travel alone to unfamiliar places, openness to encounters along the way |
| Social capital | Family and friends as support networks, participation in social and cultural activities, trust/responsiveness of government institutions |
| Self-determination | 21 statements intended to capture personal assessment of autonomy, relatedness and competencies – seven for each topic (Deci and Ryan, 2000) |

including residential choice, bicycle ownership and car availability; self-assessment of formal and informal skills needed to conduct travel, for example ease of interaction with others along the way; a set of twelve statements related to cognitive appropriation intended to gauge the participants willingness to engage in different forms of mobility such as willingness to travel for work purposes or attitudes related to travelling with children. The last two units were taken from established surveys designed to measure social capital and eudaimonic wellbeing based on self-determination theory.

The survey was administered through an online panel and telephone survey with over 1,000 responses, with age and residential location used to control the sample composition with respect to the general population of women in Israel. Half of the women lived in households with a partner and children. Whereas 850 women had access to a car, only 156 had access to a bicycle or motorcycle. About 600 women had moved homes three to five times, half served in the army away from home and/or travelled extensively abroad with their parents, and only 40 per cent did not live close to where they grew up. The women showed a clear preference for modes that were autonomous, in the order of driving, walking or riding the bus, though cycling is a very under-developed mode in Israel. Getting a lift was the least preferred mode. Approximately half of the women ranked themselves as competent at planning a trip using buses or getting to an unknown location, and communications with others along the way, but only a third felt that they could find a short-cut or handle a complex schedule of multiple destinations. Cognitive assessment for different mobility projects was distributed fairly evenly across those who were very willing, somewhat willing, and somewhat unwilling. Travelling with children without car was the exception, with over 60 per cent finding this type of travel activity very difficult. However, women who did use a bicycle (n=96) or those that served away from home in the army (n=444) were both less likely to find travelling with without a car difficult (cyclists/non-cyclists – F=5.521, p=.019; army service far/middle/close to home × 2=70.6, p<0.001). To the extent that this last summary scale can be related back to experiences and mobility inputs, the survey can contribute to establishing an ordinal motility scale as a dependent variable that is responsive to mobility histories, predictive of access, skills and appropriation and valued through the increased freedom of choice. Assuming that the relationship of motility to other capital and to wellbeing gives the reason why to promote motility, the relationships brought forward in the motility section provide operational tools. By estimating an ordinal scale of motility, and knowing what contributes most, policy makers can assess the current status, evaluate potential interventions for improving motility, and then verify if the policy interventions were indeed effective.

## 5. CONCLUSIONS AND NEXT STEPS

The use of combined methods is central to operationalising motility as a transport policy objective. The strength of the qualitative analysis is in the discovery and openness of the technique. It is a medium that brings forth the diversity of experiences and individual perspectives, while allowing a tracing of common themes without standardisation. Based on grounded theory, it does not presuppose any theoretical relationships or observations, but allows these to come from the participants. The explanations and rationales, what connects input variables to the phenomena, comes from the actors. Finally, the method is responsive and can adapt to new information. Similar to the research context, as a policy tool this format can be used in small groups at the community level to understand the cultural and social context of mobility behaviour serving to promote motility. By taking into account the different needs and perspectives, local level design and decision making can be sensitive and inclusive. For example, this method can be relevant in ensuring access to community services or local transit centres.

However, transport policy is more often focused on connecting communities and regions and even the meso-scale can make focus groups and community-based process unwieldy and difficult. Moreover, the appropriate level of analysis may require typologies, smoothing over some of the individual differences, relying on some level of abstraction as necessary to be able to balance a variety of needs and interests. Qualitative processes can only serve in a more limited role. The need for more representation requires different tools. Therefore, it is important to be able to assess needs and identify dynamic process through survey techniques. Moreover, it is necessary to have a short-hand set of questions, so that motility can be integrated into survey programmes that have multiple objectives.

In order to create a set some guidelines for an accepted practice the research survey will have to answer these questions:

- Which types of mobility experiences might contribute most to motility?
- What is the role of long distance travel in comparison to more daily encounters as a source of identity formation and motility?
- What measurable elements best reflect motility?
- What components of motility contribute the most value in promoting personal wellbeing?

The initial findings indicate that motility can be counted as a benefit of travel activities. This can be a combination of as a strategic framing for personal choices and/or as a positive externality resulting post facto in greater individual freedoms and potential for self-realisation. Thus, it becomes worthy of incorporating this consideration in transport policy. What types of transport policies promote motility? Are there certain investments or services more prone to promote motility and could motility considerations result in different policy choices? Does this differ across different population groups and what delineates these groups? The challenge is how to incorporate these considerations in the planning process and in policy decision making. Narratives are insufficient for answering these questions. The survey is an attempt to identify useful tools to provide an ordinal scale of motility and personal wellbeing from travel experiences.

Motility as a policy tool can be helpful in promoting more sustainable transport systems, related to active modes, short trips and group travel. It also establishes a justification for giving access to travel opportunities not linked directly to travel demand, based on the benefits of a wider range of personal experiences necessary for growth and development. Social capital derived from transport as an activity, not only that related to increased activity levels, can contribute to acceptance of diversity, socialisation and community cohesiveness (Wilson, 2011; Jones et al., 2012). Travel becomes about personal freedoms and choices, not unlike access to education and other basic human rights, shifting transport planning away from predict and provide and towards standards and entitlements. These issues can become more important as transport becomes more complex with new modes and increasing integration of information and communications technologies (Sheller, 2014). Furthermore, as new technologies and services now entering the market gain greater market share there is a risk of increasing the gap between the centre and periphery. Many of these new offerings rely on actual travel patterns using the power of big data to optimise service supply to high volume, frequently used routes, where user fees can support the business model. Conversely, these new offers may not be as readily available in other areas.

Further research is essential to fully operationalise motility as a tool for transport policy. It is necessary to identify how motility is expressed across different population groups (e.g. men at different ages), and to find the points of overlap and divergence between the different groups. The long exploratory survey format needs tuning, selecting the most effective questions and finding other variables or questions that might be useful. Likewise different policy initiatives, such as educating children to active and independent transport, inducing a willingness to try something new for adults, improved conditions for walking, improved bus transport etc. need to be tested for their contribution to increased motility to identify a set of means for promoting more sustainable transport that gives wider attention to social sustainability.

## ACKNOWLEDGEMENTS

This research is funded by the Office of the Chief Scientist, Ministry of Transport, State of Israel.

# REFERENCES

Abou-Zeid, M. and Ben-Akiva, M. (2012) Well-being and activity-based models, *Transportation*, 39(6), 1189–1207, doi: 10.1007/s11116-012-9387-8.

Becker, G. (1962) Investment in human capital: a theoretical analysis, *Journal of Political Economy*, 70(5), 9–49.

Collantes, G. and Mokhtarian, P. (2007) Subjective assessments of personal mobility: what makes the difference between a little and a lot?, *Transport Policy*, 14(3), 181–192, doi: 10.1016/j.tranpol.2006.12.002.

Collin-lange, V. (2014) My car is the best thing that ever happened to me: automobility and novice drivers in Iceland, *Young*, 22(2), 185–201, doi: 10.1177/1103308814521620.

De Vos, J. et al. (2013) Travel and subjective well-being: a focus on findings, methods and future research needs, *Transport Reviews*, 33(4), 421–442, doi: 10.1080/01441647.2013.815665.

De Witte, A. et al. (2013) Linking modal choice to motility: a comprehensive review, *Transportation Research Part A: Policy and Practice*, 49, 329–341, doi: 10.1016/j.tra.2013.01.009.

Deci, E. and Ryan, M. (2000) Basic psychological need satisfaction scale – in general. Available at: www.psych.rochester.edu/SDT.

Flamm, M. and Kaufmann, V. (2006) Operationalising the concept of motility: a qualitative study, *Mobilities*, 1(2), 167–189, doi: 10.1080/17450100600726563.

Geurs, K. and van Wee, B. (2004) Accessibility evaluation of land-use and transport strategies: review and research directions, *Journal of Transport Geography*, 12(2), 127–140, doi: 10.1016/j.jtrangeo.2003.10.005.

Green, W. et al. (2014) What's in their baggage? The cultural and social capital of Australian students preparing to study abroad, *Higher Education Research and Development*, 4360, 1–14, doi: 10.1080/07294360.2014.973381.

Gustafson, P. (2014) Business Travel from the traveller's perspective: stress, stimulation and normalization, *Mobilities*, 9(1), 63–83, doi: 10.1080/17450101.2013.784539.

Hopkins, P. (2010) *Young People, Place and Identity*. London: Routledge.

Jaeger, M. (2009) Equal access but unequal outcomes: cultural capital and educational choice in a meritocratic society, *Social Forces*, 87(4), 1943–1971, doi: 10.1353/sof.0.0192.

Jones, A. et al. (2012) Rethinking passive transport: bus fare exemptions and young people's wellbeing, *Health and Place*, 18(3), 605–612, doi: 10.1016/j.healthplace.2012.01.003.

Kaufmann, V. (2011) *Rethinking the City: Urban Dynamics and Motility*. Oxford: Routledge.

Kaufmann, V. and Widmer, E. (2006) Motility and family dynamics: current issues and research agendas, *Zeitschrift für Familienforschung*, 18(1), 111–129.

Kaufmann, V., Bergman, M. and Joye, D. (2004) Motility: mobility as capital, *International Journal of Urban and Regional Research*, 28(4), 745–756, doi: 10.1111/j.0309-1317.2004.00549.x.

Kaufmann, V. et al. (2015) Conclusions, in Viry, G. and Kaufmann, V. (eds) *High Mobility in Europe*. London: Palgrave Macmillan, pp. 209–218.

Kesselring, S. (2006) Pioneering mobilities: new patterns of movement and motility in a mobile world, *Environment and Planning A*, 38(2), 269–279, doi: 10.1068/a37279.

Kronlid, D. (2008) Mobility as Capability, in Priya, T. and Cresswell, T. (eds) *Gendered Mobilities*. New York: Routledge, pp. 15–34.

Levy, J. (2014) Inhabiting, in Lee, R. et al. (eds) *The Sage Handbook of Human Geography*. Los Angeles: Sage Reference.

Martens, K. (2012) Justice in transport as justice in accessibility: applying Walzer's "Spheres of Justice" to the transport sector, *Transportation*, 39(6), 1035–1053, doi: 10.1007/s11116-012-9388-7.

Nordbakke, S. (2013) Capabilities for mobility among urban older women: barriers, strategies and options, *Journal of Transport Geography*, 26, 166–174, doi: 10.1016/j.jtrangeo.2012.10.003.

Ory, D. and Mokhtarian, P. (2005) When getting is there half the fun? Modelling the liking for travel, *Transportation Research Part A: Policy and Practice*, 39(2–3 Spec. Issue), 97–123, doi: 10.1016/j.tra.2004.09.006.

Reardon, L. and Abdallah, S. (2013) Well-being and transport: taking stock and looking forward, *Transport Reviews*, 33(6), 634–657, doi: 10.1080/01441647.2013.837117.

Schwanen, T. and Wang, D. (2014) Well-being, context, and everyday activities in space and time, *Annals of the Association of American Geographers*, 104(4), 833–851, doi: 10.1080/00045608.2014.912549.

Schwanen, T. et al. (2015) Rethinking the links between social exclusion and transport disadvantage through the lens of social capital, *Transportation Research Part A: Policy and Practice*, 74, 123–135, doi: 10.1016/j.tra.2015.02.012.

Sen, A. (2007) Capability and well-being, in Hausman, D. (ed.) *The Philosophy of Economics*, 3rd edn. Cambridge: Cambridge University Press, pp. 270–285, doi: 10.1017/CBO9780511819025.

Sheller, M. (2014) The new mobilities paradigm for a live sociology, *Current Sociology Review*, 62(6), 789–811, doi: 10.1177/0011392114533211.

Shliselberg, R. and Givoni, M. (2016) Cultural differences in children's one mile mobility, *Built Environment*, 42(4), doi: 10.2148/benv.42.4.554.

Shliselberg, R. and Givoni, M. (2017) Motility as a policy objective, *Transport Reviews*, 1–19, doi: 10.1080/01441647.2017.1355855.

van Wee, B. (2016) Accessible accessibility research challenges, *Journal of Transport Geography*, 51, 9–16, doi: 10.1016/j.jtrangeo.2015.10.018.

Vincent-Geslin, S. and Ravalet, E. (2015) Socialisation to high mobility?, in Viry, G. and Kaufmann, V. (eds) *High Mobility in Europe: Work and Personal Life*. London: Palgrave Macmillan, pp. 83–100.

Viry, G. and Vincent-Geslin, S. (2015) High mobility over the life course, in Viry, G. and Kaufmann, V. (eds) *High Mobility in Europe: Work and Personal Life*. London: Palgrave Macmillan, pp. 83–100.

Viry, G., Vincent-Geslin, S. and Kaufmann, V. (2015) Family development and high mobility: gender inequality, in Viry, G. and Kaufmann, V. (eds) *High Mobility in Europe*. London: Palgrave Macmillan, pp. 153–179.

Wilson, H. (2011) Passing propinquities in the multicultural city: the everyday encounters of bus passengering, *Environment and Planning A*, 43(3), pp. 634–649. doi: 10.1068/a43354.

Witter, R. (2010) Public Urban transport, travel behaviour and social exclusion – the case of Santiago De Chile, *12th WCTR*, pp. 1–23.

Witter, R. (2012) *Public Urban Transport, Mobility Patterns and Social Exclusion – The Case of Santiago de Chile PAR*. Ecole Polytechnique Federale de Lausanne.

# 20. Exploring the links between mobility capital and human flourishing in Buenos Aires
*Florencia Rodriguez Touron*

## 1. WHY DOES MOBILITY CAPITAL MATTER?

The world has reached levels of unprecedented urbanisation and urban systems have become increasingly complex, with forecasts showing this process will deepen in the future (World Bank, 2009). In this context, transport plays a pivotal role as the backbone of the urban structure, not to mention its function as a global linker (Dimitriou, 2005). If "transport is unique because it contributes to the success or failure of nearly everything else" (Owen, 1964, p. 20) and its impact on the systems of production, circulation and distribution is manifest, it must thus have an influence on our prosaic daily lives.

The relevance of urban networks as "spaces of flows" (Castells, 1996) gives rise to one of the key elements of the current structure of inequalities: our (differential) capacity to be mobile. Even in the era of multiple mobilities (Urry, 2007), being able to move through space curbs our potential "access to needs and wants" (Beyazit, 2011, p. 123), to the point where scholars have claimed that mobility should be considered a fundamental entitlement or basic human capability (Kronlid, 2008).

Kaufmann, Bergman and Joye (2004) have incorporated the term motility to fill the conceptual interstice between social and spatial mobility. It provides a holistic view on the topic, reaching further than narrower concepts such as transit, transport or even mobility. Motility combines physical aspects, such as the ability to access opportunities spatially, with social aspects of mobility, such as the ability to move through the social hierarchy. In other words, this construct encompasses potency and act by defining our capacity to move (not only our actual movements) as a form of capital.

Motility draws attention to the perverse effects of the social distribution of movement capital in terms of inequalities, finding common ground with the Capabilities Approach and its focus on people's potential to convert capabilities into functionalities (Sen, 1995). It is therefore suitable to examine the complexity of the mobilities phenomenon and overcome the classic infrastructure-based approaches to transport assessment. The motility framework integrates three dimensions (Kaufmann et al, 2004), which delineate our capacity to be mobile, namely:

- Access: opportunities that can be reached given available transport and communication infrastructure, existing land use patterns, socio-economic position, and other constraints.
- Competence: the realm of skills and abilities, which can be physical, cognitive and organisational.
- Appropriation: how actors perceive, interpret and evaluate access and skills – based on motives, values and habits – and act in consequence.

The first aspect of motility resembles the notion of accessibility defined by Geurs and van Wee as "the extent to which land-use and transport systems enable (groups of) individuals to reach activities or destinations by means of a (combination of) transport mode(s)" (2004, p. 128). The authors use the term access when referring to the person's perspective (as in the motility framework) and accessibility when using a location perspective. Regarding the 2nd and 3rd aspects of motility, the links between these two and well-being remain almost unexplored by transport literature when it comes to the study of the general population, which will be the focus of this chapter.

## 2.   THE IMPORTANCE OF WELL-BEING IN TRANSPORT

At this stage, there is extensive consensus among scholars that transport is intrinsically related to societal well-being (Banister et al, 2011). Yet, definitions of well-being are manifold, and transport literature has almost exclusively privileged those emergent from the utilitarian tradition (Ettema et al, 2011; De Vos et al, 2013) which find more common ground with the classic roots of transport theory and the presumedly over-arching notion of utility. Even if few applications can be found within the field, the eudaimonic approach (Ryff, 1989; Waterman et al, 2010) offers great opportunities to reach a better understanding of human well-being since it focuses on the factors that make human beings flourish and certainly relates to the motility framework in the sense that "well-being, construed as growth and human fulfilment, is profoundly influenced by the surrounding contexts of people's lives" (Ryff and Singer, 2008).

A recent line of research suggests that the ultimate goal of transport policy should be to improve well-being, rather than to increase mobility (Stanley and Stanley, 2007). Focusing on subjective experience is a way to overcome resource-based approaches, whose limited nature does not allow a full comprehension of the well-being phenomenon. An equal level of infrastructure or income "can still leave much inequality in our ability to do what we value doing" (Sen, 1995, p. 8). Within the field of Psychology, the theoretical work regarding the definition of well-being is profuse; however, the intrinsic value of subjectivity in its assessment is a common standpoint. Whilst the hedonic framework seeks "the subjective experiences of pleasure irrespective of the sources from which that pleasure is derived" (Waterman et al, 2010, p. 42), the eudaimonic perspective addresses the allegedly veritable sources of well-being, of which pleasure is only a possible consequence. Rooted in Aristotle's philosophy (1925), eudaimonic thinkers do not regard happiness as an end in itself, but focus on the realisation of one's "daimon" or true self: "the subjective experiences of feelings of expressiveness (eudaimonia) are a by-product of engaging in actions consistent with the development and expression of one's best potentials and the pursuit of intrinsic goals" (Waterman et al, 2010, p. 42).

One key contribution of the eudaimonic perspective is that, as it derives from the above, it incorporates social aspects to the understanding of individual well-being, whilst in the hedonic view the social dimension of human development is disregarded. Acknowledging people's contexts is also relevant to understanding well-being in the light of inequalities. As Ryff and Singer (2008) state, "well-being, construed as growth and human fulfilment, is profoundly influenced by the surrounding contexts of people's lives, and as such, the opportunities for self-realisation are not equally distributed" (2008, p. 14). This idea certainly encompasses the Capabilities Approach and indirectly with the motility framework since, for both, individual outcomes are influenced by the uneven distribution of opportunities, which is eminently a social matter.

Following Sen, Martha Nussbaum (2003) has emphasised how relying solely on individual preferences can be problematic, since people's horizons of possibilities and expectations are constrained by their position in society, often reflecting unjust conditions. Crettaz and Sutter (2013) have empirically explored the impacts of "adaptive preferences", showing how well-being measures are affected by downward adaptation, or when "the underdog learns to bear the burden so well that he or she overlooks the burden itself" (Sen, 1984: 309 cited in Crettaz and Suter, 2013, p. 140). These limitations of the utilitarian focus on individual preferences and satisfaction justify the need to "make claims about fundamental entitlements that are to some extent independent of the preferences that people happen to have" (Nussbaum, 2003, p. 34).

Concerning the treatment of well-being within the transport field, the literature has been increasingly incorporating subjective measures (Camfield, 2006), but chiefly on the hedonic side. The potential of the eudaimonic perspective has been gaining growing theoretical recognition (Delbosc, 2012; De Vos et al, 2013; Reardon and Abdallah, 2013), but empirical research is still scarce, with the exception of the work of Stanley et al (2011) and Vella-Brodrick and Stanley (2013). Since understanding how being mobile can affect people's possibilities of "flourishing" is still a pending matter for transport studies, this chapter aims to contribute to the exploration of the eudaimonic approach. Nevertheless, it is recognised that research into transport and well-being has more to gain from a complementary strategy, combining both approaches rather than subscribing exclusively to one (Ryff and Singer, 2008; De Vos et al, 2013).

Within this broader frame, the following question stands: how does motility impact on the eudaimonic well-being of individuals?

## 3. LESSONS FROM BUENOS AIRES CITY

In order to test the hypothesis that higher levels of motility correlate with more well-being at the micro-level, a survey was conducted in four areas of the City of Buenos Aires, characterised by having differential levels of transport infrastructure and income levels, which are thought to influence people's motility. Transport infrastructure has been measured in terms of density of public transport (metro, train, tramway and bus routes) and cycling facilities (both public bicycle system and cycle path network), since the road network does not present substantial differences within the City. Therefore, transport infrastructure will from this point onwards mean public transport and cycling infrastructure coverage.

The City of Buenos Aires is a particularly interesting case study, since it contains a heterogeneous sample of different levels of motility in a limited territory. Unlike the suburban areas, which follow the car-dependent urban sprawl model, the City presents a strong correlation between transport infrastructure and income (GCBA, 2009). The northern fringe has the best infrastructure and is the wealthiest area, the medium fringe is a middle-class area with an average level of coverage, and finally the southern fringe is the historically less advantaged area with the poorest infrastructure. All sections show relatively better coverage when closer to the CBD (central business district) on the East

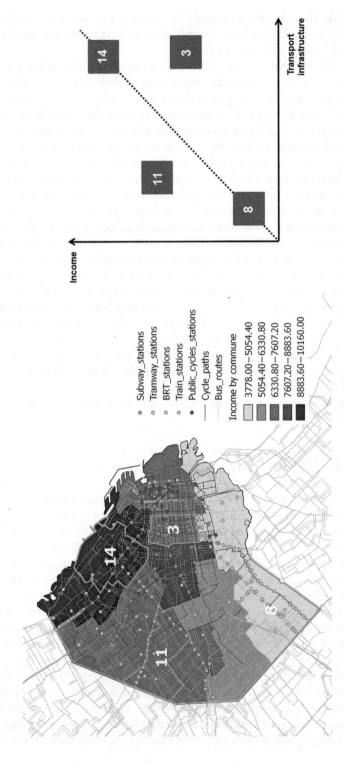

*Source:* Author's formulation based on shapefiles by GCBA, 2010 Census data, and 2014 Annual Survey CABA.

*Figure 20.1   Level of transport infrastructure and income per commune, CABA*

side, but the differences remain visible. Communes 3, 8, 11 and 14 were selected to represent the different combinations of socioeconomic and transport indicators as follows:

**Commune 14**: This area is characterised by the highest average income of the city and it is densely populated. It is well served by the three main public transport modes, and also has good conditions for sustainable modes, since it is relatively close to the CBD and located in the "northern corridor", which attracts the highest economic activity in the city and shows high urban complexity. The cycling infrastructure is also one of the best in the city. Finally, it is expected to have a high motorisation rate (disaggregated data is not publicly available), since this has been proven to correlate positively with income (ENMODO, 2010; Gartner, 2011). In a nutshell, Commune 14 is well-served and wealthy.

**Commune 8**: Situated in the most depressed area of the city, Commune 8 shows the lowest average income (37 per cent of the highest value) and a significant proportion of its population lives in poverty. The area is not satisfactorily integrated into the CBD, since the bus coverage is relatively scarce, and the level of service of the tramway and train line that reach the commune is extremely poor (7.5 and 20 minutes of headway, respectively). A light BRT corridor arrived to the area in 2013. The availability of cars in the household is nevertheless expected to be very low. In sum, Commune 8 is poorly served and economically disadvantaged.

**Commune 3**: This area is situated in a privileged geographical location, adjoining the CBD. Consequently, it enjoys the highest number of subway stations, a well-developed bus network and a good bicycle infrastructure, as well as high population density. For historical reasons, Commune 3 constitutes a middle-class area. The NBI numbers reflect small clusters of squatted dwellings and illegal sub-rental, rather than informal settlements. Motorisation rates are expected to be middle to low, both because of the income level and the abundance of transport options. Commune 3 is therefore a well-served middle-class district.

**Commune 11**: Composed of typical middle-class neighbourhoods, Commune 11 shows an average income close to the city's mean. It is poorly connected to the CBD, with no direct mode except the bus, which has a relatively poor level of coverage. This area limits the city's conurbation and exhibits a residential profile, with corridors of commercial activity but less urban complexity than in the North. The motorisation rate is also expected to be middle to low. In brief, Commune 11 is a middle-class area with relatively poor transport options.

## Survey Design: The Motility and Flourishing Scales

The purpose of the survey was to examine the relation between motility and well-being in the four communes selected for analysis. The chosen technique was an IVR (Interactive Voice Response) survey, with a total of 805 effective cases. IVR is an automated surveying technology that allows a computer to interact with respondents through the telephone, playing a previously recorded set of questions and fixed answers from which respondents have to choose by pressing numbers on their keypads. The automated nature of this technique has limitations in the sense that questions should remain as short and simple as possible, answers fixed and few (Dillman and Christian, 2005), and the total number of questions should preferably remain below 15 because they are more susceptible to breakoffs (Tourangeau, Steiger and Wilson, 2002).

As far as the questionnaire design is concerned, a motility dimension was designed to complement the identification of different levels of motility at the geographical level, by measuring individual self-reported motility, inspired by the methodological guidelines suggested by Flamm and Kaufmann (2006) and the empirical research on transport disadvantage conducted by Delbosc and Currie (2011a, 2011b), and Vella-Brodrick and Stanley (2013).

The result was a five-point Motility Scale which aims to measure the degree of difficulty people face when performing their daily travels, where one is very difficult and five is very easy. In consequence, higher overall values would correspond to higher motility levels. The Motility Scale covered the most relevant factors affecting motility suggested by the literature, although they relate mostly to the access and competence dimensions of motility, and do not claim to be exhaustive. The eight items included in the scale are summarised in Table 20.1.

As far as the eudaimonic well-being measurement is concerned, owing to the constraints of IVR mentioned above, using a combination of indexes in the way that previous studies have done (Ryff, 1989; Waterman et al, 2010; McMahan and Estes, 2011) was out of reach. However, research has shown a correlation between the different eudaimonic well-being measures (Diener, 2010), and therefore using only one was considered sufficiently rigorous. Therefore, the Flourishing Scale was deemed appropriate for an IVR in terms of length and simplicity.

The original seven-point Likert scale proposed by Diener et al (1985) was adapted to a five-point scale. Using this scale, the respondents had to indicate their degree of agreement with the following statements: (i) I lead a purposeful and meaningful life; (ii) My social relationships are supportive and rewarding; (iii) I am engaged and interested in my daily activities; (iv) I actively contribute to the happiness and well-being of others; (v) I am competent and capable in the activities that are important to me; (vi) I am a good person and live a good life; (vii) I am optimistic about my future; and (viii) People respect me.

Finally, a set of descriptive sociodemographic characteristics relevant to the research objective was also added to enrich complementary analysis. The construct was validated with semi-structured interviews.

**Travel Behaviour in the Four Communes**

Results from the survey (see Table 20.2) show that public transport is the most utilised mode among respondents.[1] Commune 3, which enjoys the best infrastructure, expectedly displays the highest level of transit use and the lowest level of car usage. Comparing the two "middle class communes", 3 and 11, it can be seen that there is a relationship between infrastructure provision and travel behaviour, since in commune 11, with similar income levels, people use their cars more. The share of sustainable modes (walking and cycling) is higher in commune 14, with no significant differences among the rest of the areas.

---

[1]    The data presented here should not be interpreted as the definitive modal split for each commune since the sample is not designed to that end, but it is indicative of the trends within communes.

*Table 20.1   Motility Scale*

| Item | Description | Operationalisation |
| --- | --- | --- |
| Introduction of the scale | | On a scale from 1 to 5, where 1 is very difficult and 5 is very easy, how easy is it for you . . . |
| 1. Transport availability | The availability of transport options (private, public, or non-motorised) to fulfil the person's mobility needs, whichever they are. | . . . to travel when you want to? |
| 2. Travel time | The capacity of the mobility system to make desired trips in a time a person judges reasonable. | . . . to get to places in a reasonable time? |
| 3. Access to activities | The capacity of the mobility system to connect a person with any activities he/she wishes to undertake. | . . . to reach all the activities you wish to undertake? |
| 4. Time poverty | The availability of time a person enjoys in order to carry out the trips he/she needs or desires, taking into account their daily obligations and routine. | . . . to find the time to make the trips you would like to? |
| 5. Cognitive understanding | The capacity of the person to understand how to use the mobility system to reach the places they desire, which depends on the system legibility and individual appropriation capacity (which can vary according to education level, age, ethnicity or other factors). | . . . to easily understand how to get to places you wish to go? |
| 6. Reliability | The capacity of the mobility system to make a person's actual trip equal the planned trip. This relates to public transport services (reliable intervals/predictive arrival/no service interruptions) and private mobility (unpredicted events that interrupt traffic flow). | . . . to move around in a reliable way, without inconveniences? |
| 7. Personal safety | The person's perception of safety when he/she is travelling in any mode, including road and personal safety. | . . . to move around feeling safe? |
| 8. Cost of transport | The capacity of the person to afford the trips they need to undertake given the offer provided by the mobility system. | . . . to cover the cost of transport? |

Surprisingly, commune 8 has the highest car usage, which could be slightly overestimated because of the exclusion of informal dwellers from the sample, but also suggests the existence of forced car ownership (Banister, 1994) due to poorer transit infrastructure.

It should be said that the motives that 59.1 per cent of respondents gave to explain their modal "choice" were cost and being the only option they had; both related more to need than to the act of freely choosing from a given set of options. This means there are nuances with regards to travel experience hidden within groups of users that can seem at first sight homogenous, such as car or transit users.

*Table 20.2   Modal choice by commune*

| Mode | Commune | | | | |
| | C3 | C8 | C11 | C14 | Total |
|---|---|---|---|---|---|
| Private car | 12.7% | 24.1% | 19.8% | 14.6% | 17.8% |
| Public transport | 75.1% | 65.8% | 66.8% | 66.3% | 68.6% |
| Walking | 2.0% | 2.0% | 1.5% | 4.0% | 2.4% |
| Cycling | 5.4% | 5.0% | 7.4% | 8.5% | 6.6% |
| Taxi | 2.9% | 0.0% | 2.5% | 4.0% | 2.4% |
| Motorcycle | 1.0% | 0.0% | 0.5% | 0.5% | 0.5% |
| Other | 1.0% | 3.0% | 1.5% | 2.0% | 1.9% |
| Total | 100.0% | 100.0% | 100.0% | 100.0% | 100.0% |

*Source:*   Author's formulation based on survey.

**The Motility and Flourishing Scales**

The results of the Motility Scale (see Table 20.3) show a relation between the commune –meaning the level of transport infrastructure and income – and people's level of motility. The differences are subtle but consistent, commune 8 having the lowest level and commune 14 the highest, as expected. The difference between communes 3 and 11 is minor; however, commune 3 shows better levels of motility, validating the hypothesis leading the definition of the area of study. In addition, standard deviation values show that for commune 14 results are the least variable (5.69 for the general score), whilst in commune 8 variability increases (6.83), suggesting that in the latter the population is slightly less homogenous.

The components which scored the lowest were safety, which is usually cited by Buenos Aires citizens as one of their main concerns, since the city observes high levels of inequalities, and attacks against personal safety, such as muggings, are frequent. The enjoyment of public spaces while moving around the city is therefore undermined by this factor. Another relevant aspect is the cost of transport, which is particularly compelling in commune 8 because of the lower income levels its dwellers possess. Travel time and time poverty are highly associated, revealing that the amount of time people spend on their daily travels logi-cally affects their capacity to find the time to undertake the activities they desire. The only exception is commune 14, where time availability does not seem to be as problematic, due to the shorter distance to travel attractors. Reliability also scores low, which is understandable given the lack of real-time information on buses (which constitute 80 per cent of the public transport share) and heavy traffic for road users, besides the recurrent service interruptions in guided modes. The other variables all score above 3, the highest being cognitive appro-priation, or the capacity of people to understand the network and make the trips they need. One exception is the difficulty in accessing activities in commune 8 (2.69), which exposes the reinforcement of the relation between being mobile and fully participating in society.

The Flourishing Scale (Table 20.4) does not respond, as the Motility Scale, to eliminate commune variation (even though well-being levels are slightly higher for commune 14), which is understandable since well-being is a complex phenomenon which contains social and individual dimensions. Standard deviation values show, however, there is a higher

*Table 20.3 Mean and standard deviation values for the Motility Scale in the four communes*

| Motility scale | Commune | | | | | | | | | |
|---|---|---|---|---|---|---|---|---|---|---|
| | C3 | | C8 | | C11 | | C14 | | Total | |
| | Mean | SD | Mean | SD | Mean | SD | Mean | SD | Mean | SD |
| **General score** | **23.64** | 6.67 | 22.26 | 6.83 | **23.50** | 6.07 | **24.47** | 5.69 | **23.47** | 6.37 |
| Travel capacity | 3.18 | 1.36 | 2.99 | 1.33 | 3.14 | 1.27 | 3.09 | 1.27 | 3.10 | 1.31 |
| Travel time | 2.83 | 1.24 | 2.73 | 1.36 | 2.85 | 1.19 | 2.98 | 1.21 | 2.85 | 1.25 |
| Access to activities | 2.95 | 1.26 | 2.69 | 1.26 | 3.12 | 1.29 | 3.29 | 1.20 | 3.01 | 1.27 |
| Time poverty | 2.86 | 1.35 | 2.74 | 1.26 | 2.81 | 1.20 | 3.11 | 1.23 | 2.88 | 1.27 |
| Cognitive appropriation | 3.62 | 1.26 | 3.42 | 1.41 | 3.57 | 1.26 | 3.55 | 1.23 | 3.54 | 1.29 |
| Reliability | 2.87 | 1.22 | 2.81 | 1.34 | 2.89 | 1.13 | 2.87 | 1.16 | 2.86 | 1.21 |
| Safety | 2.38 | 1.32 | 2.36 | 1.37 | 2.47 | 1.27 | 2.59 | 1.26 | 2.45 | 1.31 |
| Cost of transport | 2.94 | 1.41 | 2.51 | 1.36 | 2.66 | 1.21 | 3.00 | 1.28 | 2.78 | 1.33 |

*Source:* Author's formulation based on survey.

*Table 20.4 Mean values and standard deviation for the Flourishing Scale in the four communes*

| Flourishing scale | Commune | | | | | | | | | |
|---|---|---|---|---|---|---|---|---|---|---|
| | C3 | | C8 | | C11 | | C14 | | Total | |
| | Mean | SD | Mean | SD | Mean | SD | Mean | SD | Mean | SD |
| **General score** | **29.74** | 6.73 | **29.86** | 6.76 | **30.04** | 6.14 | **30.52** | 5.75 | **30.04** | 6.36 |
| Purpose in life | 3.28 | 1.36 | 3.12 | 1.34 | 3.08 | 1.31 | 3.32 | 1.18 | 3.20 | 1.30 |
| Social relations | 3.80 | 1.23 | 3.57 | 1.35 | 3.76 | 1.31 | 3.77 | 1.20 | 3.73 | 1.27 |
| Engagement | 3.51 | 1.33 | 3.82 | 1.27 | 3.74 | 1.21 | 3.87 | 1.10 | 3.74 | 1.24 |
| Contribution to others | 3.62 | 1.26 | 3.82 | 1.18 | 3.68 | 1.16 | 3.76 | 1.07 | 3.72 | 1.17 |
| Competence | 4.20 | 1.15 | 4.14 | 1.25 | 4.23 | 1.03 | 4.33 | 0.89 | 4.22 | 1.09 |
| Self-respect | 3.79 | 1.22 | 3.69 | 1.31 | 3.86 | 1.13 | 3.88 | 1.12 | 3.81 | 1.20 |
| Optimism | 3.61 | 1.37 | 3.83 | 1.35 | 3.72 | 1.26 | 3.82 | 1.24 | 3.75 | 1.31 |
| Respect from others | 3.93 | 1.24 | 3.86 | 1.30 | 3.96 | 1.09 | 3.76 | 1.16 | 3.88 | 1.20 |

*Source:* Author's formulation based on survey.

variance in less advantaged communes. It can also be argued that adaptive capacity plays a role in the homogeneity of these results, in the sense that the context in which a person is developed shapes their needs and expectations causing downward (or upward) adaptation (Sen, 1984). Further qualitative research is needed to explore this hypothesis.

The synthesized nature of this scale gives a reliable "overall psychological well-being score" (Diener, 2010, p. 153), but in contrast does not permit the assessment of each component of well-being independently. However, it is worth noting that the worst performing variable, purpose in life, is indeed one of the pillars – according to Ryff and Singer (2008) – of eudaimonia. The value of competence, which is how people evaluate their mastery in everyday activities, enjoys in contrast the highest scores.

**Influential Factors on Motility**

A multiplicity of factors can affect people's motility. Apart from the variables comprised in the Motility Scale, the survey included a series of individual characteristics that could influence the indicator. A multiple regression was therefore conducted (Table 20.5) where the dependent variable was the general score of the Motility Scale (the sum of the eight components) and the independent variables of those individual characteristics that were judged to have an impact on the indicator.

The multiple correlation is predictably not strong enough, since the value of motility depends directly on the score of the different components rather than on exogenous variables. Nevertheless, Table 20.5 presents some interesting influences from the controls included. The first one is the effect of the commune, significant at the 0.10 level, where belonging to areas with better transport infrastructure (in this case communes 3 and 14)

*Table 20.5    Linear regression Y=motility; X=control variables of the survey*

| **Regression statistics** | | | | |
|---|---|---|---|---|
| Multiple correlation coefficient | 0.311807193 | | | |
| R^2 | 0.097223725 | | | |
| Adjusted R^2 | 0.084700978 | | | |
| ST error | 6.096377025 | | | |
| Observations | 805 | | | |
| | *Coefficient* | *ST error* | *T stat* | *Probability* |
| Constant | 19.1759412 | 0.9794662 | 19.577951 | 0.00000000 |
| **D-commune*** | 0.761227316 | 0.4384488 | 1.7361827 | 0.08291992 |
| **D-privatecar**** | −2.180116097 | 0.6541098 | −3.332951 | 0.00089914 |
| **D-sustainablemodes**** | −1.313876978 | 0.7813696 | −1.681505 | 0.09305857 |
| **D-motivechoice***** | 2.515684003 | 0.5005252 | 5.0260884 | 0.00000062 |
| **Age-group** | 0.492412099 | 0.2823203 | 1.744161 | 0.08151848 |
| **Educ-level** | 0.361874 | 0.1494196 | 2.4218648 | 0.01566438 |
| **D-retired** | 1.410929698 | 0.6074632 | 2.3226588 | 0.02044972 |
| **D-disability** | −1.693143282 | 0.6595787 | −2.567007 | 0.01044040 |
| D-gender | 0.395982341 | 0.4863546 | 0.8141844 | 0.41578374 |
| D-caravailable | 0.645044933 | 0.51243 | 1.2587963 | 0.20847436 |
| D-unemployed | −0.705171453 | 0.9092441 | −0.775558 | 0.4382413 |

*Notes:*
* Dummy where 1 = belongs to commune 14 and 3; 0 = belongs to communes 1 and 8.
** Dummy where 1 = private car / sustainable modes (walking and cycling) are the principal mode used.
*** Dummy where 1 = motive of modal selection is related to choice rather than need (comfort, speed, health, environmental concern and enjoyment).

*Source:*   Author's formulation based on survey.

positively affects the level of motility, supporting the analysis of the Motility Scale in the previous subsection.

In terms of modal choice, owning and using a private vehicle as a daily form of transportation correlates negatively with the level of motility. Although this fact can appear counterintuitive, several factors can possibly be influencing it: the existence of forced use; the presence of "upward adaptation" of preferences and expectations (as the mirror effect of downward adaptation cited in Section 2) by this group of users, given that car use is related to social status (Steg, 2005); the heavy traffic and the concomitant longer time travel, which was cited repeatedly in the semi-structured interviews; and finally the fact that no suburban area was surveyed, where the effect of car ownership in motility is expected to be much stronger. Sustainable modes also correlate negatively (although less significantly) with motility, which suggests again the presence of forced choice. This leads to the strongest correlation of this section, which reveals that people who select the way they travel for reasons more related to choice than to need, are expected to have 2.5 more points in the Motility Scale.

As far as sociodemographic indicators are concerned, the strongest characteristic undermining motility is having a disability, which raises the issue of universal accessibility of the transport systems as a priority. Being retired has a positive effect on motility, which contradicts to a certain extent the existing literature but also suggests that time availability (and reversely time poverty) is a defining aspect of motility. Qualitative studies should be carried out to explore this matter. Age and education level show a weaker relation to motility, while gender, car availability and being unemployed proved to be not significant.

### Exploring the Links Between Motility and Eudaimonic Well-Being

In order to link the two scales, a series of statistical operations were conducted. After finding that simple and multiple regression were showing positive results, errors were clustered by commune in order to account for the potential correlations of the unobservables within each group of observations. Additionally, principal components analysis (PCA) was applied to both the Motility and the Flourishing Scale. The objective of implementing the PCA technique was, through orthogonal transformation, to correct the possible correlations within each scale, giving as a result a collection of values derived from uncorrelated variables (or principal components). The first component, utilised in the following regressions, accounts for the highest variability of the data. Another advantage of this procedure is that it rescales the distribution, making it closer to normal (with a mean of 0 and a standard deviation of 1). Not only does this improve the robustness of the regression but also facilitates its interpretation, since instead of having an array of values from 5 to 40 (as in the original scales), they range from –4 to 4, making the effects of variables more readable.

Considering the variables that had proved to be significant in the multiple regression, a set of iterations was conducted in Stata in order to find the best specification for the regression model. Besides motility, the variables gender, age and disability[2] were utilised.

---

[2] Commune was also tested using each commune as a dummy variable to confirm that the way it was previously measured was not biased, giving a consistent negative result.

*Table 20.6    Best model specification (with PCA)*

**Regression statistics**

| Observations | 805 |
|---|---|
| R-squared | 0.199 |
| Commune FX | YES |
| ll | −1544 |
| Robust Err, NO | |

| VARIABLES | Eudaimonic well-being – component 1 | | |
|---|---|---|---|
|  | **Coefficient** | **ST errors** | **Probability** |
| Constant | −0.270 | (0.137) | <0.01 |
| **Motility – component 1** | 0.381 | (0.025) | <0.01 |
| **Age = 30 to 49** | 0.598 | (0.205) | <0.1 |
| **Age = 50 to 65** | 0.6 | (0.215) | <0.1 |
| **Age = 65+** | 0.637 | (0.249) | <0.1 |
| **Gender (Male=1)** | −0.618 | (0.051) | <0.01 |
| **Disability** | −0.763 | (0.107) | <0.01 |

*Source:*   Author's formulation based on survey, using Stata.

The variable age was disaggregated into three different dummies for each age category, rather than using age group, which gave more refined results (see Table 20.6). As Ryff and Singer (2008) demonstrate, there is a correlation between age and well-being. However, some aspects tend to increase, such as environmental mastery, whilst others tend to decrease, such as purpose in life. The latter create the deceleration of the curve's slope. The gender effect is stable, with the limitations described for the previous regression, and the effect of disability continues to be highlighted, which underlines the criticality of this dimension.

The most salient corollary of this analysis is that an increase in one point of motility will increase eudaimonic well-being by 0.38, significant at the 0.01 level, which is the same as saying that allowing people to enhance their capacity to be mobile will develop their capacity to realise themselves. This conclusion has remained stable throughout the different statistical procedures attempted, contributing to the robustness of the results.

All things considered, the quantitative analysis applied to the survey has delivered valuable results to contribute to the debate regarding motility and eudaimonic well-being. The relation between structural conditions and individual choices has been explored through the modal choice analysis. The purposefully constructed Motility Scale has proven to be effective for the measurement of motility taking into consideration the constrains of the data collection method, having produced insightful results in the context of Buenos Aires but which could also be potentially replicable in other latitudes. Finally, the validation of the link between motility and eudaimonic well-being has relevant consequences for research in the field, and raises a range of questions worthy of further inquiry.

## 4. FURTHER PATHS WORTH EXPLORING

Firstly, as regards the study's methods, the proposed Motility Scale can only be a starting point, since it was designed in order to fulfil the requirements of the surveying technique. It would be worthwhile developing a more holistic quantitative measure, which could broaden the range of aspects in consideration and deepen their understanding. One of the pillars of motility, appropriation, was only partially tackled in the scale and it still constitutes a pending issue in the domain of transport studies. Further quantitative and qualitative research is needed to develop the motility framework at the micro-level in all its complexity.

Secondly, in the same way that transport literature has developed instruments to measure hedonic well-being in relation to travel, it would be valuable if this interest translated into future investigations regarding eudaimonic well-being, tailoring the measurement of the latter to the research objectives of the transport field. The use of a concise scale has proven fruitful in this study, but different combinations of existing and new eudaimonic scales should be explored further in research to arrive at a deeper and more robust interpretation of the phenomenon. If human well-being is effectively the ultimate goal of transport planning, a better understanding of well-being, embracing its multiple definitions with their theoretical backgrounds, is thus essential.

Thirdly, even if the study contributes to the existing literature by having linked the concept of motility to eudaimonic well-being through quantitative research, results are context-specific and cannot be automatically translated to other urban realities. The fact that an unequal distribution of mobility capital – a consequence of a general uneven allocation of resources within an urban area – has an impact on the people's possibilities of self-development should be further supported in future research, applying the methodology to larger samples and diverse contexts, to enhance its validity. In that vein, it would be advantageous to conduct a more comprehensive survey, using a combination of CATI and face-to-face interviews. This will allow not only capturing informal settlements, which are highly extended throughout the cities of the Global South, but also extending the number of dimensions the survey can cover.

Finally, the conclusions presented in this chapter suggest broader implications for transport policy. The capacity of people to decide which mode to utilise, rather than being forced to use one, has proven to have a positive impact on people's motility. This raises concern about the areas without mode diversity, alongside the financial restrictions of accessing the different modes when available, suggesting that transport policy should therefore aim to diversify and enhance mobility on the offer side, in order to better suit individual needs (certainly without losing sight of environmental goals), and consider subsidising mechanisms to ensure access. Furthermore, the utility of self-reported information has been highlighted by the existing literature and supported by this study, showing the need to incorporate subjective measures as a way to better inform the decision-making process. In that way policy will be more effective in attaining its goal, which should be enhancing people's capacity to access urban opportunities, consequently helping them reach their maximum potential.

# REFERENCES

Abou-Zeid, M. et al (2012) Happiness and travel mode switching: findings from a Swiss transportation experiment. *Transport Policy*, 19, 93–104.
Ajzen, I. (2011) The theory of planned behaviour: reactions and reflections. *Psychology and Health*, 26:9, 1113–1127, DOI: 10.1080/08870446.2011.613995.
Anable, J. (2005) "Complacent car addicts" or "Aspiring environmentalists"? Identifying travel behaviour segments using attitude theory. *Transport Policy*, 12, 65–78.
Aristotle (1925) *The Nicomachean Ethics*, D. Ross, Trans. NY: Oxford University Press.
Banister, D. (1994) Equity and Acceptability Question in Internalising the Social Costs of Transport. OECD/ECMT Seminar Internalising the Social Costs of Transport, Paris.
Banister, D., Anderton, K., Bonilla, D., Givoni, M. and Schwanen, T. (2011) Transportation and the environment. *Annual Review of Environment and Resources*, 36, 247–270.
Beirao, G. and Cabral, J. (2007) Understanding attitudes towards public transport and private car: a qualitative study. *Transport Policy*, 14, 478–489.
Bergstad, C. et al (2011) Subjective well-being related to satisfaction with daily travel. *Transportation*, 38, 1–15. DOI 10.1007/s11116-010-9283-z.
Beyazit, E. (2011) Evaluating social justice in transport: lessons to be learned from the Capabilities Approach. *Transport Reviews*, 31, 117–134.
Camfield, L. (2006) The why and how of understanding subjective wellbeing: exploratory work by the WeD group in four developing countries. WeD Working Paper 26.
Camfield, L., Crivello, G. and Woodhead, M. (2008) Wellbeing research in developing countries: reviewing the role of qualitative methods. *Social Indicators Research*, 90, 5–31, DOI 10.1007/s11205-008-9310-z.
Castells, M. (1996) *The Rise of the Network Society*. Oxford: Blackwell Publishers.
Clarke, M. (2006) Measuring human well-being in Thailand: a normative social choice approach. *Journal of the Asia Pacific Economy*, 11:2, 151–167, DOI: 10.1080/13547860600591028.
Collins, D. (2003) Pretesting survey instruments: an overview on cognitive methods. *Quality of Life Research*, 12, 229–238.
Crettaz, E. and Suter (2013) The impact of adaptive preferences on subjective indicators: an analysis of poverty indicators. *Social Indicators Research*, 114, 139–152, DOI:10.1007/s11205-013-0388-6.
Currie, G. et al (2010) Investigating links between transport disadvantage, social exclusion and well-being in Melbourne. Updated results. *Research in Transportation Economics*, 29, 287–295.
De Vos, J. et al (2013) Travel and subjective well-being: a focus on findings, methods and future research needs. *Transport Reviews*, 33:4, 421–442, DOI: 10.1080/01441647.2013.815665.
Delbosc, A. (2012) The role of well-being in transport policy. *Transport Policy*, 23, 25–33.
Delbosc, A and Currie, G. (2011a) Exploring the relative influences of transport disadvantage and social exclusion on well-being. *Transport Policy*, 18, 555–562.
Delbosc, A and Currie, G. (2011b) The spatial context of transport disadvantage, social exclusion and well-being. *Journal of Transport Geography*, 19, 1130–1137.
Diener, E. (2009) *The Science of Well-Being: The Collected Works of Ed Diener, Volume 1*. Dordrecht: Springer.
Diener, E. (2010) New well-being measures: short scales to assess flourishing and positive and negative feelings. *Social Indicators Research*, 97:2, 143–156.
Diener, E. et al (1985) The satisfaction with life scale. *Journal of Personality Assessment*, 49:1, 71–75, DOI: 10.1207/s15327752jpa4901_13.
Dillman, Don A. and Christian, L. (2005) Survey mode as a source of instability in responses across surveys. *Field Methods*, 17:1, 30–51.
Dillman, D., Smyth, J. and Christian, L. (2009) *Internet, Phone, Mail, and Mixed-Mode Surveys: The Tailored Design Method*. Chichester: Wiley.
Dimitriou, H.T. (2005) Globalization, Mega Transport Projects and the Making of Places. Paper presented to 2005 Annual Transportation Research Board Meeting, Washington, DC.
Duarte, A. et al (2010) Experienced and expected happiness in transport mode decision making process. *12th WCTR*, July 11–15, Lisbon, Portugal.
Ettema, D. et al (2011) Satisfaction with travel and subjective well-being: development and test of a measurement tool. *Transportation Research Part F*, 14, 167–175.
Flamm, M. and Kaufmann, V. (2006) Operationalising the concept of motility: a qualitative study. *Mobilities*, 1:2, 167–189, DOI: 10.1080/17450100600726563.
Gartner, A. (2011) Estudio sobre tasa de motorizacion. Relaciones y determinantes. Apostillas técnicas C3T, Buenos Aires: UTN.
Geurs, K. and van Wee, B. (2004) Accessibility evaluation of land-use and transport strategies: review of research directions. *Journal of Transport Geography*, 12, 127–140.

Graham, S. and Marvin, S. (2001) *Splintering Urbanism: Networked Infrastructures, Technological Mobilities and the Urban Condition*. NY: Routledge.

Hausman, D. (2011) *Preference, Value, Choice and Welfare*. Cambridge University Press, http://dx.doi.org/10.1017/CBO9781139058537.

Holman, N. and Rydin, Y. (2012) What can social capital tell us about planning under localism? *Local Government Studies*, 39:1, 71–88.

Hotelling, H. (1933) Analysis of a complex of statistical variables into principal components. *Journal of Educational Psychology*, 24:7, 498–520.

INDEC (2015) Definiciones y conceptos utilizados en los cuadros. Sistema de estadísticas sociodemográficas. Available in www.indec.mecon.ar/.

Janda, L., Janda, M. and Tedford, E. (2001) IVR test and survey: a computer program to collect data via computerized telephonic applications. *Behaviour Research Methods, Instruments and Computers*, 33:4, 513–516.

Jensen, M. (1999) Passion and heart in transport – a sociological analysis on transport behaviour. *Transport Policy*, 6, 19–33.

Kahneman, D., Diener, E. and Schwarz, N. (1999) *Well-Being: The Foundations of Hedonic Psychology*. NY: Russel Sage Foundation.

Kaufmann, V., Bergman, M. and Joye, D. (2004) Motility: mobility as capital. *International Journal of Urban and Regional Research*, [Online] 28:4, 745–756.

Kronlid, D. (2008) Mobility as capability, in Uteng, T. and Cresswell, T. (eds) *Gendered Mobilities*. Aldershot and Burlington: Ashgate Publishing, pp. 15–33.

Krossnik J. and Presser, S. (2010) *Question and Questionnaire Design. Handbook of Survey Research*, 2nd edn. Emerald Group Publishing Limited.

Levy, C. (2013) Travel choice reframed: "deep distribution" and gender in urban transport. *Environment and Urbanization*, 25:1, 47–63.

Lyons, G. (2003) The introduction of social exclusion into the field of travel behaviour. *Transport Policy*, 10, 339–342.

Mahoney. L. (2012) Moods and Modes: How Transport Modal Choice Impacts Subjective Wellbeing. UTSG conference, Aberdeen.

McAllister, F. (2005) Wellbeing concepts and challenges. Sustainable development research network, DEFRA.

McMahan, E. and Estes, D. (2011) Measuring lay conceptions of well-being: the beliefs about well-being scale. *Journal of Happiness Studies*, 12, 267–287, DOI: 10.1007/s10902-010-9194-x.

Nelson, A. and Allen, D. (1997) If you build them, commuters will use them: association between bicycle facilities and bicycle commuting. *Transportation Research Record*, 1578, 79–83.

Nordbakke, S. (2013) Capabilities for mobility among urban older women: barriers, strategies and options. *Journal of Transport Geography*, 26, 166–174.

Nussbaum, M. (2003) Capabilities as fundamental entitlements: Sen and social justice. *Feminist Economics*, 9:2–3, 33–59.

Owen, W. (1964) *Strategy for Mobility*. Westport, Connecticut: Greenwood Press.

Patton, M. (1990) *Qualitative Evaluation and Research Methods*. Newbury Park CA: Sage Publications.

Piccirillo, J. and Giormenti, B. (2012) Implementacion del Metrobus en la ciudad de Buenos Aires. Parte 1: reflexiones sobre los sistemas BRT. UTN, C3T.

Putnam, R. (2000) *Bowling Alone. The Collapse and Revival of American Community*. New York: Simon and Schuster.

Raje, F. (2007) Using Q methodology to develop more perceptive insights on transport and social inclusion. *Transport Policy*, 14, 467–477.

Reardon, L. and Abdallah, S. (2013) Well-being and transport: taking stock and looking forward. *Transport Reviews*, 33:6, 634–657.

Ryan, R. and Deci, E. (2001) On happiness and human potentials: a review of research on hedonic and eudaimonic well-being. *Annual Review of Psychology*, 52, 141–66.

Ryff, C. (1989) Happiness is everything, or is it? Explorations on the meaning of psychological well-being. *Journal of Personality and Social Psychology*, 57:6, 1069–1081.

Ryff, C. and Singer, B. (2008) Know thyself and become what you are: a eudaimonic approach to psychological well-being. *Journal of Happiness Studies*, 9, 13–39, DOI 10.1007/s10902-006-9019-0.

Salvia, Agustín y Donza, Eduardo (1999) Problemas de medición y sesgos de estimación derivados derivados de la no respuesta a preguntas de ingresos en la EPH (1990–1998). *Asociación Argentina de Especialistas de Estudios del Trabajo/ASET*, (18), 93–120.

Sen, A. (1995) *Equality of What?* Oxford Scholarship Online, DOI: 10.1093/0198289286.001.0001.

Sen, A. (2003) Development as capabilities expansion, in Fukuda-Parr, S. et al, *Readings in Human Development*. New Delhi and New York: Oxford University Press.

Smith, N., Hirsch, D. and Davis, A. (2012) Accessibility and capability: the minimum transport needs and costs of rural households. *Journal of Transport Geography*, 21, 93–101.

Social Exclusion Unit (2003) Making the Connections: Final Report on Transport and Social Exclusion: Summary. London: Office of the Deputy Prime Minister.

Stanley, J. and Stanley, J. (2007) Public transport and social policy goals. *Road & Transport Research*, 16(1), 20–30.

Stanley, J. et al (2011) Mobility, social exclusion and well-being: exploring the links. *Transportation Research Part A*, 45, 789–801.

Steg, L. (2005) Car use: lust and must: instrumental, symbolic and affective motives for car use. *Transportation Research Part A*, 39, 147–162.

Steg, L. and Vlek, C. (2009) Encouraging pro-environmental behaviour: an integrative review and research agenda. *Journal of Environmental Psychology*, 29, 309–317.

Steg, L., Vlek, C. and Slotegraaf, G. (2001) Instrumental-reasoned and symbolic-affective motives for using the motor car. *Transport Research Part F*, 4, 151–169.

The International Well-being Group (2013) *Personal Well-being Index*, 5th edn. Melbourne: Australian Centre on Quality of Life, Deakin University.

Tourangeau, R., Steiger, D. and Wilson, D. (2002) Self-administered questions by telephone: evaluating interactive voice response. *The Public Opinion Quarterly*, 66:2, 265–278.

UNTREF (2015) Hacia una política de transporte de calidad en el AMBA: diagnóstico y recomendaciones. Informe interno Uiversidad de Tres de Febrero.

Urry, J. (2007) *Mobilities*. Cambridge: Polity.

Uteng, P. (2006) Mobility: discourses from the non-western immigrant groups in Norway. *Mobilities*, 1:3, 437–464, DOI: 10.1080/17450100600902412.

Vastfjall, D. and Garling, T. (2007) Validation of a Swedish short self-report measure. *Scandinavian Journal of Psychology*, 48:3, 233–238.

Veenhoven, R. (2006) The four qualities of life: ordering concepts and measures of the good life, in McGillivray, M. and Clark, M. (eds) *Understanding Human Well-Being*. Tokyo, NewYork, Paris: United Nations University Press, pp. 74–100,

Vella-Brodrick, D. and Stanley, J. (2013) The significance of transport mobility in predicting well-being. *Transport Policy*, 29, 236–242.

Waterman, A. et al (2010) The questionnaire for eudaimonic well-being: psychometric properties, demographic comparisons, and evidence of validity. *The Journal of Positive Psychology*, 5:1, 41–61.

World Bank (2009) Systems of cities. Harnessing urbanization for growth and poverty alleviation. Sustainable development network urban and local government anchor, www.worldbank.org/urban.

Wu, W. (2015) Rail access and subjective well-being: evidence from quality of life surveys. *Journal of Comparative Economics*, 43, 456–470.

# PART V

# CONCLUSIONS

# 21.  What next? Reflections for research and practice
*Karst Geurs, Moshe Givoni, Beatriz Mella Lira and Robin Hickman*

## 1.   TOWARDS SUBSTANTIVE EQUITY

Levels of social inequity are rising in cities globally – and there is increasing interest concerning how to reverse these trends, and what the role of transport might be. This edited collection examines how transport systems and infrastructure investments lead to inequitable travel behaviours, with different socio-demographic groups using particular parts of the transport system and accessing varied activities and opportunities. Transport planning has conventionally focused on providing for increased levels of mobility, initially in terms of highway capacity for the private car, but increasingly with infrastructure provision for public transport, walking and cycling. The distribution of use of the transport systems and activities that follow has often been overlooked, assuming that all population cohorts have similar opportunities of use. At best, the concern for equity has been on procedural issues (Hay, 1995), e.g. whether a transport project is delivered in a fair manner. This has clearly not resulted in a social equitable transport system, with a fair level of access to transport, opportunities, livelihood, education, and resources for all members of society. Our understanding of social equity issues, in relation to transport, is still being developed. There are difficulties in understanding many important issues, including: what an 'appropriate' level of social equity is, how this can be measured, how and why this might differ by person and context, and even over time. Following this, we may seek to develop appropriate policy responses in different contexts. In the end, we wish to understand how transport projects can be more effectively used to improve social equity. Helping to achieve social equity has not conventionally been seen as the domain of the transport planner but, in our unequal contemporary societies, this goal has become critical.

The aim of this book is to explore the spatial and social equity impacts associated with transport systems, city planning and infrastructure investment, using international case studies. The contributions cover the main dimensions of equity as identified in the literature (e.g., Levinson, 2010; Thomopoulos et al., 2009; van Wee and Geurs, 2011). One important dimension is horizontal versus vertical equity. Horizontal equity concerns the provision of equal resources to individuals or groups considered equal in ability and is related to the concepts of fairness or egalitarianism. Vertical equity concerns the redistribution of resources between individuals of different abilities and needs and is related to the concepts of social justice and inclusion. The inequity of contemporary life demands a strengthened focus on vertical equity. A second typology is equity of opportunity and equity of outcome. Equity of opportunity concerns the extent to which population groups gain equal levels of access to opportunities, such as jobs, education and healthcare. Transport equity of outcome implies that society ensures that disadvantaged people actually succeed in getting a high quality job, education and healthcare. Consider all of the countries we live in – and there is little of this form of substantive equity.

## 2.   TRANSPORT AND INEQUALITY

Several of the case studies presented in Parts II and III of this volume address the role of public transport in reducing transport inequalities for urban poor, women, children and elderly people. Scheurer and Curtis (Chapter 3) show that advantaged population groups (using metrics such as income, education and employment) consolidate in and capitalise on public transport-accessible inner areas, and disadvantaged groups tend to concentrate in outer suburban areas (mostly away from the city centres, scenic waterfronts and river valleys) where public transport access is patchy. Liu (Chapter 4), using a case study in Chongqing, highlights that generally poor, established residents, rural migrants and those without a car, are most likely confined to their local area if there is insufficient supply of public transport. Smeds (Chapter 6) studies the implications of the spatial unevenness in public transport provision in London on schoolchildren's travel to school. She concludes that a lack of investment in public transport provision for peripheral urban areas can result in families being locked in to car-dependency and be more likely to drive children to school. Lopez and Biona (Chapter 10) show that public transport accessibility and affordability are both important dimensions in healthcare accessibility in Metro Manila. Inequities are significant for low-income peripheral residents unable to access preferred healthcare facilities. Beyazit and Sungur (Chapter 11) show that undereducated women workers in unskilled jobs living in the periphery of Istanbul experience the highest levels of unequal mobilities compared to other working groups. Cao et al. (Chapter 15) also find clear indications of gendered transport inequalities in lower and higher income areas in Beijing. Non-car owners in low-income areas experience constraints in job and educational opportunities and the resources available to them.

These results highlight the importance of vertical transport equity issues. However, transport equity analysis become more complex if research goes beyond cross-section data analysis, and developments in transport equity or the impacts of transport interventions on equity of opportunity or equity of outcomes are examined. Several chapters discuss whether transport inequalities can be reduced with public transport investments. Firstly, the research highlights the complex and methodologically challenging task of equity analysis. Secondly, the contributions in the book also contribute to knowledge on outcome equity. In the literature, there is general agreement that everyone deserves equity of opportunity but there is less agreement over equity of outcome, and even less evidence on the role of transport investments in enhancing outcome equity (van Wee and Geurs, 2011). Contributions in the book highlight gentrification as an important outcome resulting from changes in equity in opportunities. Scheurer and Curtis conclude (Chapter 3) that public transport investments alone will not be able to address the differences in public transport accessibility between different social groups. Melbourne's spatial and socio-economic structure, with the more advantaged groups living and moving to centrally located areas and the disadvantaged groups having few other options than to occupy the periphery, mean that serving the poorer groups by public transport becomes very difficult. Bothe and Skytt-Larson (Chapter 9) examined the outcome equity impacts of the Copenhagen metro, a large-scale public transport investment which opened in two phases between 2002 and 2007. Data for the period 1992–2012 is used to examine if the metro impacted on socio-economic characteristics of the existing population, and in-movers and out-movers in metro-served and non-metro served areas. The research concludes that the introduction of the metro did not have strong socio-economic impacts, and did not gentrify metro-served areas. Socio-economic development in the metro area was highly dynamic and can only be understood in relation to a range of other influencing factors, including the quality of existing housing stock and newly built housing. Wu et al. (Chapter 5) show that high speed rail investments in China are positively correlated to economic growth in different regions but, at the same time, are associated with social inequality at urban and regional scales. Urban commuters benefiting from reduced travel times displace lower income local residents for which housing becomes unaffordable around many high-speed railway stations. Deboosere et al. (Chapter 2) examine the evolution of employment accessibility between 2001 and 2011 in the Greater Toronto and Hamilton Area and attempt to connect the concepts of equity of opportunity and equity of outcome. They measure the impacts of the development of transit accessibility on income and unemployment rates of population segments by income class, concluding that increases in employment accessibility by public transport has resulted in income increases in low and medium income areas, and income decreases in high-income areas. The authors speculate that urban developments (densification, mixed land uses) associated with changes in transit services may have de-gentrified high-income areas as wealthier people move to the suburbs. Hence there are very different trends being experienced in different contexts.

These contributions in the book thus show that the economic and social equality impacts of large-scale investments in public transport are very context dependent, reflecting political, policy, institutional, urban development and cultural structures. Reducing transport inequalities requires long-term transport planning interventions framed around clear social inclusion goals, in combination with effective urban policies such as social housing. In addition, some authors discuss the importance of small-scale public transport investments, such as bus feeder services in low-density and socio-economically disadvantaged areas. Similarly, in the literature, there is some evidence that suggests that targeted small-scale public transport initiatives have been successful in enabling people to access new employment opportunities and facilitate other important activities, such as health visits, educational attendance and leisure and social activities (Lucas et al., 2009). However, there is generally a lack of evidence on what type and combinations of transport investments are successful in improving outcome equity, and indeed what level of outcome equity should be aimed for.

## 3.   REFLECTIONS FOR RESEARCH AND PRACTICE

There is much interest in research on the economic, environmental and social impacts of transport projects – usually for new projects being built, e.g. urban metros. The contributions in this book show that social equity analysis is a complex and methodologically challenging task, with new theoretical approaches being tested. Yet, still, there is a need for research on new and more comprehensive appraisal frameworks which better reflect social issues. There are many research directions that researchers can explore. It should be clear that in many future research avenues, interdisciplinary and multidisciplinary research is most likely to improve our understanding on transport-related social equity, as multiple factors are involved. Theoretical contributions from psychology (e.g. the role of attitudes) and sociology (e.g. wider structural issues – social and cultural norms, politics) have broadened the debate, so we can understand that transport investments have different impacts, and are modified by individual preferences and societal structures.

Banister et al. (Chapter 14) argue that the notion of 'time is money' still dominates thinking on transport through the commodification of time and monetisation of travel time savings. Although accessibility, or the ease of reaching destinations, is increasingly being used in research and practice as a key means of analysis, dominant accessibility indicators used in research (e.g. location-based measures such as gravity-based and cumulative measures) focus on measuring travel time as the transport component of accessibility. A shift towards 'reasonable travel time' is needed, recognising that how travellers value travel time goes beyond minimising travel time and some travel time can be reclaimed and made productive, e.g. in-train travel time. Improving the journey experience should be prioritised over the reduction of travel times, particularly where public transport can be made more comfortable, enjoyable or productive than the car. In the literature, there seems to be growing discussion for this broader perspective to be reflected in transport appraisal – perhaps improved journey experience becomes the basis for appraisal, certainly for the non-car modes. Experimental research conducted by the Netherlands Railways, for example, shows that consciously perceived stimuli, such as music, advertising and infotainment at railway stations, and comfortable trains with relaxing music, result in a positive appraisal of time and a more pleasant journey experience for train users (Galetzka et al., 2017; Van Hagen et al., 2014). Geurs et al. (2016) show that improving bicycle routes to stations, providing free bicycle parking facilities, improved walking experiences and times at stations, and improvements in the perceived quality of railway stations in the Netherlands has stronger impacts on train ridership and potential job accessibility for train users than frequency increases of local trains. Alongside, there has been research on the components of the public transport journey experience, including instrumental, affective and symbolic factors (Carreira et al., 2014; Hickman et al., 2015). However, more research is needed to include journey time experiences in accessibility analysis and modelling, and to examine the social equity implications. It is likely that perceived journey times and experiences vary more strongly between population groups than differences in value of time estimations.

Even though there has been an increasing amount of critique on the use of travel time as the basis for transport appraisal, few are suggesting different ways forward, beyond multi-criteria analysis (MCA). Te Boveldt et al. (Chapter 17) suggest to further develop multi-actor MCA tools into participatory evaluation methods, which goes beyond the underlying utilitarian philosophy dominating current appraisal frameworks, allowing decision makers to make their own vision on equity, ethics and sustainability. Cao et al. (Chapter 15) and Mella Lira (Chapter 16) similarly suggest a wider set of social indicators, including travel safety, physical fitness, emotions, body integrity, senses and access to employment opportunities, can be used to reflect social issues in project appraisal. Several definitions and measurements of social equity are used, ranging from statistical indicators (such as Gini coefficients, Atkinson index, Palma ratio and Theil index), spatial equity approaches examining modal equity, or differences in the spatial distribution of accessibility. The Capabilities Approach, highlighting individuals' opportunities for travel and actual participation in activities is applied in the transport field. Mobility Capital, or Motility, is also used, focusing on the capacity to engage in travel and the intrinsic value of travel experiences (see Shliselberg and Givoni, Chapter 19, and Rodriguez Touron, Chapter 20). The mobility capital approach can be used to examine the role of travel experiences in promoting well-being.

The Capabilities Approach and Motility Approach show much potential to be applied in transport, but there are obvious difficulties in application as they cannot be measured by observable network performances or observed travel behaviour. Further research is needed to test these and other conceptual frameworks as tools for transport policy, and also to further understand the variations in travel and activity participation across different population groups. As noted earlier, many equity studies address equity in a static manner using cross-sectional data. There is a strong need for more research measuring changes in social equity over time and the impacts of policy measures, in particular using more comprehensive social equity indicators. We can test whether social inequalities, individual capabilities and motilities are decreasing or increasing over time, for which population groups, and examine which measures can help to reduce inequalities. In particular, the objective of well-being should be further utilised to help to understand the role of transport in contributing to better cities and improving quality of life. We need a greater refinement of what social development might mean in transport, including clearer thresholds of social progress, social distribution, social equity and social justice. More examination is also needed on conflicts between different dimensions of transport equity. A particular decision may seem equitable when evaluated in one way, but inequitable when evaluated in another.

To move beyond the conventional focus in transport planning, on increasing mobility, initially by the private car, but also by public transport and other modes, means we need to move away from mobility metrics such as vehicle kilometres travelled (VKT), travel time, and time is money. This has led to investment in projects that enhance levels of mobility – and there has been relatively limited consideration given to other important policy objectives, such as transport's contribution to environmental, social and spatially-specific objectives. There is a need for greater realisation in transport planning practice that the transport projects being built, and the transport systems in existence, have very large distributional impacts – perhaps we are building transport systems mainly for the wealthy groups.

More recent research on transport-related social equity has focused on the concept of accessibility, examining the spatial distribution and availability of different opportunities. Wachs and Kumagai (1973), decades ago, proposed a cumulative opportunity index to measure employment accessibility for different population segments (by income and employment class) for use as a social indicator to measure the quality of urban living. Indeed, the development of accessibility as a key means of analysis and indicator, is a great step forward from the previous focus on mobility metrics. A diverse set of accessibility instruments have been developed, used by local, regional and national governments in many countries internationally. These include simple and straightforward accessibility indicators, such as spatial separation measures (e.g. distance or travel time), cumulative accessibility and gravity-based measures (Papa et al., 2016). Most practitioners are convinced of the usefulness of accessibility instruments as they generate new and relevant insights (Silva et al., 2017). However, there are several barriers that impede the use of accessibility instruments in planning practice. There are few technical, financial and user-friendliness problems, but mainly organisational barriers and a lack of institutionalisation of accessibility instruments at the heart of the implementation gap (Silva et al., 2017). The use of accessibility instruments to study social equity impacts in practice is less frequent. Equity in transport is often not the core concern of mainstream project appraisal – other policy objectives are also important. Equity is usually a small concern of appraisal and is usually dealt with by a form of multi-criteria analysis given the difficulty of including it in cost benefit analysis (Di Ciommo and Shiftan 2017). In particular, there is a lack of standardisation and guidance on the evaluation of social equity impacts. The UK is one of the few, and maybe the only country, that has national guidelines on the evaluation of the distributional impacts of transport projects and social impact appraisal (DfT, 2014; DfT, 2015). However, the evidence and guidance remains weak, and the extent to which social and distributional appraisals have impacted decision making on transport investments in the UK is less certain.

The traditional transport planning approach is based on a rational actor approach, driven by the systems analytic approach to problem solving (Stopher and Stanley, 2014). The approach starts with setting basic values and goal setting, identification of problems to be tackled, formulation of alternatives, valuation of alternatives against a set of criteria, and the selection of the optimal policy solution or package of policies, implementation, monitoring and ex-post evaluations. Recent guidelines on 'ideal' decision making processes in transport planning (Emberger et al., 2008) and Sustainable Urban Mobility Plans (Wefering et al., 2013) follow this planning cycle, albeit with more detailed steps. However, these approaches do not provide guidance on the inclusion of social equity issues. We call for much more consideration here. Conceptual approaches such as the Capability Approach offer much potential in transport planning in helping us to understand the difference between capability (the real opportunities for travel and activity participation) and functionings (actual travel and participation) but need to be applied to test the problems in application. There is a growing understanding that the rational approach to transport planning is too simplistic, such as through the contributions of behavioural economics. For example, Higgins (Chapter 18) examines behavioural economics concepts, focusing on non-rational decision making, to examine public opposition to equitable transport planning, involving taking road space from the car to cycling. To date, there is little evidence of applications of broader behavioural economics approaches within transport planning.

A shift from a travel time paradigm to a broader set of transport policies is needed, and this can include social indicators. This would need to prioritise, as noted above, the door-to-door journey experience rather than travel time as a partial picture of the journey experience. Also, the emergence of well-being as a critical policy objective, with hedonic and eudaimonic definitions, and even temporal dimensions over life stages (motility). These approaches offer many possibilities for appraising projects against experience, quality of life and well-being goals rather than more conventional metrics. Hence, an improved understanding of social equity issues is beginning to emerge and perhaps a wider set of social indicators can be used in a more participatory, even deliberative, approach to project appraisal, with transport projects prioritised against local policy criteria (Dean et al., 2018).

In the end, we require more equitable levels of participation in activities and the chance for all to live the 'good life'. Transport planning has a key role to play in helping to achieve and support outcome equity – it helps facilitates access to activities. But, as ever, we need to regularly refine our approaches to analysing travel behaviours, and to appraise and implement projects, to ensure we are progressing against contemporary issues. Our renewed focus should be to ensure that new and existing transport projects and systems help to progress against important societal goals, including more equitable lives, doings and beings.

## REFERENCES

Carreira, R., Patrício, L., Natal Jorge, R. and Magee, C. (2014) Understanding the travel experience and its impact on attitudes, emotions and loyalty towards the transportation provider – a quantitative study with mid-distance bus trips. *Transport Policy*, 31, 35–46.

Dean, M., Hickman, R. and Chen, C.-L. (2018) Testing the effectiveness of participatory MCA: the case of the South Fylde Line. *Transport Policy*, online: https://doi.org/10.1016/j.tranpol.2018.10.007.

DfT (2014) Social Impact Appraisal. TAG Unit A4.1. London, UK.

DfT (2015) Distributional Impact Appraisal. TAG Unit A4.2. London, UK.

Di Ciommo, F. and Shiftan, Y. (2017) Transport equity analysis. *Transport Reviews*, 37(2), 139–151.

Emberger, G., Pfaffenbichler, G, Jaensirisak, S. and Timms, P. (2008) 'Ideal' decision-making processes for transport planning: a comparison between Europe and South East Asia. *Transport Policy*, 15(6), 341–349.

Galetzka, M., Pruyn, A., Van Hagen, M., Vos, M., Moritz, B. and Gostelie, F. (2017) The pyschological value of time. Two experiments on the appraisal of time during the train journey. European Transport Conference, Barcelona.

Geurs, K., La Paix Puello, L. and van Weperen, S. (2016) A multi-modal network approach to model public transport accessibility impacts of bicycle-train integration policies. *European Transport Research Review*, 8(4), 1–15.

Hay, A. (1995) Concepts of equity, fairness and justice in geographical studies. *Transactions of the Institute of British Geographers*, 20, 500–508.

Hickman, R., Chen, C.-L., Chow, A. and Saxena, S. (2015) Improving interchanges in China: the experiential phenomenon. *Journal of Transport Geography*, 42, 175–186.

Levinson, D. (2010) Equity effects of road pricing: a review. *Transport Reviews*, 30(1), 33–57.

Lucas, K., Tyler, S. and Christodoulou, G. (2009) Assessing the 'value' of new transport initiatives in deprived neighbourhoods in the UK. *Transport Policy*, 16(3), 115–122.

Papa, E., Cilva, C., te Brommelstroet, M. and Hull, A. (2016) Accessibility instruments for planning practice: a review of European experiences. *Journal of Transport and Land Use*, 9(3), 1–20.

Silva, C., Bertolini, L., te Brömmelstroet, M., Milakis, D. and Papa, E. (2017) Accessibility instruments in planning practice: bridging the implementation gap. *Transport Policy*, 53, 135–145.

Stopher, P. and Stanley, J. (2014) *Introduction to Transport Policy. A Public Policy View*. Cheltenham: Edward Elgar.

Thomopoulos, N., Grant-Muller, S. and Tight, M. (2009) Incorporating equity considerations in transport infrastructure evaluation: current practice and a proposed methodology. *Evaluation and Program Planning*, 32(4), 351–359.

Van Hagen, M., Galetzka, M. and Pruyn, A. Th. (2014) Waiting experience in railway environments. *Journal of Motivation, Emotion, and Personality*, 2(2), 41–55.

van Wee, B. and Geurs, K. (2011) Discussing equity and social exclusion in accessibility evaluations. *European Journal of Transport and Infrastructure Research*, 11(4), 350–367.

Wachs, M. and Kumagai, T. (1973) Physical accessibility as a social indicator. *Socio-Economic Planning Science*, 6, 357–379.

Wefering, F., Rupprecht, S., Bührmann, S. and Böhler-Baedeker, S. (2013) *Guidelines. Developing and Implementing a Sustainable Urban Mobility Plan*. Brussels: European Commission.

# Index